FROMMER'S

FAMILY TRAVEL GUIDE

NEW YORK CITY WITH KIDS

by Bubbles Fisher

PRENTICE HALL TRAVEL

NEW YORK • LONDON • TORONTO • SYDNEY • TOKYO • SINGAPORE

FROMMER BOOKS

Published by Prentice Hall General Reference
A division of Simon & Schuster Inc.
15 Columbus Circle
New York, NY 10023

ISBN 0-13-334731-1

Design by Julie Linden
Maps by Geografix Inc.

Manufactured in the United States of America

FROMMER'S NEW YORK CITY WITH KIDS '92-'93
Editor-in-Chief: Marilyn Wood
Senior Editor: Judith de Rubini
Editors: Alice Fellows, Paige Hughes, Theodore Stavrou
Assistant Editors: Suzanne Arkin, Peter Katucki, Lisa Renaud
Managing Editor: Leanne Coupe

Contents

Maps

Dedication

For Eddie and our 47 years together through my thick and his thin. But for accidents of geography, our grandchildren would have been sixth-generation New Yorkers.

To Michael and Kate Schulte of Glencoe, Illinois and Martha's Vineyard, Massachusetts; Benjamin and Daniel Fisher of Basking Ridge, New Jersey; Hannah, Isabel, Sarah, and Nettie Rose Freed of Santa Monica, California; Maxwell and Joanna Fisher of Phoenix, Arizona; and other similarly deprived children who do not live in New York; this book is dedicated in the hope that one doesn't have to live here to love it.

Our gratitude to Nancy and David, Andrew and Robin, Robert and Penny, and Judith and Lance for making us grandparents. With the privilege came love and happiness we have never experienced in such abundance.

L'chaim! To life!

Thank You, Thank You, Thank You

Thank you, Marilyn Wood, for believing I could do this book again.

Thank you, Helen Donovan Lazarnick, for faultless fact-checking.

Thank you, Judy de Rubini, for everything.

Foreword

This is the book to guide you and your child to every place and everything worth experiencing in kids' New York.

To maximize use of this book, read it cover to cover. This will allow you to select the places you "must go." The secret to a great day in New York City is structure. Plan, plan, plan.

This edition is the result of months of research. The 2 weeks prior to publication were spent rechecking every listing. As of this writing, everything is in place.

However, New York is in a financial crunch. You must call every place you plan to visit before you plan the day. Hours change, and places close.

There is no editorial "we" in this book. I researched it, I wrote it, because I needed it. There is much gratuitous advice because I am a grandmother; grandmothers provide either words of wisdom or chicken soup. If you are a grandmother, read every word. If you are not a grandmother, read every word and turn to prayer.

I have no interests, financial or personal, in any person, place, or thing mentioned in this book.

There are memorable fringe benefits to well-planned time with kids. Conversation flows with shared expereiences. Feelings about dim sum and dinosaurs segue into discussions of feelings on more personal subjects.

The sharing of feelings between grown-ups and children is what life is all about. Touch the rungs of life's ladder together; you can't reach back for a passed rung.

Enjoy *New York City with Kids*. Enjoy New York. Enjoy each other.

Who ordered the chicken soup?

INVITATION TO THE READERS

In researching this book, we have come across many wonderful establishments, the best of which we have included here. We are sure that many of you will also come across family-friendly hotels, restaurants, shops, and attractions. Please don't keep them to yourself. Share your experiences, especially if you want to comment on places that have been included in this edition that have changed for the worse. You can address your letters to:

Bubbles Fisher
Frommer's New York City with Kids '92-'93
c/o Prentice Hall Travel Books
15 Columbus Circle
New York, NY 10023

A DISCLAIMER

Readers are advised that prices fluctuate in the course of time and travel information changes under the impact of the varied and volatile factors that affect the travel industry. Neither the author nor the publisher can be held responsible for the experiences of readers while traveling. Readers are invited to write to the publisher and author with ideas, comments, and suggestions for future editions.

SAFETY ADVISORY

Whenever you're traveling in an unfamiliar city or country, stay alert. Be aware of your immediate surroundings. Wear a moneybelt and keep a close eye on your possessions. Be particularly careful with cameras, purses, and wallets, all favorite targets of thieves and pickpockets.

What This Book Will Do for You and Yours

This book will make Manhattan manageable, New York knowable. It is not the usual book of lists. The specifics of everything and every place worthy of your time is in your hands. You didn't even know the questions, and now you have the answers. New York with kids is easy and it's fun. This city is a child's paradise—from pram to prom. Read ahead and plan your trip.

Who Needs This Book?

Don't say "Not me" in order to save the purchase price, or for the mere pleasure of talking to a book. Take this mini-test.

1. Have you ever said to a child, "I'll give you something to cry about"?

2. Have you ever said to yourself, "Who needs this?"

3. Have you ever yearned for selfish, lazy weekends spent wallowing in the pages of *The New York Times*? Do you dream of uninterrupted, unshared days?

If you answered "yes" to 1, 2, or 3, you are a parent. If you answered "no" to 1, 2, or 3, you're a lying parent. Either way, you're an eligible purchaser.

This book is for divorced parents, single parents, joined-at-the-hip parents, parents of parents, New York parents, out-of-town parents, acting parents, and nonparents.

Who needs this book? Everyone who loves kids and loves New York.

A Briefing for All Adults

In the Contents you'll see a chapter titled "For Lucky Kids Who Live in New York" and a chapter called "Primer: How to Prepare for a Kid's Visit." If you have not, as yet, been captivated by the style and content of this book (and I'll be damned if I know why you haven't), you might say, "These are not to be read by me." Au contraire! These chapters are for all of you.

You paid for the whole book. There is information for you. Honest.

How This Book Is Organized

The format of this book is so simple that it borders on idiocy. Everything and every place is listed under categories. These categories have listings. These listings include, among other information, suggested ages. No one knows your child better than you. If you feel an age designation doesn't apply to your youngster, trust your own instincts. However, if ages for tours, for example, are designated with a minimum age requirement, respect it. These folks are serious.

ABBREVIATIONS

AOTW   as of this writing

g.c.   grandchild or grandchildren or grand child
              or grand children

PTA   prior to arrival (of your g.c.)

Them or They the parents of your g.c.

Huh   New Yorkese for the mother of your g.c.
              (used most frequently when referring to
              daughters-in-law)

Himmm   the father of your g.c.

Prime Time the time lapse between scheduled and actual
              arrival of your g.c.

CHAPTER 1

Primer:
How to Prepare
for a Kid's Visit

Plan, plan, plan outings for you and your kids. This is best done if you visit one general locale per day. Dragging kids from area to area is just that—a drag. Children over 7 years should provide their input when you plan. Children under 7 should be given choices, as many as two. Not more. They buckle.

Never announce final plans until the day arrives. There could be snow, an MTA strike, a canceled performance, or an invasion of locusts. The fun of this city is that you just never know. Keep in mind that surprise beats disappointment every day of the week.

The Buildup, Prior to Arrival

Much of the joy of travel lies in anticipation. Excitement increases as the day of departure comes closer. For "you who are about to receive" a young visitor, help the excitement along.

CAMPAIGN STRATEGY

1. A picture postcard of New York. Send one a day to your g.c.
2. A T-shirt by mail: "I Love New York," "Mini-Visitor," and so on.
3. For g.c. sports fans, send a cap or shirt emblazoned with the logo of a New York team. The Giants will do.
4. A photograph of you looking at both the clock and calendar.

Any one or all of these moves establishes the anticipation being felt, a they-are-waiting-for-me mood.

How about this? Multiple-choice questionnaires. Not everyone is a brain surgeon and not everyone can read. Have Them read these to your g.c. Underlining ability is universal.

Examples:

1. I like: boats   trains   subways   walking   barefoot
2. I like: puppets   movies   sulking   shows with live people
3. I like: spaghetti   broccoli   chicken   medicine   pizza

Just keep those cards and letters going!

PTA—Travel Arrangements

If your g.c. is arriving by plane, unaccompanied, tight arrangements are a must. If he doesn't see you at that arrival gate, his apprehension will continue for the entire visit. Don't blow this.

If you are meeting an under-12 solo passenger, let's review the rules. Children under age 5 may not travel alone by plane. Children ages 5 through 7 may travel alone only on direct flights (no changes of aircraft). Children ages 8 through 11 are accepted for all travel (including connecting flights, provided that arrangements are made well in advance with the airline to ensure supervision). This supervision will cost extra.

If you are meeting an under-12 flying-alone passenger, a predesignated adult is the only person to whom the airline personnel will release a child. This predesignated adult must have proper proof of identification. Flight details must be worked out well in advance. Remember, details of the return flight must be just as clear as the arrival plans.

If getting there is half the fun (as they say), it can also be no fun at all. Don't be ashamed to keep in touch with the airline about arrival times, departure times, and so on. One of the joys of the world of computers is that you never reach the same person twice. You won't be embarrassed by being anxious or repetitive.

At airports, don't be deterred by signs that read "Only Passengers with Tickets Beyond This Point." Explain that your "cargo" is to be met and signed for by you at the arrival gate.

For younger children, a helium balloon in your hand will be amusing and make you more visible. For those 10 and older, please maintain a low profile. They are at the brink of that lovable period of life when they yearn to be orphans.

Car and limousine services are a good thought if you are going to or from the New York airports. We've all heard the horror stories about out-of-towners being "taken for a ride." These are, of course, the exceptional stories and that's why they made the newspapers.

Here are two companies I use that are slightly more than a cab as far as prices but well worth the extra money. The cars are clean and in good repair and the drivers are very pleasant. Both companies accept credit cards. They can be reached 24 hours a day, 7 days a week. The *Yellow Pages* list other companies that perform the same services. These, I found, were well priced.

🍎 **Carmel Car and Limousine Service:** (tel. 662-2222) or toll free (tel. 800/435-0018)

Their price AOTW to New York is $15 from LaGuardia, $24 from Kennedy, $25 from Newark. Add tolls, tips, and $5 for being met inside the terminal by your driver. Going to the airports is slightly less. If you need a station wagon they'll provide one for a few dollars more. Please iron out all these details when you make your reservations. There is an extra charge for rush hour, 5pm to 7pm.

🍎 **Tel-Aviv Private Car & Limousine Service:** (tel. 777-7777 or 505-0555) or toll free (tel. 800/222-9888)

Their prices are about $3 higher than the prices of Carmel. However, the prices change quite frequently. Call the toll-free numbers to make your own perfect decisions.

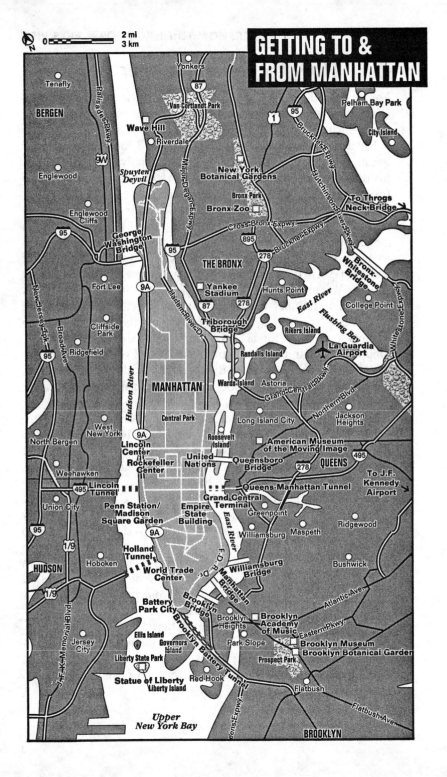

How to Welcome Your G.C.

You've picked up your guest. He has had the "open-arms welcome" and is about to take up residence in his new environment. Do this with preparation, humor, and a touch of class.

For a boffo entrance, how about a 2 × 3 foot poster of your guest? It can be terrific if you include his family, but never, never his dog or cat. This is the one memory of home guaranteed to produce just the wrong response—homesickness.

This is a catalog item, so allow a few weeks for delivery. Send any photograph, black and white, color, or 35mm. It can be 2¼ × 2¾ inches small to 8 × 10 inches large. No negatives accepted. If you write your name and address on the back of your photograph, it will be returned to you under separate cover. Here are your choices: You may order a poster in color, 20 × 30 inches for $9.99. The catalog number is p7667. You may select a black-and-white poster, 2 × 3 feet for $7.99. The catalog number is p2054. Poster mounts cost four for $1.69. The catalog number is S5026. Shipping and handling are extra. Add $2.90 if your order is under $14. Add $3.90 if your order is $14 to $23. Mail your photograph, your check, the catalog number, and your return address to Walter Drake, 9036 Drake Building, Colorado Springs, CO 80940.

If you're not into mail order, then do it in New York. There are many places that do posters and you'll find them in your *Yellow Pages.* If your fingers are not up to walking, try Independent Printing, 215 E. 42nd St. (between Second and Third avenues), New York, NY 10017 (tel. 689-5100). A 2 × 3-foot black-and-white poster will cost you $19.95. If you choose to have it mounted, add an extra $12. Independent does a very fine-quality poster. The same rules for photographs for Walter Drake apply to Independent. Why not take your photo and your money over to Independent and make your decision? The store is open from Monday through Friday, from 8:30am to 5:30pm. It will take 10 working days from the time you order your poster until you may pick it up. I did not include sales tax. They will.

If the above items sound too large, here's a peachy alternative. Decorate your refrigerator, or any other metal surface, with 3 × 5-inch photographs of your guest. Write or call Lillian Vernon, 510 South Fulton Ave., Mount Vernon, NY 10550-5067 (tel.

914/633-6300). Her 24-hour order department will tell you all about the 3 × 5-inch Lucite frames with magnetic backs: three frames per box for about $6 per box. Catalog number LV9843. Shipping and handling costs $2.95 if your order is $10 or under and $3.95 if your order is $20 or under.

What else? You could make "Welcome" signs, blow up balloons, draw funny pictures—get into it.

Playthings to Have on Hand

"Idle hands are the devil's workshop," so they say. Since you cannot offer the south 40 acres of your apartment for plowing, here are suggestions for necessary toys.

FOR THE LITTLE ONES (UNDER 3 YEARS)

Be extra careful with your selections for this group. Avoid toys with pieces small enough to go in the mouth. Avoid anything with points. Avoid toys that may break. If you can break it, so can your g.c. If you're unsure of the safety of a toy for a particular age group, call the U.S. Consumer Products Safety Commission Hotline, toll free nationwide 800/638-CPSC, Monday through Friday from 8:30am to 5pm.

There are products sold for children that look adorable but are dangerous—very dangerous. Please, please be careful. Here are some toys that are safe and fun (you remember fun?):

1. A bag of wooden clothespins. You give these to children without the bag, of course.

2. Plastic blowup beach balls with nonremovable stoppers.

3. Books, books, books. There are bedtime books and bathtime books.

FOR 3- TO 10-YEAR-OLDS

If I don't strike a responsive chord in the following suggestions, try Lillian Vernon's catalog (see earlier section on welcomes). The offerings are nicely priced and the suggested ages are realistic.

1. Have a supply of coloring books, paper, crayons and crayoffs, children's scissors, and Scotch tape handy. Keep old gift boxes, ribbons, magazines, and catalogs for collages.

2. Toss a sheet long enough to reach the floor over a bridge table. This creates a small, private room. Kids talk to themselves in the seclusion of their condo. They aren't embarrassed. Some days you may use it.

3. Kids from 2 to forever love dressing up. If you have an old wig, its time has come. Also fans, jewelry (check for loose stones, points, etc.), old pocketbooks, shoes, clothes that glitter and trail. Throw in some Crayola Kidmetics and they'll have fun (supervise the Kidmetics).

4. For the younger kids, get that old standby, Candyland. The older kids still love Monopoly. These two board games never lose their appeal.

5. Nintendo or Game Boy are a must. Have your g.c. bring his.

6. If you have a personal computer, check to see if you have games appropriate for your g.c.'s age.

The best thing for children to play with is another child. PTA, contact people you know with local g.c.'s of the same age. Arrange introductions. Ask Huh to contact friends she has in your area with kids your guest's age.

VIDEOTAPES TO RENT OR BUY

If you are not sure of what to buy or rent, contact: **KIDSNET**, P.O. Box 5959, Takoma Park, MD 20912 (tel. 202/291-1400). Your school or library may subscribe to this nonprofit service. Videotapes are categorized by age, evaluations, and NEA recommendations.

There are shops all over town to rent and buy videos, patronize your neighborhood store; the nearest is the best.

How to Run a Small Person's Hotel

PTA, you must plan for your guest's sleeping, eating, and clothing storage. You'll get really good at it.

REST ASSURED

To sleep in a bed other than one's own is an adjustment. Arrange for your beauty's sleep and you will both rest assured.

The U.S. Consumer Product Safety Commission I referred to earlier does more than tell you if a toy is safe. Our happy Feds, so dedicated to producing weapons to terminate life on this planet, are keeping abreast of public needs when it comes to consumer products. Please call or write for free pamphlets on "Safety of Children." They are mailed promptly, written clearly, and have all the information you absolutely need.

U.S. Consumer Product Safety Commission
Washington, DC 20207
(tel. toll free 800/638-CPSC)

You'll get from them the buyer's guide, *It Hurts When They Cry.* Carry this with you when you go to rent, buy, or borrow equipment. If you don't have your buyer's guide, here's the bottom line:

1. Make sure crib slats are no more than 2⅜ inches apart.
2. Allow no more than two of your fingers to fit between the mattress and the crib.
3. Port-a-cribs are wonderful, but safe only for children smaller than 35 inches tall.

Little ones are more content when surrounded by the familiar. Have Them toss crib bumpers and favorite crib toys in the suitcase.

As for your g.c.'s most favorite and most important "blankee" or "nonny," he's sure to have it (or them) in hand. Don't lose or misplace it or you and he will never sleep again. Strong enough statement? I hope so.

FOR THE CRIB GRADUATE

Young, small, and lightweight children like to sleep on a futon. Should your g.c. fall, it's a short trip. Futons are easily stored and useful. Whip one out when you have an unwelcome grown-up guest—it guarantees no more than a one-night visit.

If you think your youngster is bed-ready, but you're not quite sure, consider bed guards. They fold flat and are easily stored. Write Lillian Vernon, 510 South Fulton Ave., Mount Vernon, NY 10550-5067 (tel. 914/633-6300), and purchase it with a credit card. One bed guard is $16.98; two bed guards are $29.98. To cover shipping, add $3.95 for one or $4.95 for two. The catalog number is 661708.

Whatever he sleeps on, sneak a large rubber sheet under the mattress pad or bottom sheet. Children far from home (like 5 miles) often have "accidents," as they are called.

Chair Care: Let's Turn Our Sights to Table Heights

If your g.c. is booster-seat size, let your fingers do the walking and put the Manhattan *Yellow Pages* on an armchair. With, of course, a belt to serve as a seat belt.

THE STORAGE STORY

If your drawer space is already on overload, line up a few matching topless boxes. This will provide easy access for kids to reach their clothes, a nice plus for small people.

STROLLERS

If your g.c. uses a stroller, have Huh or Himmm send it or bring it along with your g.c. This will save you money and will save your g.c. anxiety—it's easier to deal with your own set of wheels.

HOW TO BEG, BORROW, OR BUY ALL OF THE ABOVE

Where do you get these things? Well, there are always discount stores (listed), or secondhand stores (listed), or borrowing is still a great arrangement (not listed). If you do buy and don't want to store this stuff, donate it to your favorite charity thrift shop (another spot to look for it PTA). Enjoy the tax benefit and the whole thing will cost very little.

If you are sure you want to rent a crib, or a high chair, it's easy.

Call Furniture Temporaries (tel. 534-0610). It's $24 a month for a crib, $18 for a high chair.

A ROOM OF ONE'S OWN

Rig up some private sleeping area. If you have a screen, good. A rope strung up and draped with a sheet does a nice job. In a city that sells and rents space by the square inch, I have assumed you do not have a guest room. If you do have a guest room, swell. Ignore makeshift arrangements that don't apply to you, you lucky person.

Loading the Larder

First you'll eat, then we'll talk! We are concerned here with a little something to keep body and soul together—not meals. Kids are peculiar about food. Check with Huh or Himmm PTA. Find out not only what he eats but what brands. Let's talk about peanut butter: (a) health-food store or supermarket? (b) Skippy or Peter Pan? (c) chunky or smooth? A mismatch means you'll eat the peanut butter. You don't need it on your hips. I know this sounds esoteric. I know we were raised on "the children are starving" doctrine. You're buying for the kid—buy right.

Apple juice. Frozen? Bottled? Natural? Not at all? Have raisins, tuna, fruit, carrots, milk, bread, cereal, butter, eggs, jelly, hamburger and rolls, catsup, potato chips, and natural fruit bars on hand and you'll have a little something at the ready.

How to Get the Most Out of This Time Together

There are others of our ilk who would not enjoy a g.c. or two to be house-guested and entertained. Those people have fled to Florida, closeted themselves in condos that fly the Flag of Liberation— "Adult Community." This is not you or you wouldn't be reading this.

This visit together will be the best if you do it right. The best way to start is with rule bending. If your g.c. is subject to rigid rules at home, you should let up a bit. If his home life is overly permissive, lay a few rules on him. This does not negate the views of Huh and Himmm. It merely indicates that your relationship is different. The environment is different. You are different from his parents. These rules are indigenous to this place and this time. They understand very quickly. And they enjoy the change.

I consider myself the queen of consumerism. I love presents. Mostly, I love giving them to kids. But I try to put it in perspective. Think of gifts as you think of vitamins—never more than one a day. If you're nothing but a toy dispenser to your g.c., and the palms of your hands bleed from rope burn induced by shopping-bag handles, you're blowing it. You are his present. He is yours.

If, post visit, you return to Them a spoiled brat instead of the nice child they sent you, you're in big trouble. It will be a long time, or never, before they allow you to mess their kid up again. Watch it.

Restraint is essential. Plan only one big event per day. An abundance of riches is overwhelming. If you're pushing too hard, the strain will overtake the pleasure and nothing will be good.

Planning is an absolute. Many of the best things in New York require reservations or tickets. If you change plans, cancel reservations; other children may be anxiously waiting. Once more: Never tell your g.c. of your advance planning.

Spend time with your g.c.'s relatives who live in the area. If your g.c. has cousins, allow them enough time to get to know each other. The nuclear families miss a great deal of love and friendship by staying nuclear.

Don't lose sight of the best part of the visit. With you, your g.c. will enjoy undivided attention, uninterrupted conversations, and a chance to make choices (kids have too many choices made for them). Schedule your days to include time to get to know each other—quiet time. Don't reveal any of the things you two discuss to anyone. (This takes discipline on your part!)

Don't ever, *ever* say or imply disapproval of his parents, his sibs, his school, his hometown, or his dog. This includes raised eyebrows, twisted mouth, and small gasps. Kids see everything—and sense more.

Your g.c. will learn to trust you. Your relationship has endless potential. He is your connection to the future. You are his connection to the past.

Preparation for Gramma and Other Hostesses and Hosts

Be sure you have comfortable shoes or sneakers. Use a shoulder bag—carefully. Put the strap on your shoulder and across your chest, the bag under the opposite arm and in front of you. You're used to having something in your hand. This time it won't be your pocketbook, but another hand. Why risk losing one or the other? Preoccupied ladies are prime targets for criminals.

PTA, cancel all engagements. Your teeth won't rot if you cancel that dental appointment.

Put your g.c.'s name, your address and phone number, and your local police precinct's phone number on your g.c.'s person. Please, out of view—you do not want the world to greet him by name, nor do you want him to look like a crate of oranges ready for shipment. We know you won't be separated, but do it anyway. It's important you feel secure. If you don't, you will transmit your anxiety to your g.c.

If you need to use public lavatories, take him to the ladies room. If he's too old for that one, let him use the men's room. Keep your eye on that door. Has it been longer than three minutes? Call him. Four minutes? Go get him!

Baby-sitters

This visit is not an endurance contest. If you need a break from the routine of togetherness, so does your g.c. A need for a manicure, lunch with another adult, or just time alone is nothing to be ashamed of. Do it before you yearn for the 8 × 10-inch glossy on the piano instead of the real kid. Don't be a martyr. To enjoy a great painting, you must step back. To enjoy your g.c., step away for a few hours. Strategic withdrawal is a maneuver to be respected. You'll both be refreshed by the break.

Tell your g.c. the sitter's name and describe exactly how they are to spend the day (the park, a walk, reading, baking a cake). Tell him when you are returning—and be prompt.

Leave your phone number (if possible) or the number of a friend of yours who will be at home. Don't forget the number of the physician. Advise the sitter of activities and conversation to avoid with your g.c.—and have a nice day.

Advise the agency in advance if you want a sitter to take him out, to play, to lunch, to go to a museum, and so on. No excuses. Here's how to find a sitter.

All of the agencies listed are licensed by New York City. There is a 4-hour minimum on each booking.

Avalon Registry, 116 Central Park South, New York, NY 10019 (tel. 245-0250)
Fee: A baby nurse costs $10 per hour; a sitter for children under 6 weeks old is $8 per hour, 7 weeks to 6 months is $7 per hour, over 6 months is $6 per hour. Add $1 per hour for each sibling
Transportation Fee: $2 each way until 8pm, $5 each way after 8pm. Cash only
Hours: Daily from 8am to 10pm.

Avalon is good at last-minute bookings. Of course they prefer 24 hours' notice, but don't we all? It's nice to know where to get a baby nurse.

Babysitter's Guild, 60 E. 42nd St., Suite 912, New York, NY 10017 (tel. 682-0227)
Fee: $7.50 to $12 per hour. Price depends on location and language requirement. Add 25¢ per hour for each additional child. Cash only
Transportation Fee: $4 each way; $6.50 if your sitter leaves after midnight
Hours: 9am to 9pm daily

This agency has been in business for 50 years. References are checked before they employ anyone. All their sitters speak English; however, if you have a bilingual child or a child who does not speak English, advise the Babysitter's Guild. Among their personnel there are 16 languages spoken. If you need someone on short notice, call and they will try to oblige. They prefer 24-hours' notice.

My g.c. spent a day in the park with a lady from this agency and had a wonderful time.

Fox Agency, 30 East 60th St., New York, NY 10021 (tel. 753-2686)

Fee: $8 to $10 per hour. Price depends on sitter's experience. Add 10% of the total for an agency fee
Transportation Fee: Bus fare before 9pm, cab after 9pm. Cash only
Hours: 8am to 8pm Monday to Friday
   If you prefer a baby nurse or a traditional nanny, Fox will provide them.

🍎 **Gilbert Child Care Agency, Inc.,** 115 W. 57th St., New York, NY 10019 (tel. 757-7900)
Fees: $8 per hour for infants up to 3 months; $7 per hour for infants 3 to 9 months; and $6.25 per hour for children 9 months and older. Add $1 per hour for each sibling. Add $2 per hour for each unrelated child. Cash only
Transportation Fee: $4 each way before 8pm, $8 after 8pm
Hours: 9am to 5pm Monday through Friday
   P.T. Child Care, a baby-sitting service for 42 years, merged with Gilbert Child Care Agency, Inc. Unlike some of their clients, these firms were not born yesterday. They provide sitters "from A to Z," to quote their representative. You may request, and they will provide, multilingual sitters. Specify if your child prefers a young or older sitter.
   The earlier you call to book, the better. If you call by 3pm, Gilbert will produce a sitter that evening. If you need a sitter for the weekend, you must have your request in no later than Friday. Gilbert Child Care Agency is closed every Saturday and Sunday.

Lend-a-Hand, 200 W. 72nd St., New York, NY 10023 (tel. 362-8200)
Fee: $10 charge for one-time use; $60 for a 6-month membership; $100 for a 1-year membership. The sitter's charge is $10 per hour. Checks or cash
Transportation Fee: $2 each way and cab fare after midnight
Hours: 9am to 5pm daily, Saturday till noon
   Lend-a-Hand has been in the biz for almost 20 years. They are especially good if you're in a last-minute crunch. Their people are in the 20s-to-40s age group.

Lynn Agency, Inc., 2067 Broadway, New York, NY 10023 (tel. 874-6130)
Fee: $8 per hour for infants up to 3 months; $7 per hour for

children 3 months and older. Add $1 per hour for each additional child 10% of the total is added for the Lynn Agency. Checks or cash accepted

Transportation Fee: $2 before 9pm, $6.50 after 9pm
Hours: 9am to 5pm Monday to Friday

The Health and Safe Return of Your G.C.

You know those cards that read, "do not bend, fold, or mutilate"? Well, this is pretty much the same thing. The little bugger must be returned in the same condition in which he was received. Improved is acceptable.

Answers are easy. The questions are hard. Here they are and you may take full credit. They, his folks, will be really dazzled by your ability to think ahead. Don't you believe this separation is easy for Them (in some cases it must be like taking off a hair shirt), but They are apprehensive, and will appreciate your concern for things that will never happen.

PTA, ask Them if, in case of illness, you should contact your own physician or would they rather have you contact a New York physician referred by their doctor. If they opt for plan "B"—their own physician's referral—be sure they give you the referred name, address, telephone number, and hospital affiliation. Whether this doctor is selected by you or Them, call him PTA. Give the physician your g.c.'s name, the name of the referring physician, and the dates your g.c. will be in town. Ask the doctor for his office hours, how you can contact him at other times, and which hospital you should use in case of an emergency.

Your next brilliant request is for Them to send you a notarized letter granting you the legal right to authorize medical and/or surgical treatment while their child is in your care. Don't take an attitude—this is a dirty job, but you have to do it. This letter of authority is a must in case you are unable to contact Them. Assure Them no moves will be made prior to attempting to reach either or both parents of your charge. This is for use only when time is a consideration. According to the Health and Hospitals Corporation, "Grandparents have the right to authorize (medical/surgical treatment) after all attempts to reach parents fail." (See "Medical Advice," in this chapter.)

The big one is out of the way. On to the little nigglers. Have Them send his blood type; a list of all allergies, vitamins, medications, nose drops, salves; a list of over-the-counter or prescribed medication; toothbrush and paste, shampoo, and soap. You must be sure of these things, because you don't want to introduce a product that can cause an allergy.

Kidproofing Your Home

The best way to get this job done is on your knees. Room by room, drawer by drawer. This is, of course, for the under-5 crowd, but older g.c.'s do some surprising things. Would you believe 10-year-olds sitting on a window ledge? Sharpening a pencil with your most lethal knife? Heading for the elevator to "look around the neighborhood" (at night)? Not to mention examining pills that look like M&Ms. A youngster's mentality is an uncharted area. Watch it!

KITCHEN

Keep your dishwasher locked—caustics adhere to the machine. Elevate all knives to unreachable new heights. Remove ladders and step stools that might aid a climb to stove tops. Use a piece of elastic to twist around the knobs or handles to that wonderful neighborhood under the sink that has everything poisonous, and to cupboards containing breakables.

BATHROOMS

Best to keep the door closed. Your hamper and your toilet seats serve purposes you've forgotten—they're used to climb to the medicine chest. So get a shoe box and put medications, razors, and face creams out of reach. Why face creams? Do you really need a mural on your bedroom wall? If you have hot rollers or hair dryers, stash them. Please, no telephones, TVs, or radios, unless they are those special waterproof radios.

NIGHT TABLES

Do they look like another Duane Reade pharmacy? Clean them out—and don't overlook the treasures in your handbag.

DOORS & WINDOWS

Be sure your windows are locked. For air, open them from the top. Don't be a bore—I know all about (1) being short (before, after, or during osteoporosis), (2) having no strength in your hands, and (3) the "shmeerer," who painted them shut. Ask Grampa or some other strong person (hah!) to do it. Try your super.

Be sure there's an unreachable door lock. Even if the lock is "too complicated for a little one," tape it! You'll see what's too complicated.

OTHER ROOMS

The title of this book was going to be "Knew York on Your Knees." Another unused title was "I Wuv New York." That has absolutely nothing to do with this exercise—I just wanted to see how it looked in print.

Now, on your knees. If you see a table corner that might just fit your g.c.'s eye, go to your hardware store and buy inexpensive corner protectors called "kinder-gards." The Meissen, the Baccarat, the antique bric-à-brac—store them away. Lamps you love? Replace them with others. Thrift shops always have some uglies real cheap.

If electric outlets are open, put covers over them. Hardware stores and five and dimes stock these items. Cigarette lighters and match strikers go off to the mothballs. If there is a way to tape closed tuners on TVs, stereos, and VCRs, do it. One visit from a knob-and-button-loving toddler guarantees a visit from the repair-man.

Push-in locks on doors are a natural for toddlers. Inexpensive, plastic doorknob covers are sold for this purpose. When you see an actor in a film heave a shoulder against a locked door and gain entry at once, remember, it's not your shoulder. A locked-in-a-bathroom toddler has a power over excluded adults he will not easily relinquish. Avoid the confrontation.

Take a few long, hard looks at your home. Think of potential pitfalls. Look again.

Medical Advice

It is best to have the name of a reputable pediatrician on hand for your g.c. when he's visiting New York. New York friends are also good sources for referrals, or contact any of the below-listed hospitals for such a referral (PTA).

This is for more than the basic maintenance. Emergency rooms are difficult places unless you call your doctor before you go to one. He will arrange to meet you himself or send a surrogate. Otherwise, there is a strong possibility you will wait many difficult hours for treatment.

If your child requires stitches, remember two words: plastic surgeon. The hand that holds the needle should have the qualifications.

This form was recommended by a registered nurse at a pediatric emergency room. If the child you are caring for is not your son or daughter, it is a must. Type it up yourself with the name of your hospital and all other pertinent details, and then have Them sign it.

It's best if all involved live in New York and can do this at the hospital in advance. If this is not possible, however, do it your way, but be sure there is notarization of signatures of all those people who sign these forms.

According to a hospital representative, "No invasive treatment will be done unless a parent can be notified," but "In the case of

(Name of) Hospital
(Address)

Date: _____

I hereby authorize the (name) Hospital to admit and treat my child, _____,
in the Ambulatory Care Department, whether or not accompanied by me.

_____
(Signature of Parent or Guardian)
Home Phone Number: _____
Business Phone Number: _____

_____
(Witness's Signature)

Allergies: _____

Medications Taken: _____

Other Information: _____
_____
_____

Date of Last Visit: _____
_____

extreme life-threatening emergency, doctors will take responsibility until the parent can be notified." So what have we accomplished? Doctors and lawyers tell me these forms "may not be binding, but will facilitate treatment."

Let me clear up one more matter. In situations with divorced parents, if you have custodial care, be sure you have forms from both parents. And one more time: Always notify your own physician before you go to any emergency room. Otherwise you'll be there for hours.

Medical Services—Alternatives to Emergency Rooms

If you do not have a New York doctor and your physical problems are far from life threatening, there are immediate-care facilities available. Bring cash, a check, a credit card, and your insurance card.

Also bring along a medical history of your g.c., so that the medical folks will know something about the child's background.

EAST SIDE

New York Hospital's Urgent Care Center, 520 E. 70th St., east of York Avenue, New York, NY 10021 (tel. 746-0795)
Fee: $94.50. Most insurance accepted. They will bill you
Hours: 8:30am to 11pm Monday to Friday; 12 to 8pm Saturday and Sunday

This is a place for quick treatment to minor problems. Enter through the N.Y. Hospital Emergency Room. The wait should not be more than 20 minutes. Board-certified physicians. Lab tests and X-rays available.

Doctor's Walk-In, 57 E. 34th St., between Madison and Park Avenues, New York, NY 10016 (tel. 683-1010)
Fee: $55
Credit Cards: AE, MC, V
Hours: 8am to 6pm, Monday to Friday; 10am to 2pm Saturday
   Board-certified specialists available by referral. Internists on the premises.

WEST SIDE

Immediate Medical Care of Manhattan, 152 W. 72nd St., between Columbus Avenue and Broadway, New York, NY 10023 (tel. 496-9620)
Fee: $75
Credit Cards: AE, MC, V
Hours: 8am to 8pm Monday to Friday; 10am to 6pm Saturdays and holidays; 12 noon to 5pm Sundays
   General practitioners. No more than a 30-minute wait.

Roosevelt Hospital's Urgent Care Center, 58th Street at Ninth Avenue, New York, NY 10019 (tel. 523-6765)
Fee: $20 to $75
Credit Cards: None. Most insurance accepted. They will bill you
Hours: 9am to 9pm Monday to Friday; 1pm to 8pm Saturday and Sunday
   This facility is manned by Roosevelt–St. Luke's Hospital staff physicians. You will be seen by highly qualified people.
   Note: I despise this whole segment, but caring for a child is like getting married. The things you think of before are never the things you think of afterward. Things you think of afterward are, well, you know.

Emergency Numbers

LIFE-THREATENING EMERGENCIES

For accidents, ambulance, fire, first aid, or police, dial 911 or the operator.

AMBULANCE

For life-threatening emergencies: 911.

The paramedics will decide if the patient is in bad enough condition to require a hospital. If they feel a hospital is your destination, they will take you to the closest medical facility.

For transportation to a hospital of your choosing (if it isn't the nearest facility), you may call the following or other such companies for a private ambulance. You will also pay for the service.

Keefe & Keefe (tel. 988-8800)
Park Ambulance (tel. 543-5100)
Scully-Walton (tel. 542-0740)

NEW YORK CITY HOSPITALS

An asterisk (*) indicates hospitals where pediatricians are on duty in the emergency room.

Beekman Downtown Hospital (New York Infirmary), 170 William St.
Emergency services: 312-5070

*Bellevue Hospital Center, First Avenue and 29th Street
Emergency services, pediatrics: 561-3025
Emergency services, adults: 561-3015
General information: 561-4141

Beth-Israel Medical Center, First Avenue and 16th Street

Emergency services: 420-2840
General information: 420-2000

Cabrini Medical Center, 227 E. 19th St.
Emergency services: 995-6620
General information: 995-6000

***Columbia Presbyterian Medical Center,** 622 W. 168th St., between Broadway and Fort Washington Avenue
Emergency services, pediatrics: 305-6628
Emergency services, adults: 305-2255
General information: 305-2500

Hospital for Joint Diseases (Beth Israel Medical Center), 380 Second Ave., at 17th Street; and the Orthopedic Institute, 301 E. 17th St., at Second Avenue
General information: 598-6000

Lenox Hill Hospital, 100 E. 77th St., between Park and Lexington avenues
Emergency services and
General information: 439-2345

Manhattan Eye, Ear, and Throat Hospital, 210 E. 64th St., between Second and Third Avenues
General information: 838-9200

Mount Sinai Medical Center, 100th Street and Fifth Avenue
General information: 241-6500

New York Hospital, The Cornell Medical Center, Emergency Pavilion, 510 E. 70th St., between York Avenue and East River Drive
General information: 746-5454

New York University Medical Center, 560 First Ave., at 33rd Street
Emergency room: 340-5550
General information: 340-7300

St. Clare's Hospital, 426 W. 52nd St., between Ninth and Tenth avenues
General information: 586-1500

St. Luke's–Roosevelt Hospital Center, 428 W. 59th St., at Ninth Avenue
General information: 523-4000
—1111 Amsterdam Ave., at 114th Street: 523-4000

St. Vincent's Hospital and Medical Center, W. 11th St., at Seventh Avenue
General information: 790-7000

PHARMACY (24-HOUR)

Kaufman's, in the Beverly Hotel, Lexington Avenue and 50th Street (they promise "speedy delivery")
Prescriptions: 755-2266 or 755-2267

OTHER EMERGENCY NUMBERS

Consumer Information: If you are not sure if a product is safe, general information for the U.S. Consumer Product Safety Commission is toll free 800/638-CPSC (Monday through Friday from 8:30am to 5pm).

Dental Emergency Service: 679-3966, after 8pm

Doctor's Home Referral Service: 718/745-5900

Drug Abuse Hotline (New York State): toll free 800/522-5353

Lost and Found
Taxi: 374-5084

Poison Control Center: 340-4494

Police Precinct: 374-5000 for the precinct telephone number in your neighborhood. Your local precinct will provide emergency assistance. If a prescription, required at once, must be obtained, call your local precinct.

Travelers Aid Society: 944-0013

CHAPTER 2

Coping with the City

New York—or at least the island of Manhattan, the major visitor's area—is 12 miles long from the southern end to the northern end and 2½ miles wide at the widest point. Not including lower Manhattan, addresses on avenues—running north and south—are easily located by using the directory below.

Addresses on streets—running east and west—are identified by "East" and "West" designations. Fifth Avenue is the dividing line. The lower the number, therefore, the closer you are to Fifth Avenue. Tuck a street directory in your wallet and you'll never get lost.

STREET DIRECTORY

To locate an avenue address:

1. Cancel the last figure of the address.
2. Divide by 2.
3. Add or subtract the key number below.

4. The answer is the nearest numbered cross street, or damned close to it.

Key Numbers

Ave. A	Add 3
Ave. B	Add 3
Ave. C	Add 3
Ave. D	Add 3
First Ave.	Add 3
Second Ave.	Add 3
Third Ave.	Add 10
Fourth Ave.	Add 8
Fifth Ave.	
Up to 200	Add 13
201 to 400	Add 16
401 to 600	Add 18
601 to 775	Add 20
776 to 1286	Cancel the last figure and subtract 18
1287 to 1500	Add 45
Above 2000	Add 24
Ave. of the Americas (6th Ave.)	Subtract 12
Seventh Ave.	Add 12
Above 110th St.	Add 20
Eighth Ave.	Add 10
Ninth Ave.	Add 13
Tenth Ave.	Add 14
Amsterdam Ave.	Add 60
Audubon Ave.	Add 165
Broadway	Subtract 30 (23rd to 192nd Sts.)
Central Park West	Divide by 10 and add 60
Columbus Ave.	Add 60
Convent Ave.	Add 127
Edgecombe Ave.	Add 134
Fort Washington Ave.	Add 158

Lenox Ave.	Add 110
Lexington Ave.	Add 22
Madison Ave.	Add 26
Manhattan Ave.	Add 100
Park Ave.	Add 35
Pleasant Ave.	Add 101
Riverside Dr. (up to 165th St.)	Divide by 10 and add 72
St. Nicholas Ave.	Add 110
Wadsworth Ave.	Add 173
West End Ave.	Add 60
York Ave.	Add 6

You noticed! Some avenues are not listed. There are good reasons. A quick example of why: When the World Trade Center was being built, the by-products of the excavation were dumped into the Hudson River. Aha! Less river, but more land. And that was the beginning of Battery Park City. As for lower Manhattan where the city began, it just kind of grew. Thus, some areas don't fit any formulas.

But let's go back for more geography. . . . When the flower children of the 1960s moved to the cold-water flats of the Lower East Side, this area east of Broadway and south from 14th Street to Houston Street was renamed the East Village. (Cute, no; just geography tampering!)

In the 1970s the area south of Houston Street, between Lafayette Street and Sixth Avenue, became known as SoHo (streets *so*uth of *Ho*uston). Much of this area was also designated as a National Historic Landmark District thanks to its cast-iron loft buildings dating back to the mid-19th century.

The *tri*angle *be*low *Ca*nal Street, developed with the need for affordable housing in the SoHo vicinity, was called TriBeCa. The 1970s gave us NoHo (Houston Street north to Astor Place, from Broadway to the west to the Bowery to the east). The 1980s gave us LoBro (*lo*wer *Bro*adway, north from Canal Street to Houston Street).

Should you encounter the term Alphabet City, know that it encompasses the Lower East Side streets from Houston to

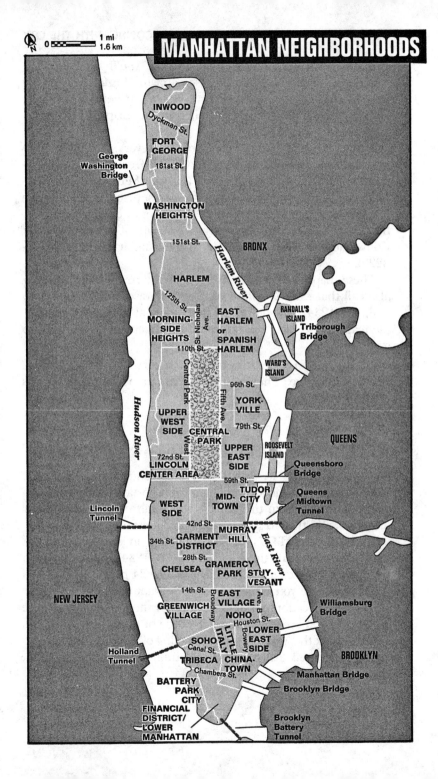

MANHATTAN NEIGHBORHOODS

1 mi
1.6 km
0

INWOOD
Dyckman St.
FORT GEORGE
181st St.
George Washington Bridge
WASHINGTON HEIGHTS
151st St.
Harlem River
BRONX
HARLEM
125th St.
St. Nicholas Ave.
MORNING-SIDE HEIGHTS
110th St.
EAST HARLEM or SPANISH HARLEM
RANDALL'S ISLAND
Triborough Bridge
Central Park
WARD'S ISLAND
96th St.
Fifth Ave.
YORK-VILLE
UPPER WEST SIDE
CENTRAL PARK
79th St.
Central Park West
UPPER EAST SIDE
ROOSEVELT ISLAND
QUEENS
72nd St.
LINCOLN CENTER AREA
59th St.
Queensboro Bridge
TUDOR CITY
Queens Midtown Tunnel
Lincoln Tunnel
WEST SIDE
MID-TOWN
42nd St.
MURRAY HILL
East River
34th St.
GARMENT DISTRICT
28th St.
Broadway
GRAMERCY PARK
CHELSEA
STUY-VESANT
14th St.
EAST VILLAGE
Ave. B
NEW JERSEY
GREENWICH VILLAGE
Broadway
NOHO
Houston St.
LOWER EAST SIDE
Williamsburg Bridge
SOHO
Canal St.
LITTLE ITALY
Bowery
Holland Tunnel
TRIBECA
CHINA-TOWN
BROOKLYN
Chambers St.
Manhattan Bridge
BATTERY PARK CITY
Brooklyn Bridge
FINANCIAL DISTRICT/ LOWER MANHATTAN
Brooklyn Battery Tunnel

Hudson River

14th Street, Avenues A through D. You'll find all the traditional downtown areas (Chinatown, Little Italy, etc.) plus Manhattan's more northerly reaches (Chelsea, Midtown, Upper East and West Sides) detailed in our map of Manhattan areas.

Readers, not to worry! You can find every street with the Metropolitan Transit Authority's (MTA) free Manhattan subway and bus maps. To get them, call the MTA (tel. 718/330-1234, a 24-hour number) to find the closest place to pick up your maps or get them from a subway token booth operator or MTA bus driver. You can also pick them up at the New York Convention and Visitors Bureau, at 2 Columbus Circle (tel. 397-8222).

These maps are very handy, even if you're walking. You may also call that same 24-hour number for travel information. (tel. 718/330-1234). If you're just not good at reading even simple maps, these folks will tell you how to get where you want to go.

Of course, every bookstore and newsstand sells in-depth directories of this genre. They're fine, but my money is made on this publication.

Getting Around Town

My special thanks to Robert Bernstein and Donald Sussman, representatives of the Metropolitan Transportation Authority. All access information in this book is the result of their time, their attention, and their responses to all my questions.

Please put the MTA's telephone number in your wallet so you have it ready at all times (tel. 718/330-1234). You will reach courteous, knowledgeable, efficient people 24 hours a day. If you tell them where you are and where you want to go, they will give you precise directions for either the bus or the subway. The choice is yours. If you are not sure which mode of transportation would be better, ask the MTA. If you're thinking of using the subway and you're concerned if the station or the train is safe, ask. They speak the truth.

HOW TO PAY THE FARE ON BUSES AND SUBWAYS

Subway and bus fares are $1.25 one way. Buses require exact
change (no pennies) or tokens. People over 65 may show their
Medicare cards and pay half price: 65¢. Children under 6 ride free
with an adult. Each adult is permitted no more than three children
under age 6 as free riders.

Subway turnstiles accept tokens only. Subway tokens are bought
at subway toll booths. These booths often have long lines. Be wise
and buy bags of tokens known as "ten-paks." Tokens are not
refundable. If you're 65 or over you must see the person at the toll
booth before you use a token. He or she will give you a pass for
your return trip; good for six months. Children under 6 ride free
by ducking under the turnstile. Hold hands getting on and off
whatever mode of transportation you use.

BY BUS

The MTA bus map provides you with bus routes. Buses have
numbers that are displayed on the front of the bus. Your map will
give you the bus stops for each route. Look at maps displayed at
bus stops. If your bus number is not posted, you have selected the
wrong bus stop. Look at the map again. Remember, in New York
all buses do not stop at all bus stops.

If you are traveling east or west and will need to transfer to a bus
traveling north or south, or a reverse route, you must request a
transfer for each of your companions and yourself when you pay
your fare.

Bus travel is fine. The windows are clean and it allows you to see
the city. It is a horrible experience during rush hours: 6:30am to
9:30am and 3:30pm to 6:30pm. It is even worse in the subway and
a cab is difficult to get at these hours. The great thing about this
city is one can always find something to do in any neighborhood:
see a movie, go into the stores or museums, get something to eat,
visit a library. If you are traveling with less flexible little ones, you
must schedule yourself to avoid public transportation during rush
hours.

BY SUBWAY

We each have our own word for this mode of transportation. Mine is "subwary," because wary is what you must be. First, avoid rush hours. You and your youngster can be separated by the rush of humanity. Stand firm. Hold onto a pole and each other. Watch your belongings. A favorite ploy used by thieves is to jostle your youngster. As you look to your victim, you can be ripped off.

There is a sign posted that designates the safest (everything is relative) area to wait for your train during off-hours (non rush hours). Read it and do it. Stand up against the wall (as the saying goes) and away from the track. If your youngster is new to this mode of travel, brief him before the descent.

The subways are dirty, dangerous, and unreliable. But it's often the only game in town. When the grid is locked on the streets above, when you are beyond walking distance, when you cannot get a cab, there is but one option—the subway.

You must remain alert to the people around you when you're in New York, and more alert when on the subway with kids.

I've provided you with all the "cons." Here are the subway "pros." It is the quickest, most efficient, and most direct way to travel.

The following are the numbers and letters of the subway lines: Numbers 1, 2, 3, and 9 travel the IRT system (Broadway–7th Avenue) on the west side of Manhattan. Numbers 4, 5, and 6 travel the IRT system on the east side of Manhattan. The number 7 IRT train goes east and west: It travels from Times Square to Grand Central Terminal and on to Queens and Shea Stadium. If you want to transfer from the West Side IRT system to the East Side IRT, use the train marked "S" as a shuttle between Times Square and Grand Central Terminal.

The A, B, C, D, E, and F trains are part of the IND system (Eighth and Sixth Avenue trains) and travel on the west side of Manhattan. The N and R trains are part of the BMT system and travel on the west side of Manhattan. The J and M trains are also BMTs and travel on the east side of Manhattan. The L train of the BMT goes crosstown on 14th Street and on to Brooklyn.

BY TAXI

If time and money mean nothing to you, try to get a cab in rush hour. If you achieve your goal, you'll sit forever in traffic while the meter ticks your coins away.

Public transportation is $1.25 a pop, yet it doesn't take you to your front door. If you are a group of three and the traffic is not too bad, a taxi will be the most economical and most comfortable way to travel. If your child is terrified of crowds, take a taxi.

A taxi is available when the light is lit on top of the cab. If the off-duty "radio call" light is lit as well, it won't stop for you.

Every taxi has a medallion number above the light and inside the taxi. No taxi driver is permitted to refuse to take you to your destination when it stops for you. If the driver says, "Not going that way" or refuses to take you by wording it in a less charming way, jot down that number on top of the cab and register your complaint with the Taxi and Limousine Commission (tel. 382-9301). If you have a problem with the driver while in the cab, take his name as well as his medallion number.

Most people have good experiences with taxis and their drivers. I'm just giving you the facts.

Taxi drivers are not required to change any bill larger than $10. Well, at least they don't require exact change—yet.

BY FOOT

New York is a walking city. Walking is the quickest, best, and most exciting way to see the sights. Take the toddlers in their strollers. Children who are older will be showing you the sights. Kids are visual, and there's so much to see on the streets.

While walking, be careful of the bicycle riders. They are dangerous. There seems to be no regard for pedestrians, red lights, or oncoming cars. It's not predictable where or when they'll be coming at you.

There also seems to be an amazing nonchalance on the part of motorists in regard to red lights. Be careful. Don't assume for a hot second that because you have the green light, you're safe. You're not. Be vigilant—for you and your companion.

It would be irresponsible not to make you aware of the pitfalls.

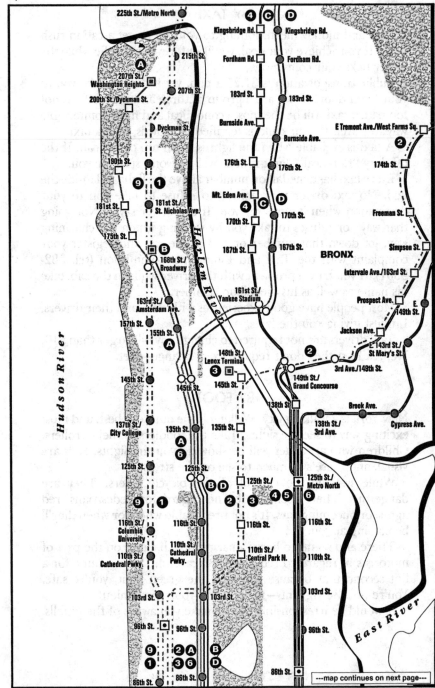

---map continues on next page---

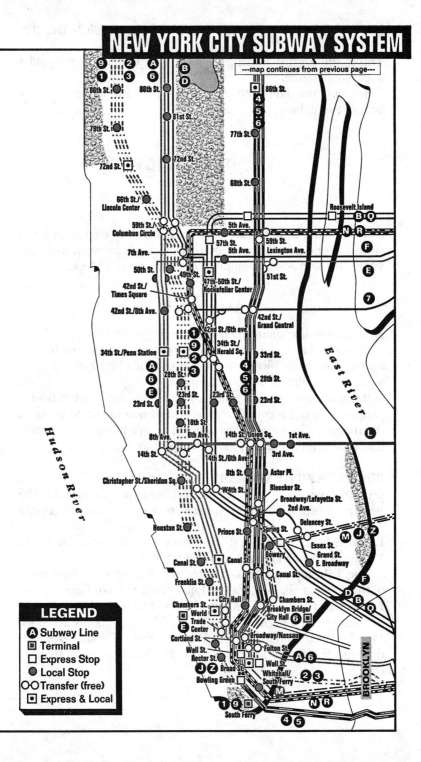

NEW YORK CITY SUBWAY SYSTEM

---map continues from previous page---

LEGEND

- **A** Subway Line
- **⊡** Terminal
- **□** Express Stop
- **●** Local Stop
- **OO** Transfer (free)
- **⊡** Express & Local

This is still a great walking city. Do it by neighborhoods and I know you'll agree.

But leave the days filled with rain, sleet, snow, ice, and intense heat to the stalwart postal people.

Things to Know

WEATHER

New York has a temperate climate. It's usually coldest in January and February. Those months it averages between 26° and 40°F. July and August temperatures can rise to 90°+F.

BATHROOMS

Basic advice: Use them when and where you find them.

Museums are dependable places. Department stores too, of course. Hotels are nice. Assume the attitude of a paying guest to avoid the hostility of the management.

If you and the kids are going to the theater, any theater, from a puppet show to Lincoln Center, use bathrooms prior to going to the theater. The lounges are jammed before the show. Intermission time is even worse. This is the absolute truth.

BROADWAY THEATER DISTRICT. In the Times Square area, prior to a Broadway show, try the **Marriott Marquis Hotel** (1535 Broadway, near 45th Street. It has a rest room on each of its eight levels.

LINCOLN CENTER AREA. There are bathrooms in **Avery Fisher Hall,** open from 10am to 11:30pm.

The **Library and Museum for the Performing Arts** (near 65th Street) is another option. Enter from Lincoln Center Plaza North, which is the uptown side of the Metropolitan Opera House, or enter from 111 Amsterdam Ave. The rest rooms are open Monday and Thursday from 10am to 8pm; Tuesday, Wednesday, and Friday from noon to 6pm, and Saturday from 10am to 6pm.

ROCKEFELLER CENTER AREA. In the **RCA Building, 30** Rockefeller Plaza, the bathrooms are open weekdays from 8am to 7pm.

   Saks Fifth Avenue (Fifth Avenue at 50th Street), has very nice facilities—the ladies' room is on the fourth floor and the men's room is on six.

CITICORP CENTER AREA. In the **Citicorp Center** (153 East 53rd St., between Lexington and Third avenues), on the lower level next to Alfredo's restaurant, you'll find the bathrooms. They're open Monday through Friday from 7am to midnight, Saturday and Sunday from 8am to midnight.

   Crystal Pavilion (805 Third Ave. at 50th Street), is open Monday through Saturday from 8am to 11pm.

   The **Waldorf-Astoria Hotel** (50th Street, between Park and Lexington avenues), is another choice. Why not go first class?

   Of course there are the shops. **Tiffany's** (57th Street and Fifth Avenue), bathrooms on the mezzanine level. **Bloomingdale's** (59th Street, between Lexington and Third avenues), men on five and ladies on four and seven. **Macy's** (34th Street between Broadway and Eighth Avenue), has lots of lavatories, but don't use the second-floor facilities. **Bergdorf Goodman** (Fifth Avenue at 58th Street), the ladies' rooms are on four and seven and the men's room is on five. My most favorite is the ladies' room at **Lord & Taylor** (38th Street and Fifth Avenue)—a marble monument to wasted space.

CHAPTER 3

How to Find Out What's Happening for Kids

For fabulous and free events, follow my lead and get the suggested reading from the Convention and Visitors Bureau, Central Park, and the N.Y. Public Libraries. All this and more on the following pages.

Publications

QUARTERLY

🍎 **Convention and Visitors Bureau of New York City, 2** Columbus Circle, New York, NY 10019 (tel. 397-8222)
Hours: 9am to 5pm Monday through Friday

A quarterly calendar of events is available here. They'll mail you one on request. Everything is listed in their calendar, but before you include something scheduled as part of your itinerary, call the place you're planning to visit—often there are changes. These are very helpful people and a good, good source. They have discount theater tickets, and booklets and pamphlets from sites and attractions around the city.

🍎 **Central Park calendar of events,** Central Park Conservancy, 830 Fifth Ave., at 64th Street, New York, NY 10021 (tel. 360-2766)

Stop at the Dairy, mid-park at 65th Street, or Belvedere Castle mid-park at West 79th Street, to pick up this free quarterly calendar.

It includes "events, activities, and special things to watch for." You will find so much available for kids of all ages that your mind will boggle. Don't be without this. Central Park is a hub of activities and entertainment for children.

BIMONTHLY

🍎 **Lincoln Center calendar of events,** c/o Sunny Levine, 70 Lincoln Center Plaza, New York, NY 10023 (tel. 875-5400)

Put 52¢ in postage stamps on a self-addressed envelope with your request for the Lincoln Center calendar of events to the above address. You will receive your informative calendar of all that is happening at Lincoln Center.

🍎 *Walks and Workshops,* free programs led by the Urban Park Rangers (tel. 427-4040)

Call the Rangers and they will put you on their mailing list. If time is short, pick up a copy in Central Park at the Arsenal, the Belvedere Castle, or the Dairy. *Walks and Workshops* is a must if you are in New York with kids.

MONTHLY

🍎 *Events for Children,* The New York Public Library, Fifth Avenue and 42nd Street, New York, NY 10018, or any branch library.

This publication will be yours, free, if you stop in at any branch library. Again, you won't believe how much is happening for kids at the many libraries.

WEEKLY

* *New York* **magazine,** 755 Second Ave., at 40th Street, New York, NY 10016 (tel. 880-0700)
They publish 50 times a year. Absolutely everything going on in New York is covered in the section titled "Events." The children's calendar is in the section titled "Other Events."

* *Village Voice,* 842 Broadway, at 12th Street, New York, NY 10003 (tel. 475-3300)
This weekly newspaper is to be found on the newsstands every Wednesday. It covers off- and off-off-Broadway theaters better than any other. It has a load of information on what's going on for kids all over town, and covers lower Manhattan in depth. Good reading right through. Focus on the section titled "Kid's Stuff" for your g.c.

DAILY

* *New York Times,* 229 W. 43rd St., New York, NY 10036 (tel. 556-1234)
You really needed a guidebook to be told about this publication, right? Just a reminder to pay special attention to *The New York Times* "Weekend Guide" in the Friday "Weekend" section. You cannot be without this for street fairs, parades, special happenings, and current goings-on at the museums. And more.

* *New York Newsday,* 2 Park Ave., New York, NY 10016 (tel. 725-3600)
An informative daily with good columnists and lots of grown-up news. As for the kids, let me quote *New York Newsday:* "A special feature every day, a full color section every Sunday. All about kids, written by kids. Full of games and stuff."

Telephone Information

Don't forget the 1 before you dial an area code other than 212.
Any phone number without a designated area code is 212!

Bryant Park Arts Line (tel. 382-2323)
They provide daily recorded announcements of performances—only music and dance.

Central Park, Belvedere Castle (tel. 772-0210)
This number is specifically for children's activities.
Hours: 11am to 4pm Tuesday, Wednesday, Thursday, Satur-
day, and Sunday; 1pm to 4pm Friday. Closed Monday

The Dairy, the visitors information and resource center (tel.
794-6564)
Hours: 11am to 4pm Tuesday, Wednesday, Thursday, Saturday,
and Sunday; 1pm to 4pm Friday. Closed Monday

Urban Park Rangers, Central Park (tel. 427-4040)
Hours: 9am to 5pm daily.
Note: If the tape is on, call back or leave your number and they will
return your call.

Convention and Visitors Bureau of New York City, 2
Columbus Circle, New York, NY 10019 (tel. 397-8222)
Hours: 9am to 5pm Monday through Friday
   If you have any questions, don't hesitate to call—they couldn't
be more cooperative. If you stop by, you'll find booklets and
pamphlets from sites and attractions around the city. And discount
theater tickets as well.

Lincoln Center, call 877-2011 for current events, 580-4356
for visitor's services, and TDF's NYC ON STAGE 768-1818
for cultural happenings.

New York Public Libraries, Office of Children's Services
(tel. 340-0906)
Hours: 9am to 5pm Monday through Friday. Closed Saturday and
Sunday

Donnell Library Center, Central Children's Room (tel.
621-0636)

Hours: 12:30 to 8pm Monday; 12:30 to 5:30pm Tuesday; 9:30 to 5:30pm Friday; 1 to 5pm Saturday

🍎 **The New York Public Library at Lincoln Center,** the Children's Room, 2nd floor (tel. 870-1633); for older children (tel. 870-1630)
Hours: Children's Room 2 to 5:45pm Monday, and Wednesday to Friday; 1 to 4pm Saturday
   The Library at Lincoln Center is open on Saturday and reservations are a must for their programs. For information (tel. 870-1630).

🍎 **Jefferson Market Public Library** (tel. 243-4334)
   Hours: Children's Room, 2:30 to 5:30pm Monday to Thursday, 1 to 5pm Saturday. Closed Friday and Sunday
Library Hours: 10am to 6pm Monday, 1 to 6pm Tuesday and Thursday, 1 to 8pm Wednesday, 10am to 5pm Saturday. Closed Friday and Sunday
   For the public library near you, see the *NYNEX* white pages listed under New York Public Library. Unfortunately, there is no recorded announcement of library activities. It is too bad that the monthly library publication *Events for Children* (see page 41) advises "programs are subject to change," but does not include the telephone numbers of each public library.

Sports Events

🍎 **Madison Square Garden,** Seventh Avenue, between 32nd and 33rd streets, New York, NY 10001 (tel. 465-6000)
   For everything you need to know regarding basketball, hockey, wrestling, and other special events such as tennis, dog shows, and horse shows. For tickets, there's the box office or Ticketron (tel. 399-4444).

BASEBALL TEAMS

🍎 **New York Mets,** Shea Stadium, Flushing, NY 11368 (tel. 718/507-6387), (tel. 718/507-8499) for automated ticket and schedule information

New York Yankees, Yankee Stadium, Bronx, NY 10451 (tel. 293-6000)

BASKETBALL TEAMS

New York Knicks, Madison Square Garden, Seventh Avenue, between 32nd and 33rd streets, New York, NY 10001 (tel. 465-6000)

New Jersey Nets, Brendan Byrne Arena, The Meadowlands, East Rutherford, NJ 07073 (tel. 201/935-8888)

FOOTBALL TEAMS

New York Giants, Giants Stadium, The Meadowlands, East Rutherford, NJ 07073 (tel. 201/935-8222)

New York Jets, Giants Stadium, The Meadowlands, East Rutherford, NJ 07073 (tel. 516/538-7200) for everything

ICE HOCKEY TEAMS

New York Islanders, Nassau Coliseum, Uniondale, NY 11553 (tel. 516/794-4100)

New York Rangers, Madison Square Garden, Seventh Avenue, between 32nd and 33rd streets, New York, NY 10001 (tel. 465-6000)

TENNIS

Newspapers will herald the coming of the big tennis events and where they'll be played.

U.S.T.A. National Tennis Center, Flushing Meadows Corona Park, Queens (tel. 718/271-5100)

WRESTLING

Madison Square Garden, Seventh Avenue, between 32nd and 33rd streets, New York, NY 10001 (tel. 465-6000)
Check your newspapers or call for dates and names of wrestlers.

CHAPTER 4

Holidays, Parades, Street Fairs & Special Events

You have to know where, when, and what for New York happenings, because there are so many so often that you can miss loads of fun only blocks away.

For parade dates, routes, and times, don't hesitate to call the Convention and Visitors Bureau, Monday through Friday (tel. 397-8222). For information on all street activities, street performances, street fairs, art shows, and more, call 566-2506. For information on monthly park activities, call 860-1809. This includes Damrosch Park behind Lincoln Center if you're tracking down Lincoln Center Out-of-Doors.

From late April until October there are outdoor activities all over town. April is when the street entertainers emerge, and stay until October. Street fairs proliferate in these months and are jolly!

Parade dates change from year to year, but usually remain in the month for which they are scheduled. (Could you take the St. Patrick's Day Parade out of March? Of course not!)

The public spaces at the World Financial Center at Battery Park City have free performances year-round. Look in your Friday *New York Times* weekend section for schedules.

January

❧ Chinese New Year and Chinese New Year Parade
Dragons draggin' through the streets of Chinatown are not to be missed. They won't be if you read the introduction to this chapter one more time so you know where and when parades take place.

As if this parade weren't enough, Chinese restaurants all over the city, and especially in Chinatown, serve special New Year's dinners. Save this for the older kids—younger ones lack the patience or the stomach size to make it through these.

❧ Grand Prix Tennis Tournament
This biggy is at Madison Square Garden. Call 563-8300 to get specifics on the schedule and ticket avaiability and prices.

❧ Ice Capades
A wonderful show for all ages. Every year they bring something special and new. Check the Madison Square Garden well in advance to get great seats during their 14-day visit (tel. 563-8300 for more information).

Note: Some years they arrive in February.

❧ Winter Festival
Central Park strikes again! Look in your *Good Times* for this one-day winter wonderland. Not to worry if it's snowless—they make it. They instruct you how to ski cross country (well, from Fifth Ave. to Central Park West, anyway) and other seasonal fun things.

February

❧ A.A.U. National Track and Field Championships
Preteen and teenage jocks wait for this one to come to Madison Square Garden. Call 563-8300 for more information.

Chinese Lantern Day
Chinatown with children on parade—and lots more. Is there anything kids like more than seeing other kids? Of course not.

Empire Cat Show
This takes place at Pier 90, Hudson River at 50th Street. If your child is a cat-lover, he'll go mad. If you're allergic to felines, you'll go mad, too. Be careful—some of these beauties are for sale.

Presidents' Day
There's always something for Abe and George. Don't bother sending gifts. Watch the papers for parades and other celebrations.

Westminster Kennel Club Show
This is still the classiest production in New York. The dogs are magnificent. But for real style, the handlers should get the ribbons. The audience is swellegant, too. If your youngster has the patience and wants to go, it's a treat. If you have cable TV, you can save the money and get the feel of grandeur at Madison Square Garden. Call 465-6000 for more information.

March

The Easter Parade
Fifth Avenue from Central Park (59th Street) down to Rockefeller Center (50th Street). Chic and style have been replaced by costumes and exhibitionism. The expression "Easter Parade" is left over from New York's elegant period when the gentry would promenade down the avenue to see and be seen. No one ever marched in parade style—they sauntered. Now they are on rollerblades.

Note: This is listed under March, but Easter often arrives in April.

The Easter Show
It's at Radio City Music Hall, of course (50th Street and Sixth Avenue; tel. 247-4777). For tickets and program information or Ticketron information call 399-4444. For Ticketron tickets with a credit card call 947-5850. Dancing bunnies and dancing

Rockettes—and a seasonal spectacle for the family. Get your tickets in advance. Avoid the rush.

🍎 Egg Rolling in Central Park
This, too, could take place in April. Saturday, the day before Easter Sunday, they have egg rolling on the Great Lawn in Central Park from 9am to 3pm. You do not need to worry about your g.c.'s finery—the eggs are wooden or plastic.

🍎 Ringling Bros. and Barnum & Bailey Circus
It's all in this book (see "Circuses" in Chapter 10, "That's Entertainment"). Don't miss the Circus Parade (not scheduled or announced under this title). The kids and you will be enthralled as they march the animals from their point of New York arrival to Madison Square Garden (that's why it's called the Circus Parade). If you don't find the date, the route, and the hours in your usual sources, call the Garden (tel. 465-6000) or the Convention and Visitors Bureau (tel. 397-8222).

🍎 St. Patrick's Day Parade
The march is March 17 on 5th Avenue. Starting time is 11am. Days before, you can watch the white street line on Fifth Avenue turn to green. (Well, it's almost spring—a lot of things are starting to turn green.) The parade route is from 44th Street north to 86th Street, with much activity on the steps of St. Patrick's Cathedral at 50th Street. If you want to see every breathing New York politician, here's your big chance.

April

🍎 Broadway Show League Softball
The teams in this league are made up of theater folk. The quality of the softball skills is questionable, but it's fun. They play at the Hecksher Diamond in Central Park, 62nd Street, on Thursday at noon and 2pm from the middle of April through July. Just look for the team shirts—maybe *Cats* vs. *The Phantom*.

🍎 The Greek Day Parade
Fifth Avenue is mighty attractive when it's dotted with the

native Greek costumes. The children are not to be believed. You'll never see whiter white than their stiff skirts (boys too) or blacker, more beautiful eyes (boys too).

Sports
New York's favorite sport, baseball, begins at Shea Stadium for the Mets and Yankee Stadium for the Yankees.

Street Entertainment
Weather permitting, of course, you'll find these performers all over town. Here are some key locations: Battery Park and Wall Street—weekdays at noon; Central Park—at two places every day, the mall and the zoo entrance; Fifth Avenue—from Rockefeller Center to Central Park (59th Street), every day at noon and 5pm; Metropolitan Museum of Art—every day groups come and go, but you may be sure they're there at lunch hour; the 42nd Street Library—every day at lunch hour for sure, and when the weather is good, the audience (escapees from offices) is large; Theater District—at every theater at intermission for matinee and evening performances.

May

Armed Forces Day Parade
Fifth Avenue turns into an armed camp. Even the tanks take to the street. The reviewing stand at 65th Street overflows with the military.

Brooklyn Bridge Day Parade
Marchers and bands come over the bridge. The bridge is magnificent, and when the weather is good, it's a special event.

Martin Luther King, Jr., Memorial Day Parade
This is huge and most impressive—on Fifth Avenue.

Ninth Avenue International Food Festival
This has gotten to be such a winner it runs Saturday and Sunday. It stretches from 37th to 57th Streets on Ninth Avenue, with ethnic foods as far as you're able to see. The odors of all different kinds of foods are tantalizing. Guaranteed indigestion if

you and your g.c. eat enough. There are street performers, balloons, and more stuff to buy. A big crowd. A big, happy crowd. If you have a toddler, take him in his stroller. You'll have lots of company on wheels.

Norwegian Independence Day Parade
A lovely Fifth Avenue event. The participants are blond and beautiful. It's true!

Washington Square Outdoor Art Show
Across from Washington Square Park at 4th Street and Fifth Avenue, but it spreads down the side streets and over to Sixth Avenue on the west side, LaGuardia Place to the south, and who knows where this will end?

It goes for three weekends. It starts at the end of May and goes into June. It's a revelation. My g.c. happen to love this one. I'm not sure if they find the art or the spectators more fascinating. Bring the stroller if you have little ones. If the weather is great, hold on tight to your kids, or bring a leash. Crowds are murder on "togetherness." You'll find the exact dates in *New York* magazine and the *Village Voice* for sure.

Ye Old Village Fair
Greenwich Village has a street fair for blocks. And they have a special street just for kids. The fair takes place between Seventh Avenue and Hudson Street, but the tentacles spread. Follow the crowds for fun, entertainment, and face-stuffing.

It takes place in the middle of the month—keep an eye out in your *New York Times* Friday edition so you don't miss this one. Take the babies, the strollers, and everybody else.

You Gotta Have Park
This is the Saturday and Sunday event from 10am to 6pm that is the civic-minded, park-loving New Yorker's outing. Everybody is welcome to sweep and clean up the park.

Softball games with teams made up of TV soap opera cast members, actors and actresses from Broadway shows, and just plain civilians add to the fun. Paul Newman sells popcorn.

The spirit is what makes it all fun. As many as 10,000 volunteers take part. There are booths set up by the Central Park Conservancy to solicit donations to ensure the upkeep of our dearest treasure—Central Park.

June

🍎 Central Park
The theater and musical events both indoors and outdoors in the park begin in this month. The traffic is limited to bikes, skates, skateboards, walkers, runners, and horse-drawn carriages. No cars. The longest and largest picnic—Central Park in the summer.

🍎 Museum Mile Festival
From 6 to 9pm on the first Tuesday evening in June, the museums from 82nd to 105th streets invite everyone for a free visit. And you feel like a special guest. Any participating museum will be happy to give you further information if you telephone. Kids 9 years and older will like this because it adds to their feeling of New York sophisticate.

🍎 Puerto Rican Day Parade
The floats on Fifth Avenue are colorful and the music is wonderful. This parade always terminates in a participant's picnic in the park. If you like ethnic food, the vendors have their wagons on 59th Street and Fifth Avenue.

🍎 Rockefeller Center
Stop by for the free outdoor concerts at lunchtime.

🍎 Salute to Israel Parade
Fifth Avenue is the parade ground. A spirited, well-attended affair. There are more Jewish people living in New York than in Tel Aviv.

🍎 St. Anthony Festival
A *molto bene* outing on Sullivan Street near Houston Street. Inhale—you'll locate it. Great Italian food, great Italian spirit. More of New York's *dolce vita*. Ever see pastry fried in a huge garbage pail? And the kids will go for it. Go at night—even with little ones—it's more fun. There are rides, too!

World Trade Center Plaza
A broad spectrum of entertainment for you and the kids. Jugglers, mimes, musicians, and other talented performers. And it's free.

July

American Crafts Festival
This is not just a huge crafts show. For you and your kids there is also a children's festival with entertainment—puppets, clowns, singing. There are also craft demonstrations the young folks may never have seen. Okay, when was the last time you saw a spinning wheel at work, or wool woven from the very sheep shorn for the occasion? This takes place the first two weekends in July at Lincoln Center (64th Street and Broadway). There's no charge.

Entertainment for Kids in the Park
In Central Park, and other city parks in July and August, the Department of Parks and Recreation has mobile entertainment units visit playgrounds and other areas in the parks with a full load of entertainers, arts and crafts, and sports stuff. They have it all. Look in your *Good Times* for the dates. For more information, call 397-3156.

Independence Day
Contrary to rumors, the Fourth of July celebrations existed before the 1986 Miss Liberty fête—and they continue. Fireworks are done by R. H. Macy (they do more than the Thanksgiving Day Parade for New York). Head for the FDR Drive at 9pm on the Fourth. Not to worry—there are no cars from 14th to 51st streets.

There's a day-long festival downtown as well. Catch it at Battery Park, unless you like speeches. For oratory and more, go to City Hall.

Italian Street Festival
Music, gaiety, and happy times dominate at Carmine and Bleecker streets in southern Greenwich Village.

Jazz at the South Street Seaport
Your older kids will dig this. Jazz groups perform for four

weeks—from July 15 through August 15—on Friday and Saturday evenings at 8pm. You must arrive hours earlier for your first-come, first-served, free tickets. No problem keeping entertained at the Summer Seaport. Check the boat schedule—they also have jazz cruises if your youngsters are real aficionados.

Mostly Mozart
For six weeks, from the middle of July through August, evenings at Lincoln Center in Avery Fisher Hall (64th Street and Broadway; tel. 874-2424). Lincoln Center Out-of-Doors is free.

What did this city do before Lincoln Center (BLC)? Take the kids of all ages to the outdoor concerts. Use good judgment for the Avery Fisher Hall nights. Puhlease—there are people who wait all year for this festival, so no noise, of course.

Nathan's Famous Hot Dog Eating Contest
This is held at the Coney Island restaurant (Surf and Stillwell avenues; tel. 718/266-3161 for information, or 869-0600 to register a participant). They accept only 30 contestants, but the real fun is watching. Then you can explore Coney Island.

South Street Seaport
This is the height of the South Street Seaport season. The boats are running, the performers are at the piers (jugglers, clowns, magicians), and right through August free entertainment abounds in all the public spaces. Weekdays from noon to 6pm and weekends from 11am to 8pm, on Pier 17 you'll see the best of the street performers.

August

Greenwich Village Jazz Festival
This is for your older kids because it's not all out-of-doors. You visit various Greenwich Village clubs to see some of the jazz groups (only the best) perform. There are films and lectures as well. It runs for 11 days at the end of the month. You can get the prices—some places are free, and some are inexpensive. For more information, call 242-1785.

Lincoln Center Out-of-Doors
Dance, music, theater—all yours for the taking in the fresh (?)

air. Check for the age-appropriate performances. You'll not regret these outings. If you do, you may leave. It's free and outside, at 64th Street and Broadway. For more information, call 877-2011.

Richmond County Fair

The Richmondtown Restoration at 441 Clarke Ave., Staten Island, is well worth a visit for you and your g.c. Couple it with the fair and it's a swell outing for all ages. Country-and-western bands, square dancing, food, watermelon-seed-spitting contests, frog jumping, and diaper-changing competitions. Does this have your name on it? You betcha. This takes place for two days at the end of August (with September rain dates). They start at 11am and finish at 7pm. Admission charge of $1 for the kids and $2.50 for you alleged adults. For more information, call 718/351-1617.

Tap-O-Mania

How would your kids like to be in the *Guinness Book of World Records*? Just join the mid-August Macy's Parade of Tap Dancers. It starts at noon, and there is a rain date. Heavens, the rain would muffle the sound of the dancing feet. This is as much fun to watch as it is to be a participant. Last year there were more than 8,500 dancers. Guinness lists this as the "record for the largest line of dancers ever to tap in unison." The unison is questionable. The event is pure New York. Crazy, man! It takes place at 34th Street and Seventh Avenue near Broadway. Call 560-4377 to register.

September

Feast of San Gennaro

This is the biggest, best, and most colorful of the Italian street festivals. It takes place in the middle of September for 10 days, from noon to midnight (pick your hours according to the g.c.'s ages and stamina). The nights are prettier and more crowded. They have food you won't believe, fun things to buy, and spontaneous activities that are the best. Head for Mulberry Street in Little Italy; then follow your nose. For more information, call 226-9546.

The 42nd Street Street Fair
One Sunday in this month, from river to river on 42nd St.

Labor Day
The traditional parade is still held on Fifth Avenue, but it has really lost its pizzazz, as well as its crowds. They've all gone to the West Indian American Day Carnival, which makes its way down Eastern Parkway in Brooklyn to the reviewing stand in front of the Brooklyn Museum. It's so exciting and colorful that it exceeds parade classification. You've never seen better costumes. For more information, call 718/783-4469. Go!

Labor Day Street Fair
This is a fair on Labor Day Monday to celebrate the meaning of Labor Day. From noon to 7pm on 42nd Street between Ninth and Tenth avenues they have shows, food, and music.

New York Is Book Country
The third Sunday in September from 11am to 5pm on Fifth Avenue between 48th and 57th streets. From Madison to Sixth avenues on 52nd and 53rd streets is also Book Country. The Kids' Block is on 53rd Street between Fifth and Sixth avenues. Every bookstore, publisher, and even bookbinders have stalls, carts, or stands on the street for this big one. Clowns and balloons abound. This is a lovely fair. Take all the kids.

Once Upon a Sunday
At the Museum of Modern Art, 53rd Street between Fifth and Sixth avenues, just one day at the end of the month, from 11am to 3:30pm. They've done a whole day all for kids. The under-6 crowd is invited free. They have cartoons, stories, games, food, and more. All done with the style and care we expect from MOMA—even for a kid's outing.

Sports
The football season begins! If you doubt it, turn on your TV Monday nights.

Steuben Day Parade
The German marching day up Fifth Avenue. A good parade. Look in your *New York Times* or *New York* magazine. For more information, call 397-8222.

Third Avenue Merchants Association (TAMA) Fair

The first Sunday after Labor Day from 11am to 7pm on Third Avenue, of course, from 14th to 34th streets. While the kids are stuffing their faces or deciding which ride they would like, keep your eyes peeled for great bargains.

Third Avenue Street Festival

This takes place in the middle of the month—some years it's the same day as the Book Country event on Fifth Avenue. Finish with the books, then on to Third Avenue from 68th to 90th streets. On Sunday, of course, from 11am until about 7pm. Entertainment, food, toys, and general frolicking in the streets. If it's nice weather, you have a swell outing. Put this on your must list.

U.S. Open Tennis Championships

If your g.c. is a fan, he'll love this one. *The New York Times* ads start long before the event if you want tickets to attend. Something the kids will never forget.

Washington Square Outdoor Art Show

For a return engagement. This is around Washington Square Park and extends north to 14th Street and south to Houston Street. It takes place on Labor Day weekend and the next two weekends as well, from noon until you lose the light. It's big, varied, and fun for all.

October

Annual Village Halloween Parade

This is the most unusual parade in New York. On Halloween, October 31 at 7pm, the march starts. It begins on Sixth Avenue and Houston Street and goes up Sixth Avenue to Union Square Park, 14th Street. There is a throng of marchers that join along the way—and never in your life will you see such outlandish costumes, wigs, and makeup. This is absolutely spectacular. The music is great, and the spirit is wild. Very Wild. For older kids only.

The Columbus Avenue Street Fair

The Upper West Side citizenry provides this street fair with vitality and enthusiasm. Start at about 67th Street and walk north.

Food, entertainment, merchandise you'll covet or choose to dismiss. It's good fun. If you want to know what to wear to feel you're current and chic, just look around you.

The Columbus Day Parade
Politicians on parade. Of course there are floats (always the *Niña*, the *Pinta*, or the *Santa Maria* to celebrate the arrival of Columbus). A big turnout for the march up Fifth Avenue.

Pulaski Day Parade
This is the Polish celebration march—and it's a big one.

Rockefeller Center Skating Rink
It opens for the season at the end of this month, weather permitting. It's open 7 days a week from 9am until 11:30pm at Rockefeller Plaza, 50th Street and Fifth Avenue. Even if you can't skate, it's fun to watch. The kids can rent skates and have an instructor here, if they want to give it a go. If they're good skaters, here's a great place to show off their skills.

Sports
Welcome the basketball season with the Knicks at the Garden. The Nets are at the Meadowlands.

November

The Big Apple Circus
This circus sets up their tent behind Lincoln Center (between the Opera House and the New York State Theater, in the rear) around Thanksgiving time. They are with us through Christmas. Please don't exclude this from your Christmas or Chanukah gift list for your children. Especially for the toddlers through age 10 group. (For more information, see the section on "Circuses" in Chapter 10, "That's Entertainment.")

Christmas Star Show
This show at the Hayden Planetarium is a very special show for the holiday season. It goes on until after New Year's, and everyone raves about it. For more information, call 769-5920.

The Macy's Thanksgiving Day Parade
This is it! The big event of the year for kids. Don't tell me

"I can see it better on TV." It's just not the same. Rain or shine, heat, sleet, or snow—get out on the street. The only exception is if you have a friend of a friend who is able to wheedle you a window spot on Central Park West or someone's office on Broadway.

The parade starts on 77th Street and Central Park West, travels south to Columbus Circle, then to Broadway, and on down to its final resting place, Macy's at 34th Street and Broadway.

If you don't know the meaning of the word *spectacular*, here's your big chance to enhance your vocabulary. If you have little ones, get a curb spot early. It's worth the wait.

For extra pleasure, watch them inflate the balloons on Wednesday night. It takes just about all night to do the job. It gets done in the 70s on Central Park West. It's not just for kids, you know.

New York Marathon
If you want to see camaraderie at its zenith—come to the marathon. Runners from all over this country and the rest of the world assemble for this 26.6-mile run on city pavement through five boroughs. They are cheered from Staten Island right to the finish line in Central Park (at Tavern-on-the-Green). One of the best spots to see true grit is Central Park South, almost at the finish line. You'll see faces etched with exhaustion, hope, exhilaration, pain—it's an unbelievable experience for you and your kids. Don't miss seeing the marathon—it's thrilling. The ages and physical conditions of some of the runners will give you new respect for the courage of the participants. Save your loudest applause for the physically disabled Achilles Runners. About 6pm many of the runners finish. They're a true inspiration.

Radio City Music Hall Christmas Spectacular
The harbinger of the holiday season takes place from November into January. Join the lines at the theater (Sixth Avenue at 50th Street; tel. 247-4777 for ticket and program information; for Ticketron information 399-4444; tickets with credit cards 947-5850), well in advance for your seats. Your little ones will be wide eyed.

Veterans' Day Parade
It's November 11. Check the papers for parade information.

Window Shopping
The store windows are ready for viewing. Fifth Avenue goes all out with holiday decorations. The excitement is building.

December

American Crafts Holiday Festival
Saturday and Sunday of the second and third weekends in December at New York University Loeb Center, Washington Square and LaGuardia Place. And it's not just crafts. If your youngsters have never seen a glassblower, let them have a demonstration of a lost art. There is other entertainment, but gee, a glassblower! All ages will have a peachy time. Bring money—they sell toys and other good things. For more information, call 677-4672.

The Annual Children's Christmas Party
This is put on by the Museum of the City of New York, Fifth Avenue and 103rd Street. Make your reservations well in advance. It takes place the second Monday in December from 2 to 5pm. It's a kids' heaven. Bring your toddlers and older ones, too. This museum loves kids—this party will convince any of you doubters. For more information, call 534-1672. For the Share-the-Season Celebration, bring an ornament for the Christmas tree.

Chanukah Celebration
On the first night of this holiday, everyone is invited to the 92nd Street Y—it's at Lexington Avenue and 92nd Street. Bring all the kids. There are stories, puppet and magic shows, and the first candle is lit on the menorah. For more information, call 427-6000, ext. 233.

A Christmas Carol
This is at the Trans-Lux Theater at South Street Seaport, 210 Front St. You only thought you were familiar with this Dickens classic. Wait until you see and hear this version.

Christmas Carousel
Every year at Lever House, 390 Park Ave., at 53rd Street, the exquisite carousel is in the lobby for viewing. Little ones find it

most frustrating because they can't ride on it with Santa Claus. If your g.c. is mature enough to be a spectator and not a participant, fine. Otherwise, keep moving.

Christmas Trees
This is an eye-dazzling month in New York. Don't miss the Christmas tree at Rockefeller Center (as if it were possible), and those at the Metropolitan Museum of Art, the American Museum of Natural History, and the South Street Seaport. The tree at South Street Seaport is really alive. It's formed by carolers, positioned and dressed to look like the branches. Lovely on the eyes as well as the ears.

Holiday Windows
The windows on Fifth Avenue are a must. Especially Lord & Taylor (38th Street and Fifth Avenue) and Saks Fifth Avenue (50th Street and Fifth Avenue). The two Sundays prior to Christmas, Fifth Avenue becomes a strolling street. No cars, buses, etc. are permitted to use the avenue from 11am to 3pm on those days. The restriction is from 34th Street north to 57th Street. If you have a short companion, walk on the sidewalk early in the morning.

The Menorah on Fifth Avenue
The largest menorah in the world is 32 feet high and is at 59th Street and Fifth Avenue. A candle is lit here each night of the Chanukah festival.

New Year's Eve
The 600-pound ball descends at midnight in Times Square. It is preceded by a 90-minute laser show. I do not suggest you take the kids to join the millions of revelers; it is televised.

At midnight in Central Park, between 63rd and 69th streets, there are 6 minutes of fireworks. There is a much longer fireworks display at the South Street Seaport.

There is also a 5-mile run in the park. Runners assemble at Tavern-on-the-Green at midnight, most in outrageous costumes, and start the run at 12:30am; there are thousands of runners each year. Happy New Year in New York!

The Nutcracker
At Lincoln Center, of course (the New York State Theater,

64th Street and Broadway). This ballet is all the magic of the holiday season in one stupendous performance. From the middle of December into January is just not a long enough run for everyone to be satisfied. It's the hottest ticket in New York Christmas week—but you can always try. For more information, call 870-5570.

Rockefeller Center Tree-Lighting Ceremony
This takes place early in the month at dusk, usually around 5pm. The crowds are huge. If you're with a small child, the crush is terrific and he is sure to grow impatient. An older child may enjoy the crowds, the anticipation, and the excitement. It is nifty to be there when it's lit—especially for those of you who are unable to handle the sorting of lights on a tabletop tree. How do they manage this? It all takes place at 50th Street and Rockefeller Plaza; for more information, call 489-3000.

South Street Seaport
A singing Christmas Tree! The weeks before the holiday there are carolers arranged to look like a tree. Usually a weekend entertainment, but as the big day comes closer, their appearances are more frequent. Call (tel. 732-7678) for the schedule.

Waldorf-Astoria Hotel Lobby
If you want to see some of the prettiest decorating of the Christmas season, enter on the Park Avenue (at 50th Street) side and go through the lobby. It's lovely.

Atriums, Plazas & Parks

Regrouping and resting are integral components when touring New York. Any decisions made in the midst of the pedestrian traffic will be losers. Take a few minutes for a breather at any of the places below. For information on street activities and performances call 566-2506.

The following listings are geographical, from north (uptown) to south (downtown). For activities in Central Park, see Chapter 9.

Since 1961, New York City has provided an incentive program to builders of commercial space; in exchange for public space, builders may add 20% more floor space beyond the amount normally permitted. In 1975, the city became smarter. Guidelines for builders were included with specific requirements for seating, planting, and lighting.

The most relaxing spaces are those with waterfalls.

East Side, Up to Down

Carl Schurz Park, 86th Street and East End Avenue
It stretches from 82nd Street to 89th Street. It's maintained in

perfect condition since it lies in the shadow of Gracie Mansion—the home of Hizzoner the Mayor. This is a fine, large, well-equipped park/playground where the kids can run free.

Grand Army Plaza, 58th Street to 60th Street on Fifth Avenue

This was designed by Thomas Hastings (1911) as a gateway to Central Park. The south end has the Pulitzer Fountain, sculpture by Karl Bitter. The plaza is intersected by 59th Street. The north end has the golden Augustus Saint-Gaudens horse with General Sherman astride. Grand Army Plaza is a key location for vendors, demonstrators, performers, and us plain civilians. A good place to hang out.

Place des Antiquaires, 135 E. 57th St., at Lexington Avenue

A very beautiful building. If you've escaped from Bloomingdale's, this will give you a moment to catch your breath.

AT&T Building, Madison Avenue and 56th Street

This is covered space with lovely white iron chairs and tables. No problem here even if it's raining. They often have musical entertainment. Ask the folks at InfoQuest if there is anything on the agenda. Don't forget to visit InfoQuest. See Chapter 8.

IBM Building, the Bamboo Court, 56th Street and Madison Avenue

This is a beautiful space enhanced by huge pots with exquisite seasonal plants. The towering trees make one feel he is in a lovely wooded spot. There's a little snack bar with great coffee and pastries, and sandwiches for the children. You might even catch a musical group performing. No definite schedule.

Trump Tower, 56th Street and Fifth Avenue

On the fourth and fifth levels there are outside gardens where you might be in time for a fashion show or some other event. At the lower level (the building's—not yours!) you may sit at the snack bar, providing you partake of refreshments sold in this oasis. The wall of water is spectacular.

Seagram Plaza, 54th Street and Park Avenue

Though intended as a fitting entrance to a spectacular building, this is a key location for sitting, talking, and brown-bagging it. In good weather this vast space is teeming with people sitting on the steps and other places they are able to find room—all catching the "rays." A fun thing to do.

Citicorp Center, Lexington Avenue, between 53rd and 54th streets

The Market at Citicorp has lots of entertainment, plenty of seating, and three floors of shops, restaurants, and snack bars. Do look at St. Peter's Church in this building. The interior was designed by Louise Nevelson.

520 Madison Avenue, on 53rd Street

A waterfall awaits you here in the middle of the city.

Park Avenue Plaza, from 52nd to 53rd streets between Madison and Park avenues

Enter this indoor plaza from either street and enjoy the waterfall and perhaps a spot of tea.

Paley Park, 53rd Street, between Fifth and Madison avenues

The ultimate vest-pocket park. Opened in 1967, this is one of the first miniparks. The waterfall is 20 feet high. There are tables and chairs where you may enjoy your brown-bag or street-bought lunch to the salubrious sound of rushing water. It is set back from the street, and seeing it for the first time is much like finding $10 on the sidewalk.

The park is closed in January and February. From May 1 to November 1, it is open from 8am to 7pm. From November 2 to April 30, it closes at 6pm. It is never open on Sunday.

Paley Park is on the land formerly occupied by the Stork Club. Put that in your memorabilia/trivia ledger.

Tishman Building, 666 Fifth Ave., at 52nd Street

You'll hear nothing in this space other than the sound of rushing water and the hum of polite conversation.

Greenacre Park, on 51st Street, between Second and Third avenues

This is the most spectacular of the atriums with a waterfall. Not to worry about waste; the 2,000 gallons of water used per minute are recirculated. There are usually lots of moms with carriages and strollers here to view the 25-foot waterfall and enjoy the food provided by the on-premise restaurant—hot dogs, chili dogs, pasta, salads, and more. All of it good. Lovely plantings, as well as tables and chairs that are movable to catch the sun rays, make this an ideal plotzing place in clement weather.

Olympic Tower, 51st to 52nd streets and Fifth Avenue
There is public seating at this indoor atrium where you'll be soothed by the sounds and images created by the waterfall.

Crystal Pavilion, 50th Street and Third Avenue
Hours: Monday through Saturday
At this three-tier atrium, there are flashing neon lights, disco music, and plenty of seats. With two waterfalls, a gondola elevator, and lots of plants and flowers, this is a really glitzy place.

Helmsley Palace, Villard Houses, 50th Street and Madison Avenue
Hours: 24 hours daily
The Villard Houses are the public space for the hotel. Marble halls, staircases, and art are worth a look. No seating.

Rockefeller Center, Channel Gardens, Fifth Avenue and 50th Street
This is a central location to be sure. During Easter time the scent of the lilies will intoxicate you. At Christmas season you'll be trampled.
Note: The best view of the Christmas tree is from the Ladies Room at Saks Fifth Avenue that faces west.

Chemcourt, 47th Street and Park Avenue
Hours: 24 hours daily
That's not a real man hailing a cab—it's a sculpture titled *Taxi.* This is a three-story greenhouse atrium with trees and flowers provided by the New York Botanical Garden. There are terraced pools, too. Not for sitting, but swell for looking.

Dag Hammarskjöld Plaza I, 47th Street and Second Avenue
Summer sitting with a waterfall and music at noon.

Dag Hammarskjöld Plaza II, between 46th and 47th streets on Second Avenue

More space than seats. They do have lots of huge sculptures—
but you can't sit on them.

Park Avenue Atrium, 45th and 46th streets, between Park
and Lexington avenues
Hours: Monday through Friday from 8am to 6pm
   This 23-story atrium with a glass-enclosed elevator will provide
you and the kids with a fine view of the 245-foot sculpture *Winged
Gamma.* No seating, but the elevator and the views make it worth a
stop if you're in the area.

Ford Foundation, 42nd Street, between First and Second
avenues
Hours: Monday through Friday from 9am to 5pm
   When you visit the U.N., don't miss this. Within the walls of this
10-story glass house are trees, plants, and a pool. The skylight and
the floor will make you feel like you're in a huge, beautiful
greenhouse. You are.

Whitney Museum at Philip Morris, 42nd Street and Park
Avenue
Hours: Monday through Saturday from 11am to 6pm (on Thursday to 7:30pm)
   This is a Whitney Museum satellite exhibit space. There are free
tours, a sculpture court, and an indoor garden. You can also buy
yummy desserts at the snack bar. I know I promised you just
sitting, but I had to sneak in some atriums that are too good to
miss.

Bryant Park, Fifth Avenue and 42nd Street
   Directly behind the library it is face-lifting time. AOTW a
restaurant is under construction. This charming park is in the
process of being reclaimed and restored to its original pastoral
beauty. By publication date, it should be all ready for you.

Grand Hyatt Hotel, 42nd Street between Vanderbilt and
Lexington avenues
   If you're in the neighborhood, drop in to see this indoor atrium
with a waterfall in a most dramatic setting.

Highpoint Plaza, 250 E. 40th St., at Second Avenue
   The high point of a visit here is to view the waterfall.

Madison Square Park, Fifth Avenue, between 23rd and 26th streets

This lovely site was where the first Madison Square Garden was built. The second was at 50th St. and 8th Avenue. The third and present Madison Square Garden is at 33rd Street and 7th Avenue. Now that you know all this, pull up a bench and chill out.

West Side, Up to Down

Riverside Park, 72nd to 145th streets, between Riverside Drive and the Hudson River

This park comes and goes, geographically speaking. There are intersections that wipe it out entirely (72nd Street, 79th Street, etc.). There are swings, seesaws, and other things for kids in various locations. Some parts of Riverside Park are lovely and some are filthy holes. Pick your spot with care.

Strawberry Fields, Central Park West and 72nd Street

This is Yoko Ono's memorial to the late John Lennon. It is an International Peace Garden as well as a playground. Unfortunately, there are people who continue to steal the plaque.

Strawberry Fields is directly across the street from the Dakota Apartments. Every teenager with whom I've done New York has asked to see this site.

Lincoln Center Plaza, Broadway and 65th Street

The ledge around the fountain is a soothing spot. Plans are in the works (I've been told) for more seating in this area.

The island of land on Broadway that divides the north and south traffic has benches at every corner. They were once key locations decades ago. This is where the local gentry exchanged gossip and enjoyed the weather while the trolley cars provided the background music. Unfortunately, today these benches now sit in filth—crack vials, garbage, and worse.

Fisher Park, between 54th and 55th streets on Sixth Avenue

With a waterfall, a big kite sculpture, and chairs and tables, this spot is an oasis.

🍎 **Equitable Center,** Equitable Life Assurance Building, 51st to 52nd streets and Seventh Avenue
Hours: Monday through Friday from 11am to 6pm (on Thursday to 7:30pm), and on Saturday from noon to 5pm

This is an atrium that is a satellite branch of the Whitney Museum. The proportions of this space will knock your socks off. The entrance to this 53-story building is an 80-foot arch. Roy Lichtenstein's *Mural with Blue Brushstroke* (68 × 32 feet) fits this atrium space perfectly.

The lack of seating is unimportant when compared to the paintings, the sculpture, and the beauty of this atrium.

🍎 **Exxon Park,** 49th to 50th Streets, between Sixth and Seventh avenues

Here is a space for some fine summer sitting. On Tuesday and Thursday at noon, you and the office lunch-hour crowd may share the joy of the free concerts. There is a counter to buy food and drinks. A waterfall 20 feet high and 46 feet long is also nothing to sneeze at.

🍎 **McGraw-Hill,** 48th to 49th streets, between Sixth and Seventh avenues

A summer place. There are benches, a snack bar, and a waterfall for the kiddies to walk under. Yes—under! The waterfall that separates the street from the park is 40 feet wide and 20 feet tall. Surely this is worthy of your attention.

🍎 **Union Square Park,** 14th to 17th streets, between Park Avenue South and Broadway

When they brought this park back from a slum, they even built condos and co-ops for the birds and the squirrels. Greenmarkets are held every Friday, Saturday, and Wednesday. Plants, flowers, vegetables, and fruits are sold. They also have programs here for kids, where they learn about plants and nutrition. Call the Department of Parks and Recreation (tel. 408-0100) and they'll tell you all about it.

Downtown

🍎 **Washington Square Park,** Fifth Avenue and University Place
This is the NYU campus among other things. It is the heart of

Greenwich Village and busy all the time. In summer there are concerts, dancing, and all sorts of goings-on; some are planned and some are unplanned. The sun has only to shine and spontaneous performances of music, mime, and magic occur.

For programs for the kids, call 408-0204. Enjoy the playground. The Washington Square Arch was designed by Stanford White. There is a way to get inside, but it's not open to the public.

Washington Market Community Park, Chambers and Greenwich streets
In this spot there is a gazebo and climbing equipment for the kids, and trees, flowers, old-world charm for you.

Louise Nevelson Plaza, Maiden Lane and William Street
If you love her work, don't skip this when you're in the Financial District. The trees, the benches, and the aesthetics will help you unwind.

Trinity Church Gardens, Wall Street and Broadway
If you're determined not to waste a second with just resting, come sit here—the final resting place for Alexander Hamilton, Robert Fulton, and other famous people. Make your stay shorter.

Bankers Trust Plaza, Greenwich and Liberty streets
This soothing downtown resting place has a grand waterfall.

Wall Street Plaza, 88 Pine Street
In the heart of the Financial District beats a waterfall. A wise place to invest time.

Hanover Square, Hanover and Pearl streets
A little place with benches. That's all, folks. It does have historical merit—but this chapter is for R & R.

Columbus Park, Mulberry and Baxter streets
Chinatown's play area. Playground equipment.

City Hall Park, Broadway, Park Row and Chambers Street
This is one of the parks toured by the Urban Park Rangers. It sits in the shadow of City Hall, a lovely building. When the weather is good, it does attract a throng.

World Trade Center Plaza
Beautiful sculpture, lots of seating, food and snacks available, and entertainment (free) when the weather is cooperative. It's too large to miss when you're doing the World Trade Center, the World Financial Center, and Battery Park City.

South Street Seaport, Fulton Street and the East River
There's always a place to sit, to eat, to look, in all weather. Outdoors when it's nice, the place bubbles over with constant entertainment. Indoors, counter after counter of self-service ethnic foods.

The Esplanade, Battery Park City at the World Financial Center, between West Street and the Hudson River
Enter through the World Financial Center. This building cost $1.5 billion (not a typo, it's billion). The esplanade is absolutely not to be missed. The sandboxes, the sculpture, the views are all described in detail in Chapter 6. If ever you trusted me, go for this one.

Winter Garden, World Financial Center at Battery Park City
This is the most spectacular public space ever built in New York City. When the city wanted to impress Lady Di, they held the reception in her honor here. For details turn to Chapter 6. Please put this on your "must see" list. Words do not do it justice.

Battery Park, the southern tip of Manhattan Island
When the weather is warm the place to be is here! It catches all the winds. The views are only spectacular. People-watching is the activity. A key location.

Bowling Green, the most southern tip of Broadway
This was the first park in New York City. See where the only street that goes through the entire city originates. Well, if you are a trivia collector it's important.

Brooklyn

Prospect Park, Eastern Parkway and Grand Army Plaza, Brooklyn (tel. 718/788-0055 for information on park events;

718/788-8500 for the Environmental Center; 718/287-7400 for the Urban Park Rangers)
Access: By bus—call the MTA (tel. 718/330-1234) for the schedule of the Culture Bus Loop 2. By subway—2, 3, or 4 to Grand Army Plaza.

Bounded by Ocean Avenue, Parkside Avenue, Prospect Park West, and Prospect Park Southwest, Prospect Park is huge—526 acres to be exact. The same safety rules for Central Park apply even more rigidly to Prospect Park because it's so vast. A brief review of the rules: Don't stray from the well-used areas, don't carry or wear things of value, and leave the park before sunset.

If you're visiting the Brooklyn Museum, you are but a short walk from the park. If you're visiting the Brooklyn Children's Museum the walk is a bit longer. The routes are the same: follow Eastern Parkway.

The Grand Army Plaza is the most visible entrance to the park. And why not? It was designed by Frederick Law Olmsted and Calvert Vaux. These men designed Central Park in Manhattan before they designed Prospect Park (they believed the latter to be their masterpiece) and they repeated the Grand Army Plaza theme. In the center of the plaza you'll see the **Soldiers and Sailors Memorial Arch,** which you can climb (only on spring and autumn weekends) for a wonderful view of Brooklyn and Manhattan.

The activities in this park are endless. They have a rink for ice skating, roller-skating paths, playgrounds, boats to row around the lake, picnic areas, a carousel, and bridle paths for horseback riding.

They have a zoo (and I mean a magnificent zoo!), with elephants and camels and the like. "Magnificent" applies to the murals of Kipling's *Jungle Book* that decorate the walls of the brick buildings. There's also a zoo with farm animals.

There is a cafeteria and rest rooms. Bring those strollers and diapers.

CHAPTER 6

Sites & Skyscrapers: New York's Finest from A to Z

Special buildings are New York. Try this for giggles—show your g.c. how to cut through buildings to avoid getting wet on a rainy day. At 56th Street and Madison Avenue enter into the AT&T covered walk-through to 55th Street. Cross Madison Avenue, stay exposed until 54th Street, head east and go through the Lever House on Park Avenue and 54th Street; exit on 53rd Street. Enter Park Avenue Plaza building (spectacular lobby with a waterfall) on 53rd Street between Park and Madison avenues; exit on 52nd Street. On 52nd Street, go to 40 E. 52nd into the Security Pacific Plaza building. Exit on 52nd Street and cross to the Helmsley (hotel); exit on 50th Street. Now, a choice. Either head west and go through Saks Fifth Avenue if you want to continue downtown

(50th to 49th streets, Fifth and Madison avenues) or head east and go through the lobby of the Waldorf-Astoria (enter on Park Avenue; exit on Lexington Avenue).

The point of this silly exercise is to focus on buildings that one enters on one street and exits on another. It will startle the kids, catch them up in the magic pursuit—and it's a splendid way to travel many blocks without realizing how much ground you're covering. You'll find yourself, and the kids, continuing to look for more of these expansive, and grand, tunnels all over town.

Always look up when walking around New York, but be careful crossing streets. The nicest things happen on the tops of buildings. They are sure to ask you, "What is that little house on top of the building?" The answer, nine times out of 10, is that it's an architectural device to house building "necessaries" (water units, etc.) in the most attractive way.

Another question that will come up is about people. People sitting around in nice weather. People on the steps of the Seagram Building eating lunch, or brown-bagging it at the Pulitzer Fountain. People in the IBM Building Bamboo Court or across the street at the AT&T atrium when it's raining. People who work indoors desperately need to be outdoors to retrench.

This is your chance to tell your little pal about public space. You can explain the arrangement the city has with builders: They have extra floors in exchange for public space.

When the Seagram Building was erected, it was recognized how badly public space is needed. From day one the steps and other outdoor areas of the Seagram Building have been dense with New Yorkers seeking the sun and fresh (?) air on nice days.

The American Telephone and Telegraph Building, World Headquarters, Madison Avenue (between 55th and 56th Streets), New York, NY 10022 (tel. 605-5500)
Access: Bus—M1, M2, M3, M4, M5, M6, M7, M10, M27, M28, M32. Subway—4, 5, 6, N, or R to 59th Street; E or F to Fifth Avenue
InfoQuest Center: Wednesday through Sunday from 10am to 6pm, on Tuesday to 9pm
Architects: Philip Johnson and Andrew Burgee
As new as tomorrow in concept but the top is a design borrowed

from the old. It's flawless in design and workmanship. Peek in the elevators if you doubt. Kids gasp at the lobby's "Golden Boy."

For more information on the InfoQuest Center, see Chapter 8.

The Bronx Zoo, Fordham Road (Bronx River Parkway), Bronx, NY 10460 (tel. 367-1010)

Access: By bus, call 652-8400 for schedule and fare information. On the BxM11, Liberty Lines Bus, which runs on Madison Avenue; stops are 28th Street, 37th, 40th, 47th, 54th, 63rd, 84th and 99th streets. Returns via 5th Avenue.

By train and bus call 532-4900 for schedule and fare information. From Grand Central Terminal take Metro-North to Fordham Station and the Bx9 bus to Southern Boulevard zoo entrance.

Bus and subway—2 or 5 subway to 180th Street, Bronx Zoo/Bronx Park Station, walk east; D train to Fordham Road, change to Bx12 bus going east on Fordham Road, exit Southern Boulevard and walk east on Fordham Road to Ramney gate entrance.

Subway—2 express to Pelham Parkway, walk west to Bronxdale zoo entrance; or 5 express to E. 180th Street and transfer to 7th Avenue line 2 train to Pelham Parkway, walk west to Bronxdale zoo entrance.

Admission: April to October, Friday to Monday, $4 for adults, $2 for ages 2 to 12, free for under 2; November to March, $2.50 for adults, $1 for ages 2 to 12, free for under 2; Tuesday, Wednesday, and Thursday by donation or free

Hours: Monday through Saturday from 10am to 5pm, Sundays and holidays until 5:30pm; November through March until 4:30pm

Ages: All

Children's Services: Bring your stroller (or rent one). Diaper change facilities available. Food may be brought or bought. Don't forget your camera

This is at least a full day's outing. It is the oldest and the largest zoo in any city in the United States.

Animals in cages are repugnant to most of us. The Bronx Zoo has all of its animals living in replicas of their natural habitats. They look happy, well fed, and well cared for.

The Children's Zoo is absolutely thrilling. You and your g.c. can walk on trails through woods and marshes. And there's a petting zoo, too!

You may ride the Bengali Express in the Wild Asia exhibit. It's a 2-mile ride on the monorail with more wilderness than one could ever imagine in the Bronx. There is a tour guide to identify animals, birds, and fauna.

Reservations are required (tel. 220-5141) for the free, guided walking tours given only on Saturdays and Sundays. They are conducted by the Friends of the Zoo.

Tickets for the Children's Zoo are not sold after 4pm on Monday through Saturday; Sundays and holidays Children's Zoo tickets are not sold after 4:30pm.

The winter season is from November 1 to March 31. All rides are closed, the Bengali Express guided tour is closed, and there are no Animal Theater Shows.

Don't forget to visit the World of Darkness. Here night has been reversed to day so you're able to see the magnificent birds flying around in a jungle setting. You *can* fool Mother Nature.

The Bronx Zoo is almost 300 acres. Plan how you're going to spend your day. Call for a brochure or get one at the Convention and Visitors Bureau at 2 Columbus Circle, Monday to Friday.

Brooklyn Botanic Gardens, 1000 Washington Ave. (at Eastern Parkway), Brooklyn, NY 11225 (tel. 718/622-4433)
Access: Subway—2, 3, or 4 to Eastern Parkway; D or Q to Prospect Park
Admission: Free; donation if you wish in winter. Conservatory, April through September, adults $2, children under 12 and senior citizens $1
Hours: October through March, Tuesday through Friday from 8am to 4:30pm, on Saturday, Sunday, and holidays from 10am to 4:30pm; April through September, Tuesday through Friday from 8am to 6pm, on Saturday, Sunday, and holidays from 10am to 6pm
Children's Services: Strollers are good. Diaper changes available

If not hands-on, this is certainly nose-on. You may walk on grass so lush that it looks like a putting green, with bountiful trees to rest under and flowers to sniff to your heart's content.

If you and your g.c. have need for a bucolic experience—a day of nature's green and the sky's blue—head for Brooklyn. Do make a point of visiting the Steinhardt Conservatory.

🍎 **Central Park Zoo,** Fifth Avenue at 64th Street, behind the Arsenal (tel. 861-6030)
See section in Chapter 9.

🍎 **The Chrysler Building,** 405 Lexington Avenue, at 42nd Street, New York, NY 10017 (tel. 682-3070)
Access: Bus—M15, M27, M32, M42, M101, M102, or M104. Subway—B, D, Q, or F to 42nd Street; 4, 5, 6, or 7 to Grand Central Terminal (42nd Street)
Architect: William Van Allen (1930)

If your g.c. is into cars, terrific buildings, and a good story, this is it in one neat package.

When the Chrysler Building was under construction in 1930, Walter Chrysler, the automotive tycoon, thought that when his building was completed, it would be the tallest skyscraper in New York. However, 40 Wall St. was under construction at the same time. Yasuo Matsui, the architect for 40 Wall, surreptitiously added two extra feet in order to be taller than you-know-what. Well, Walter, not to be outdone, secretly had a stainless-steel spike assembled, raised it through the roof, had it bolted into place, and thereby added 123 feet. The prize: the tallest skyscraper in the world. (How do you like them apples, Matsui?) How fleeting was Walter's glory! In May 1931, the Empire State Building opened and it loomed 200 feet above the Chrysler Building.

The Automotive Tower (a/k/a Chrysler Building) has stylized motor designs at each setback. At the fourth setback the building flares out and gargoyles loom in the style of radiator caps. A brickwork frieze around the structure depicts wheels with radiator caps. The brick designs were taken from hubcaps.

The automotive-style lights in Van Allen's original plans were added in 1981. Don't overlook the magnificent African marble triangle in the lobby. (Don't think we'll be seeing that again.) The paneled elevators are something wondrous. Open till 6pm.

The Con Ed Conservation Center (tel. 599-3435) in the lobby (open Tuesday through Saturday from 9am to 3pm; free admission; all ages) has exhibits about methods of energy conservation. There is more to it than this. Wouldn't you like to know why smoke rises from the manholes on New York's streets?

🍎 **Citicorp Center,** E. 53rd Street, between Lexington and Third avenues, New York, NY 10022
Access: Bus—M15, M27, M28, M32, M101, or M102. Subway—E or F to Lexington Avenue; 6 to 51st Street
Architects: Hugh Stubbins & Associates (1977)

When a few blocks away, look up. It looks like a tin whistle. This is a perfect example of how great architecture and well-planned space, plus a sharing attitude (g.c., please emulate), can change a neighborhood. Citicorp built it and it became so popular they rented space across the street to house their bank. (Reason enough to bank with them?) It's a joy to sit outside and people-watch in good weather, or do the same inside in all weather. St. Peter's Church in the building has a most beautiful Louise Nevelson interior. It can be seen through the windows on the Lexington Avenue side at 54th Street. There are shops (Conran's for one), bookstores, and food counters galore. There is often music in the afternoon. It seethes with joyous activity.

Saturday entertainment is free and varied. Giggles galore in this spacious environment are year round for all ages.

🍎 **Commodities Trading,** 4 World Trade Center, New York, NY 10048 (tel. 938-2000)
Access: Bus—M1, M6, M10, M22, or X25. Subway—1, N, or R to Cortlandt St.; A, C, or E to Chambers St.–World Trade Center
Hours: 9:30am to 3pm
Architects: Minoru Yamasaki and Associates (1973)

There is a visitor's gallery overlooking the floor of the exchange. You can see the traders in cotton, coffee, cocoa, and others wheeling and dealing. You can even hear it. The g.c. will absolutely flip—even if he doesn't comprehend the action or the lingo. Do you? You can see plenty Monday through Friday from 9:30am to 3pm. For tour information (tel. 938-2025), ask for Katie. If you're in the area—and you will be—take a look.

🍎 **The Daily News Building,** 200 E. 42nd St., New York, NY 10017 (tel. 210-2100)
Access: Bus—M15, M16, M42, M101, M102, M104, M106, X25 to 42nd Street. Subway—4, 5, 6, or 7 to Grand Central Terminal (42nd Street). S shuttle goes from Times Square to Grand Central

Architects: Howells & Hood (1930); Harrison & Abramovitz (1958 addition)

Before you put a foot in the building, look up. At first glance it looks like just a slab. It isn't—it has setbacks. Look above the entrance at the decorative work. It's most impressive. Not the sort of decorative work one sees on new buildings, to put it mildly.

Plan on spending a bit of time in the lobby to soak in the detail. There is a huge revolving globe 12 feet in diameter. Now look down. The floor is done as a huge compass. Study it and see how far from New York other countries and other parts of the United States are by airplane. There is a clock in the lobby that shows the time differences in 17 zones.

One world in one lobby. The new buildings in this city define the magnificence of the good, old buildings in New York. No better example than this.

The Empire State Building, 34th Street and Fifth Avenue, New York, NY 10016 (tel. 736-3100)
Access: Bus—M1, M2, M3, M4, M5, M6, M7, M16, or M32, M34, or cross-town bus. Subway—6 to 33rd Street; B, D, F, N, Q, R, 1, 2, or 3 to 34th Street
Admission: $3.50 for adults, $1.75 for children
Observatory Hours: 9am to midnight (except Christmas)
Ages: 5 years and up
Architects: Shreve, Lamb & Harmon (1931)

To see this view takes three elevator rides. You go express to the 80th floor, then to the 86th floor for outdoor-terrace views, and a third elevator to the 102nd floor where there's a small glass-enclosed room at the top.

The 34th Street ticket office has a "Visibility Notice"—if the day is less than clear, come back another day. Not to see these views under optimum conditions would be sad. The nighttime view has to be the most idealized vision of New York that exists.

And don't forget to visit the Guinness World Records Exhibit Hall, as if your g.c. would let you miss this winner!

Flatiron Building, 175 Fifth Ave., at 23rd Street and Broadway, New York, NY 10010 (no telephone)
Access: Bus—M1, M2, M3, M4, M5, M6, M7, M16, M32, M104, or

M26 cross-town bus to 23rd Street. Subway—6, F, N, or R to 23rd Street

Architects: D. H. Burnham & Co. (1902)

The limestone exterior has never appeared more pristine. The wonder of this building is its shape (it does look like a flatiron). From different sides, one gets different feelings. It looks like a slab, it looks like a triangle, and it looks just great. Part of its special appeal is the setting and all the surrounding open space. This is that complicated point where Broadway crosses Fifth Avenue— and the point where both of these streets seem to open up and provide an opportunity to see this freestanding, surprisingly shaped building.

The detail is French Renaissance, and now—for the first time in my long memory—it's easy to see the definition and the intricacy of the work. It's beautiful and it's fun. It was meant to be named the Fuller Building, but that just didn't have a chance. Sorry, Mr. Fuller.

Grand Central Terminal, E. 42nd Street, between Lexington and Vanderbilt avenues, New York, NY 10017

Access: Bus—M1, M2, M3, M4, M5, M15, M32, M42, M101, M102, M104, or X25. Subway—4, 5, 6, 7, or S to Grand Central Terminal

Architects: Warren & Wetmore Engineers; Reed & Stem Sculpture and Clock, Jules Coutan

The U.S. Supreme Court declared this a landmark in 1978; otherwise it would have gone the way of Penn Station. (Let this be a lesson to your g.c. of the power of individuals to join forces to protect their environment.) The thought of losing this beaux arts treasure galvanized the citizenry and the landmarks preservationists into action, so now it's yours to see.

To get the full impact, come in from Vanderbilt Avenue, stand at the top of the staircase, and just gaze for a while. Don't overlook the lower levels—the ceiling and floor tiles are magnificent. Many kids are no longer familiar with trains—sad, sad. (See Chapter 18 for a description of the Oyster Bar; otherwise there's plenty of commuter food.)

The Municipal Art Society (tel. 935-3960) conducts free tours on Wednesdays at 12:30pm. Meet outside Chemical Bank's Commuter Express.

Guinness World Records Exhibit Hall, in the Empire State Building at 34th Street and Fifth Avenue, New York, NY 10016 (tel. 947-2335)
Admission: $5.50 for adults, $3.50 ages 3 to 11.
Hours: 9am to 10pm daily
   Nobody can resist this one. Your g.c. will be dazzled by the biggest, the smallest, the longest, the shortest, the mostest museum. Head for the concourse with your g.c. if he's more than 3 years old. My recommendation on this one is as high as the building itself.

The IBM Building, 590 Madison Avenue, between 56th and 57th streets, New York, NY 10022 (tel. 407-3500, or toll-free 800/426-3333 nationwide, for information)
Access: Bus—M1, M2, M3, M4, M5, M28, or M32. Subway—Q to 57th Street; E or F to Fifth Avenue
Hours: The atrium is open from 8am to 10pm daily
Age: Check for appropriate exhibits
Architect: Edward Larrabee Barnes (1983)
   Enter this building from Madison Avenue (the 57th Street entrance is for businesspeople; it is guarded and requires ID). On the lower level is the Gallery of Science and Art. They have had fabulous shows. Check for appropriate interest—some are very special.
   The Bamboo Court has the Botanic Garden shop if you want to buy some seeds to plant. All sorts of entertainments take place in the atrium at various times. You have but to inquire. Wednesday at 12:30pm is a given. The seasonal plantings in this space are breathtaking. The trees that reach the top of the atrium boggle the mind. The little circular bar sells the best cup of coffee in New York.

Lincoln Center for the Performing Arts, 63rd to 65th streets, along Broadway, New York, NY 10019 (tour information tel. 877-1800, ext. 512; main number tel. 877-2011)
Access: Bus—M5, M7, M10, M11, M30, M66, M103, or M104 to

Broadway and 64th Street Subway—1 to 66th St.–Lincoln Center; A, B, C, or D to 59th St.–Columbus Circle
Architects: Wallace K. Harrison, Max Abramovitz, Philip Johnson (1960)

Lincoln Center has three main buildings: the Metropolitan Opera House, the New York State Theater, and Avery Fisher Hall. The Juilliard School and Theater, Alice Tully Hall, Bruno Walter Auditorium (Library), the Mitzi Newhouse Theater, the Vivian Beaumont Theater, and the New York Public Library at Lincoln Center complete the physical complex that is built around a magnificent plaza.

The 1-hour tour of Lincoln Center departs from the concourse level (downstairs). Admission is $6.75 for adults, $5.50 for students, and $3.75 for children ages 6 to 13 and senior citizens. Tours are given from 10am to 5pm daily (call at 9:30am for the schedule; it changes all the time). If this tour is the only way to get inside these buildings, okay. However, walking around the complex and peeking in windows is less clinical. A Lincoln Center exec feels that "the tours introduce children to the tremendous vitality and variety of the artists of America's first performing arts center." The tour visits the Metropolitan Opera House, Avery Fisher Hall, and the New York State Theater. There the youngsters will see how "opera, symphony, and dance thrive side by side in these beautiful theaters." This, again, from the same exec who obviously loves Lincoln Center. Don't we all?

If you're able to schedule it, don't miss it. Six years and older sounds right to me.

Metropolitan Opera House, Lincoln Center, 63rd to 65th streets, along Broadway, New York, NY 10019 (tel. 769-7000)
Admission: Tour $6 for adults, $3 for students
Hours: Monday through Friday at 3:45pm, on Saturday at 10am
Ages: 10 years and up

The Metropolitan Opera Guild gives the backstage tours of Lincoln Center. If your g.c. is old enough, this is a tour! It's a spectacle. The logistics of the Opera House boggle the mind—it's really exciting. The older g.c. will be captivated. Reservations well in advance are a must.

Allow at least two weeks to be sure you'll have a place.

Reservations are difficult, especially at school vacation times. If you call 582-3512, have three dates in mind and your credit card in hand. If you write, send a stamped self-addressed envelope, a check payable to the Metropolitan Opera Guild, and your three or four selected dates to Backstage Tours, Education at the Met, 1865 Broadway, New York, NY 10023. Tickets are $6 per adult, $3 for students (enclose a copy of the student's ID). Arrive about 10 minutes before scheduled time of departure. If you haven't made advance reservations and received confirmation, it never hurts to call and ask if there is space for you and yours.

New York Aquarium, Surf Avenue at W. 8th Street, Brooklyn, NY 11224 (tel. 718/265-3246, for information tel. 718/266-8711)
Access: Subway—D or F to W. 8th Street (Brooklyn)
Admission: $4.75 for adults, $2 for children under 12
Hours: October through April from 10am to 4:45pm; May to September until 5:45pm on weekends and holidays

It took a whale of a lot of money to restore the aquarium, but the city officials did a fabulous job. Exhibits include the mysterious Bermuda Triangle. There is a shark tank. See New York's only Pacific walrus and his friends enjoy their daily feed. During May through September sea lions and dolphins perform in the Aquatheater. During October through April, the beluga whales and the sea lions are the Aquatheater stars.

There are places to eat; buy your food or brown-bag it. If you choose the Aquarium restaurant or the snack bar, fine. If you bring those brown bags to the outdoor picnic area, don't bring tuna fish. Its mother may be watching (sob, sob). Great spot for all ages. Bring the stroller for the little one.

The New York Botanical Garden, Enid A. Haupt Conservatory, Bronx, NY 10458 (general information tel. 220-8700; travel directions tel. 220-8779; exhibition information tel. 220-8778)
Access: Train—Metro North from Grand Central Terminal to Botanical Garden station. Train tickets include admission to the Enid Haupt Conservatory. Fare for adults, $6.50; children under 16, $3.50. Subway—C or 4 to Bedford Park Boulevard, take the

Bx19 bus eastbound to Webster Avenue or walk about eight blocks east to the Botanical Garden

Note: One fare for the subway and one more fare for the bus

Hours: Conservatory, Tuesday through Sunday from 10am to 4pm. Grounds open April 1 to October 31 from 10am to 7pm, November 1 to March 31 from 10am to 6pm

Admission: The grounds, display gardens, and walking trails are free. Contributions are appreciated, and needed. The admission charge to visit the conservatory is $3.50 for adults, $1.25 for children 6 to 16, free for under 6. Free admission Saturday from 10am to noon

Children's Services: No strollers in the conservatory. Checking service available. No brown bags. Yes, diaper change

Somehow we forget what individuals have done for the quality of life in this city—Brooke Astor, Enid Haupt, the Rockefellers, the Wollmans, other families and individuals who remain anonymous. This is Ms. Haupt's splendid gift.

The conservatory is a Victorian crystal palace made up of 11 glass pavilions. Cactus, herbs, ivy, and citrus flourish under glass (you don't even need good weather for this). The outdoor gardens have seasonal displays: native plants, herbs, roses, and a pine barrens area.

You may eat at the Snuff Mill Restaurant for very little money if you opt for a sandwich or a box lunch. For those who want a day-in-the-country feeling, it is only magnificent.

The train excursion will delight any age child, as will the crystal palace. You don't have to be accompanied by Luther Burbank to enjoy this. If you feel your g.c. has become overstimulated by your city activities, change the pace with this outing.

New York Stock Exchange, 20 Broad St. (visitors entrance), New York, NY 10005 (tel. 656-5168)

Access: Bus—M1, M6, M15, M98, X23, X25, or X92. Subway—2, 3, 4, or 5 to Wall Street; N or R to Rector Street; J, M, or Z to Broad Street

Hours: Monday through Friday from 9:20am to 4pm

Architects: George B. Post (1903); Trowbridge and Livingston (addition, 1923)

This is a club with about 1,400,000 members. The actual

trading takes place on the ground floor. The visitors' gallery on the third floor gives a perfect fishbowl view. And it's exciting to watch.

If you are visiting the Exchange during school vacations, you'd better be in line early. There is a film and the last showing is at 3:30pm. There are exhibits but nothing is as dramatic as the view of the madness on the Exchange floor when you look down from your gallery perch on either of the two tiers open to visitors.

Old Merchant's House, 29 E. 4th St., between Lafayette Street and the Bowery, New York, NY 10003 (tel. 777-1089)
Access: Bus—M1, M5, or M6 to 4th Street Subway—6 to Astor Place; R to 8th Street; A, B, C, D, E, F, N, or Q to W. 4th Street. Closed in August
Hours: Sunday from 1 to 4pm (groups, other days)
Admission: $2 for adults; $1 for students; children, free
Built in 1832, this row house now stands in mint condition waiting for your visit. For a perfect example of how life was once lived by a well-heeled merchant and his family, visit this treasure. It is a revelation of the architecture, the furnishings, and the life-styles that existed when this neighborhood was farmland.

The Pan Am Building, Park Avenue and 46th Street (north side of the building), New York, NY 10017 (tel. toll free 800/348-8000)
Access: Bus—M1, M2, M3, M4, M5, M15, M32, M101, M102, or X25. Subway—4, 5, 6, 7, or S to Grand Central Terminal
Architects: Emery Roth and Sons, Pietro Belluschi, and Walter Gropius (1963)
Have your children look up. Walk them through the arcade to the south side of the building. Now explain to them the business of selling air rights. Selling space in the sky? Our sky? It does have a Steven Spielberg–esque quality. Reinforce the idea with a stroll north on Park Avenue. See the Helmsley Palace looming over Park Avenue (more air rights).

Rockefeller Center, 47th to 50th streets between Fifth and Sixth avenues, New York, NY 10020
Access: Bus—M1, M2, M3, M4, M5, M6, M7, M27, M32, or M104.

Subway—B, D, or F to 48th to 50th streets–Rockefeller Center; R or N to 49th Street
Architects: Reinhard and Hofmeister; Corbett, Harrison, and MacMurray; Hood and Fouilhoux (1931–1940)

This is New York at its finest. The architecture, the ornamentation, the absolute splendor continue to overwhelm these myopic eyes. Twenty-two acres house 19 buildings. The entire center is joined by an underground concourse that children find amazing.

In order to really appreciate these buildings you must take the only two tours still available to the public: the NBC Studio Tour and the Radio City Music Hall Tour.

Let's talk about the Rainbow Room on the 65th floor of Rockefeller Center. If Mom and Dad are here together, it's time to read about baby-sitters in this book. If you love Gershwin and glitz, and money is no object, go for it. Your older kids could see 1940s glamour (with an intentional "u"). It has been completely restored to its original opulence complete with revolving dance floor and continuous music. A reservation is an absolute must (tel. 632-5000).

If you don't find this costly enough, try the new Rainbow and Stars nightclub at the same location. It's even more expensive and features star performers.

NBC Studio Tour, Concourse Level

The NBC studios are located in the RCA Building at 30 Rockefeller Plaza, between Fifth and Sixth avenues at 50th Street (tel. 664-4000). Tours are given Monday through Saturday from 9:30am (for groups) or 10am (for individuals) to 4:30pm at a cost of $7.25 per person. Tickets go on sale at 9am. Tours are for age 6 and older. This is a rule. They are sold on a first-come, first-served basis.

The tour takes 55 minutes and it feels like 5 minutes. You'll visit the studios, see special props, browse through makeup rooms, see technical devices, and meet Van Go. Van (let's call him by his first name) is a mobile unit used for sports coverage by NBC camerapeople.

Three kids on each tour are chosen to act. The guides are surely aspiring actors. Their voices do project. The kids will like seeing themselves on TV. Don't look at yourself—you'll appear 10 pounds heavier.

☙ *Radio City Music Hall Tour*

Located at 1260 Avenue of the Americas (Sixth Avenue), at 50th Street (tel. 623-4041 for tour desk), Radio City Music Hall is a part of the Rockefeller Center complex. The interior of the music hall was designed by Donald Deskey, but let's not overlook the guiding genius of Samuel Lionel Rothafel, or "Roxy" as he was then known to the world.

Hours: Monday through Friday from 9:30am to 4:30pm, Saturday from 10am to 4:30pm, Sunday from 11am to 4:30pm. No tours given during the Christmas and Easter seasons.

Admission: $7 per person

Ages: All ages welcome; no strollers on tours. You can check them. You must call to check the tour times. They are often changed or canceled if there is a big production or a rock concert in the works

Present yourselves in the lobby at box office number one; this is the Tour Desk Box Office. Do not wait in line on 50th Street; that line is to buy performance tickets. Tell the usher or doorperson standing at the Sixth Avenue entrance where you are heading and he or she will let you enter.

The tour lasts one hour, which just isn't long enough to take it all in. There's an explanation of the history and architecture of the building, as well as a description of the productions and a real look around. There was never such a beautiful building as this: the Grand Foyer with its 24-karat gold-leafed ceiling; the famous Mighty Wurlitzer, the largest theater organ in the world; the 60-foot proscenium arch inspired by an ocean sunset. And if you think your boys won't marvel at the underground hydraulic system, I'll accept any wager. This is the only place one continues to revisit that remains as large as it was in childhood memory—an empty theater has such a mysterious quality. An overwhelming experience! What can I say to force you to take this tour?

☙ **South Street Seaport,** 19 Fulton Street (at the East River), New York, NY 10038 (tel. 732-7678, or SEA-PORT)

Access: Bus—M15. Subway—2, 3, 4, 5, J, M, or Z to Fulton Street; A or C to Broadway–Nassau Street

Admission to the Museum: $6 for adults, $4 for senior citizens, $3 for children.
Hours: Daily, 10am to 6pm in summer, to 5pm in winter
Note: These hours are for the museum and some boats. Please watch the newspapers for announcements of entertainment, fireworks, special boat rides, and all sorts of things. Or call 669-9424 and they will tell you everything
Architects: Benjamin Thompson Associates (Phase I, 1983; Phase II, 1985)

When you arrive at South Street Seaport, "Today's Events" are posted south of Pier 17 and a copy of "Broadside," South Street Seaport's calendar of events and programs, is available. This is New York's largest (11 blocks) and most expensive restoration. Along the pier and cobblestone plaza is a museum, a theater, a restored print shop, boats to visit, restaurants, and shopping galore. In season there's entertainment, and after 5pm the place is taken over by the Wall Street crowd.

Two main buildings are monuments to consumerism! Fulton Market, at Beekman and Fulton streets, is packed with shops. You'll see counter after counter of ethnic foods on the second level. Pier 17, at Fulton Street and the East River, has even more, and higher-priced, shops than Fulton Market.

On a nice day the seaport is fun. It's very close to the World Trade Center, New York Stock Exchange, Chinatown—an easy day to plan for an older g.c. For younger ones, one of these outings is plenty. Take a stroller. See Chapter 7, "Touring the Town."

Now on the National Register of Historic Places, this restoration must be seen. (See Chapter 8, "Museums"; Chapter 10, "That's Entertainment," and Chapter 12, "Shopping for Toys"; for more.)

The Statue of Liberty, Liberty Island and Ellis Island (tel. 363-3200 or 363-3267 for information, tel. 269-5755 for ferry information)
Access: Ferry—from Battery Park and South Ferry, Circle Line Ferry (tel. 269-5755). Bus—M1, M6, or M15 to South Ferry. Subway—4 or 5 to Bowling Green; R to Whitehall Street or N to South Ferry

Admission: Includes ferry fare. $6 for adults, $3 for children 3 to 17

Hours: 9am to 5pm daily

Architect: Frederic-Auguste Bartholdi

Engineer: Gustave Eiffel

Base: Richard Morris Hunt

Inscription: Emma Lazarus (from her poem, "The New Colossus")

Dedication: October 28, 1886

Rededication: July 4, 1986

Ages: C'mon everybody! Strollers and all.

Notes: The ferry leaves every hour on the hour from Battery Park. No reservations. Tickets and ferry space is on a first-come, first-served basis. Before you buy boat tickets be sure to ask how long a wait you'll have on Liberty Island to reach the crown. More than one hour, don't go! The ferry goes to Ellis Island after it stops at the Statue of Liberty. From Ellis Island, it returns to Battery Park. See Chapter 8, "Museums," for information of the Ellis Island Immigration Museum.

Liberty Island has viewing platforms, a museum with exhibits, a mall and plaza, concession building, and a picnic area. If the weather is nice, brown-bag it. Not to worry if you don't. If you're bringing a toddler, do bring a stroller.

Though the statue was a gift from France, the money for the base was collected by donations made by U.S. citizens. When you recover from the awesome sight of the Lady, take a moment to reflect. Jeanne de Pusieux, who later became Madame Bartholdi, was the model for the statue's figure. The face was modeled on the face of Bartholdi's mother—a terrifying lady. The figure has a suggestion of forward stride (ah, body language), which intensifies the feeling of protection and strength she exudes. Proportions of the island as a setting in relation to the statue increase the power of the Lady. And the base is equal in brilliance of design to the statue.

The interior is elegant as well as functional. In 1916 the Germans blew up a munitions depot less than half a mile away and the statue survived the blast—intact. The huge doors depict the restoration of 1986 and are not to be overlooked.

The seven points of her crown represent the seven seas and continents. Don't you love pointless trivia? Here's more. The lighthouse at the Suez Canal was the original site chosen by Bartholdi for the behemoth lady. Ahh, c'est la vie, Fred.

When you see the doorless souvenir shop, you'll know a pit stop is inevitable. Even this has a history—it was opened in 1930 by the Hill family and is still operated by this dynasty.

The United Nations, First Avenue between 42nd and 48th streets, New York, NY 10017 (tel. 963-1234)

Access: Bus—M15, M27, M42, M104, or M106. Subway—4, 5, 6, 7, or S to Grand Central Terminal

Architects: International Committee of Architects chaired by Wallace K. Harrison (1952); Le Corbusier was responsible for the concept of three buildings

The United Nations is composed of the General Assembly Building, the Secretariat Building, the Hammarskjöld Library, and the Conference Building. The Rockefellers donated the land for the U.N. and the Ford Foundation the land for the library.

For your older g.c. who is genuinely interested, it's possible to attend meetings of the Councils and General Assembly (usually early September until shortly before Christmas). Tickets are free and given out until the line exceeds the tickets (read the *New York Times* for "Daily Agenda").

The Delegates' Dining Room is open to the public at lunch hour (space permitting). There are gift shops with souvenirs from all nations.

The best part of the U.N. (personal and g.c. viewpoint) is the commanding presence of the exterior with flags flying, the free-standing, unobstructed Secretariat Building, and the austere authority of the main lobby. This can be enjoyed by children of all ages. See Chapter 7, "Touring the Town." The internal operations are a bit overwhelming.

Winter Garden, at the World Financial Center, Battery Park City (tel. 945-0505)

The most magnificent public space ever built in New York City is Winter Garden at the World Financial Center. Larger than Grand Central Station and 110 feet high, it is breathtaking. The roof is glass and the floors are marble. There is a 60-foot staircase that gives one the feeling of being in a Greek amphitheater.

There are 16 palm trees in Winter Garden. They were raised in

Hawaii, nurtured in California, and transported across the United States by a convoy of trucks. With pit stops to tend the cargo, examinations of the trees by representatives of animal and wildlife groups at state borders, and the usual mechanical problems with trucks, this operation took more than one year.

Well, the trees are now 45 feet high and appear to be thriving in Winter Garden. Which proves of course that you can fool Mother Nature. All it requires is time and money.

Winter Garden has free scheduled entertainment. All programs are first rate. There is nothing about this environment that could tolerate anything less than the best. Call the telephone number listed above for particulars.

I have been accused of hyperbole in my writings. Winter Garden and the entire World Financial Center defy anything less than superlatives. See for yourselves.

The Woolworth Building, 233 Broadway, at Barclay Street, New York, NY 10048 (tel. 553-2000)
Access: Bus—M1, M6, M9, M10, M15, M22, M101, M102, X25, X90, or X92 to Broadway and Barclay Street. Subway—2 or 3 to Park Place; 4, 5, or 6, or Z to Brooklyn Bridge; A, C, E, J, or M to Chambers Street; N or R to City Hall
Architect: Cass Gilbert (1913)
Note: A short walk from the World Trade Center. You may use this as your destination point as well as the above

Here is a building in perfect condition, and it was always thus. The Woolworth family built this at a cost of $13.5 million. That was a whole bunch of nickels and dimes in those days. The pride the organization and the Woolworth family felt for this building is reflected in its condition. The company still retains the building. It's still their main headquarters. Most unusual. And it never, ever, had a mortgage.

This was the world's tallest building from 1913 until 1930 when the Chrysler Building took the title briefly (see Chrysler Building or Empire State Building in this chapter for a good story).

The outside is a masterpiece, Gothic in style, with wonderful detail. The lobby will take your breath away and make you laugh at the same time. This lobby is three stories high decorated with Byzantine-style mosaics and (look higher) frescos. Take your eyes from this and the stairway if you want to giggle. On the Barclay Street side of the building, under the crossbeams, are caricatures—Mr. Woolworth counting his coins and Mr. Cass holding a model of this building.

🍎 **World Financial Center,** between the Hudson River and West Street, and between Vesey and Liberty streets, Battery Park City, New York, NY 10006 (tel. 945-0505 for information on free arts and entertainment programs)
Architect: Cesar Pelli for Olympia & York
Access: Bus—M9 or M10. Subway—1, N, or R to Cortlandt Street–World Trade Center, or the A, C, or E to Chambers Street–World Trade Center. Enter U.S. Customs House and cross the north footbridge to enter the World Financial Center

The master plan for Battery Park City was conceived by Alexander Cooper and Stanton Eckstut. Before I describe the WFC, let me tell you about BPC. Battery Park City began when the landfill excavated to build the World Trade Center was dumped into the Hudson River. Two and a half decades and $4 billion later, voilà! There are now 4,000 apartments housing 6,000 permanent residents. There are 20,000 people employed at BPC. When construction is completed, there will be 12,000 apartments, housing a projected 35,000 people, and 8 million square feet of office space. This does not include public space, parks, stores, or restaurants. BPC at completion will cover 92 acres of land. The World Trade Center and its plazas are not part of BPC; the marinas and yacht basins are in BPC.

The WFC is composed of four separate buildings of different girth, height, and roof design. They are joined by corridors. There are parks, public spaces, restaurants, and shops.

Visit Winter Garden and move right along to the north end of the esplanade. On the fence in big, brass letters are quotations from Frank O'Hara and Walt Whitman. Well worth reading.

The esplanade, with a view of the river and New Jersey, is on the west side of the WFC. When completed it will join Battery Park at the south end. Head south. Stop at Albany Street and see the Ned Smyth sculpture titled *Upper Room.* The kids will find it user friendly and good for climbing. Continue south to South Cove. There are two sandboxes, dune grass, huge rocks for the kids to climb, child-size water fountains, and a black iron structure. Climb the staircase to get an even better view of the Statue of Liberty. When you come down, walk out to the boardwalk and face the construction. It is an interpretation of Miss Liberty: head, crown, and all. The staircase is built in the style of the Eiffel Tower in Paris, which was the model for the interior of the Statue of Liberty. This structure was designed by Mary Miss and Stanton Eckstut. The landscape architect was Susan Child.

If it's a nice day, get sandwiches at Au Bon Pain and brown-bag it on the esplanade. If the weather is uncooperative, eat at Minters listed in Chapter 18.

WFC has three tenants occupying office space: American Express, Dow Jones, and Merrill Lynch. Maybe that's why it's named World Financial Center.

If you don't want to see the most breathtaking setting, enhanced by exquisite buildings and executed by skilled craftspeople, then avoid the World Financial Center. Well, it is a book for kids so I opted for a negative approach to encourage your visit. You know, reverse psychology.

The World Trade Center, 1 World Trade Center, New York, NY 10048 (tel. 466-4170)
Access: Bus—M1, M6, M10, M22, or X25. Subway—1, N, or R to Cortlandt Street; A, C, or E to Chambers Street–World Trade Center
Note: See Windows on the World in Chapter 18. Twin towers 110 stories high. Exhibition space is on the mezzanine of Building One as well as the lobbies of One and Two World Trade Center. In good weather, check out the action at the 5-acre plaza

The concourse is Manhattan's largest indoor shopping mall, with shops, services, restaurants, and snack bars. Food is available everywhere. If you want it with a view, check the prices before you take a table.

World Trade Center Observation Deck, 2 World Trade Center, New York, NY 10048 (tel. 466-7397 for reservations and information for the Observation Center, 466-4235 for information on children's activities, and 466-4170 for general information on activities)
Access: Bus—M1, M6, M9, M10, M22, or X25. Subway—1, N, or

R to Cortlandt Street; A, C, or E to Chambers Street–World Trade Center
Admission: $3.50 for adults, and kids over 13. $1.75 for children ages 6 to 12, children under 6 are free
Hours: 9:30am to 9:30pm daily
Architects: Minoru Yamasaki and Associates (1973)
Note: See Windows on the World in Chapter 18

Here you're 107 floors (a quarter of a mile) up in the air. Walk to the open-air rooftop and you've made it to the highest outdoor observation area on earth. This is really awesome. The wonderful thing is that the windows have outlines of the buildings you are viewing so you know exactly what you're seeing.

Be sure it's a clear day for this outing. Often this part of New York may be fogged in, though it may be clear in other areas.

Don't miss this (as if it were possible). And don't miss the History of Trade Exhibit on the Observation Decks, or the art: Masayuki Nagare's double pyramids at the entrance, James Rosati's *Ideogram,* the Miró tapestry, Nevelson's *Sky-Gate New York* wall sculpture.

During December there are daily puppet shows at noon. Call to double-check. The week before Christmas, Santa is waiting for your g.c. daily on the Observation Deck. The week before Easter, the Big Bunny himself will greet your kids.

CHAPTER 7

Touring the Town

A sure-fire way to get a handle on the overall geography of this city and the diversification of neighborhoods is a bus tour. For panoramic splendor, board a boat.

Call for current schedules. Many tours change with the seasons. Do tell the person with whom you speak the age of your fellow traveler. If your companion is short, as in age, select a tour that is short, as in duration. Two and a half hours is plenty. Consider the tour listings as you would a menu; select what you prefer.

For neighborhood walks, take your youngster's hand in yours and go! Do it before his hand is too large to fit in yours.

Sightseeing by Bus & by Boat

To get an overall picture of New York, bus and boat are the ways to go. The air is up to you!

BY BUS

The Gray Line Sightseeing Association, Inc., 900 Eighth Avenue, at 54th Street, New York, NY 10019 (tel. 397-2600)

Access: Bus—M1, M2, M3, M4, M5, M6, M7, M10, M11, M16, M28, M32, M104. Subway—B, D, or E to Seventh Avenue; N or R to 49th Street; A, C, or D to Columbus Circle

Admission: $15 for a 2½-hour tour, 25% less for children under 12

Hours: Summer tours from 9am to 4pm, winter tours from 9am to 2pm

Credit Cards: AE, M, V

Please call or write for a brochure. Tours, times, and prices vary. The buses are positively lush—clean and comfortable with good views available through big, clean windows. The guides are good for giggles as well as information.

On the flip side, these tours run from 2 hours to eternity, so select carefully! AOTW, the best is tour no. 1. For $15 you get Times Square, the Garment Center, Herald Square, Greenwich Village, the Bowery, Chinatown, the Financial District, the World Trade Center, the United Nations, and Rockefeller Center. It takes about 2½ hours. This is the maximum amount of time any age can endure. Strollers are accepted for storage. No bathroom facilities on buses.

Short Line Tours, 166 W. 46th St., between Sixth and Seventh avenues, New York, NY 10036 (tel. 354-5122)

Access: Subway—B, D, F, or Q to Rockefeller Center

Admission: Varies depending on tour

Hours: Year round, call for schedules

Credit Cards: AE, M, V

They have wonderful tours and a good many in the 2- to 2½-hour time period. $15 for adults, $11.25 for ages under 12. They also have a 4½-hour Grand Tour and a helicopter tour (call for details). No bathroom facilities.

BY BOAT

Circle Line, Pier 83 (42nd Street at the Hudson River), New York, NY 10036 (tel. 563-3200)

Access: Bus—M11 or M42. Subway—A, C, or E to 42nd Street

Admission: $16 for adults, $8 for children under 12. Children under 2 ride free.

Hours: 9:30am to 5:45pm daily. Boats depart every 45 minutes from the beginning of March through December. The schedule varies November through March. There are night cruises. Call.
Credit Cards: AE, M, V
Ages: All ages

Be sure your youngster is up to a 3-hour boat ride. Most children love it. The guides are very entertaining. This 35-mile ride provides a singular view of the harbor and the city. Kids 3 years and over can easily ship out on this one. For toddlers, bring some crayons and paper. Feel free to brown-bag it. Soda and snacks are sold aboard. The boats are very comfortable, and you don't feel confined. Needless to say, it's best when the weather is nice and the day is clear. Collapsable strollers may be brought aboard—and there are bathrooms, so don't fret.

This trip is my number one choice in the boat and bus sightseeing selections.

Touring Around Town

Prior to planning your tours, check Chapter 6. In the interests of expediency, tours of those sites and skyscrapers are included in the appropriate listing.

A few of the "must sees" are to be found in Lincoln Center, the New York Stock Exchange, and Rockefeller Center. There are many more in this chapter. Do not overlook the tours conducted by the Metropolitan Museum of Art, the Museum of Natural History, the New-York Historical Society, and the Museum of the City of New York.

There are all kinds of tours available to see this vast city. Included here are also group tours (who says you have to go it alone?) and walking tours for the robust. There are more tours available in New York. See the weekly listings in *New York* magazine and the Friday *New York Times*.

The listings emblazoned with the symbol "$$$$" in this chapter are very expensive.

Backstage on Broadway, 228 W. 47th St., New York, NY 10036 (tel. 575-8065)

Access: Bus—M1, M2, M3, M4, M5, M6, M7, M10, M27, M32, M104, or M106. Subway—1 to 50th Street, N or R to 47th Street
Admission: $7 for adults, $6 for students
Hours: Monday through Saturday at 10:30am—"usually"
Ages: 13 years and up

This is a tour for teenage g.c.'s. The tours are conducted by Broadway professionals (actors, directors, stage managers). Tours are all in Broadway theaters and this is where you'll meet your lecturer. The people who run these tours know where and who the lecturer is about 10 days in advance.

You must reserve long in advance because many tours are taken by groups. However, you never know. You and the older children really interested in theater will love this one.

Carnegie Hall, tour window at 154 W. 57th St., between 6th and 7th avenues (tel. 247-7800, general information)
Admission: $6 for adults, $3 for children under 12 accompanied by an adult, $5 for students and senior citizens
Hours: Tuesday and Thursday, at 11:30am, 2pm, and 3pm

Here's a 40-minute tour that will encourage the kids to practice, practice, practice. Carnegie Hall has been doing business at the same corner for more than a hundred years. This 2,800-seat auditorium has hosted the best, even the Beatles.

Enjoy discussions and anecdotes of the history of Carnegie Hall. Best of all are the stories of behind-the-curtain happenings.

Central Park—the Dairy (tel. 397-3156), the Urban Park Rangers (tel. 427-6100), or tips and tours tape (tel. 360-3444)

Call these numbers for information on walks and talks. Sign up and join the crowd that's going.

The rangers have a Sunday walk (rain or shine) for 90 minutes. In the fall there's a bird-watching walk to see the southern migration of the birds. The rangers have early-riser wildlife walks at 6am to view the rabbits, raccoons, and woodchucks.

Either call or be sure to get your free quarterly publication, the Central Park *Good Times.* This calendar will provide you with all the information you'll need. I know you've read this before, but I just don't want you to miss out on these wonderful free walks and talks. You can't do better anyplace else.

🍎 **Con Edison Energy Museum,** 145 E. 14th St., at Irving Place (tel. 460-6244)

Admission: Free

Hours: Tuesday through Saturday from 10am to 4pm

Electricity in the past, the present, and the future. Not overstated, is it?

🍎 **Federal Reserve Bank,** 33 Liberty St., at Wall Street, New York, NY 10005 (tel. 720-6130)

Access: Bus—M1, M6, M15, X25, X90, or X92. Subway—2, 3, 4, or 5 to Wall Street; J, M, or Z to Broad Street

Admission: Free

Hours: Monday through Friday from 10am to 3pm

Ages: 15 years and up

You must reserve at least one week in advance. The tour takes 1 hour and is enlightening. Tourists get a good basic idea of what central banking is all about—plus a visit to the gold vault.

🍎 **Fraunces Tavern Museum,** 54 Pearl St., corner of Broad Street, New York, NY 10004 (tel. 425-1778)

Admission: $2.50 for adults, $1 for children under 12

Hours: Call from 10am to 4pm Monday to Friday for information

See the 18th-century Manhattan of Samuel Fraunces. Walk around and visit the taverns that Mr. Fraunces operated and the places that he frequented in those days before the American Revolution. It's short and sweet and presents an interesting point of view.

This is not an everyday happening so you will have to call for the schedule. There are two walks. They start at the Fraunces Tavern Museum and you can do both at once. A quickie.

🍎 **New York Big Apple Tours, Inc.** (tel. 691-7866)

There is no address given because they arrange to meet you at specific starting points. These tours are given in French, German, Italian, and Spanish. Advance reservations required for all tours. Call and they will tell you all you want to know—in English. However, the tours are conducted only in foreign languages.

🍎 **New York City Mounted Police,** Unit Headquarters, 42nd Street between 11th and 12th avenues (tel. 239-9352)

Admission: Free
Hours: Depending on availability of police troops and by appointment; 7 days a week from 9am to 5pm
Ages: 5 and older

The Mounted Police have six barns throughout the boroughs where you may visit. They keep 90 Morgan horses for the 142 troopers. The tours are very informal, the men conducting these are anxious to answer any questions the kids may have.

It's a great visit on many levels. You not only get to see the horses, meet the people who handle them, but it also gives great insight into city traffic problems and the management of crowds, which the Mounted Police and their steeds do so well.

92nd Street YM-YWHA, Lexington Ave. and 92nd Street, New York, NY 10128 (tel. 996-1100)
Access: Bus—M18, M101, or M102. Subway—4 or 5 to 86th Street, 6 to 96th Street

Let's clear the air. There are certain organizations in this city that do things better than anyone else. The 92nd Street Y has long set the standard for similar organizations nationwide. For good reasons. They consistently provide new methods to develop the minds and bodies of New Yorkers of all ages. Whatever they offer, they never disappoint. They have group tours for ages 10 and over. Their schedule and places of visitation vary.

Advance registration is required for the Y tours; get your head together and take one or two. They do a Jewish Lower East Side tour that is for teenagers because it takes 3½ hours; the cost is $15. There is a 3-hour tour of the West Village for $10 and, of course, there are tours for younger kids.

If touring is what you want to do then do it by foot with the 92nd Street Y. I know I'm repetitive. I know I keep telling you how great the 92nd Street Y programs are. Why, you might think, do I even give other listings? The answer is your schedule might not coordinate with the Y's schedule. You might want to see parts of the city the Y is not doing.

The tours I list are all good. I have eliminated three times as many tours as I have listed. I do not just give names. I give you the top of the heap. The 92nd Street Y is the top of the heap's heap.

🍎 **Post Office Tours,** New York Post Office, J.A.F. Building, Room 3023, New York, NY 10199-9641 (tel. 330-3288 for Communications office)

Access: Varies—you will be advised of the location of the post office you will be touring

Admission: Free

Ages: 5 to 12 years may visit the local delivery stations that are nonmechanized; ages 13 and older may take tours of the mechanized post offices

If you have time, write to Miss Silva at the above address. If you're in a hurry, call Miss Silva at the listed number.

The Communications Department prefers two weeks notice but they will be happy to cooperate in any possible way. The tours take between 30 and 40 minutes and kids must be accompanied by an adult. I was also advised that "you need not be a group. A tour will be arranged for any adult with even one child." The post office is anxious for every citizen to be made aware of how his post office and the U.S. mail functions.

They are flexible about visiting hours. If you request a visit to a specific post office, it's okay if the age requirements are met.

There is no charge for any tour. It's included in the price of postage stamps, I guess. You are very welcome to take this tour—they really want you and the kids.

Organized Walking Tours

For walking and talking tours, check your usual sources: the weekend section of *The New York Times,* on Fridays, and *New York* magazine. The museums and the 92nd Street Y are dependable sources. See the Lower East Side Tenement Museum and read about their tours.

🍎 **Look for the Wild Foods Tours,** "Wildman" Steve Brill (tel. 718/291-6825)

In case you have not read about him in the newspapers, Mr. Brill is a unique human being. He believes, and his tours delineate, that many of the things we consider weeds, or less, are edible foods. His tours are a revelation. Steve Brill will help you find chicken mushrooms, butternuts, cherries, and more. Mr. Brill has been banished from Central Park.

You will have to call "Wildman" for schedules, meeting places (often out of Manhattan), instructions on what to take with you, and the basic rules. His tours are definitely winners.

Municipal Art Society, 457 Madison Ave, between 50th and 51st streets, New York, NY 10022 (tel. 935-3960)

Access: Bus—M1, M2, M3, M4, M5, M6, M7, M10, M28, M32, or M104 to 50th Street. Subway—1 to 50th Street or N or R to 49th Street. The MAS is on the east side of Madison Avenue. Enter the gates of the Villard Houses courtyard, which is also the way to enter the Helmsley. The MAS entrance is on the north side of the courtyard

Admission: $14 per person

Hours: Scheduled on some Sundays from 1 to 4pm April through September

Ages: 11 years and up, generally (some are good for younger; ask when you call for schedule)

Note: After you receive your schedule, send your check. Include your phone number, as they call to confirm reservations and advise on meeting places of tours

Depending on the tour, you meet at their headquarters—you have to ask when you make your arrangements. They have extremely well-qualified people conducting their tours. They concentrate on neighborhoods, landmark buildings, and more.

Museum of the City of New York, 103rd Street and Fifth Avenue, New York, NY 10025 (tel. 534-1672, ext. 206—Walking Tours, Public Affairs Department)

Admission: $10 per person

Hours: Sundays, March through October (rain or shine)

These tours are good for children over 10 years of age. They are fine tours for those interested in more than superficial viewing: a little history, a little architecture, and a good outing.

Singer Tours, 130 Saint Edward St., Brooklyn NY 11201 (tel. 718/875-9084 from 7 to 11pm)

Lou Singer is the most fabulous person with whom to take a tour of New York City. There isn't anything the man does not know about this city, from architecture to zabaglioni. Food for the soul, or food for the stomach, Mr. Singer is the guide.

Singer Tours are best known for noshing. The Lower East Side is the turf. Bagels and lox on Houston Street (pronounced like it looks, "*house*-ton"). Cheeses at Ben's, pickles at Gus's (pronounced "goose"). Schapiro's Kosher Winery, candy on Essex Street, cake in Little Italy. Clearly not a tour for people with little stomachs, but your older kids will eat it up. This tour costs about $25 per person, not including food. A shorter version is less expensive and covers the Second Avenue Deli, a Jewish cemetery, and various other places.

There are lots of options. The above tours leave from Manhattan. He has tours in other boroughs as well. Ethnic culture, artistic institutions, history, or heartburn—Lou Singer is the man to contact.

Singer Tours does "It's All Yours" custom tours for a group of one to six people. It takes 6 hours and costs $150 for the entire outing. Whatever tour you select, you've chosen the right man.

Small Journeys, Inc., 114 W. 86th St., Rm. 12B, New York, NY 10024 (tel. 874-7300)—$$$$
They will arrange "special services" for children. Walking tours, bus tours, all sorts of things. You may even request a multilingual guide. It's costly for just a couple of people. However, if you're traveling with a large group it makes good sense. You know, I want to cover all your bases.

South Street Seaport Museum Tour, 171 John St., between South and Front streets (tel. 669-9405)
Would you like a tour of the Fulton Fish Market at 6am? If you are an early riser, this tour takes place the first and third Thursday of every not too cold month. It costs $15 a person and takes 90 minutes. This is the time to be at the Fulton Fish Market to watch the fish store owners and restaurant food buyers pinch the fish and negotiate prices. This outing is guaranteed to clear your sinuses, or close them permanently.

Don't worry if you're not going to be in New York on a Tuesday or a Thursday; the Fulton Fish Market is open Monday through Friday to everyone. The Seaport Museum offers other tours. Reservations are required for all their tours.

🍎 **Talk-A-Walk,** Sound Publishers, Inc., 30 Waterside Plaza, New York, NY 10010 (tel. 686-0356)

No more calls, folks, we have a winner. Talk-a-Walk makes cassettes that contain 3-hour walking tours. And they come with maps. At $9.95 (plus $2.50 for shipping) each, they're worth every penny.

The *Across the Brooklyn Bridge* cassette comes with a good map, travel directions, and more. The other tapes cover the downtown area: *World Trade Center to Bowling Green* (LM1-2), *Customs House to Seaport Museum* (LM3-4), and *Seaport Museum to World Trade Center* (LM5-6).

These cassette tours are so good that they are now used for cities abroad. Contact Gerald J. Morse at the above address and phone number. There will be more coming, I'm sure.

Though planned for adults, they can be enjoyed by a bright 6-year-old and up. Older kids (about 10 years) will love them. The lazy ones can sit and listen—forget the walk.

Try it—you'll be amazed. And don't hesitate to conduct your own! With this book, it'll be a piece of cake.

🍎 **United Nations Tours,** First Avenue, between 42nd and 43rd streets, New York, NY 10017 (tel. 963-1234)

Access: See "The United Nations" in Sites & Skyscrapers chapter. Use the entrance to the U.N. at 46th Street and First Avenue for the tour desk

Hours: The tours of the U.N. are given fairly continuously from 9:15am to 4:45pm on Monday through Friday during the winter months. From the end of March until the end of October, the tours are given 7 days a week from 9:15am to 4:45pm. No tours are given on holidays

Admission: $5 for adults, $4.50 for senior citizens, $3.50 for children

Note: No tours are given at the U.N. when major political events are on the agenda. No children under age 5 are permitted on the tours

🍎 **Urban Park Rangers** (tel. 427-4040 or 427-6100)

They have tours and they have workshops every Saturday and every Sunday. Call for the schedule and the suggested age of the participants. If you ask for their seasonal bulletins, *Walks and Workshops*, they will be mailed to you free of charge.

Their tours are unique. Before Halloween, they visit historic cemeteries in New York. Their bulletin reads as follows: "Dig up old friends or make new ones. Meet at Trinity Church at 7pm." Now, what 8-year-old-or-over kid wouldn't dig this outing?

They have "wakeup early" tours to Hallet Nature Sanctuary, rambles in Riverside Park, climbs to visit Manhattan's best star-gazing spot. You must make reservations.

I've written so much about Central Park and the rangers—what can I say to make you go? Send me your address—I'll come and get you. Anything so you become familiar with the Urban Park Rangers programs. They're in all the New York parks.

Walking Tours of Chinatown, 70 Mulberry St., New York, NY 10013 (tel. 619-4785)

These tours are 90 minutes. They cost $8 per person, $3 for students and senior citizens. They leave at 10am and 1pm from the second floor of the above address. Call and check the schedules. If you are planning to join the tour you must make a reservation.

On this outing you will learn the history of Chinatown as well as receive a mini-education on present-day Chinatown. It's good basic training for the neighborhood, and it's nice to understand what you are seeing. The entire Lower East Side south of the Manhattan Bridge to Baxter Street is now Chinatown.

If you haven't been to Chinatown in a while, you won't believe how it has expanded. Mulberry Street is the only street considered Little Italy. You will notice the Walking Tours of Chinatown office is on Mulberry Street. Ciao.

Walk New York

If you're a native New Yorker, the title of this section is a rhyme (wahk noo yahk).

The walks detailed below cover some really interesting old parts of the city that are a bit complicated to explore with just a map. Some of the longer walks are broken into sections so you can choose just how much walking is suitable for you and yours on a particular day. Before you walk any streets, look in Chapter 6, "Sites & Skyscrapers," if you want to plan your excursions around special places.

This section concludes with the area that symbolizes the excitement and glamour of the entertainment capital of the world— Times Square, the theater district.

LOWER MANHATTAN

From South Street Seaport to Battery Park

This stroll starts at the seaport and winds through the financial district to the World Trade Center and Battery Park City. Add another 20 minutes to walk from Battery Park City to reach Battery Park.

Obviously the time you spend on this outing depends on the number of stops to visit buildings, to eat, to shop. This is up to you and yours. Children 8 years and older can do this in a, well, in a walk. Take your toddlers in a stroller.

Do all of this walk or part of this walk, as you wish. If you cannot complete this in one day, try to complete it another time. This is an area in which to savor the sites. There is just too much good stuff in this part of town to skip over.

North and South of the Seaport

Start this walk at the South Street Seaport, at Fulton and Front streets. To see what this part of Manhattan was like prior to the restoration, walk 3 blocks north on Front Street to Pecks Slip. En route you will see and smell the still-used (but shrunken) Fulton Fish Market, where buyers from restaurants and fish stores come shopping at about 6am every day. When you reach Pecks Slip, face north and see the *trompe l'oeil* (French for "fool the eye") mural of the Brooklyn Bridge painted on a building wall, executed by Richard Haas. Other al fresco building murals, by disciples of Mr. Haas or the master himself, decorate the walls in the downtown area.

Look around Pecks Slip a bit to see what was, then walk back (south) on Water Street (one block west of Front Street) to Fulton

Street to really start this tour. Continue another block south on Water Street to 127 John St. It's not possible to miss this fun house. On the side of this building facing Fulton Street is a playground. On the north side is a huge digital clock, and a blue-and-white-striped awning is over the main entrance. Sewer conduits hold neon lights, and the terrace has funny-shaped chairs that are extremely comfortable. This building was done in 1971 by a developer named Mel Kaufman, obviously a fun guy.

Continue south on Water Street to no. 55—Vietnam Veterans Plaza, the site of the New York Vietnam War Memorial. Etched into the glass-brick memorial are messages and letters from men and women veterans. Many visitors leave notes here. At dusk the memorial, lit from within the glass, is a most moving sight.

Back north on Water Street to Fulton Street and westward ho!

Restaurant Note

A secret to be shared—for munchies head for Fulton Street: McDonald's, Burger King, pizza places, pasta spots, and Mrs. Field's Cookies to mention but a few. Let's not be hasty in the munchie selections. Head for a tiny, fast-food spot at 67 Fulton St. named Ruben's Empanadas. An empanada is a pastry filled with cheese, chicken, or beef, etc.—light as a butterfly. Sit on a stool or munch as you march. On a cold day they're terrific handwarmers as well as good eating. (Ruben's is closed on Sunday.)

Fulton to Nassau Streets

Walk west (away from the East River) on Fulton Street to Gold Street. On your left (south) side, a few steps below Fulton on Gold Street is a building with the word "Excelsior" etched in the brick over the entrance. This was built in the 1880s as an electric generating plant. New York was wired for electrical service in 1883 and this power station was one of the first built in the United States. It is now (you guessed!) a condominium. Gold Street may be called a street, but it's actually an alley with aspirations, typical of this part of Manhattan.

Back to Fulton Street and westward 2 blocks to Nassau Street. On the northwest corner of Nassau and Fulton streets is the

0 | 100 m
0 | 110 y

Manhattan Bridge

Brooklyn Bridge

Market St.

East Broadway

Henry St.

Madison

Catherine St.

Oliver St.

FDR Drive

Pier 18

Pier 17

Fulton Fish Market

Pier 16

19

St. James Place

Park Row

Dover St.

Peck St.

Water St.

Front St.

SOUTH STREET SEAPORT HISTORICAL DISTRICT

Pell St.

Mott St.

Worth St.

Baxter St.

Frankfort St.

Ferry St.

Cliff St.

Fulton St.

Burling Slip

Pearl St.

Maiden Lane

Bayard St.

Mulberry St.

Columbus Park

Hogan Pl.

Police Plaza

24

23

22

21

Centre St.

Lafayette St.

Spruce St.

Beekman St.

Gold St.

John St.

Ann St.

Dutch St.

Williams St.

Maiden Lane

Nassen St.

John St.

Federal Plaza

Duane St.

Reade St.

Chambers St.

20

17

City Hall Park

Theatre St. Row

Park Row

Fulton St.

Broadway

Chase Manhattan Plaza

11

Broadway

16

13

Dey St.

Cortlandt St.

Church St.

St.

Church St.

Worth St.

Thomas St.

Duane St.

Warren St.

Murray St.

Park Pl.

Barclay St.

Vesey St.

WORLD TRADE CENTER

14

Liberty St.

Cedar St.

Thames St.

Albany St.

Leonard St.

West Broadway

Varick St.

Franklin St.

Hudson St.

Jay St.

Reade St.

Chambers St.

Harrison St.

Greenwich St.

West Side Highway

West St.

15

BATTERY PARK CITY

West St.

Path Tubes

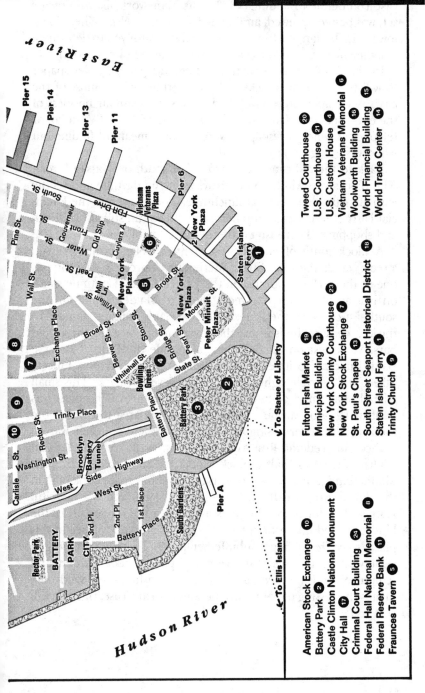

LOWER MANHATTAN

East River

Pier 15
Pier 14
Pier 13
Pier 11
Pier 6

South St.
FDR Drive
Vietnam Veterans Plaza
2 New York Plaza

Pine St.
St.
Gouverneur
Front St.
Old Slip
Water St.
Cuylers A.
Pearl St.
William St.
Mill Ln.
4 New York Plaza
5 New York Plaza
Broad St.
Wall St.
1 New York Plaza
Moore
Peter Minuit Plaza
Exchange Place
Broad St.
Pearl St.
Stone St.
Beaver St.
Bridge St.
State St.
Whitehall St.
Staten Island Ferry

Bowling Green
Battery Park
Trinity Place
Rector St.
Washington St.
Carlisle St.
Brooklyn Battery Tunnel
Side Highway
West St.
West
1st Place
Battery Place
3rd Pl.
2nd Pl.
South Gardens
Pier A

Rector Park
BATTERY PARK CITY

Hudson River

↙ To Ellis Island
↓ To Statue of Liberty

American Stock Exchange ⑩
Battery Park ②
Castle Clinton National Monument ③
City Hall ⑰
Criminal Court Building ㉔
Federal Hall National Memorial ⑧
Federal Reserve Bank ⑪
Fraunces Tavern ⑤

Fulton Fish Market ⑲
Municipal Building ㉑
New York County Courthouse ㉓
New York Stock Exchange ⑦
St. Paul's Chapel ⑬
South Street Seaport Historical District ⑱
Staten Island Ferry ①
Trinity Church ⑨

Tweed Courthouse ⑳
U.S. Courthouse ㉑
U.S. Custom House ④
Vietnam Veterans Memorial ⑥
Woolworth Building ⑯
World Financial Building ⑮
World Trade Center ⑭

cast-iron Bennett Building (1873)—its framework, like an Erector set, was bolted, screwed, and welded all in iron. (*Note:* When doing lower Manhattan, it's fun to carry a magnet with you to determine whether or not a building is really constructed of cast iron.)

In the 1800s, the Bennett Building was part of "Newspaper Row," the northern blocks of Nassau Street, where most of the city's newspapers were published. It was the glamour business of the era—see if the kids can fathom a world without TV, radio, or telephones, when newspapers were the only means of finding out what was going on in the world.

Back to the old drawing board. Walk south on Nassau Street. The blocks you will be on are carless in the daytime and seethe with activity particularly at lunchtime. The folks from the Financial District lunch and shop here; those who can still afford lunch and shopping. There isn't a trendy store for blocks.

A block south of Fulton Street between Nassau and William streets stands the John Street Methodist Church, at 44 John St., one of the earliest churches in the United States. Continue south on Nassau Street for one more block to Maiden Lane. On the southeast corner is the Federal Reserve Bank Building, famous to the kids because this is where the government houses all those gold bars. Walk east on Maiden Lane alongside the Federal Reserve Bank Building to its eastern end and you will arrive at Liberty Street and a lovely sight—the Louise Nevelson Park. This small triangle has three of her magnificent sculptures. The park was built in 1979 by various corporations in the area to combat the food carts that were using this land to park and sell their wares.

Face the Federal Reserve Bank, then walk to your left on William Street for half a block. Climb the steps to visit 1 Chase Manhattan Plaza. This was the first large public space to be built in the downtown area. It was completed in 1960 and is a merciful resting place for those who work in the area and for you. Turn the kids loose and take a breather. The first sight you will see at this plaza is *The Trees,* a huge Dubuffet sculpture. There is a submerged pool west of the sculpture with a Japanese rock garden and sculpture by Isamu Noguchi. The old wishing-well syndrome invites the tossing of coins into the water. In any case, this one will cost you.

Wall Street

Walk west past the pool and down the steps on the other side of the plaza to Nassau Street. Turn left and continue south for 2 blocks to Wall Street. At Wall and Nassau streets is the Federal Hall National Monument, with a huge statue of George Washington. For good reason. This is where Washington was inaugurated in 1789 as the first president of the United States. This building is open to the public.

Stand on the steps of the Federal Hall and look south on Broad Street to the New York Stock Exchange Building to your right. Walk to your west on Wall Street to Broadway. Dead ahead lies the cemetery (tee hee), and Trinity Church will close the vista at Broadway and Wall Street. En route to the church at 1 Wall St., at the corner of Wall Street and Broadway, is the Irving Trust Building. During weekday business hours, walk in and see a handsomely decorated lobby of red and gold hand-done mosaics. In 1930, this was the original banking room for the Irving Trust Company. I fell on this one by error, but it's a beauty.

From here, cross Broadway to Trinity Church and its graveyard. Stop and visit the small museum in the church. In the graveyard the tombstones make interesting reading because the names are those of the families that built New York, as well as of statesman Alexander Hamilton and inventor Robert Fulton. The church and graveyard are among the most valuable pieces of real estate in the world. North of the church, on Broadway on the left are two Gothic-style office buildings built in 1907 to complement Trinity Church. Architects say complement; I say dwarf.

City Hall and Lower Broadway

At Broadway and Liberty Street you won't be able to miss the big orange Noguchi sculpture. Continue down the hill at Liberty Street to the World Trade Center if you're in a mad rush. I wouldn't be in a rush—instead I'd head north at Broadway and Liberty Street. The destination is easily seen; a few trees stand 4 or 5 blocks in the distance. The trees indicate City Hall Park and City Hall. Open to the public.

Directly across from City Hall is the Woolworth Building, whose lobby is absolutely not to be missed. It's open even on weekends, when the very friendly guards will let you enter. Now go west on Liberty Street to the World Trade Center.

World Trade Center and Battery Park City

The World Trade Center is well covered in Chapter 6, "Sites & Skyscrapers." Not included in depth are the lower regions of the building.

More people use this area than live in an average small town. People who work in the area use the shops, dining areas, fast-food places, and banks in this building. It's an amazing sight at the end of the day to see people on their way to the subway buying flowers, candy, books, and a clean shirt to wear tomorrow. Worth seeing any time of the day.

Read about the World Financial Center and Winter Garden in Chapter 6 and then move right along. Battery Park City is bounded on the south by Battery Park, on the east by West Street, and on the west by the Hudson River. The northern border is Vesey Street, but this will change as building continues. The first building, Gateway, was being erected when Stanton Eckstut and Alexander Cooper, the men who designed the master plan for BPC, returned to the drawing board. Richard Kahan was head of the Battery Park City Authority and all three men felt changes were in order. Eckstut and Cooper developed plans for lower and more graceful buildings. They decided the best public spaces were important. Careful consideration was given to the magnificent space on the Hudson River. View Winter Garden, the plaza, and the courtyard and the esplanade to see the ultimate in public spaces.

Stand on the esplanade and face west. On the Hudson River, looking from south to north, you will see the Statue of Liberty, Ellis Island, and a red building that was an old train depot. On the New Jersey embankment you will see buildings that are part of Newport City. This is a big, new, residential and commercial development in Jersey City. The green building is an old renovated building that is leased to a Japanese company.

The boats, scurrying back and forth, carry New Jersey commuters to and from Wall Street. AOTW the marinas and yacht basins are still under construction. The extension of the BPC esplanade to Battery Park has several blocks left before completion.

If you still feel you have a 5-minute walk left in you, head south to Battery Park. Its well-benched promenade invites you to sit and watch the boats and the water and just relax. Unless you decide to take the ferry and go to Liberty Island and see the Statue of Liberty and Ellis Island, and . . . that's all folks.

NOHO

Houston Street to Astor Place

Let's begin our walk at Houston Street and Broadway, at the southwest corner, with a building that is a sure eyebrow-raiser. On the Houston Street side (as if you could miss it) is a purple-painted wall with a geometric arrangement of turquoise projections. When Houston Street was widened, an adjoining building was sliced off and this wall was left in its wake. Those projections are exposed structural plates that allowed the building to remain standing. The Public Art Fund stepped in and retained an architect to create something interesting with the remains. This was accomplished by the addition of projecting rods to the structural plates. These, and bright-colored paint, have created a monument of function and design.

Walk north on Broadway. At no. 647 is a little eatery called Bitable that features health foods, which sounds dreary but isn't. If you need a fast-food fix, try this. Continue north on Broadway. At Bond Street is Wings, a shop with good casual clothing (sweats, jeans, etc.) for kids of all ages, and you, too. On the northeast corner of Bond Street, the red-brick building was the original Brooks Brothers Clothiers. In 1873 they moved in and left in 1883 to go "uptown" to 24th Street. Ed Debevic's fabulous diner is at 661 Broadway, between Bleecker and Bond streets. Glance down the side streets as you walk, many of these former factory buildings were renovated into condominiums.

Continue north on Broadway and see the mixture of stores that sell fabric remnants standing cheek by jowl with restaurants such as Blue Willow, Bayamo, and others (see Chapter 18). At Broadway and 4th Street is Tower Records (see Chapter 14). Continue north and you'll pass the many stores of Unique Clothing Company. Just beyond Unique is ACA Joe (for sweatshirts), another "in" shop for your teenagers; now on to Astor Place.

Turn right on Astor Place and walk east. Look in the window of the Astor Place Hair Designs (see Chapter 16). At the east end of Astor Place is Lafayette Street. Look to the north and you'll see a huge black Rosenthal sculpture that turns on a pivot. Beyond this to the north is the Astor Place IRT subway station kiosk. Although it was built as part of the Astor Place renovation, this very beautiful kiosk actually is an authentic copy of the one that had been torn down years ago.

Look to the south on Lafayette Street and on the east side of the street is the Public Theater. In the imposing building that was formerly the Astor Library, the late Joe Papp established a culture supermarket with the best of plays, films, and Shakespeare at realistic prices.

Cooper Union

On the south side of Astor Place at Lafayette Street is Cooper Union, built in 1850 by Peter Cooper to provide poor boys (as once he was) with free education. (The free education is still available; affordable housing for the students is a problem.)

Mr. Cooper had amassed a fortune in the iron business, among his other investments. Thus the internal beams in this building are old railroad rails and the building is, as they say, made of iron.

On the south end of Cooper Union is a round cylinder. Mr. C. knew the elevator was coming, so he built this to house the future lift. What he didn't know was that elevators would be square. This created a problem for the Otis Elevator Company, but they did ultimately fit a square peg into a round hole.

In the basement of Cooper Union is the Great Hall, where Abraham Lincoln spoke when he campaigned for the presidency of the United States. Under each seat in the Great Hall is a hole. It was Mr. Cooper's plan to put ice in the basement, fans in each hole, and provide his version of air conditioning.

It is important to remember that lectures, such as Lincoln's

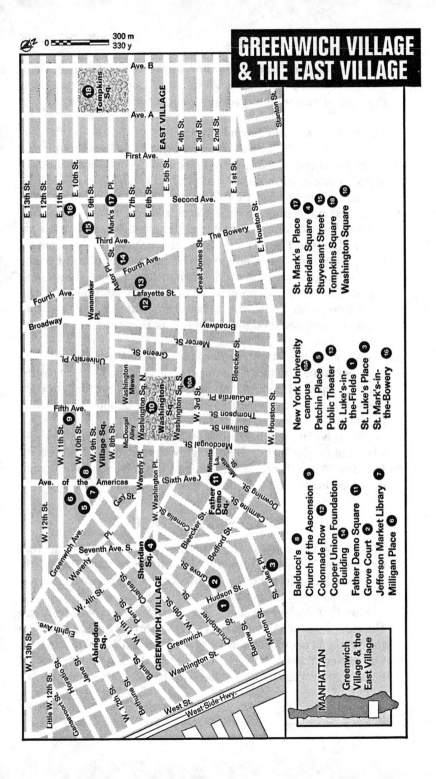

GREENWICH VILLAGE & THE EAST VILLAGE

0 ___ 300 m
___ 330 y

Ave. B

Tompkins Sq.

Ave. A

EAST VILLAGE

Stanton St.

E. 4th St.
E. 3rd St.
E. 2nd St.

First Ave.

E. 13th St.
E. 12th St.
E. 11th St.
E. 10th St.
E. 9th St.

E. 5th St.
E. 7th St.
E. 6th St.

E. 1st St.

St. Mark's Pl.

Second Ave.

E. Houston St.

The Bowery

Third Ave.

Great Jones St.

Astor Pl. St.
Fourth Ave.

Wanamaker Pl.

Lafayette St.

Fourth Ave.

Broadway

Broadway

University Pl.

Greene St.
Mercer St.

Bleecker St.

W. 3rd St.

Washington Mews

Washington Sq. N.

Washington Sq.

Washington Sq. S.

LaGuardia Pl.

W. Houston St.

Fifth Ave.

McDougal Alley

Village Sq.
W. 8th St.

Thompson St.
Sullivan St.

W. 11th St.
W. 10th St.
W. 9th St.

Waverly Pl.

Washington Pl.

Macdougal St.

Minetta La.
Minetta St.

Ave. of the Americas

(Sixth Ave.)

Father Demo Sq.

Downing St.

W. 12th St.

Gay St.

Cornelia St.

Camine St.

Greenwich Ave.

W. Washington Pl.

Bleecker St.
Bedford St.

Seventh Ave. S.

Waverly

Pl.

Charles St.

Sheridan Sq.

Grove St.

St. Luke's Pl.

W. 13th St.

Eighth Ave.

Horatio St.

Jane St.

Abingdon Sq.

Bank St.

W. 11th St.

Perry St.

W. 10th St.

GREENWICH VILLAGE

Christopher St.

Hudson St.

Little W. 12th St.
W. 12th St.
Bethune St.
Gansevoort St.

Greenwich

Morton St.
Barrow St.

Washington St.

West St.

West-Side Hwy.

Listings

St. Mark's Place (17)
Sheridan Square (4)
Stuyvesant Street (15)
Tompkins Square (18)
Washington Square (10)

New York University campus (10A)
Patchin Place (5)
Public Theater (13)
St. Luke's-in-the-Fields (1)
St. Luke's Place (3)
St. Mark's-in-the-Bowery (16)

Balducci's (8)
Church of the Ascension (9)
Colonnade Row (12)
Cooper Union Foundation Building (14)
Father Demo Square (11)
Grove Court (2)
Jefferson Market Library (7)
Milligan Place (6)

MANHATTAN

Greenwich Village & the East Village

given in this hall, were the prime source of entertainment and group socializing in the late 1800s. Peter Cooper was, no doubt, thinking of new ways to provide comfort for the audiences.

St. Mark's Place and Second Avenue

St. Mark's Place (actually a continuation of 8th Street) runs east from Third Avenue. Between Third and Second avenues on St. Mark's Place is one wild store after another. See Trash & Vaudeville in Chapter 11 for the full impact.

At Second Avenue and St. Mark's Place, take a long look around. Second Avenue once had elegant mansions that were torn down after the Civil War because the owners of these homes headed uptown. Tenements replaced the mansions and became homes for the newly arrived German immigrants. They were replaced by the Jewish immigrants of the early 20th century. The town houses on St. Mark's between Second and First avenues remained and were bought by physicians; this street was renamed Doctor's Row.

Walk south (turn right) on Second Avenue. Directly across from Love Saves the Day (see Chapter 11) is a Ukrainian eatery named Kiev. It's open 24 hours a day and is a late-night meeting place for the neighborhood residents. An interesting group. The food is hearty and very inexpensive.

This is NoHo, north of Houston Street, in a nutshell. To those who dispute the name, these neighborhoods are still the Lower East Side, Astor Place, the East Village. But this book reflects what it's called now.

GREENWICH VILLAGE

Most New Yorkers will agree (if they agree on anything) that Greenwich Village is bordered by 14th Street on the north, Houston Street on the south, Broadway on the east, and the Hudson River on the west.

The East Village occupies the territory east of Greenwich Village—bounded by 14th Street on the north, Houston Street on the south, Broadway to the west, and the East River to the east. Older New Yorkers call this area part of the Lower East Side; it became known as the East Village in the late '60s when many of the cool but indigent flower children moved there because rents were soaring in the Village. (When someone refers to "the Village," that usually means Greenwich Village.) If you are properly confused . . . so is everybody else.

A bit of history and trivia (they are difficult to separate). In the 1920s and 1930s, the Village was the neighborhood of low rents and high principles. Artists and writers worked and lived in this area. Political movements and ideologies were freely espoused in the bars and coffeehouses that were then so plentiful and so well attended. That was then. Now for now.

Washington Square

Greenwich Village is dominated by New York University, the largest real estate owner in the area. The campus is Washington Square Park. Before it was Washington Square Park, it was Potter's Field, a burial ground for the poor. The Washington Square Arch was built on the bones at the southern tip of Fifth Avenue. The full flavor of Greenwich Village is to be savored here when the weather is good. For true madness, attend the biannual art shows (see Chapter 4).

The row houses on the north side of Washington Square are as handsome as they were in the time of Henry James. To see an exquisite small area, walk north on Fifth Avenue on the east side of the street and peer into a small alley called Washington Mews.

Heart of the Village

Continue north on Fifth Avenue to 8th Street. Turn left on 8th Street and go west to Sixth Avenue, passing a tacky conglomeration of shoe stores, clothing shops, and eateries. Sixth Avenue, one of the main Village arteries, is loaded with more shops, food places, street merchants, and all forms of commercialism.

Note: Sixth Avenue was renamed the Avenue of the Americas during the Roosevelt years. This gesture was to honor our Pan-American policy. Sixth Avenue is, and always will be, Sixth Avenue. Despite what is written on the sign/street posts, that's the way it is.

Crossing Sixth Avenue westward, you'll find that 8th Street has become the Village Square and continues diagonally as Greenwich Avenue, also a major shopping street. The Victorian Gothic tower-topped fantasy to your right is the Jefferson Market Public Library, and a good stopping-off place for storytelling hours and other kid-related activities. Worth a stop. The lovely garden at the Village Square is a community project, one of the prettier ones around town.

The first street on your left past Sixth Avenue is Christopher, a key street in the Village with unexpected intersections and crossings. Walk west on Christopher to Gay Street, a small winding street 1 block long (typical of many such in Greenwich Village). Walk back to Christopher Street and continue west to Sheridan Square, site of another pretty community garden (no entrance, sorry) as well as small theaters, nightclubs, shops, and restaurants.

At Sheridan Square turn left (south) on Seventh Avenue. Continue past Bleecker Street, then south to Bedford Street, and turn left on Bedford. This street has tiny houses, the most representative of the 19th century to be found in New York. They are something seen in picture books, and this is what the Village is about. A few steps to the right of Seventh Avenue (westward) will bring you to the tiny Edna St. Vincent Millay House, only 8 feet wide.

From this point, retrace your path northward. Don't hesitate to explore side streets along the way. There are many and they're all attractive and worth your attention.

The entire area is fairly safe because there are so many people on the streets. This doesn't mean to suggest that you become careless with your youngster or your pocketbook or wallet. It means because it gerrymanders you will no doubt become lost. Not to worry. Ask how to get to Sixth Avenue and use it as your home base.

Union Square

To see what is really new in this part of town, head for the northeast part of Greenwich Village. Go back to 8th Street and Sixth Avenue and walk east on 8th Street to University Place. Turn left (north) on University Place and walk to 14th Street and Union Square Park.

For the purists among us, yes, the park does run from the north side of 14th Street to 17th Street, somewhat north of Greenwich

Village. I have my reasons for including it, and here are a few. Union Square Park has a playground and a greenmarket on Wednesday and Saturday mornings (early afternoon, too, on Saturday). One may buy plants and flowers here, and fresh-from-the-farm produce. The New York Parks and Recreation Department (tel. 397-3177) has a program for young children at 9:30am on Wednesday and Friday (AOTW). Call and recheck the times when you make your reservations. The program is free and the kids will see a show, take part in games, and more. They will also tell the youngsters about gardening as they learn about agriculture and nutrition while touring the greenmarket. There are other types of entertainment here, so call and check the schedule because much of it is for older children as well.

If this seems a bit sketchy, it's meant to be. My concern was that you not miss the charming architecture, the commercial areas, and the changes at the northern end (Union Square). For aimless wandering, Greenwich Village is a key spot. Take a stroller for the toddlers. Look in the shopping and restaurant chapters to see if there are places you want to visit, such as Kiddie City on Union Square.

SOHO

The area is bounded by Houston Street to the north, Canal Street on the south, Sixth Avenue to the west, and Lafayette Street to the east. SoHo came into its own as the center of the 1950s New York art scene. Space once occupied by manufacturers was large and cheap. Many of the artists were able to buy their space at low prices and remain. When prices began to skyrocket, many others fled to less pricey areas. Lots of good galleries are here.

SoHo is 26 blocks of intense, high-priced shopping places. Clothing, arts, crafts, antiques, collectibles, jewelry, and even pots and pans. There are lots of places to eat, either in sitting or walking positions.

Take the toddlers in strollers. For them it's nothing. For the older kids who will absolutely have to see SoHo, here we go. Walk south from Houston Street on West Broadway. Before you have reached the next block (Prince Street) you will have seen 25 (honest!) places to spend your money.

MANHATTAN
SoHo, TriBeCa, Little Italy & Chinatown

Alternative Museum **7**
Chatham Square **10**
City Hall Park **13**
Columbus Park **11**
Confucius Plaza **9**
Duane Park **14**
First Shearith Israel **12**
Independence Plaza **15**
The Museum of
  Holography **5**
New Museum of
  Contemporary Art **3**
New York Chinatown
  History Project **8**
New York Earth Room **1**
The Police Building **4**
San Gennaro Church **6**
Singer Building **2**
Washington Market
  Park **16**

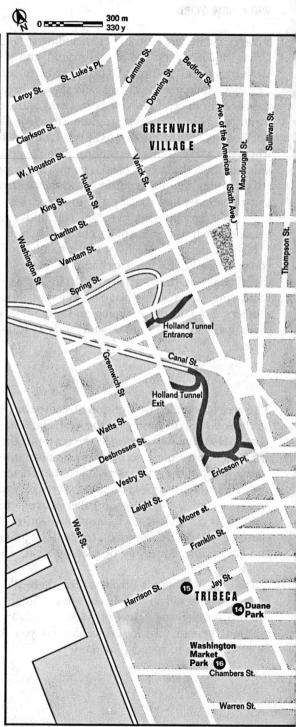

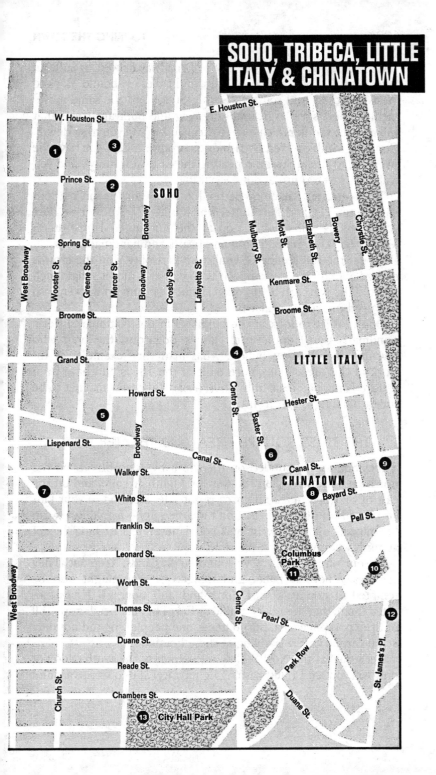

SOHO, TRIBECA, LITTLE ITALY & CHINATOWN

W. Houston St.

E. Houston St.

1

3

Prince St.

2

SOHO

Broadway

Mulberry St.

Mott St.

Elizabeth St.

Bowery

Chrystie St.

Spring St.

Kenmare St.

West Broadway

Wooster St.

Greene St.

Mercer St.

Broadway

Crosby St.

Lafayette St.

Broome St.

Broome St.

Grand St.

4

LITTLE ITALY

Howard St.

Centre St.

Hester St.

5

Broadway

Baxter St.

Lispenard St.

Canal St.

6

Canal St.

9

Walker St.

CHINATOWN

8 Bayard St.

7

White St.

Pell St.

Franklin St.

Leonard St.

Columbus
Park

Worth St.

11

10

West Broadway

Thomas St.

Centre St.

Pearl St.

12

Duane St.

Park Row

St. James's Pl.

Reade St.

Church St.

Chambers St.

Duane St.

13 City Hall Park

At Prince Street go either east to Broadway or west to Sullivan Street—either way, shops, eateries, and galleries abound. Back to West Broadway and south to Spring Street and the same movements. There's a playground at Spring and Sullivan streets that will give the toddlers a chance to break loose (and you to sit down). Continue south on West Broadway to Broome and, if you have the strength, to Canal Street, repeating the east/west forays, and you will have covered just about everything.

The teenagers will enjoy Betsey Johnson, Canal Jean Co. (both in Chapter 11), and Parachute, which is at 121 Wooster St. The younger kids will enjoy a stop at the Enchanted Forest at 85 Mercer St. They have "books and beasts and handmade toys."

To get the full feeling of vitality and frivolity, join the crowds doing SoHo on the weekends. If the weather is nice it's that much better. The places in SoHo open at noon or 1pm on weekends so you need not set your alarm.

Don't forget to look at the buildings in this National Historic Landmark Cast-Iron District. James Bogardus, the man who invented the cast-iron building, has many fine examples of his work in this area. They were built in the 1800s and have been restored and look maaahhhvelous. (*Note:* Take your magnet to be sure a building is cast iron.)

THE TIMES SQUARE AREA AND THEATER ROW

Times Square is bounded on the south by 42nd Street, on the north by 50th Street, on the west by Eighth Avenue, and on the east by Sixth Avenue. This area is not safe. Hold on to your kids and watch your belongings. Don't wear jewelry—a gold Rolex can be snipped off your wrist and you'll never feel a thing except anguish when you check the time.

In your wanderings you will pass two playlands: Keep out! They are sleazy beyond belief and dangerous. You might also be tempted to stop at T-shirt stores and stuff stores. If I have not listed them, they are not adorable or fun. They are head shops, full of drug paraphernalia, porno items, and people who did not dine at Le Cirque before arriving at these boutiques.

Let's start at the New York Times Tower at the south end. Not only will you see 14,800 flashing lights travel 360-foot trips around the building spelling out news flashes, but there's also a 20- × 40-foot computer-generated art display that flashes a 35-second electronic art exhibit every 20 minutes. The *New York Times* is no longer in that building (it's now on 43rd Street west of Seventh Avenue).

Walk north on Broadway to visit the Marriott Marquis Hotel, on Broadway between 45th and 46th streets. The lobby is on the eighth level. It has a most impressive revolving clock. The glass elevators will give you a panoramic view of Times Square and a ride for the kids. Continue north to 47th Street and Duffy Square where TKTS is located if you wish to see a show (see Chapter 10).

Theater Row

This is located on 42nd Street between Ninth and Tenth avenues. It's an important segment of the entertainment scene. The productions here are far more innovative than what is being produced in the 36 Broadway theaters. This is because Theater Row has smaller theaters, tighter budgets, and takes smaller financial risks. Tickets for productions in all nine theaters in this compound may be purchased at Ticket Central on the south side of 42nd Street near Ninth Avenue.

While you're in this area, look at the McGraw-Hill Building on the south side of 42nd Street, between Eighth and Ninth avenues. Designed by Raymond Hood and built in 1930, it's a classic example of the modern architecture of the period.

For kids who are real theater aficionados, make a pit stop at the Theater Arts Bookshop at 405 W. 42nd St. Though most of the stock serves professionals rather than us civilians, they do have splendid posters. Hours are Monday through Saturday from 10am to 8pm, on Sunday from noon to 3pm and 5 to 7pm. Call them at 564-0402 if you wish to know more.

CHAPTER 8

Museums

Museums provide the best good times for the least money. They become addictive. But a good rule is don't stay more than 2 hours. Let your kids leave while they still want to see more. This rule does not apply to the Children's Museum of Manhattan. Too bad they don't allow sleeping bags. Check programs to learn of special films, exhibits, and other happy events.

Museum shops are treasure troves for toys, books, games, and more. The Children's Museum of Manhattan has great stuff, and they gift wrap. The Museum of the City of New York and the Metropolitan Museum of Art stock a varied selection of records, dolls, and toys. Many of these are under $5. The American Museum of Natural History has many, many gift shops. A 25¢ snake can bring immeasureable joy to the right kid.

American Craft Museum, 40 W. 53rd St., between Fifth and Sixth avenues, New York, NY 10019 (tel. 956-3535)
Access: Bus—M1, M2, M3, M4, M5, M6, M7, or M32. Subway—E or F to Fifth Avenue
Admission: $3.50 for adults, $1.50 for students, free for children under 12

Hours: Wednesday through Sunday from 10am to 5pm, (on Tuesday to 8pm), closed between exhibitions
Ages: All ages
Children's Services: Strollers permitted, diaper change possible, no food
Architects: Kevin Roche for the building, Fox and Fowle for the museum

The American Craft Museum is the first condominium/museum. The former home of ACM was a 53rd Street town house. It was traded to E. F. Hutton in exchange for this permanent home in the Hutton Building. The 15,000 square feet of viewing space is spread on four levels. The curving staircase enfolds a handsome atrium. (If you look out the windows on the upper levels of the Craft Museum, you look into the windows of the Matisse Gallery at MOMA. Guess what you see from the Matisse Gallery?)

This luxurious space permits large exhibits in perfect surroundings. Ceramic sculptures, carved wooden floor displays, and fiber hanging pieces are shown here to perfect advantage. Do not overlook the small jewelry exhibit tucked in the corner of the west side of the first level.

They do very special shows at ACM. Inquire about hands-on special events for kids.

American Museum of Immigration, Statue of Liberty National Monument, Liberty Island, New York, NY 10004 (for ferry information tel. 269-5755; for general park information tel. 363-3267)
Access: To ferry by bus—M6 to South Ferry. Ferry—Battery Park—South Ferry. Subway—1 to South Ferry, 4 or 5 to Bowling Green, R or N to Whitehall Street.
Admission: Ferry passage is $6 for adults, $3 for kids under 18. Ferry passage includes Museum admission
Hours: Every day from 9:30am to 3:30pm, closed Christmas. The last ferry leaves Battery Park for Liberty Island at 3pm. During summer and holidays there are extended hours
Note: All ferries go to Ellis Island and Liberty Island.
Ages: All ages

Children's Services: Strollers permitted, food available, diaper change possible

This is housed in a structural addition (1986) to the base of the Statue of Liberty and depicts the history of American immigration in three parts.

The first part of this permanent collection examines the years between the founding of Jamestown in 1607 and the opening of Castle Garden (known to our crowd as Kesilgarten) in 1855. It includes the Black American Room and the plight of the "reluctant immigrant." There is a short movie titled *Crossing the Ocean,* and a display of clothes worn by immigrants arriving during this time period.

The second section deals with the years from 1855 to 1890 and the arrival of the Scandinavians, the Asians, and the migration of the peoples from Eastern Europe westward across the United States. The last display in the museum covers the years 1890 to the present. Want to find out what the busiest immigration year was? 1907.

The final portion is titled "And Still They Come." What a perfect opening gambit for a discussion with your older kids on the subject of changing attitudes toward immigrants.

American Museum of the Moving Image, 35th Avenue, at 36th Street, Astoria, New York, NY 11106 (tel. 718/784-0077).

Note: Travel time to AMMI is about 25 minutes each way. It is quick, it is easy, and there are several ways to get there

Access: (tel. 718/784-4777 for travel information) Bus—from Second Avenue and 59th Street, Steinway Transit Bus 0101, to 35th Avenue, Astoria. Leaves every 15 to 30 minutes 24 hours a day. Fare, one way, $1.15. Subway—N to Broadway station in Astoria. Turn right on 36th Street to 35th Avenue to AMMI; E or F to Queens Plaza station where you transfer to R or G train to Steinway Street; or R or G train from Manhattan to Steinway Street. Turn right at 35th Avenue to 36th Street, 2-block walk to AMMI

Admission: $5 for adults; $2.50 for students with ID and children; $1 for each theater admission, which is on a first-come, first-served basis

Hours: Tuesday to Friday noon to 4pm, Saturday and Sunday noon to 6pm

Note: There are special programs, films, and lectures, at the Riklis Theater and the Warner Communications Room. These hours have nothing to do with museum hours. Call for schedules and information

Ages: Best for children 10 and older

The American Museum of the Moving Image is dedicated to every facet of film production. From the silents to Spielberg, it's all here.

The first level is used for changing exhibits. There are two state-of-the-art theaters located on the ground floor. The Riklis Theater seats 193 people. It is the ultimate in film theater design because so many types of film, including old nitrate, may be viewed here. Film buffs may view 70mm, 35mm, 16mm, and super 8mm films.

The 60-seat Warner Communications Screening Room is a place to view films and video formats. The second floor houses the permanent Behind the Screen installation. This covers the people and the professions involved in both TV and filmmaking. The third floor covers everything you want to know about video and much more.

AMMI is the first museum in the United States "devoted to the art, history, and technology of motion pictures, television, and video." Don't be put off by that stilted quote—this place is fun. Visit the mirror that reflects your image in costumes of famous stars; Marilyn Monroe's dress from the *Seven-Year Itch* may be your style.

Visit Tut's Fever. This is a riotous spoof of the 1920s movie palaces. The installation was created by Red Grooms and Lysiane Luong. Mae West sells the popcorn; the seat covers are Rita Hayworth as Cleopatra. Check the schedule for films shown here.

Memorabilia, equipment, and demonstrations of the creation of special effects in filmmaking, and lots more. The gift shop is outrageous. Things from 50¢ and up. For $300 you may have your very own hand-painted seat cover of Rita that you will covet. Maybe.

There is a place for coffee and a bit more. There are lots of places to eat on Steinway Street, from MacD's to a real diner. Ask at the desk when you buy your tickets.

You're going to like AMMI. The only other facility similar to this is in London. Put "must see" next to AMMI if you are doing museums with older kids.

American Museum of Natural History, Central Park West and 79th Street, New York, NY 10024 (tel. 769-5000; for children's activities tel. 769-5315)

Access: Bus—M10, M17, or M79. Subway—B or C to 81st Street, 1 to 79th Street

Admission: Suggested donations are $4 for adults, $2 for children. If you are visiting the Hayden Planetarium (tel. 769-5901), buy these tickets first and museum admission is included

Hours: Sunday, Monday, Tuesday, Thursday from 10am to 5:45pm; Wednesday, Friday, and Saturday to 9pm. Check the hours for special areas: People Center, Discovery Room, and Natural Science Center

Children's Services: Strollers permitted (checkroom); food available, diaper change possible

Plan in advance for this one. This building is enormous, so decide if your visit is to be to the Natural Science Center, the People Center, the Hall of Pacific People, the Reptile Hall (with dinosaurs), or the Hall of Ocean Life (with the big, blue hanging whale). Decide if you're going to opt for mammals or meteorites— but whatever, acquaint yourself with the floor plan. For information about the planetarium, see the Hayden Planetarium listing in this chapter.

The Discovery Room is the favorite of little children. Line up for tickets at the information desk promptly at 11:45am. The room accommodates only 25 lucky kids at one time for these hands-on exhibits. Your little ones will also enjoy the Gems Room in the Hall of Minerals and Gems.

Be sure to visit the Naturemax Theater if their timetable jibes with yours (tel. 769-5200). The screen is 60 feet wide and the films are very exciting. Tickets are extra; you may pay for these when you pay your admission. Be sure you are staying for the film; tickets are not refundable. Daytime tickets for Naturemax Theater are $4 for adults, $3 for students, $2 for children.

There are double features on Friday and Saturday evenings at 6 and 7:30pm. Tickets for evening Naturemax pictures may be purchased in the 77th Street lobby from 6pm on. Because admission to the museum is free after 5pm on Friday and Saturday, you have to pay for the movie tickets only: $6.50 for adults, $3 for kids. Speaking of weekends, there are many drop-in activities. The Studio Art Workshops is a find. Again, check in advance for information.

The second floor of the AMNH has a particularly worthwhile shop for moderately priced books and other good kid things. Educational stuff is disguised well.

There is good eating on Columbus Avenue or in nice weather brown-bag it in the park. There are always hot dog wagons and other stuff in the area. You'll know them by their wheels or that irresistible odor of grease. The dining in the museum is too noisy in the main lunchroom where the school kids eat. The dining room, with tablecloths, is pretentious, slow, and pricey.

The American Museum of Natural History is so full of wonders that it is difficult to leave. Don't ruin your day by going on overload. Frequent visits are a far better choice.

Asia Society, 725 Park Ave., at 70th Street, New York, NY 10021 (tel. 288-6400)

Access: Bus—M1, M2, M3, M4, M101, or M102. Subway—6 to 68th Street

Admission: $2 for adults, $1 for students

Hours: Tuesday through Saturday from 11am to 6pm, on Sunday from noon to 5pm

Ages: "All welcome"

Children's Services: No strollers, no food, no diaper change

This rose-colored granite building was designed by Edward Larrabee Barnes and it's a masterpiece, but there's no reason to go to the Asia Society if you don't have youngsters who are well-behaved and keep their hands in their pockets.

It will be of no surprise to anyone to know that the Asia Society was founded under the guidance of John D. Rockefeller III to "promote an . . . understanding and appreciation of Asian culture" (1956). There are stone sculptures from Southeast Asia, Indian bronzes, Chinese and Japanese paintings and sculpture (among other things). The youngsters will most admire Ganesha, the elephant-headed Hindu god of good luck. The exhibits vary when loans from other museums and individuals are accepted for exhibition.

This is for people interested in and respectful of Asian culture. Inquire about their on-premise film programs.

Note: If you have a sixth-grade g.c., consider the videotapes produced by the Asia Society, available for purchase (two almost-half-hour videos are $17.50, the set) from them. They are excellent tapes on travel in Asia with a Japanese sixth-grade student as the tour guide.

Aunt Len's Doll and Toy Museum, 6 Hamilton Terrace, at 141st Street and St. Nicholas Avenue, New York, NY 10031 (tel. 926-4172)
Access: Bus—M3, M4, or M101. Subway—A to 145th Street
Admission: $3 for adults, $1 for children
Hours: By appointment
Children's Services: No strollers, no food, no diaper change, no cameras

Aunt Len is Lenon Holder Hoyte. What you will see is her private collection. She has thousands of dolls of all types, from candybox to character dolls. She also has everything that goes with them to share with you. Your 3-years-and-older g.c. will think she's in doll heaven.

This museum is Ms. Hoyte's town house. Space is a consideration, so an appointment is a must. Because she does this all herself, you will want to make a donation above the admission price.

Brooklyn Children's Museum, 145 Brooklyn Ave. (St. Mark's Avenue), Brooklyn, NY 11213 (tel. 718/735-4432 or 718/735-4400)
Access: Subway—4 to Nevins Street, 3 to Kingston Avenue; then walk 1 block west to Brooklyn Avenue and 6 blocks north to the museum
Admission: Suggested donations are $2 for adults, and 50¢ for children
Hours: Monday, Wednesday, Thursday, and Friday from 2 to 5pm; Saturday, Sunday, and holidays from 10am to 5pm; closed Tuesday
Ages: Toddlers and up

Children's Services: No strollers (check them), no food, diaper change possible

You will have no need to limit the time of your stay in this museum. The activities are participatory and hands-on. The biggest plus is that if your kids are several different ages, there are still plenty of activities for all of them.

Learning experiences are happy times. The Brooklyn Children's Museum does everything with a playful quality. Not to be overlooked are the early-childhood playroom and the music room.

The thrust in the exhibits is the environment, nature, and science. Whether the message is transmitted by tunnel travel, animals, water, or steam, it is designed to be a learning experience. You cannot be too young or too old to enjoy the Brooklyn Children's Museum.

They have special programs and exhibits; you will inquire, right? Founded in 1899, this is the world's first museum for children.

Brooklyn Museum, 200 Eastern Pkwy., Brooklyn, NY 11238 (tel. 718/638-5000 for general information, ext. 225 for Museum Education; ext. 374 for detailed information)

Access: Subway—2 or 3 to Eastern Pkwy.–Brooklyn Museum; 4 or 5 to Nevins Street, then cross the platform and transfer to the 2 or 3 (AOTW there's work being done at the Nevins Street station; call the MTA to check on its status.)

Admission: $4 for adults (suggested donation), $2 for students over 12 years with ID, under 12 free with an adult

Hours: Wednesday through Sunday from 10am to 5pm

Children's Services: Strollers permitted; Museum Café open weekdays from 10am to 4pm, on Saturday from 11am to 4pm, and on Sunday and holidays from 1 to 4pm; diaper change possible

The permanent collection has a lovely sculpture garden, plus Islamic, Asian, and Egyptian art, costumes, textiles, period rooms (kids love these), and decorative arts. Also American and European painting and sculpture.

For kids there are free drop-in art workshops year round, with special events during school vacation periods. On Saturday from 11am to 1pm they have Arty Facts for children 4 years and older with an adult, plus storytelling, dramatics, and other activities. For children 6 to 12 years, every Saturday and Sunday at 1pm in the Grand Lobby, join the crowd for the What's Up? program.

Children even have their very own gift shop. The Kids Mart is filled with interesting and unusual toys and great stuff.

🍎 **Children's Museum of Manhattan,** 212 West 83rd St., between Broadway and Amsterdam Avenue, New York, NY 10024 (tel. 721-1234)

Access: Bus—M5, M7, M10, or M11. Subway—1 to 79th Street, B or C to 81st Street

Admission: $4 for children and adults

Hours: Tuesday through Friday from 1pm to 5pm, Saturday and Sunday from 10am to 5pm. Closed Monday, Thanksgiving, Christmas, and New Year's. Summer hours from Memorial Day through Labor Day, Tuesday through Sunday from 10am to 5pm, closed Monday

This remarkable museum must be seen to be appreciated.

The lower-level exhibition hall has interactive exhibits for preschoolers and accompanying adults that include an undersea water world, a city market, a city building, and a sandy beach.

The CMM has a media studio where kids can produce videotapes. There is a full-sized TV studio and control room where they are transformed into technicians and actors.

There is a children's theater where, on weekends, they have dancers, musicians, puppeteers, and children's theater groups.

There is an early childhood center where little ones learn about colors, textures, and nature in a space that encourages climbing and touching.

Self-discovery is a main theme at this museum and they do it all so well.

The gift shop is run by Audra Herman and it is astounding how many good things are available in a small space ranging in price from 15¢ to $100. The shop's inventory parallels the exhibits. However, one can always buy art supplies here from one paintbrush to an entire kit. There are party favors from $2 to $5 that are worthwhile gifts to replace the usual bag of junk. They gift wrap free of charge!

If you are in New York with a youngster under 12, don't miss a visit to the Children's Museum of Manhattan. It has an attentive, loving staff, and excellent hands-on exhibits in child-pleasing space.

The Cloisters, Fort Tryon Park (Fort Washington Avenue near 190th Street), New York, NY 10040 (tel. 923-3700)
Access: Bus—M4 (I insist!). Subway—A to 190th Street and walk through the park (not on your life)
Admission: Suggested "voluntary donation," $6 for adults $3 for students
Hours: Tuesday to Sunday, November through March, from 9:30am to 4:45pm; April through October, from 9:30am to 5:15pm. Closed Monday, Thanksgiving, Christmas, and New Year's
Children's Services: Strollers, no food, diaper change possible. Bring those brown bags

This is a center for special events for children. When you inquire about them, ask about the tours. Fort Tryon Park was an old Rockefeller estate that was gifted to the city, and the northern part of this land was reserved for the Cloisters. This was in 1930 and that generous Rockefeller was John D. Rockefeller, Jr.

The Cloisters looks like an ancient monastery—Romanesque and Gothic in feeling. There is a parapet and the kids will enjoy a walk on this—the views are terrific. On the main floor the kids will like the Camping Room, where there's a 15th-century bird cage and equally ancient mousetrap on St. Joseph's workbench. On the ground floor, the Bonnefont Cloister provides a fine view of Fort Tryon Park—and there's a small medieval herb garden.

The Cloisters has a Belgian block driveway. The blocks were moved there from the streets of New York. This city wastes nothing (ha, ha!). The park covers 62 acres and overlooks the Hudson River. Your g.c. will be pleased to learn there were once Indian camps on this site. It's the place to see the Hudson, the George Washington Bridge, and the Harlem River. This is not the safest part of the city. Go early and leave a little earlier.

Cooper-Hewitt Museum, 2 E. 91st St., at Fifth Avenue, New York, NY 10128 (tel. 860-6868)
Access: Bus—M1, M2, M3, M4, M18, or M19. Subway—4, 5, or 6 to 86th Street

Admission: $3 for adults, $1.50 for children, free for all on Tuesday after 5pm
Hours: Tuesday from 10am to 9pm, Wednesday through Saturday to 5pm, and on Sunday from noon to 5pm
Ages: 6 years and up
Children's Services: No strollers, no food, diaper change possible
   The former Carnegie mansion is now the Cooper-Hewitt. The building is almost experience enough. This is the Smithsonian Institution's National Museum of Design. Terrific exhibits, and some even include "searches." Check in advance on what's being shown. They really like children here.

Ellis Island Immigration Museum, Family History Center (tel. 264-4451; for travel information from Battery Park tel. 269-5755; from Liberty State Park in New Jersey tel. 201/435-9499)
Access: Ferry—from Battery Park and South Ferry. Bus—M1, M6, M15 to South Ferry. Subway—4 or 5 to Bowling Green, R to Whitehall Street or N to South Ferry
Note: The first ferry stop is the Statue of Liberty, then Ellis Island. The ferry does not stop at the Statue of Liberty on the return trip. If you're doing both you must do the Statue of Liberty before Ellis Island
Architects: Boring & Tilton, completed in 1900
Architects for the restoration: Beyer Blinder Belle and Notter, Finegold & Alexander, completed in 1990
Admission: Includes the Statue of Liberty $6 for adults, $3 for children under 12
Hours: 9am to 4:45pm daily
   It has taken 8 years and $156 million to make this restoration the longest in time and the most expensive of any building in this country. It was worth it.
   Ellis Island was the immigrant's point of arrival for 32 years, from 1892 to 1924. It has been restored to roughly duplicate the way it looked in the years 1918 to 1924.
   The Registry Room, originally built in 1918, is your point of entry. It is awesome. Try to imagine how it looked to the exhausted immigrants. Get your tickets to see the 27-minute film. It will give

you special insight for the rest of the tour. The kids will like the hands-on Family Album Kodak Exhibit on the lower level.

You can buy food at the snack bar, eat on the terrace, and enjoy the views. The gift shop is next to the snack bar.

Don't miss the Wall of Honor with the names of immigrants immortalized by their descendants in bronze plaques. As you walk down the three-sectioned "staircase of separation" just off the Registry Room, you are retracing the steps of immigrants who were directed to ferries to Manhattan, to trains to the west, or to detention rooms on the island. The impact of this experience is very moving.

Your visit to Ellis Island will stay with you always. Wow!

Forbes Magazine Galleries, 62 Fifth Ave., at 12th Street, New York, NY 10011 (tel. 620-2389)

Access: Bus—M1, M2, M3, M5, or M14. Subway—4, 5, or 6 to 14th Street; 1, 2, or 3 to 14th Street; N to Union Square; F to 14th Street

Admission: Free

Hours: Tuesday, Wednesday, Friday, and Saturday from 10am to 4pm (Thursday is reserved for group tours)

Ages: 5 years and up

Children's Services: No strollers, no food, no diaper change

Malcolm Forbes of magazine and balloon fame has struck again! A treasure trove of the unusual, the exquisite, and the priceless (how gauche!). Your g.c. will be wide-eyed at the display of toy soldiers. Toy boats aren't too tacky either. And much more. Please don't overlook this. People of all ages are captivated. It's small and special.

Guggenheim Museum, 1071 Fifth Ave., at 89th Street, New York, NY 10128 (tel. 360-3500 or 360-3513)

This museum will reopen late in the spring of 1992. Stay tuned for further details in the next edition. In the meantime call the museum directly for current information.

Hayden Planetarium at the American Museum of Natural History, Central Park West and 79th Street, New York, NY 10024 (tel. 769-5920)

Access: Bus—M10, M17, or M79. Subway—B or C to 81st Street or 1 to 79th Street

Admission: $4 for adults, $3 for students, $2 for children under 12. Admission to the Planetarium allows free admission to the museum

Hours: Sky shows, Monday through Friday at 1:30pm and 3:30pm; Saturday at 11am, and hourly from 1 to 5pm, Sunday, hourly from 1 to 5pm. Not on the hour, so check the schedules.

Ages: No children under 2

Children's Services: No strollers, no food, no diaper change

The weekend Laser Rock show is Friday and Saturday at 7:30pm, 9pm, and 10:30pm. Tickets for these shows are $6. They go on sale at the 77th Street lobby starting at 6pm. These shows are a big happening, so if you're planning to go, get your tickets early. This is especially true during school vacation periods. There are also special shows for preschool kids for which you absolutely must make a reservation (tel. 873-5714).

At Christmas time there is a very special star show, and check "Lucky Kids" chapter for information on lectures on astronomy. This is a humdinger of a planetarium. I know, because I've slept through planetarium shows all over the country. Well, it's a dark place, with comfortable seats, and that's how it is.

The IBM Gallery of Science and Art, 590 Madison Ave., between 56th and 57th streets, New York, NY 10022 (tel. 745-3500)

Admission: Free

Hours: Tuesday to Saturday from 1am to 6pm

Ages: Depends on the current exhibit

This is a small and very beautiful space. The focus here is on quality. The theater on the lower level shows films that provide in-depth information on the exhibits.

The IBM Gallery is a soothing environment and their programs are excellent.

InfoQuest Center, American Telephone and Telegraph Building, World Headquarters, 550 Madison Ave., between 55th and 56th streets, New York, NY 10022 (tel. 605-5555)

Access: Bus—M1, M2, M3, M4, M5, M6, M7, M10, M27, M28, M32, or M104. Subway—E or F to Fifth Avenue

Admission: Free

Hours: Wednesday through Sunday from 10am to 6pm, on Tuesday to 9pm; closed major holidays

The InfoQuest Center is spectacular! A science and technology museum eight levels high and 18,000 square feet big. AT&T never does things on a small scale, bless them.

Ride the glass elevator up and work your way down InfoQuest's multilevel exhibit of high-tech fun! You'll receive an Access Card that you personalize on a touch-screen computer. The Access Card is your key to unlocking the mysteries of the Information Age. The center's 40 interactive exhibits are devoted to Photonics, Microelectronics, and Computer Software—all this and two robots, too!

Photonics is the technology of moving and managing information over beams of light sent through hair-thin glass fibers. See your own voice as it travels over a glass fiber.

Microelectronics is a fancy word for computers on a chip. The technology of microelectronics packs millions of electronic components onto an area the size of a postage stamp! Here, explore microchips yourself or go on a journey with "Alice in Microchipland."

Computer Software is a set of instructions written by a human programmer that tells a computer what to do. Gor-don explains all about software as you enter this area. There are a dozen fun video games here that let you test your "software" against ours.

At InfoQuest the focus is on involvement. Audience participation is at its zenith—robots respond to hand clapping or button pushing with amazing results. Kids will have the opportunity to program their own rock videos. And would you believe a display 80 feet large on which you see a name travel around the world through undersea cables, microwave (you thought it was an oven?) links, and orbiting satellites. How does it sound so far?

The staff is warm, attentive, bright, and responsive. You only have to ask for assistance and explanations. Kids of the '90s require neither of these because they were born into the age of electronics.

Those of you born prior to 1970 could have a problem. Work it out here; that's what museums are for.

Mark this "absolutely must see." For kids 12 and older, this is my number one selection. These older kids, really involved in the world of high tech and state of the art, find InfoQuest "awesome." Younger kids will have a swell time, too.

🍎 **International Center of Photography,** 1130 Fifth Ave., at 94th Street, New York, NY 10128 (tel. 860-1777)
Access: Bus—M1, M2, M3, or M4. Subway—6 to 96th Street
Admission: $2.50 for adults, $1 for children
Hours: Tuesday from 11am to 8pm, Wednesday through Friday from noon to 5pm, Saturday and Sunday from 11am to 6pm; closed Monday
Ages: Any age that understands and wants to see photographs

This is the only New York museum that exhibits only photographs. Well, there is a branch at 77 W. 45th St. It is located in the International Paper Building and the admission is free (tel. 536-6443), but I thought you'd be on Museum Mile and this would be more convenient. If you want to see outstanding photography and special exhibits visit ICP.

🍎 *Intrepid* **Sea Air Space Museum,** Pier 86, Hudson River, at 46th Street and Twelfth Avenue, New York, NY 10036 (tel. 245-2533)
Access: Bus—M11 or M42. Subway—A, C, or E to 42nd Street
Admission: $7 for adults, $4 for children
Hours: Wednesday through Sunday from 10am to 5pm (last admission sold at 4pm)
Ages: 5 years and up

This former World War II aircraft carrier majors in history! Films are shown that pertain to ships, satellites, communications, etc., and are included in your admission price.

Since Desert Storm, attendance at the *Intrepid* has increased tremendously. On exhibit are planes used in the war in the Persian Gulf. They have a scud on exhibit.

There are also exhibits that focus on travel in space, naval aviation, and more. Exhibits and films change frequently.

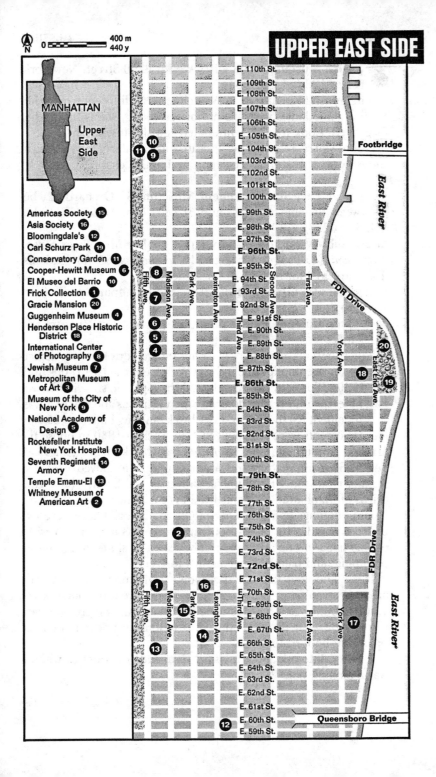

UPPER EAST SIDE

N
0 — 400 m
0 — 440 y

MANHATTAN
Upper
East
Side

Americas Society (15)
Asia Society (16)
Bloomingdale's (12)
Carl Schurz Park (19)
Conservatory Garden (11)
Cooper-Hewitt Museum (6)
El Museo del Barrio (10)
Frick Collection (1)
Gracie Mansion (20)
Guggenheim Museum (4)
Henderson Place Historic
   District (18)
International Center
   of Photography (8)
Jewish Museum (7)
Metropolitan Museum
   of Art (3)
Museum of the City of
   New York (9)
National Academy of
   Design (5)
Rockefeller Institute
   New York Hospital (17)
Seventh Regiment (14)
   Armory
Temple Emanu-El (13)
Whitney Museum of
   American Art (2)

E. 110th St.
E. 109th St.
E. 108th St.
E. 107th St.
E. 106th St.
E. 105th St.
E. 104th St.
E. 103rd St.
E. 102nd St.
E. 101st St.
E. 100th St.
E. 99th St.
E. 98th St.
E. 97th St.
E. 96th St.
E. 95th St.
E. 94th St.
E. 93rd St.
E. 92nd St.
E. 91st St.
E. 90th St.
E. 89th St.
E. 88th St.
E. 87th St.
E. 86th St.
E. 85th St.
E. 84th St.
E. 83rd St.
E. 82nd St.
E. 81st St.
E. 80th St.
E. 79th St.
E. 78th St.
E. 77th St.
E. 76th St.
E. 75th St.
E. 74th St.
E. 73rd St.
E. 72nd St.
E. 71st St.
E. 70th St.
E. 69th St.
E. 68th St.
E. 67th St.
E. 66th St.
E. 65th St.
E. 64th St.
E. 63rd St.
E. 62nd St.
E. 61st St.
E. 60th St.
E. 59th St.

Fifth Ave.
Madison Ave.
Park Ave.
Lexington Ave.
Third Ave.
Second Ave.
First Ave.
York Ave.
East End Ave.

East River

FDR Drive

Footbridge

Queensboro Bridge

Jewish Museum, 1109 Fifth Ave., at 92nd Street, New York, NY 10128 (tel. 399-3344)

The Jewish Museum, AOTW, is closed. No different from other Fifth Avenue ladies who are no longer young, she is having her face lifted. Look for the rejuvenated Jewish Museum in 1993.

Not to worry. Many of her treasures are available for viewing at the New-York Historical Society, listed in this chapter.

Lower East Side Tenement Museum, 97 Orchard St., between Broome and Delancey streets, New York, NY 10002 (tel. 431-0233)

Access: Subway—F to Delancey Street, or J or M to Essex Street
Admission: $1. Program tickets $10 for adults, $5 for students. Tours are $12 for adults, $6 for students
Hours: Tuesday through Friday from 11am to 4pm, Sunday from 10am to 3pm
Note: This museum and its programs are best for 10 years and older folks

The programs given here are films or live performances depicting life for the immigrants in New York from the late 1800s until the 1930s. The tours are conducted through the still-vital Lower East Side; the tour leader describes the way it was and where it was.

A tenement is a five- or six-story brick building built on a 25-foot lot. Tenements were first built in New York in 1830 to house the arriving immigrants and later the free blacks from America's South. Soon thereafter, this architectural style moved west. Dr. Kenneth Jackson of Columbia University said, "In 1900, two-thirds of Manhattan residents lived in tenements; today 10% do." These buildings had four apartments to a floor. There were two bedrooms and a 10- × 12-foot living room. As many as 13 or 14 people lived in one apartment. They slept in shifts, used outside plumbing, and paid $10 per month for rent.

If you and your kids are descended from immigrants, and you are unless you're an American Indian, you owe it to yourselves to visit the Lower East Side Tenement Museum. It will give you new respect for what people endured as well as an understanding of operation boot-strap.

Please call to ask about a visit. It is a study of America when it was a melting pot.

Metropolitan Museum of Art, Fifth Avenue and 82nd Street, New York, NY 10028 (tel. 535-7710 or 879-5500)
Access: Bus—M1, M2, M3, or M4. Subway—4, 5, or 6 to 86th Street
Admission: Suggested donations $6 for adults, $3 for children, under 12 free
Hours: Tuesday through Sunday from 9:30am to 5:15pm, on Friday and Saturday till 8:45pm
Ages: All ages
Children's Services: No strollers, food available but pricey, diaper change possible

On these vast premises is a junior museum. Check in advance because they have special activities and drop-in workshops. The education center has a very fine gift shop on the second floor. Please confine yourself to one area to avoid overload for you and your g.c. It's large for little feet.

The kids seem immediately drawn to the Temple of Dendur and the prehistoric Egypt exhibits. In the permanent collection they'll find American folk art, the French impressionists, arms and armor, Persian carpets, pre-Columbian art—and why go on about the world's largest museum?

The Uris Center for Education has programs for kids from ages 5 to 12. These include workshops, gallery talks and sketching, films, slide talks, drawings, classes, and lots more. These take place on Saturday and Sunday for children and their parents. Call 570-3932 for further information on this.

For ages 10 to 13, there are Saturday-morning programs and workshops. You may take the series or take one workshop. Call 570-3932, ext. 3519, for more information.

Friday evening there are gallery talks from 7pm to 8pm, and sketching for families. These are from mid-September to mid-June for young people from 5 to 12 years and a parent. Meet in the Great Hall at 7pm.

The administrators of the Met are very bright. (Surprised, right?) One woman on the staff said to me, "Adults find this place overwhelming, so we have many programs for children so they will be comfortable here."

They do a splendid job for young people at the Division of Education Services.

El Museo del Barrio, 1230 Fifth Ave., at 105th Street, New York, NY 10029 (tel. 831-7272)

Access: Bus—M1, M2, M3, or M4 to 104th Street. Subway—6 to 103rd Street

Admission: Suggested donations are $2 for adults, $1 for students, free for children

Hours: Wednesday through Sunday from 11am to 5pm

Children's Services: Strollers permitted; no food, diaper change possible

If your Spanish is *no bueno,* El Museo del Barrio means "the museum of the neighborhood." It was founded by members of the Puerto Rican community in order to keep alive their heritage. It now has expanded to include the cultures of all Spanish-speaking people.

The permanent collection includes pre-Columbian artifacts, folk art, sculptures, painting, and carvings. There are also fine examples of household implements once used in Puerto Rico.

This museum is very much alive. It is used by a theater group and as a fine arts school as well. They are especially into hands-on programs for children. Call for information on current exhibits and happenings for your youngster.

Museum of American Folk Art, 2 Lincoln Square, Columbus Avenue between 66th and 67th streets, New York, NY 10023 (tel. 977-7170)

Access: Bus—M5, M7, M10, M11, M29, M30, M103, M104 to Broadway and 64th Street. Subway—1 to 66th Street–Lincoln Center; A, B, C, or D to 59th Street–Columbus Circle

Admission: Free

Hours: Daily from 9am to 9pm

The Museum of American Folk Art, created by enclosing a very small open public space, is done in a most elegant style; stone and wood make perfect backgrounds for the displays. The lighting is excellent. The kids will much admire the 9-foot tall St. Tammany, the Indian weather vane. Whirligigs, quilts, and primitive paintings are all splendid examples of the American heritage.

The on-premise gift shop is extremely well stocked—books, blocks, dolls, jewelry, and pick-up-sticks for the kids. Lots of handmade gifts. The folk-art books available here are representative of "the most complete selection" to be found anyplace. The museum operates a second gift shop at 62 W. 50th St., between Fifth and Sixth avenues (tel. 247-5611). This is open Monday through Saturday from 10:30am to 5:30pm.

🍎 **Museum of the American Indian (Heye Foundation),** Broadway and 155th Street, New York, NY 10032 (tel. 283-2420)
Access: Bus—M4 or M5. Subway—B to 155th Street; 1 to 157th Street and Broadway
Admission: $3 for adults, $2 for children
Hours: Tuesday through Saturday from 10am to 5pm, on Sunday from 1 to 5pm; closed Monday and major holidays
Ages: 6 years and older
Children's Services: No strollers, no food, no diaper change
This is the largest collection in the entire world completely devoted to American Indian works. Most of these remain undisplayed due to the prevalent New York problem—not enough space. For years there has been talk of moving this museum to a larger and more accessible area. Unless New York provides better housing and more respect, we could lose this museum.

Despite the location and the inadequate lighting, it's still worth a visit—there are treasures to be seen. Call for a brochure, because they give many demonstrations. Navajo weavers, musical instruments, and stories of Indian work in ceramics are a few examples.

On the first floor are costumes, baskets, and weapons of the Indians from the Plains states (as they are now known), the Northeast Woodland, the Great Lakes, and the Southeast. The second floor has exhibits on Canadian Indians, Eskimo tribes, and the Indians of the Northwest and Southwest coasts of the United States. There are also archeological artifacts found in many digs in North America. The third floor has pre-Columbian art. Among these you will find everything known to Indian civilizations. Totem poles, masks, drums, headdresses, ceremonial robes, and cookware just to name a few.

🍎 **Museum of the American Piano,** 211 W. 58th St., New York, NY 10019 (tel. 246-4646)
Access: Bus—M5, M7, M10, M28, M32, M103, or M104. Subway—1, A, B, C, or D to 59th Street–Columbus Circle

Admission: Suggested donations are $2.50 for adults, $2 for children
Hours: Tuesday through Friday from noon to 4pm
Ages: 4 years and up

About 20 pianos are on display here. Check for times of miniconcerts. If your g.c. is devoted to the instrument—and you're in the area—go.

Museum of the City of New York, Fifth Avenue at 103rd Street, New York, NY 10029 (tel. 534-1672; for program information tel. 534-1034)
Access: Bus—M1, M2, M3, or M4. Subway—6 to 103rd Street
Admission: Suggested donations are $4 for adults, $2 for children, $6 for the entire family
Hours: Tuesday through Saturday from 10am to 5pm, on Sunday and holidays from 1 to 5pm
Ages: Toddlers and up
Children's Services: No strollers, no food, diaper change possible

This is a place for the entire family. Their programs change quite frequently so you will have to check for the current happenings. They do puppet festivals, concerts, tours, and demonstrations. They cover Dutch origins of New York, marine life, antique toys, to name but a few.

The permanent collection contains a most extensive selection of dollhouses, dolls, and antique toys. The collection of miniature everything (tea pots, furniture, and pets) captivated my granddaughters. My grandsons liked the dioramas and everything on marine life.

You will have to stay in touch with the Special Events Office (tel. 434-1672) for information on walking tours, concerts, talks, and workshops.

This museum is New York. Try not to miss this.

Museum of Colored Glass and Light, 72 Wooster St., between Spring and Broome streets, New York, NY 10012 (tel. 226-7258)
Access: Bus—M6 or M10. Subway—C, E, N, or R to Prince Street; 6 to Spring Street

Admission: $1
Hours: 1 to 5pm daily
Ages: 3 years and up
Children's Services: No strollers, no food, no diaper change
   Raphael Nemeth is the owner and the artist. This minimuseum
defies classification. Children love it—they feel at home. Visit it if
you're in the neighborhood.

Museum of Holography, 11 Mercer St., near Canal Street,
New York, NY 10013 (tel. 925-0526)
Access: Bus—M6 or M10. Subway—1, 6, A, C, E, N, or R to Canal
Street
Admission: $3 for adults, $1.75 for students, $1.50 for children
under 12
Hours: Tuesday through Sunday from noon to 6pm (on Thursday
until 9pm, Wednesday from 10:30am to 6pm)
Ages: 8 years and up will understand
Children's Services: No strollers, no food, no diaper change
   An absolutely complete oversimplification of holography is that
it's a lensless method of photography using a laser beam to
produce a three-dimensional image.
   Fortunately this museum explains and displays holographic
works so that you understand. It will be easier for your g.c. If you
still don't understand, there are free lectures on Thursday evenings from September to May.
   Why miss the chance to see the largest collection of holographs
in the world?

Museum of Locks, J. M. Mossman Collection of Locks, 20 W.
44th St., between Fifth and Sixth avenues, New York, NY
10036 (tel. 840-1840)
Access: Bus—M1, M2, M3, M4, M5, M6, M7, M32, M42, M104, or
M106. Subway—7 to Fifth Avenue; 1, 2, 3, N, Q, or R to Times
Square; B, D, F, or Q to 42nd Street
Admission: Free
Hours: Monday through Friday from 10am to noon and 2 to 4pm;
closed in July. Hours may vary, so call in advance to check.
Ages: 7 years and up

Children's Services: No strollers, no food, no diaper change

Antique, modern, complicated—all sorts of locks. The museum is owned by a man devoted to locks and their functions. Your g.c. will be fascinated, especially if he's considering a life of antisocial behavior. There are some rare beauties here.

I suggest the bus rather than the subway. The Times Square station is less than the garden spot of America.

The Museum of Modern Art, 11 W. 53rd St., between Fifth and Sixth avenues, New York, NY 10019 (tel. 708-9400)
Access: Bus—M1, M2, M3, M4, M5, M6, M7, M10, M27, M28, M32, or M104. Subway—E or F to Fifth Avenue
Admission: $7 for adults, $4 for students with I.D., free for children under 16 accompanied by an adult; on Tuesday by donation
Hours: Friday through Tuesday from 11am to 6pm, on Thursday until 9pm; closed Wednesday
Children's Services: No strollers, food available, diaper change possible. The museum will provide you with a baby carrier if you request one. A baby carrier, unfortunately, is not a person, but a canvas apparatus one affixes to oneself in which to carry a baby

The Museum of Modern Art has, as part of the permanent collection, the finest examples of contemporary designs for functional living, from forks to chairs. Youngsters are quite startled to see things with which they are familiar, albeit part of their households, exhibited in a museum. They are also amused by the Lichtensteins from his early newspaper comics series. If they haven't seen the works of Giacometti and Henry Moore prior to this visit, they laugh out loud. Elongation and bulk do that to people—especially small people. Children enjoy MOMA. What they see in a Picasso or a Pollock may not be what you see. Listen and you'll learn.

There are two movie theaters, so check to see if there's anything appropriate for your g.c. The food is fine. If you're lucky and the weather is nice, you might find a table in the garden. Two days of the year are set aside by MOMA just for children, call the number above for schedule.

🍎 **Museum of Television and Radio,** 25 W. 52nd St., between Fifth and Sixth avenues, New York, NY 10019 (tel. 621-6600)
Access: Bus—M1, M2, M3, M4, M5, M6, M7, M10, M27, M28, M32, or M104. Subway—E or F to Fifth Avenue
Admission: $5 for adults, $4 for students, $3 for kids under 13 and seniors
Hours: Tuesday Wednesday, Saturday, Sunday from 11am to 6pm, Thursday 11am to 8pm, Friday 11am to 6pm with screenings in the Main Theater continuing to 9pm

Every Saturday at 10am from January to June there is a program titled Re-creating Radio Workshops for "children ages 8–13" (that's a rule). At these workshops kids actually "re-create radio programs from the '30s and '40s using authentic sound effects . . ." Performances are recorded and audio cassettes are mailed to each child at no charge. Tickets for this must be purchased separately.

There are Saturday morning screenings of classic films for children. These run about 90 minutes and are perfect for kids ages 3 to 9. Even the kids in strollers are welcome inside the auditorium. The fee for these performances is the same as the admission, $4.50 for adults and $2.50 for kids. Get your tickets a half hour before the performances.

Adults have access to the library files of cataloged audiotape which contain, among other things, NBC's Radio Network programming from 1927 through 1969. Videocassettes of all the programs you loved as a kid are a wonder to youngsters who often say, ". . . you *watched this?*" The grainy, black-and-white films are treasures. The "let's wing it" school of early children's TV productions are hilarious. There are videocassette players available for viewing by two people (you and a youngster?) for an hour at a time on a first-come basis.

This magnificent building is the newest of New York museums and I urge you to visit and make use of its facilities.

🍎 **New York City Fire Museum,** 278 Spring St., between Hudson and Varick streets, New York, NY 10013 (tel. 691-1303)

Access: Bus—M6 or M10. Subway—1 to Canal Street, change to C or E to Spring Street
Admission: Free, donations accepted
Hours: Tuesday through Saturday from 10am to 4pm
Ages: Over 7

There are two floors of fire department memorabilia of buckets, uniforms, horse-drawn fire wagons, and lots more. I suggested 7 years and older because artifacts are rare and tempting, and this museum is strictly hands-off. Why put a strain on the little ones? Take the kids who are able to resist the temptation to touch.

New York City Transit Exhibit, Schermerhorn Street and Boerum Place, Brooklyn, NY 11201 (tel. 718/330-3060)
Access: Subway—2, 3, 4, or 5 to Borough Hall; walk 2 blocks south when you exit the subway. The museum was formerly a subway station, so you'll have no problem if you look for the two lights
Admission: $2 for adults, $1 for children under 17
Hours: Tuesday through Friday from 10am to 4pm, Saturday from 11am to 4pm
Ages: 3 and older
Children's Services: No strollers, no food, no diaper change

This exhibit is housed in the old Court Street Shuttle Station that was in operation from 1936 to 1946. In 1976, it was opened as part of the bicentennial celebration. In 1986, its operation was turned over to museum professionals. Now there are yearly special exhibits. Subway cars from 1903, original advertisements, old tokens, maps, turnstiles, and even pictures of former Miss Subways are here.

Best of all is a scale model of the whole subway: 460 stations. Well, maybe second best; there is also the only usable public ladies' room in the entire subway system. The gift shop features T-shirts, postcards, and Y-cut token decorations on coffee mugs as well as other unusual items.

New York Hall of Science, Flushing Meadows–Corona Park, 47-10 111th St., Corona, NY 11368 (tel. 718/699-0675; for in-depth information tel. 718/699-0005)
Access: Subway—7 to 111th Street (walk 5 blocks to 48th Avenue). Car—Long Island Expressway to 108th Street or Grand Central

Parkway eastbound to Midtown Tunnel exit (plenty of parking available)
Note: See Queens Museum
Admission: Suggested donations are $3.50 for adults, $2.50 for children, free Wednesday and Thursday 2 to 5pm
Hours: Wednesday through Sunday from 10am to 5pm
Ages: All ages, even babies, will enjoy the visual pleasures
Children's Services: Strollers checked—they will supply a baby carrier, diaper change possible, food (cafeteria) available

No more calls—we have a winner! New York had not had a permanent science museum since the 1940s when the Museum of Science and Industry closed. Wallace K. Harrison, the architect who gave us the Trylon and Perisphere at the 1939 World's Fair, designed this breathtaking space.

Most of the exhibits are hands-on—plenty to crank, pedal, and manipulate. "Feedback" has been handled brilliantly. Big kids may pedal a bike, thereby turning a full-size airplane propeller. This is linked to centrifugal weights. The biker pedals more quickly and the propeller adjusts itself to create more wind without spinning appreciably faster. Okay, you have to be there. Little ones may work a windmill by turning its directions with the flick of a switch. *Voilà!* Feedback.

A microscope (2,000 × power) allows one to see tiny dancing chips bombarded by surrounding atoms. (Ever see a bombarding atom?) There's a huge clock constructed totally from bicycle parts. The prisms, mirrors, soap bubbles, and trompe l'oeil that made an all-too-brief visit to the IBM Building are now ours to keep.

Don't lose a second. Get out to Queens. The exhibits will give you a visual understanding of science.

New-York Historical Society, 170 Central Park West, between 76th and 77th streets, New York, NY 10024 (tel. 873-3400)
Access: Bus—M10 or M17. Subway—B or C to 81st Street; 1 to 79th Street
Admission: $4.50 for adults, $1 for children under 12
Hours: Tuesday through Sunday from 10am to 5pm
Ages: 2 years and up
Children's Services: No strollers, no food, no diaper change

Exhibits of old New York and other displays the children like a whole lot. The museum does a great many special-event shows as well. They have movies and story hours for children—and a good collection of antique toys.

The hyphen in the name is for real. The first museum in the state is entitled to some privileges; since 1804 the New-hyphen-York Historical Society has invoked this one.

In the permanent collection are the *Birds of America* by Audubon and the John Trumbull portrait of Alexander Hamilton that your kids will recognize as the very same portrait reproduced on our $10 bill. They have Tiffany glass windows, furniture by Duncan Phyfe, and more.

Among their books and manuscripts and maps is the first printing of the Declaration of Independence. Of course, that's under lock and key, but it's a comfort to know it's close by. Among the permanent exhibits are "Early American Leaders," "Life in British Colonial New York," as well as "A Child's World."

The New-York Historical Society was founded for the "collection, preservation, and dissemination of history—that of New York City, New York State, and United States history in general."

They do a splendid job and are well aware of the importance of children as their (possibly) most interested visitors.

The Jewish Museum collection is on the first floor. Because of the Sabbath, this section closes at 3pm on Friday and reopens on Sunday.

Queens Museum, NYC Building at Flushing Meadows–Corona, NY 11368 (tel. 718/592-2405)
Access: Subway—7 train marked Flushing to Willets Pt. Station (Shea Stadium). Follow signs on Roosevelt Avenue to the Unisphere. This is a section of the New York City Building
Note: The best access to the Queens Museum is a short walk over a footbridge from the New York Hall of Science (see listing in this chapter)
Admission: $2 for adults, $1 for students, free for children under 5
Hours: Tuesday through Friday from 10am to 5pm, Saturday and Sunday from noon to 5:30pm; closed Monday

The thing to see at this museum is the 9,000-square-foot detail-perfect model of the five boroughs that make up the

City of New York. In case you don't know, they are Manhattan, Brooklyn, Bronx, Queens, and Staten Island. Who said I didn't learn anything at the Highland Manor School for Girls? But back to the Panorama! Every building and every street is included and the model is huge. There are also other scheduled exhibits.

If this is an outing, make it part of your trip to the New York Hall of Science. Kids under 5 will not begin to understand the panorama but older kids will be impressed.

Note: You do know this was the site of the 1939 World's Fair.

🍼 **Snug Harbor Cultural Center** (home of the Staten Island Children's Museum), 940 Richmond Terrace, Staten Island, NY 10301 (tel. 718/273-2060)

Access: Ferry and bus—Ferry to St. George Terminal (this is where the ferry docks), then the no. 40 bus to the entrance of Snug Harbor. The bus departs every half hour and the ride takes 10 minutes. The cost is $1.15 in change or a token; children under 5 are free. The ferry to Staten Island costs 50¢ (quarters only)—the toll is paid on the Staten Island side when you board the ferry to return; no charge for ride out.

Admission: Suggested donation is $2

Hours: Wednesday through Friday from 1 to 5pm, on Saturday and Sunday from 11am to 5pm

Ages: All ages

Children's Services: Strollers permitted, brown-bag your food (there are vending machines), diaper change possible

Sailor's Snug Harbor was formerly a home for retired seamen. What was once the maintenance building is now the new home of the museum. What was formerly a 5,000-square-foot museum is now housed in 20,000 square feet. When the museum had a small place in Stapleton, S.I., it had a big imagination. Their thinking and expanded space have produced a sensational new facility for New York.

Hands-on, of course. "Building Buildings" is a typical Staten Island Children's Museum environment, and here is where children examine food and shelter. They find themselves in an area in the process of construction, plumbing, and wires exposed and hanging. Blocks with Velcro backs and a flannel wall allow them to build, create, and design. It may read like a playroom, but it's a learning center. Questions are asked and answered. Wonderful communication here between kids and staff!

"Big Top Puppets" is another permanent museum show. Little ones may turn the crank on Dragon Band and the creatures play music. Press and produce a strong man lifting an elephant. Older kids are challenged by exhibits that make them ponder the worlds of physics and architecture. And staff are always present to respond to questions.

The gift shop is without a doubt the best around, with 500 items from 50¢ to $30—puzzles, construction kits, T-shirts, and an inflatable stegosaurus. Don't look that word up—go to the Staten Island Children's Museum for the answer.

South Street Seaport Museum, 207 Front St., New York, NY 10038 (tel. 669-9400)
Access: Bus—M15 to Fulton Street. Subway—2, 3, 4, or 5 to Nassau Street; J, M, or R to Broadway–Nassau Street; A or C to Fulton Street
Admission: $6 for adults, $3 for children 4 to 12
Hours: Monday through Friday from 10am to 4pm, Saturday and Sunday to 5pm

Exhibits pertaining to 19th-century sea life, with a working 19th-century print shop next door. The Children's Center (165 John St.) has kiddie-appropriate exhibits.

Admission to the museums allow you to visit historic ships, take three different tours, and see two films. Make your first inquiry about tours, workshops, and story hours. There is lots of stuff going on and much to see at South Street Seaport. All one has to do is ask lots of questions.

The Whitney Museum of American Art, 945 Madison Ave., at 75th Street, New York, NY 10021 (tel. 570-3676)
Access: Bus—M1, M2, M3, or M4. Subway—6 to 77th Street
Admission: $5 for adults, $3 for students with ID, free for children under 12 if accompanied by adult. On Tuesday free from 6 to 8pm
Hours: Tuesday from 1 to 8pm, Wednesday through Saturday from 11am to 5pm, and on Sunday from 11am to 6pm
Ages: 3 years and up
Children's Services: No strollers, food available, diaper change possible

Everything new and important done by contemporary American artists can be seen at the Whitney. The children love it because much of it is amusing.

The Calder Circus is part of the permanent collection. If they are showing the film that accompanies the circus, don't even try to move your g.c. It's a spellbinder to viewers of any age. The exhibits change often. The building is magnificent.

AOTW, the architect Michael Graves has a model of his design for the proposed expansion of the Whitney. There are plans to build on top.

Your g.c. will find the size of the elevators awesome. Watch your youngster's face if it's a new experience.

CHAPTER 9

Burn-Off

Where do the kids get all that energy? The meaningful issue is how to help the kids dispose of their energy. That's what this chapter is all about.

Archery, bowling, beaches, bike trips, day excursions, swimming, sailing, and tennis are but a few activities. There are gyms, dance, arts and crafts programs by the hour and the day for all ages.

For single parents in New York on a visit, call Kindred Spirits at the 92nd Street Y, 1395 Lexington Ave. (tel. 996-1100). Go to ball games, ice-skating parties, picnics, and museums, with other single Moms and Dads and their kids. Evening activities without the kids include cocktail parties and other festive happenings. See Chapter 20 for more details.

Central Park

Central Park is 840 acres of the world's most valuable real estate. It is bounded on the north by 110th Street and on the south by 59th Street (or Central Park South). The east side border is Fifth Avenue and the west side is Central Park West.

In Central Park you may bicycle, row a boat, sail a boat, ride the carousel, or take a carriage ride around the park. There is ice skating, roller skating, tennis, running, a zoo or two, and playgrounds forever.

There are marionettes, storytelling, workshops, music (jazz, symphony, grand opera), and Shakespeare and other theater (see "That's Entertainment").

The only way to use the park and know what's going on is to have a copy of *Central Park Map & Guide* (50¢), and a copy of Central Park *Good Times*. (They are published by the Central Park Conservancy through the office of the Central Park Administrator, New York City Department of Parks and Recreation. Calendar listings are sponsored by the New York City Department of Parks and Recreation and the Central Park Conservancy. The editorial office of the Central Park *Good Times* is located at the Arsenal, 830 Fifth Ave., Room 103, New York, NY 10021. See Chapter 3.)

The Dairy, Belvedere Castle, and the Arsenal serve as Central Park information centers. Call or visit them to get the two publications as well as the schedule of the Central Park Rangers Walks & Workshops. If you prefer to do this by mail, send a stamped, self-addressed envelope, your request for *Good Times* and the *Central Park Map & Guide* with a check for 50¢ to the Dairy, 830 Fifth Ave., New York, NY 10021.

Central Park *Good Times* is a quarterly publication with a complete calendar of special park events, descriptions, and locations. It also includes notice of future events. The *Central Park Map & Guide* is exactly that. Don't set foot in the park without these two invaluable publications. Read them before you go. You can plan a wonderful day.

Before you fling yourself into the park with wild abandon, be cautious. Carry very little money, no jewelry, and leave your credit cards at home. If you aren't sure of your cross street, look at the lamp posts. Every two or three has the cross street painted on.

Unless you are part of a scheduled evening event, leave before the sun considers setting. Stay out of isolated areas. Prudence is needed, but not paranoia. The park is loaded with mini-moms, bikers, and joggers. When the weekend weather is good, it's wall-to-wall people. It is patrolled by the rangers, Parks Enforcement Patrol, and New York's finest.

One partial quote from the *Map & Guide:* "Enjoy the park, but remember you are still in the middle of the city. Stay alert to people around you." Good advice anyplace. Central Park is the most wonderful place in New York. Use it exactly as I suggest on the next pages and you'll have to agree.

Central Park has a staff any corporation would envy. Whether employees of the Parks Department or dedicated volunteers, they make one feel secure. A super group is the Urban Park Rangers. If you're not sure how to get to your park destination, call the rangers. If you feel a bit "frightened" of the park, call the rangers. They'll give you the safest, quickest route to where you want to go. (God knows, I've done my best.)

You say that isn't enough? The rangers conduct walking tours and workshops. The tours are in and out of Central Park. Add your name to the mailing list at the Dairy or call the rangers. They want you safe and happy in Central Park. And park activities go on year round—indoors and outdoors.

There's also the Parks Enforcement Patrol (tel. 397-3082). Although the uniforms are very similar to the rangers, the PEP are authorized to take a firmer position—like a summons.

Now you know the people in the park. You have your two publications. Write down the following phone numbers and put them in your wallet:

Activities Information, daily from 9am to 5pm (tel. 427-4040)
Daily Information, Central Park (tel. 397-3156)
The Belvedere Castle, Learning Center, kids' information (tel. 772-0210)
The Dairy, calendar listings (tel. 397-3156) *Hours for the Belvedere Castle and the Dairy:* Tuesday through Thursday, Saturday, and Sunday from 11am to 4pm, Friday from 1 to 4pm, hours are extended to 5pm from spring until fall.
Urban Park Rangers, emergency and visitors service (tel. 860-1351) and activities information, daily from 9am to 5pm (tel. 427-4040)

Look for the brightly colored phone symbol. These are emer-

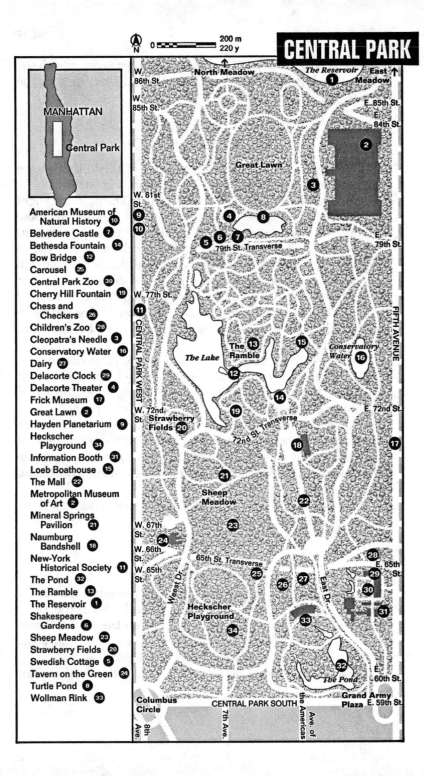

CENTRAL PARK

0 ——— 200 m
0 ——— 220 y

MANHATTAN

Central Park

American Museum of
  Natural History (10)
Belvedere Castle (7)
Bethesda Fountain (14)
Bow Bridge (12)
Carousel (25)
Central Park Zoo (30)
Cherry Hill Fountain (19)
Chess and
  Checkers (26)
Children's Zoo (28)
Cleopatra's Needle (3)
Conservatory Water (16)
Dairy (27)
Delacorte Clock (29)
Delacorte Theater (4)
Frick Museum (17)
Great Lawn (2)
Hayden Planetarium (9)
Heckscher
  Playground (34)
Information Booth (31)
Loeb Boathouse (15)
The Mall (22)
Metropolitan Museum
  of Art (2)
Mineral Springs
  Pavilion (21)
Naumburg
  Bandshell (18)
New-York
  Historical Society (11)
The Pond (32)
The Ramble (13)
The Reservoir (1)
Shakespeare
  Gardens (6)
Sheep Meadow (23)
Strawberry Fields (20)
Swedish Cottage (5)
Tavern on the Green (24)
Turtle Pond (8)
Wollman Rink (33)

The Reservoir
North Meadow
East Meadow
W. 86th St.
W. 85th St.
E. 85th St.
E. 84th St.
Great Lawn
W. 81st St.
79th St. Transverse
E. 79th St.
W. 77th St.
The Lake
The Ramble
Conservatory Water
CENTRAL PARK WEST
FIFTH AVENUE
W. 72nd St.
Strawberry Fields
72nd St. Transverse
E. 72nd St.
Sheep Meadow
W. 67th St.
W. 66th St.
65th St. Transverse
W. 65th St.
E. 65th St.
West Dr.
East Dr.
Heckscher Playground
The Pond
E. 60th St.
Columbus Circle
CENTRAL PARK SOUTH
Grand Army Plaza
E. 59th St.
8th Ave.
7th Ave.
Ave. of the Americas

gency call boxes. They will put you in immediate contact with the Central Park Police Precinct and the Medical Unit. Help will be sent to you, if needed.

READY, GET SET, GO!

Now you have your *Good Times*, your *Map & Guide*, your phone numbers, and my invaluable advice—so have a good day!

If your g.c. is stroller-age, take the stroller. The little one might not want to sit in it at first, or at last. But it's a big park and those are little legs. A stroller is also a great place to stow your gear. What gear? Well, remember the plastic beach ball I told you to buy? If the air is out, put it in your pocket. If the air is in, put it in the stroller, with or without your g.c. Take some of your finest plastic containers (throw out the cole slaw), and a few of those tired kitchen utensils you've been intending to dump. Coffee measurers are winners, plastic spoons, and a funnel for the sand—an assortment of whatever.

For the ever-impatient under-4 age group, put some cookies, fruit, raisins (not for under-2, however), and a box or two of fruit juice in a bag. Include a change of clothing, wipes, diapers if needed, and always carry plastic or paper drinking cups.

If you're going to, or may pass, a playground with water, and it's more than 80°, bring a towel and "floaties." If water isn't on your agenda, reroute yourself. If you think for one hot second you can keep your g.c. out of the water, you're wrong. He knows he has his pigeon with him.

Wear your sneakers, or any comfy, closed shoe. It's gritty. Don't dress. It's informal, you know.

BICYCLING

The park is closed to motor vehicles on weekends and in the summer months. Never ride on pedestrian paths. When the park is open to traffic, use the designated recreation lane. Always travel counterclockwise around the park. If you have any questions about biking rules, paths, and so forth, call 397-8156.

Look at your Central Park *Good Times* calendar. In the spring there is a bicycle safety clinic, a bike-a-thon, and other activities. Toddlers may ride their bikes anywhere in the park.

If your young g.c. is on his bike, trot along and beg for mercy. If your older g.c. wants to go bicycling and your varicose veins scream at the thought (show of legs, please), you have choices: (1) rent a low bike for yourself—they're less painful; (2) rent a tandem bike and share your agony; (3) don't go.

If you prefer to rent a bike and ride it to the park here are two shops; one on the east side and one on the west side.

Gene's, 242 E. 79th St. (tel. 249-9218)
You must provide $20 in cash, a driver's license, and a major credit card as a deposit. If you wish to rent a mountain bike change the $20 deposit to a $40 deposit. The mountain bikes rent for $21 a day or $6 per hour. Three-speed bikes are $10.50 a day or $3 per hour.

West Side Bicycle, 231 W. 96th St. (tel. 663-7531)
You must leave $20 in cash and have a driver's license or a major credit card. $20 a day for a three-speed bike or $4 per hour. $25 a day for a 10-speed bike or $6.50 per hour.

You can also rent bikes inside the park at the following locations.

Loeb Boathouse, at 76th Street, a bit east of midpark (tel. 517-4723)
Fee: $6 per hour; $12 per hour for tandem bikes
Hours: April through October, Monday through Friday from 10am to 7pm, Saturday and Sunday from 9am to 7pm

Pedal Carriages, Tavern on the Green parking lot, West 66th Street in the park (tel. 860-4619)
These are available weekends only, weather permitting, May through October. The price is $15 per hour. Four people will be comfortable in this, two of them better have strong legs.

THE CAROUSEL

Carousel, in midpark, at 64th Street (tel. 879-0244)
Fee: 75¢ a ride

Hours: Monday through Friday from 10:30am to 4:45pm, on Saturday and Sunday to 5:45pm

Weather permitting, this is a nostalgic treat.

GOLF

Golf in Central Park, just east of the Wollman Rink (tel. 517-4800)

Price: $6.50 adults, $3.50 children

Hours: Late spring to the end of October, Monday from 10am to 5pm, Tuesday through Thursday from 10am to 9:30pm, Friday and Saturday from 10am to 11pm, Sunday from 10am to 9:30pm

Each hole represents a different New York landmark, such as Kennedy Airport. The best-looking 9 little holes you ever did see.

Miniature Golf at 9 Bond Street, between Broadway and Lafayette Street just 2 blocks north of Houston Street (tel. 982-8600)

Price: $6 per person per game

Hours: Tuesday, Wednesday, and Thursday from 4:30pm to 12am, Friday until 1am, Saturday and Sunday from 2pm to 1am

Not in Central Park, but 18 holes of miniature golf! Not to fret if you have a wait, there is a pinball machine and a couple of video games.

This is really a bunch of fun for kids of all ages. They are often booked for private parties, so call and make sure you'll be able to play a round.

HORSE-DRAWN CARRIAGES

Horse-Drawn Carriages, Central Park South (59th Street) from Fifth to Sixth avenues

I'll prepare you—the price is $34 for 30 minutes. See "Rides for Children" in Chapter 10.

HORSEBACK RIDING

Claremont Riding Academy, 175 W. 89th St., between Columbus and Amsterdam avenues (tel. 724-5100 for reservations)

Fee: $30 per hour
Hours: Monday through Friday from 6:30am to an hour before dusk (huh?), on Saturday and Sunday to 4pm
Lessons: $32 per half-hour private lesson, 6 years and up
Credit Cards: None

"Riders must be experienced in an English saddle. No galloping." Don't let your g.c. pull the wool (saddle blanket?) over your bifocals. If he's from Arizona and tells you he's never used a western saddle and he's a very experienced rider, and you know he's only 18 months old, however verbal, call Them! Specific parental permission is needed for this one.

Claremont will not permit young children to ride outside the ring unless they are "very, very good" and accompanied by an adult. This is New York's oldest and largest riding academy with a ring.

MODEL YACHTS

Conservatory Water, 73rd to 75th streets and E. Park Drive to Fifth Avenue

Model yachts compete in races on Saturday at 10am on into the day. They're fun to watch—seasonal, of course. Or sail your own. You don't have to have a yacht. Use anything that floats (providing it has a string).

While near the water with your nonswimmer g.c., put floaties on him. If he says, "They don't fit over my sweater," put them under the sweater. More objections? Tell your g.c. he looks like Bluto from *Popeye* (will he know who that is?). If the little bugger is not to be laughed out of this, continues to protest, and doesn't know the phone number of the Child Abuse Council, pinch him. (Only a jest—don't write me!)

PLAYGROUNDS

Your *Central Park Map & Guide* includes playgrounds and letter codes. Just to make your life simpler, I walked every playground. The listings include exactly how to enter the park and in which direction to walk to find the playground of your choice. Too specific? Not for those of us unfamiliar with Central Park, or those with kids saying, "Are we there yet?"

Easily the best burn-off! The construction work on the playgrounds is constant. Call a day in advance to be certain the playground you have selected to visit is open. The Dairy and the Belvedere Castle open at 11am; you might want an early-morning start. Playground equipment is up all year. The letter codes are as follows:

Adventure Playgrounds (A). An adventure playground is one that has been renovated. It contains both traditional and wooden equipment.

Water Playgrounds (W). This is a playground with a wading pool and/or sprinklers. When the temperature hits 80° or higher, the water is on.

Food Available (F). Hot dogs, ice cream, pretzels—park munchies to spoil dinner—to the delight of your g.c.

If the playgrounds have no letter designation, they are as they read—just plain playgrounds.

East Side Playgrounds

Fifth Avenue, 67th to 68th streets (A)—enter at 67th or 68th streets and Fifth Avenue.

Fifth Avenue, 71st to 72nd streets (A, F)—enter at 72nd Street and Fifth Avenue, then bear left.

Fifth Avenue, 79th to 80th streets (W)—enter at 79th Street and Fifth Avenue.

Fifth Avenue, 84th to 85th streets (A, W, F)—enter at either 84th or 85th streets and Fifth Avenue.

Fifth Avenue, 98th to 99th streets—enter at 98th Street and Fifth Avenue.

108th to 109th streets (A, F)—enter from 110th Street and go south.

West Side Playgrounds

CPS is Central Park South (59th Street); CPW is Central Park West.

CPS and 62nd Street (Heckscher Playground)—enter at Seventh Avenue and CPS, then go north.

CPW and 67th Street (A)—enter at 67th Street and CPW.

CPW and 72nd Street (Strawberry Fields)—enter at 72nd Street and CPW.

CPW, 76th to 77th streets—enter at 77th Street and CPW, then walk south.

CPW and 81st Street (Diana Ross Playground; W)—enter at CPW and 81st Street, then walk north.

CPW, 84th to 85th streets—enter at 85th Street and CPW, then walk south.

CPW, 85th to 86th streets (A)—enter at 85th Street and CPW, then walk north.

CPW, 90th to 91st streets (W)—enter at 90th Street and CPW, then walk north.

CPW, 93rd to 94th streets (A, W)—enter at 93rd Street and CPW.

CPW, 96th to 97th streets—enter at 96th Street and CPW, then walk north.

CPW, 99th to 100th streets (A, W)—enter at 100th Street and CPW, then walk south.

Central Park North and 110th Street—enter from 110th Street.

ROWBOATS

Loeb Boathouse, northeast corner of Central Park Lake at 76th Street (tel. 517-4723)

You may rent rowboats here from April to October, daily from 9am to 6pm. You must be 16 or older and armed with proof, if you look too young. Bring a major credit card, your driver's license, and money. A deposit of $20 is required. Lifejackets are provided free of charge and must be worn. The maximum number of people in a boat is six. The charge is $6 per hour.

There is a gondola from Venice that is splendid for an evening cruise. Reservations are required and you still wait in line. The charge is $30 for 30 minutes. Romantic adventures are costly.

Now let's talk food. The Boathouse restaurant (tel. 517-3623) and Terrace dining are very special and a bit expensive. The snack bar in the same area is super and cheap. For the best crinkle french fries in New York, try these. They also have all-natural yogurt and juices. There are tables and chairs outside and it's a great spot to catch the rays in nice weather.

RUNNING AND WALKING

Running Club

🍎 **N.Y. Road Runners Club,** 9 E. 89th St., P.O. Box 881, FDR Station, New York, NY 10150 (tel. 860-4455)

This group has something for every age, with activities April through November. Contact them for schedules (the whole year at a glance) and current registration fee.

Peewee Runs

Who said you have to walk before you can run? Wrong. Put your nonwalker into a stroller and join the under-4-year-old crowd. If your 3- and 4-year-olds are accompanied by an adult, they may participate in this event. Check the schedule—they hold it several times a year.

Safari Runs

First- through sixth-graders. Usually an April event. With prizes. The kids love this.

The Reservoir

🍎 **Running at the Reservoir,** 85th Street and Fifth Avenue (east side) or CPW and 90th Street (west side)

You can do it—1.57 miles! If you and your g.c. can't, it's okay. Nobody's watching.

When running in the park, use the left lane of the roadway at all times.

ICE SKATING IN THE PARK

🍎 **Lasker Rink,** 106th Street, midpark (tel. 397-3106)
Admission: $2.50 for adults, $1.50 for children under 12; $2 for skate rentals

Hours: Monday from 10am to 5pm, Tuesday through Thursday from 10am to 9:30pm, Friday and Saturday from 10am to 11pm, Sunday from 10am to 9:30pm

The Lasker Rink is at the north end of the Central Park Lake. The Lasker and the Wollman are both managed by Donald Trump/Ice Capades. The Lasker Rink, 26,600 square feet, is half the price of the Wollman Rink and just as nice. It's fun and it's well run. It's not for the little ones at night. The big kids fly around that ice.

Wollman Rink, 64th Street, midpark (tel. 517-4800)
Admission: $5 for adults, $2.50 for children under 12; $2.50 for skate rentals. They stock all sizes including half sizes. Private skating instruction is available
Hours: Monday from 9am to 5pm, Tuesday through Thursday from 10am to 9:30pm, Friday through Sunday from 10am to 11pm

The setup is beautiful. The rink is lovely—33,000 square feet of lovely. The snack bar is clean and well run. See the hall of fame here with pictures and memorabilia of famous skaters. If you're going with little ones, try to avoid the night skating. It gets a bit dicey.

ROLLER SKATING IN THE PARK

Central Park Roller Skating, at 69th Street and the northwest corner of the Sheep Meadow

When the weather is good come here not just to skate but to see the really great skaters and skate boarders perform. Of course you may skate in other areas of the park, but you'll miss the show.

Wollman Rink (tel. 517-4800) See "Ice Skating in the Park"
Admission: $5 for adults, $2 for kids 12 and under; $2.50 for skate rentals
Hours: From mid-April through October, Monday from 10am to 5pm. Tuesday through Saturday from 10am to 11pm, Sunday from 10am to 9:30pm

Sundays and Wednesdays are family nights; $20 admits family of five or more, at least one adult, including skate rentals. Tuesdays are Cheapskate Nights from 5 to 11pm, $2.50 admission for all ages including skate rentals. Lots of special happenings. Ask for the monthly calendar of events, and roll with the good times.

ICE SKATING OUTSIDE CENTRAL PARK

Ice Studio, 1034 Lexington Ave. (at 73rd Street), New York, NY 10021 (tel. 535-0304)

Admission: $5 for 1 hour, $6 for 1½ hours; $2.75 for skate rentals

Hours: Thursday from 8:30 to 10pm, Friday from 5 to 6pm and 8:30 to 10pm, Saturday and Sunday from noon to 1pm and 5:15 to 6:15pm

The rink is 35 × 55 feet. No problem—if you're little, it looks big. If you hate to skate, you're around the rink in no time. It's cute, it's friendly, and it's fun.

Rivergate Ice Rink, 401 E. 34th St., at First Avenue, New York, NY 10016 (tel. 689-0035)

Admission: $5 for adults until 5pm, $6 after 5pm and on weekends, $2 for children under 12; $2.50 for skate rentals

Hours: Monday through Friday, noon to 10pm, Saturday and Sunday from 10am to 10pm

This is a cute little rink. The ice is good, the music is loud, and the kids like it. When they tire of skating they watch the helicopters.

Rockefeller Center, 601 Fifth Ave., at 50th Street, Rockefeller Plaza, New York, NY 10020 (tel. 757-5730)

Admission: $7 to $10 per session. Sessions vary from 90 minutes to 3 hours; $4 for skate rentals

Hours: Monday through Thursday from 9am to 10pm, Friday and Saturday from 9am to midnight, Sunday from 9am to 10pm

Note: Private skating instruction is available

Nothing is more winter in New York than ice skating outdoors in these posh surroundings. Prometheus and weary Fifth Avenue shoppers look at you admiringly. In December you often get to skate with Santa himself.

The last time we were there, the ladies room was a mess. We

were not told of the time schedule for clearing the ice. It's hardly worth mentioning that my watch was snatched. What's another watch when you see the glee and pride on the faces of your kids? None of this is sarcasm. It's a singular experience and it is not to be missed. You do not have to be a good skater. It's a memorable happening. See Chapter 18 on restaurants if you want to do it in style at the American Festival Café.

Skyrink, 450 W. 33rd St., at 10th Avenue, New York, NY 10001 (tel. 695-6557)
Admission: $7 per session; sessions vary from 90 minutes to 3 hours for everyone ; $2.50 for skate rentals
Hours: Monday through Thursday from 8:30 to 10:15pm, Friday and Saturday from 8 to 11pm. There are daytime hours but they vary from day to day so you'll have to call

How many opportunities are there to ice skate on the 16th floor? And this rink is 200 × 85 feet: the largest indoor skating rink in the city. You've eaten at places where "the truck drivers eat." Well, this is where "the ice skaters skate." Don't be startled if you run into Brian (Boitano) and Debi (Thomas). I'm absolutely not kidding.

This is a splendid place to skate. The ice is perfect and the supervision is strict. Most of the skaters are just plain folks. Don't let your kids be put off by the thought of competing with Brian and Debi.

CENTRAL PARK ZOO

Central Park Zoo, Fifth Avenue at 64th Street, behind the Arsenal (tel. 861-6030); gift shop (tel. 794-0284)
Admission: $2.50 for adults, 50¢ for children ages 3 to 12, free for children under 3
Hours: April through October, Monday to Friday from 10am to 5pm; Saturday, Sunday, and holidays from 10am to 5:30pm; May through September on Tuesday from 10am to 8pm; November through March, every day from 10am to 4:30pm

It took four years and $35 million to re-create these 5.5 acres. The first Central Park Zoo was a donated menagerie housed in wooden sheds in 1864. The second facility was built in 1934. It was a lot of cages with very sad-looking animals. This present zoo was built under the auspices of the New York Zoological Society.

The buildings are inspiring. Kevin Roche and firm did an admirable job of design. Many of the old materials were retained and incorporated into the new buildings. See the animal friezes on the exterior walls.

There are other old favorites. The sea lions' pool has been updated and it remains a major attraction, especially at feeding time. The bears have stayed on and are well housed. Don't miss them.

The small animals are housed in three exhibits representing three different climate zones: the Temperate Territory, the Tropic Zone, and the Polar Circle. Flora, fauna, animals, and birds, indigenous to their territories, are set up extremely well. The concept and the beauty of the zoo is perfect. Children about 6 years old will be able to view all of the exhibits at eye level. Children under 6 will be able to see the animals enjoying underwater activities. The pools are encased in Plexiglas for good viewing from strollers. Of course you can lift the little ones. The penguins are irresistible. The Temperate Territory is out-of-doors, and this is where you'll find the primates.

For the botany buff, try the Intelligence Garden. It allows you a ministudy of very special trees, all properly labeled.

The Zoo School has very special programs for the kids. Call Monday through Friday for more information (tel. 439-6538). The Zoo Gift Shop has lots of stuffed, oops, I mean plush animals. There are games, T-shirts, and lots of stuff. The book section has a very fine and mostly inexpensive selection of animal books for all ages.

There is a very nice snack bar with pizza and all sorts of good things. Just walk through the Intelligence Garden to find it. On nice days, eat in the garden. You may also reach the snack bar from outside the zoo; there is an entrance at the south end.

The gift shop is open when the zoo is open. Profits help support the zoo.

Let it be known and appreciated that Mrs. Lila Acheson Wallace, co-founder of *Readers Digest,* donated 8.5 million dollars to the zoo restoration. Money well spent. The zoo is wonderful.

Gymnastics, Exercise & Sports

Time out. You and the kid have been together on this New York binge long enough. He needs to be with other kids. You need a solitary hour. For the following gyms, you only have to call to check space availability, hours for your age youngster, clothing requirements (if any), prices, and to herald your coming.

Don't worry. The facilities listed are established, reliable, and safe. The personnel is experienced, skilled, and loving.

Of course you may remain for the session. Why? Give the kid a break. He'll be with his peers for a change, and you'll be "free at last, free at last." Hey, even a train stops.

Alzerreca's Sport Program, 210 E. 23rd St., between Second and Third avenues, New York, NY 10003 (tel. 683-1703)
Fees: $7 to $15, depends on the activity
Ages: 3 to 16
Soccer games, gymnastics, teen aerobics, jazz dance. They also have aerobikata—a combination of aerobics and karate. Leave him with darling Kim and Jorge Alzerreca while you relax.

Billdave Sport Club, 206 E. 85th St., between Second and Third avenues, New York, NY 10028 (tel. 535-7151)
Fees: In summer 8-week programs $2,175, 4-week programs $1,275, 2-week programs are available
Hours: Weekdays from 2 to 5pm during the school year, Saturday and holidays from 9am to 5pm. There are summer activities in mid-June and the end of August at their day camp in Riverdale
Ages: 3 to 12
For information on summer programs and for more about 85th St., speak with Bill Axelrod. The menu lists soccer, baseball, ice and roller skating, bicycling, basketball, and more. This club is 46 years old. Feel more secure?

Hackers, Hitters, and Hoops, 123 W. 18th St., New York, NY 10011 (tel. 929-7482)
Hours: Monday through Thursday from 11am to 11pm, Friday from 11am to 1am. Saturday from 10am to 1am, Sunday from 10am to 6pm
Ages: 5 and older accompanied by an adult, of course.

This is a sports center. It's 23,000 feet of space filled with nothing but activities. Miniature golf, a regulation-size basketball court with hoops, Ping-Pong tables and a batting cage for baseball. There is something called an Orbitron, a device that rolls the victim around like gyro; it's 2 tokens for a 2-minute ride but you must be 4 feet 6 inches high for eligibility. The miniature golf is 7 tokens for adults and 4 tokens for kids, basketball hoops are 3 tokens for each player for one round. Ping-Pong is 7 tokens per hour per table.

This is an outing that gets a bit pricey especially if you have a few kids in tow. Buy your tokens in $25 lots and save a few dollars.

There is a lounge where you may buy ice cream, hot dogs, and soda.

Hackers, Hitters, and Hoops is unique because of all the activities in one place. It is terrific and all age kids love it. The dads who rented the batting cages for $23 for 30 minutes and $35 for one hour were the biggest kids of all. This is a great place.

Sutton Gymnastics and Fitness Center, 440 Lafayette St., between 4th Street and Astor Place, New York, NY 10003 (tel. 533-9390)
Fees: The class time is decided by the child's ability and strength. A 1-hour class or a 90-minute class is $15.
Hours: Call to arrange time
Ages: 3 years to adults

Visiting gymnasts and nongymnasts will enjoy this experience. The gym is sunny and spacious, and the equipment consists of a beam, rings, a full-size trampoline, and parallel bars. For little novices they have tumbling classes, too.

Providing there is space in the appropriate class, your kids will burn off at Sutton. Contact Joanne Sotres for more information.

CHAPTER 10

That's Entertainment

Entertainment is forever in New York. See the weekend edition of *The New York Times* to make selections. If there is a Broadway or Off-Broadway show you must see, order your theater tickets when you order your plane tickets. See Chapter 3 for other sources of information.

How and Where to Buy Tickets

AGENCIES AND THEATER CLUBS

Bryant Park Ticket Booth, in Bryant Park on 42nd Street, between Fifth and Sixth avenues (tel. 382-2323)
Hours: Tuesday, Thursday, and Friday from noon to 2pm and 3 to 7pm, on Wednesday and Saturday from 11am to 2pm and 3 to 7pm, and on Sunday from noon to 6pm

Tickets for music and dance performances only. Turn your

radio to station WOR (710 AM) for the Radio Arts Line for information. Cash and traveler's checks only. Tickets are 50% off (plus, in some cases, a small service charge) and are same-day sales only (Monday performances may be purchased on Sunday).

🍎 **Ticket Central,** 416 W. 42nd St., New York, NY 10036 (tel. 279-4200)

Hours: 1 to 8pm daily

They represent Off- and Off-Off-Broadway theaters. Operated by Playwrights Horizon. What was once a really frightening part of the city is now an attractive, well-lit, friendly area. The coming of Playwrights Horizons was the trailblazer. Other theaters followed, and naturally, the new restaurants joined the parade.

The tickets at Ticket Central are for the neighborhood houses. Not discount, but these tickets are much less than Broadway to begin with. Check as to age-appropriate performances. Many productions for teenagers and adults, of course, are on W. 42nd St. (off Ninth Avenue).

TELETRON, TICKETRON, AND TKTS

To learn which Broadway shows have available tickets, call 800-STAGENY or 768-1818. You must do this on a Touch-tone phone. For Teletron call toll free 800/233-3123 or 239-6200.

Tickets can be ordered by phone from Telecharge (tel. 800/233-3123 or 239-6200). Telecharge is hooked into the central box office computer of the Shubert organization; they know what's available. Have your credit card ready when you call. Tickets will be mailed to you. If time is short, tickets will be held at the box office, bring your credit card for identification. The service charge is $3.75 for a New York show. Add this to the ticket price. They do not give seat locations.

Teletron has an information number in New York (tel. 399-4444) that provides callers with dates and times of performances as well as information on what show tickets are available. This same phone number will give you the locations of Ticketron outlets. If you visit a Ticketron location because you want your tickets at once, bring cash. Other times you may use your credit card. If

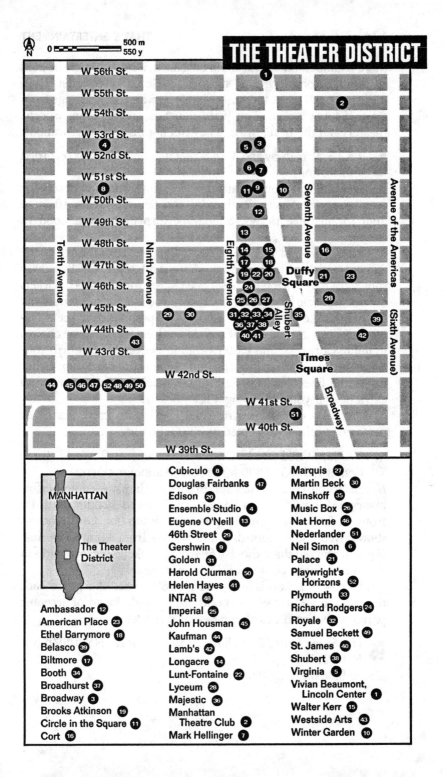

THE THEATER DISTRICT

500 m
0 ━━━━ 550 y
N

W 56th St.
W 55th St.
W 54th St.
W 53rd St.
W 52nd St.
W 51st St.
W 50th St.
W 49th St.
W 48th St.
W 47th St.
W 46th St.
W 45th St.
W 44th St.
W 43rd St.
W 42nd St.
W 41st St.
W 40th St.
W 39th St.

Tenth Avenue
Ninth Avenue
Eighth Avenue
Seventh Avenue
Avenue of the Americas (Sixth Avenue)
Broadway

Duffy Square
Shubert Alley
Times Square

MANHATTAN
The Theater District

Ambassador 12
American Place 23
Ethel Barrymore 18
Belasco 39
Biltmore 17
Booth 34
Broadhurst 37
Broadway 3
Brooks Atkinson 19
Circle in the Square 11
Cort 16

Cubiculo 8
Douglas Fairbanks 47
Edison 20
Ensemble Studio 4
Eugene O'Neill 13
46th Street 29
Gershwin 9
Golden 31
Harold Clurman 50
Helen Hayes 41
INTAR 48
Imperial 25
John Housman 45
Kaufman 44
Lamb's 42
Longacre 14
Lunt-Fontaine 22
Lyceum 28
Majestic 36
Manhattan Theatre Club 2
Mark Hellinger 7

Marquis 27
Martin Beck 30
Minskoff 35
Music Box 26
Nat Horne 46
Nederlander 51
Neil Simon 6
Palace 21
Playwright's Horizons 52
Plymouth 33
Richard Rodgers 24
Royale 32
Samuel Beckett 49
St. James 40
Shubert 38
Virginia 5
Vivian Beaumont, Lincoln Center 1
Walter Kerr 15
Westside Arts 43
Winter Garden 10

there is enough time, tickets will be mailed; if not, they will be held at the box office of the show you selected. To order from Ticketron, call 339-4444 or 947-5850. Service charges range from $2 to $4 per ticket. The price depends on the event (sports, theater) and the ticket price. They will not disclose seat locations.

TKTS, Broadway and 47th Street (tel. 354-5800 for recorded information)

Hours: Monday through Saturday from 3 to 8pm for tickets for evening performances, Wednesday and Saturday from 10am to 2pm for matinee tickets, Sunday performances from noon to closing

This is the best thing that ever happened to theater-goers! Same-day tickets to Broadway shows and some Off-Broadway shows are half price plus $2 service charge for all tickets. Tickets are not available for every show. Before you join the line, check the board opposite the cashiers' windows for postings of ticket availability. Do not go to TKTS if you do not have two or three choices in mind. Christmas and Easter vacation weeks are not worth your time; the lines are far too long and the selections are slim. Other times, the lines, however long, move quickly. Allow yourself an extra hour if you are buying TKTS tickets.

You may use cash or traveler's checks; no credit cards or personal checks are accepted at TKTS booths.

TKTS, World Trade Center Mezzanine at 2 World Trade Center (tel. 354-5800 for recorded announcements)

Hours: To purchase tickets for Broadway shows, evening performances, Monday through Friday from 11am to 5:30pm, Saturday from 11:30am to 1pm. To purchase tickets for Off-Broadway shows, Wednesday, Saturday, and Sunday from 11am to closing. You can also purchase the day *before* for weekend performances at the World Trade Center TKTS location only.

The cost of tickets is half price plus $2 service charge for each ticket. Cash and traveler's checks are the only forms of accepted payment. No credit cards, no personal checks.

Hit Show Club, 630 Ninth Ave., New York, NY 10036 (tel. 581-4211)

Hours: 9:30am to 3:30pm

Send these folks a stamped, self-addressed envelope. In return you'll receive the information you need for coupons, coupons, coupons. These may be exchanged at the box offices of theaters on and off Broadway. Large savings. Hit Shows will send you coupons for one show at a time. Be sure to ask for a list of what's available. They don't sell tickets—just discount coupons. No charge for their service.

Try it. It's only an envelope and a stamp to find out if it's for you and yours.

TICKET BROKERS

If you are desperate to see a particular show, there are legitimate ticket agents. Do try to give them as much notice as possible for the really hot tickets. Here's whom you'll pay and how much.

- **Edwards & Edwards,** 1 Times Square Plaza, New York, NY 10036 (tel. 944-0290).
  Their fee is 17½% over the price of the ticket.

- **Golden-Leblang Theater Tickets,** 150 Broadway, New York, NY 10036 (tel. 944-8910)
  The extra freight here is in the neighborhood of 30% over the ticket price.

- **Theater Services Americana,** 355 W. 52nd St., New York, NY 10019, Suite 2A (tel. 581-6660)
  Add 24½% to the price of the ticket.

The Best of Lincoln Center for Young People

Lincoln Center is the perfect place to establish a connection with the arts for your g.c. The following programs do it brilliantly. These can be the happiest experiences for you and your children of all ages.

- **American Ballet Theatre,** Metropolitan Opera House (tel. 362-6000)

The ABT appears at the end of May with the early crocus. If your g.c. has never seen a ballet, this is a perfect introduction.

🍎 **New York City Ballet,** a/k/a the NYBT at the New York State Theatre (tel. 877-2011 for information)

The New York Ballet Theatre performs the *Nutcracker Suite* in December. And what a performance! It's splendid. It is also one of the hottest tickets in town around Christmas time.

Write months ahead for these. If your g.c. is unable to attend, you'll never be stuck with these tickets. Accept any seat for any performance. Take any child over 4. Each child must have his own ticket, even if he sits on your lap.

In order to raise funds for Lincoln Center, tickets are sold at the box office at $50 above the price; this $50 is a tax-deductible donation. This is done for the *Nutcracker;* call 870-5662 for these selected seats.

🍎 **The Celebration Series—Meet the Artists,** Lincoln Center, 140 W. 65th St., New York, NY 10023 (tel. 877-1800, ext. 547 for dates, prices, and reservations, or write to the above address)

Note: There are two full-scale, original productions a year, one in March and the other in May.

Admission: $12 for each performance, $16 for the series of two

"When children are exposed to the arts at an early age, then the arts become a part of their lives." The quotation is from Jacques d'Amboise. Bravo!

The Celebration for Children at Lincoln Center has been conceived and directed by Mr. d'Amboise, the former principal dancer of the New York City Ballet and founder and artistic director of the National Dance Institute.

This is the best possible way to introduce your children to the world of live, performing arts. If they are veterans, they'll have the time of their lives because these presentations are lively and original.

🍎 **Joy in Singing and Young Artists Concert,** Bruno Walter Auditorium (tel. 870-1630)

Hours: Performances September through June on Monday, Wednesday, Thursday, and Friday at 4pm, on Saturday at 2:30pm

These are delightful, if your companion is over 10.

🍎 **Lincoln Center Plaza** (tel. 877-2011 for the hotline for Lincoln Center activities)
Lincoln Center Out-of-Doors takes place in August.

🍎 **The City of New York** (which owns the public areas at Lincoln Center) and the **Department of Cultural Affairs** provide absolutely super programs outdoors on the plaza. These are especially great for "us" because the kids are not confined. There is much going on here. Use your calendar and your head and the children will have an experience to remember.

🍎 **New York City Opera,** New York State Theater (tel. 870-5570)
If your g.c. is really old enough (you don't look it!) and ready for the opera, go for it.

🍎 **New York Philharmonic Young People's Concerts,** Avery Fisher Hall (tel. 799-9595 for information)
Admission: $6 to $20
This is numero uno for your kids. If you're uncertain about your g.c. making it through an entire concert, then opt for one of the city's greatest bargains: The New York Philharmonic holds open rehearsals at Avery Fisher Hall on Wednesday and Thursdays at 9:45am. You will need the Philharmonic's schedule (tel. 580-8700) to know which Wednesdays and Thursdays. Seats are $4 each and unreserved. If your child is noisy or restless, it's easy to leave at this price. You will find this experience captivating. The structuring of perfection is something to see and to hear.

🍎 **Happy Concerts for Young People,** Avery Fisher Hall (tel. 704-2100 for information and tickets)
Admission: From $15 to $28 per ticket, 20% discount for a subscription to all five concerts.
Hours: Five Saturdays during the school year, 11am and 1pm
Ages: 6 to 12
Tickets may be purchased at Avery Fisher Hall, Lincoln Center, 2 to 3 weeks prior to the performances. Not an easy purchase because there are many subscriptions sold.

🍎 **Bruno Walter Auditorium,** New York Public Library at Lincoln Center (tel. 870-1630 for information)

Hours: Monday, Tuesday, and Thursday from 10am to 8pm, Wednesday and Friday from noon to 6pm, Saturday from 10am to 6pm; closed Sundays and holidays

Tickets are free but are limited in number. You must apply in person on the day of the performance after 3pm (of course). On Saturday, after noon use the Amsterdam Avenue entrance.

LINCOLN CENTER TICKETS

By Mail

For a schedule, send a self-addressed envelope stamped with 52¢ to Lincoln Center Calendar, Editor, 140 W. 65th St., New York, NY 10023, or call 877-2011 for current information. If you want the schedule for a whole year send six 52¢ stamped envelopes. You'll then know what you wish to see well in advance. For late changes, check *The New York Times* or the *Village Voice.*

Having decided what you wish to see, send a check or money order made out to the theater you wish to attend—for example, not to Lincoln Center, but to Avery Fisher Hall. With this, send the date and the price seat you want. Of course include alternative dates. If you wish to designate specific rows and seats, do it. Also indicate alternative seating. Allow 3 to 4 weeks for a reply. Nonsubscription tickets go on sale 4 weeks prior to performance.

Mail to: [Name of Theater] Box Office, Lincoln Center, New York, NY 10023.

By Telephone

The following are box office listings. For daily information call 877-2011. For ticket information hotline call 787-5623.

Avery Fisher Hall (tel. 874-2424 for information, 874-6770 to charge tickets)
Hours: Monday through Friday from 10am to 6pm, on Saturday and Sunday from noon to 6pm

Vivian Beaumont Theater (tel. 239-6277 for the box office, 239-6200 to charge tickets)

Hours: 7 days a week from 8am to midnight to order by phone

The Juilliard School and Theater (tel. 799-5000 for information, 874-6770 to charge tickets)
Hours: Monday through Friday from 11am to 6pm

Metropolitan Opera House (tel. 362-6000 for information, and to charge tickets)
Hours: Monday through Saturday from 10am to 8pm, on Sunday from noon to 6pm

New York State Theater (tel. 870-5570 for the box office, 307-7171 to charge New York City Opera tickets and NYBT tickets)
Hours: Monday from 10am to 8pm, Tuesday through Saturday to 8:15pm, Sunday from 11:30am to 7:15pm

Alice Tully Hall (tel. 362-1911 for information, 874-6770 to charge tickets)
Hours: 11am to 6pm daily, until 8:30pm on performance night

Spectator Sports

MADISON SQUARE GARDEN

Madison Square Garden, 4 Pennsylvania Plaza, Seventh Avenue between 33rd and 34th streets, New York, NY 10001 (tel. 465-6000)
Hours: Monday through Saturday from 10am to 7pm, on Sunday from 11am to 7pm

Hockey, basketball, ice shows, Ringling Bros. Circus, and the thing kids are hooked on—wrestling.

For more information on sports, see "Sports Events" in Chapter 3.

Children's Theater

New York is theater and theater is New York. Children's theater has the cream of talent; while training and auditioning for stardom, overqualified, gifted performers, writers, and directors are working in children's theater. Off-Broadway theaters have 100 to 499 seats. Off-Off Broadway means fewer than 100 seats. The terms have nothing to do with geographical location.

You must call for performance schedules, ticket prices, availability, and age-appropriate information. To find out who is appearing in New York when you are appearing in New York, check *New York* magazine, and the Friday *New York Times* "Weekend" section.

Also stay in touch with the American Museum of Natural History, Brooklyn Children's Museum, Children's Museum of Manhattan, the Museum of the City of New York, and Central Park. These places are always doing something special.

Brooklyn Academy of Music, 30 Lafayette Ave., Brooklyn, NY 11217 (tel. 718/636-4130)
The BAM Opera House does performances with puppets as well as shows with live actors and actresses. They are very specific about ages at BAM, which is extremely helpful. Tickets are $3 when bought in advance and $4 when purchased at the door.

January through June there are programs for the family.

Little People's Theater Company, Courtyard Playhouse, 39 Grove St., off Seventh Avenue South, New York, NY 10014 (tel. 765-9540)
Admission: $6, phone-in reservations accepted; no tickets mailed
Hours: Saturday and Sunday at 1:30pm and 3pm
Ages: 2 to 10
You will always find information on these productions listed in *New York* magazine. Little People's Theater Company has been in the "biz" for 22 years. You may have birthday parties here before or after showtime, at no extra charge!

From September to June they do eight shows—two shows run concurrently. Audience participation and comedy are two ingredients. They do new versions of classic favorites. Reservations are a must.

New Media Repertory Company, 512 E. 80th St., New York, NY 10021 (tel. 734-5195 for information and reservations)
Admission: $5 for adults, $4 for children
This group has its very own 60-seat theater—no small trick in

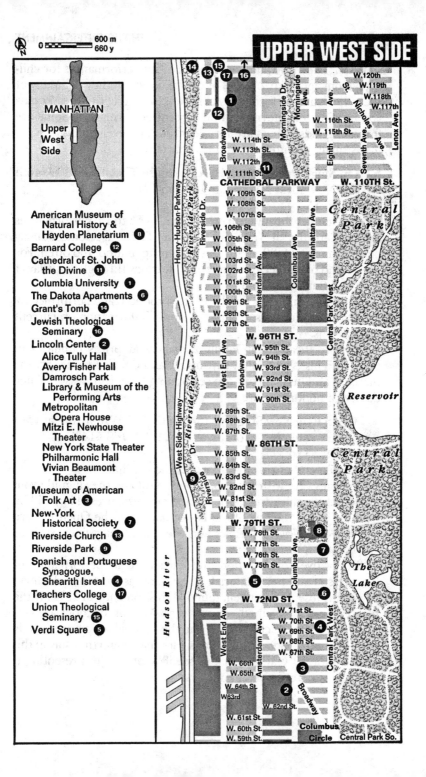

UPPER WEST SIDE

0 ═══ 600 m
    ═══ 660 y

MANHATTAN
Upper West Side

American Museum of Natural History & Hayden Planetarium ⑧
Barnard College ⑫
Cathedral of St. John the Divine ⑪
Columbia University ①
The Dakota Apartments ⑥
Grant's Tomb ⑭
Jewish Theological Seminary ⑯
Lincoln Center ②
  Alice Tully Hall
  Avery Fisher Hall
  Damrosch Park
  Library & Museum of the Performing Arts
  Metropolitan Opera House
  Mitzi E. Newhouse Theater
  New York State Theater
  Philharmonic Hall
  Vivian Beaumont Theater
Museum of American Folk Art ③
New-York Historical Society ⑦
Riverside Church ⑬
Riverside Park ⑨
Spanish and Portuguese Synagogue, Shearith Isreal ④
Teachers College ⑰
Union Theological Seminary ⑮
Verdi Square ⑤

this city. They give audience-participatory performances for children from ages 3 to 7. This, of course, is not all they do. Many of their shows are performed by children. Do not let this theater pass you by. Call for information on current performances. Some are for young kids; others are for older kids and even adults.

It's small, it's intimate, and it's charming.

On Stage Production, Hartley House Theater, 413 W. 46th St., New York, NY 10036 (tel. 666-1716)

Admission: $5

Hours: October through early May. For ages 3 to 12, performances are on Saturday at 1pm and 3:30pm. There are some Sunday performances at 3:30pm for this age group, but not too often. For age 12 and older, performances are Thursday through Saturday at 8pm and Sunday at 3pm

On Stage Children is family theater produced and performed by On Stage Productions. Contact them for information on current productions.

"Quality theater, for family audiences at prices families can afford." This is what they say, mean, and do. Lee Frank, artistic director, and his company are celebrating their 15th season. They deserve a hundred more.

Open Eye: New Stagings for Youth, 270 W. 89th St., at West End Avenue, New York, NY 10024 (tel. 769-4143)

Admission: $3 to $12

Hours: September through May, Sundays at 2pm

The ages vary with the productions. Call and they'll guide you.

For tickets, call a week prior to the performances. They will be held for you at the box office. Performances of the Open Eye are listed in *The New York Times* and the family magazines, such as *Parents and Kids Directory.*

"Innovative collaboration and excellence in performance of both classic and new material." The quote is from Jean Erdman who, with Joseph Campbell, founded this company in 1972. If the blurb sounds a bit stilted, not to worry—the productions are not. They interpret the classics well and the original scripts are exactly that—original. Good productions. How else could they stay in this business for 20 years? Check to see if what they're presenting is age-appropriate for you and yours.

❧ **The Paper Bag Players,** 50 Riverside Dr., New York, NY 10024 (tel. 362-0432)
Admission: $9 for one production, $14 for two productions when ordered at the same time

The Paper Baggers come to Symphony Space (Broadway and 95th Street) in January and February. During their 6-week visit they do two productions. They say their shows are for audiences in the 5- to 9-year-old range. Everything they do is original: book, music, costumes, dance. The casts are small in number and large in talent. This is good entertainment for all ages.

Don't wait to read about the Paper Bag Players in the *Times.* Write for a brochure, because the productions sell out very fast. This is a "nonprofit organization" supported by groups ranging from the National Endowment for the Arts to Zabar's—obviously all people of unyielding good taste.

❧ **Symphony Space,** 2537 Broadway, at 95th Street (tel. 864-5400), call Tuesday through Sunday from noon to 6pm

This theater is not exclusively for children's performances. From late December through the first week in January they feature Gilbert and Sullivan. John Reed of the D'Oyly Carte company has been the featured player with the New York Gilbert and Sullivan Production Company for the past 10 years. Let's hope he will never leave. The company is fabulous. Anyone from 6 to 106 will have a wonderful time.

❧ **Theatreworks, USA** (tel. 677-5959)

Here is an idea whose time has come! This group has introduced the "excuse-proof subscription—10 tickets you and the kids can use any time you want" for $125. If that sounds expensive, reader, divide $125 by 10.

They do 10 musical productions each season. The Promenade program is for families—ages 4 to adult. Tickets can be purchased through Theatreworks. For single or series tickets, just call. They know their schedule 2 months prior to performances.

Performances run about 1 hour. The cast? Five to eight performers. Some of their productions are appropriate for junior high and high school students, so call for a brochure.

The American Theater Association honored this company for "sustained and exceptional accomplishment" in children's theater.

More important, it's fun. They are skilled professionals doing meaningful children's theater. They are absolutely sensational and two of my g.c. were transported by their magic (ages 3—I cheated—and 9). I've run out of adjectives. Just go see for yourself. They sell out early. Move it!

Thirteenth Street Repertory Co., 50 W. 13th St., New York, NY 10011 (tel. 675-6677)

Admission: $4
Hours: Saturday and Sunday at 1 and 3pm
Ages: 4 and up

You will find the Thirteenth Street Repertory listed in *The New York Times.* Ticket reservations are a must. Call and they will be held for you at the box office.

This is an unusual company because they perform year round. They do only original musicals, and every month they do a new show. Their productions are extremely well done. I cannot recommend this happy company without smiling. You may have a birthday party, or any other kind of party, before or after the show at this theater.

For in-depth information on this group, talk with Edith O'Hara at the number listed.

Triplex Performing Arts Center, 199 Chambers St., New York, NY 10007 (tel. 618-1980; for a recorded announcement tel. 618-1900)

Admission: $5; a 10-pass booklet is good for any show
Hours: October through May, Saturdays at 11am and 1pm
Ages: 3 to 10

You will find Triplex listed in *New York Family.* Or call. Just don't lose touch with this center because they offer dance and music concerts and all sorts of theater productions.

The Triplex is part of the Borough of Manhattan Community College.

Vineyard Theater, 108 E. 15th St., New York, NY 10003 (tel. 353-3366)

Admission: $6

"A chamber theater of obvious merit"—Clive Barnes. They do children's events, chamber music, art, jazz, and theater. They also tour most of the time. Performances are usually at 12:30 and 3:30pm. The question is when. Watch the papers for information.

VYP Family Entertainment, 92nd Street YMHA-YWHA, 1395 Lexington Ave., at 92nd Street, New York, NY 10128 (for the box office, tel. 415-5440; for Y ticket charge, tel. 996-1100 for information and for the Y catalog, tel. 996-1100
Admission: $12 for preferred seating, $12 for general admission
Hours: October through May, Sundays at 1:30 and 3:30pm
Ages: 3 to 8
If you do not get your Y brochure, which is available in September, you will miss lots of good stuff. Everybody knows the 92nd Street Y does great things for families. You have to call early for tickets. VYP is for Very Young People.

The Bard

Shakespeare in the Park, Delacorte Theatre, 81st Street, west of midpark (tel. 861-7277 for ticket information)
Admission: Free
Hours: July and August, performances at 8pm daily except Mondays
Tickets are required for these performances at the Delacorte. They are distributed on a first-come, first-served basis. This takes place at the south end of the Great Lawn (80th Street, midpark). For the 8pm performance, be there around 2:30pm to collect a coupon that you exchange for two tickets at 6pm.
This is strictly for teenagers who want to see Shakespeare's work performed well.

Kings County Shakespeare Co. (tel. 718/596-9685)
This is the resident company for Celebrate Brooklyn, and it appears two weekends at each of the following in June and July: Prospect Park, Brooklyn Botanic Gardens, and Central Park. All performances are at 2pm. These are free, except for the August performances at the Prospect Park Bandshell, which require a donation.
In February and March the same group performs at St.

Michael's Church on West 99th Street, between Broadway and Amsterdam Avenue. Tickets are $8 for adults and $4 for children under 12. They also perform in February and March at the Picnic House in Brooklyn's Prospect Park.

Puppets & Marionettes

PUPPET SHOWS

Puppet shows are performed for very limited engagements. You will have to call for schedules and check the Friday "Weekend" section of *The New York Times*. For children 3 and older.

Reservations are a must. A week in advance is advised.

Macy's Puppet Theater, Macy's Department Store, 8th floor Herald Square (34th Street and Broadway), New York, NY 10001 (tel. 560-4441)

Admission: $1.50

Hours: Store hours during Christmas shopping season; shows several times a day

Delightful! Usually the adventures of Macy Mouse. Shows all day during holiday shopping.

Papageno Puppet Theater, 173 W. 81st St., New York, NY 10024 (tel. 874-3297)

Admission: $5

Hours: Some Saturdays and Sundays at noon, 1pm and 2pm

Ages: 3 and older

The apartment/theater of Susan Delery Whedon is the performance place. This talented soprano-puppeteer is the whole 45-minute show. She is also the business manager, so call for information.

Puppet Company, 31 Union Square West, at 16th Street, Loft 2B, New York, NY (tel. 741-1646)

Admission: $7

Hours: Sunday at 1pm and 3pm

Susan and Steven Wilderman, talented puppeteers, a brother

and sister team, are in charge. If your schedules jibe with theirs, don't miss Puppet Company.

Puppet Playhouse, Mazur Theater at Asphalt Green, 555 E. 90th St., New York, NY 10128 (tel. 879-3316 or 369-8890)
Admission: $3.50
Hours: Saturday and Sunday at 10:30am and noon for some shows
Ages: 3 years and older
Note: Puppet shows here are usually performed from October to May on Saturday and Sunday. Time and date schedules vary and must be checked in advance.

Come early for a good seat. The man in charge of this theater is Leonard Suib and he has been doing this for 17 years. And doing it very well I might add. There are magicians, dancers, and storytellers who perform here as well as puppets.

Swedish Cottage Marionette Theater, Central Park, CPW and 79th Street (enter at 81st Street) (tel. 988-9093)
Admission: $3
Hours: October to May, Tuesday through Friday at 10:30am and noon

You must have a reservation. Double-check the schedules—they do change. Performances run about 1 hour. All ages like these. They do many productions that are superb.

Tickets will be held at the door; reserve a week in advance. Look in your Central Park *Good Times, The New York Times,* or call the park at 360-1333.

Music

You'll have to check in Chapter 3, "How to Find Out What's Happening for Kids." Then check the sources of information for the current performances. These are a few of the "constants." New York, however, has many visiting performers and performances.

Central Park
There's plenty here—seasonal, of course: New York Grand Opera (72nd Street Bandshell, midpark); New York Philharmonic (Great Lawn); Boston Symphony (Great Lawn); informal music

188

THAT'S ENTERTAINMENT

(Dairy, loggia), on Sunday from 1 to 2:15pm; jazz (Dairy, loggia), in spring.

Lincoln Center Out-of-Doors (tel. 877-2011)
Usually at Damrosch Park on 63rd Street between Broadway and Amsterdam Avenue. All kinds of stuff. It's free. You'll have to call or watch the newspapers to find out what's happening.

Lollipop Concerts, at Florence Gould Hall, French Institute, 55 E. 59th St., New York, NY 10022 (tel. 704-2100)
Admission: $30 per ticket, $84 for the series
Hours: From October to April there are three concerts, Saturday at 10:15 and 11:30am and Sunday at 1:15 and 2:30pm. Call for the dates
Ages: 3 to 5 years
Kids get a chance to "conduct," and play rhythms with instruments. You know, it's called involvement.

SummerStage (tel. 860-1335) for the schedule
At the band shell, mid-Central Park, just south of 72nd Street there are summer activities that are free and fun. From the end of June to the middle of August, there is rock music, pop, blues, funk, and opera. Sometimes there are poetry and novel readings by the authors.

All you and the kids need is a blanket to sit on. A picnic is a good idea because you'll want to arrive early to set up the blanket in a key spot.

Sunday Family Programs, Museum of the City of New York, 103rd Street and Fifth Avenue, New York, NY 10029 (tel. 534-1672)
They have music, theater, and workshops scheduled throughout the year. Their Family Days focus on a variety of activities and themes.

Third Street Music School Settlement, 235 E. 11th St., New York, NY 10003 (tel. 777-3240)
Admission: Free for concerts
Hours: September through July
Ages: 3 and up
At the beginning of the school year, a catalog with a complete

schedule is available. There is instruction in art, music, and dance
for preschoolers.

🍎 **World Trade Center,** weekdays at lunchtime (tel. 466-4170)
for information and a free schedule

From the beginning of July through August on the plaza at the
WTC. Jazz, comedy, music, "tricksters, gagsters, and crooners."
And it's all free.

Circuses

🍎 **The Big Apple Circus** (tel. 268-3030 for information)
Admission: Tickets are from $10 to $40

The New York School for Circus Arts is responsible for this
not-for-profit masterpiece. It's a one-ring circus, performed in a
tent. In Manhattan the tent is at Lincoln Center (between the New
York State Theater and the Metropolitan Opera House, a smidgin
to the west), arriving for 10 weeks in October, and staying until the
first week in January. If this doesn't coincide with your g.c.'s visit,
don't hesitate to travel to get to it.

The setting is intimate. No seat is more than 35 feet from the
most skilled, youthful performers ever. There are not enough
superlatives for the Big Apple Circus. And the price of your ticket
helps support the Circus Arts School. My five g.c. (from 10 months
to 12 years) had the best time. So did I.

🍎 **Ringling Bros. and Barnum & Bailey Circus,** Madison
Square Garden, 4 Penn Plaza (Seventh Avenue between 33rd
and 34th streets), New York, NY 10001 (tel. 465-6000)

This is a three-ring circus that usually arrives in New York in
April and stays until June. Lavish is the key word! The show is
terrific, but the amount of overpriced souvenirs, programs, and
food is quite wearing. The best part of this circus is the arrival.
The parade, when the animals are brought to the Garden on
arrival in New York, is something to see—if you can stay up that
late at night.

The lack of information on ticket prices was not an oversight—
they change frequently. The ringside seats are, of course, absolute

heaven. At Madison Square Garden the less expensive seats allow for the panoramic viewpoint, but you sacrifice the feeling of really being there.

Films

Check your regular sources of information; *The New York Times* and *New York* magazine will list films for kids.

For what's going on in the commercial movie houses call 777-FILM. This free service will tell you what's playing where and even supply you with ratings. This is not a P.G., pretty good source, it's very good.

Museum Movies

American Museum of Natural History, Naturemax Theater, Central Park West and 79th Street, New York, NY 10024 (tel. 769-5650 or 769-5200)
Admission: $4 for adults, $2 for children

What a huge screen at Naturemax! The film subjects cover nature, science, and culture. They are excellent—both educational and entertaining. Whether the title is *Grand Canyon, Behold Hawaii,* or *Dance of Life,* you'll enjoy these movies.

Asia Society, 725 Park Avenue, at 70th Street, New York, NY 10021 (tel. 288-6400)
Admission: $2 for nonmembers, free for members and children under 12

They don't have films all the time—but when they do, they're grand. For older children.

Check schedules—some films shown here are appropriate for children.

Metropolitan Museum of Art, Fifth Avenue and 82nd Street, New York, NY 10028 (tel. 535-7710)

Art films are shown on Saturday at 12:30pm and 2pm. The Met also offers a lecture and sketching program, the Charles H. Tally lecture series for families. This is conducted by teachers working for the museum. It is held on Friday from 7 to 8pm. Children from ages 6 to 12 meet in the Uris Education Center. Programs for children and families at the Metropolitan Museum of Art are endless.

Library Movies
For an up-to-date recorded announcement of major exhibitions and events, call the New York Public Library (tel. 340-0906). They will provide you with information on films and story hours for toddlers.

🍎 **Central Children's Room,** The Donnell Library Center, 20 W. 53rd Street between Fifth and Sixth avenues, New York, NY 10019 (tel. 621-0636)
They will advise you of the films being shown here. If you call Children's Service (tel. 340-0906) they'll provide you with further information on films being shown at the Lincoln Center Library and other libraries in the city.

Elsewhere
🍎 **American Museum of the Moving Image,** 36-01 35th St., Astoria, NY 11106 (tel. 718/784-0077 for information)
Admission: $5 for adults, $2.50 for children
Hours: Tuesday to Friday from noon to 4pm, Saturday and Sunday from noon to 6pm
Ages: About 10 and up
Note: Film seating reservations are available to members only (tel. 784-4520). For accesses and further information, see the American Museum of the Moving Image listing in Chapter 8
There are three theaters: the Riklis; the Warner Communications screening room, for videos and video art; and King Tut's Fever Palace Theater, for old movie serials at 2 and 3pm.

Stories

Central Park
🍎 **Belvedere Castle, Central Park,** 79th Street south of the Great Lawn (tel. 772-0210)
Hours: Tuesday through Sunday from 11am to 5pm (on Friday from 1pm); November 1 until spring they close at 4pm

🍎 **Hans Christian Andersen Statue,** Central Park, 74th Street
   at the model boat pond (enter at CPW and 72nd Street and
walk east)
Hours: May to September, Saturdays from 11am to noon

Libraries

For programs and information on library activities, pick up a
free brochure titled "Events for Children" for the current month
at any branch library. These events include film programs, film-
strips, picture-book hours, and story hours.

🍎 **Central Children's Room,** The Donnell Library Center, 20
   W. 53rd St. (between Fifth and Sixth avenues), New York, NY
10019 (tel. 621-0636)
Hours: Monday from 12:30 to 8pm, Tuesday from 12:30 to
5:30pm, Friday from 12:30 to 5:30pm, Saturday 1 to 5pm
    From October to May they have regularly scheduled story
hours. There is a story hour for kids, ages 8 to 12, from October
through May, the first Saturday of each month at 3pm. From
October through June, at 2:30pm on Thursday, there is a
30-minute film program for preschoolers, ages 3 to 6. It's held in
the Banker's Trust Company Auditorium.
    Look in your "Events for Children" publication, or call.

🍎 **Jefferson Market Public Library,** 425 Sixth Ave., at 10th
   Street, New York, NY 10011 (tel. 243-4334)
Hours: Library—Monday 10am to 6pm, Tuesday and Thursday 1
to 6pm, Wednesday 1 to 8pm, Saturday 10am to 5pm. Closed
Friday and Sunday. Children's Room—Monday to Thursday 2:30
to 5:30pm, Saturday 1 to 5pm. Closed Friday and Sunday
    It may not look like a library, because it started life as a
courthouse (1878). The clock tower was once used to watch for
fires. There is a storytelling and story-dance toddler program. For
preschoolers, they have storytelling and films on Tuesday at 11am
and 1pm twice a month. Check for subjects and ages, and
double-check the hours. They have various programs for children
6 to 8 years old and 7 years and older. Call or stop by and pick up
your library publications.

New York Public Library at Lincoln Center, Children's Room, 2nd Floor, 111 Amsterdam Ave. at 66th Street, New York, NY 10023 (tel. 870-1633)

Hours: Monday through Friday (closed Tuesday) from 2 to 5:45pm, Saturdays from 1 to 4pm

Wonderful books, tapes, video cassettes, and records for children. They sometimes have story hours and special activities.

Comedy Clubs & Jazz Places

These listings include ages of people admitted. Young people, and young-looking people, must be prepared to be "proofed." They must have identification with a photograph affixed. If your under-21 people, or you, think a beer or an alcoholic drink might be in order because "the kid's not driving," forget it. Such indiscretions could close a club. An owner can be put out of business. Young entertainers depend on these showcases. Use your good judgment. Your bad judgment could cause a disaster.

In season, lots of good stuff happens out-of-doors, especially music. South Street Seaport is a key summer spot. Check the usual sources; pay particular attention to the *Village Voice.*

Catch a Rising Star, 1487 First Ave., near 77th Street (tel. 794-1906 for reservations)

Showtimes: Sunday through Thursday, continuous performances from 9pm to midnight, Friday night shows at 8:30pm and 11:30pm, Saturday night shows are 7pm, 10pm, and 12:30am (Showtimes change with the season, so call first.)

Prices: Sunday through Thursday $8 cover and 2-drink minimum per person, Friday and Saturday $12 cover and 2-drink minimum per person

Credit Cards: AE, traveler's checks

The minimum age for admittance is 14 years old and only when accompanied by a person 18 or older with proper ID. The "2-drink minimum" can be applied to a sandwich, a dessert, or a Coke. "Catch" has a reputation for cleaner shows than some of the clubs. Their PR representative warned me that "profanity is used." Let's get real. Profanity is used in schoolyards, too.

Chicago City Limits, at the Jan Hus Theater, 351 E. 74th St. (for reservations tel. 772-8707, to charge tickets tel. 307-7171)
Showtimes: Wednesday and Thursday at 8:30pm, Friday and Saturday at 8 and 10:30pm
Price: Wednesday and Thursday $12.50, Friday and Saturday $15
Credit Cards: AE, MC, V

If accompanied by a person 18 or over, the minimum age for admittance is 10. Why so young? No booze at Chicago City Limits. Just a bunch of talented, funny people who are very impressive. This is excellent entertainment. Remember, you must reserve your tickets in advance. This is a popular attraction, so make your plans.

Comedy Cellar, 117 MacDougal St., near Bleecker Street (tel. 254-3630)
Showtimes: Sunday through Thursday at 9pm, Friday at 9 and 11pm, Saturday at 8, 10, and midnight
Price: Cover charge and 2-drink minimum per person. Cover Sunday through Thursday $5 per person, Friday and Saturday $10 cover; drink minimum is $7 every night. Cash only.

Reservations are a must at the Comedy Cellar so call in advance. Cash is the only accepted payment. "Everyone over 21 needs ID." The management would not commit in regard to ages. However, if you are going with older kids, I doubt if you will have any problems. If you allow anyone under 21 to use alcohol, you are putting yourself and the owners in harms way. This is serious business. If you come here hungry, plan to eat their Israeli food. No sandwiches or burgers served.

Upstairs, in the Olive Tree Cafe, they show Charlie Chaplin movies continuously. No cover charge here and no live show. Downstairs is for stand-up comedians. C.C. is in the heart of the village and is a tough contract; it's always crowded.

The Comic Strip, 1568 Second Ave., near 81st Street (tel. 861-9386)
Showtimes: Sunday to Thursday from 9pm to 1am, Friday at 9pm and 11:30pm, Saturday at 8:30pm and 11:30pm
Price: Monday there is no cover but there is a 2-drink minimum; Tuesday, Wednesday, and Thursday $8 cover and 2-drink mini-

mum; Friday $12 cover and 2-drink minimum; Saturday the cover
is $14 and a 2-drink minimum
Credit Cards: AE, M, V

If you are 17 and older, you are welcome at this spot, which is
well worth the time and money. Bring a photograph ID.

Improvisation, 358 W. 44th St. (tel. 765-8266 or 765-8268)
Showtimes: Sunday through Thursday from 9pm to 4am,
Friday at 9pm and midnight, Saturday at 8pm, 10:30pm, and
12:30am
Price: Monday and Tuesday $8 cover and $8 drink minimum;
Wednesday, Thursday, Friday, and Sunday $11 cover and $8 drink
minimum; Saturday $12 cover and $9 drink minimum. Tax and
tips not included
Credit Cards: AE and traveler's checks

The Improvisation motto is "30 years of love, truth, and
laughter."

The minimum age admitted is 11, and 11 through 18 must be
accompanied by someone over 21 with ID. During the prom
season, kids use their over-21 limo drivers as their over-21
chaperones. During school breaks, The Improv has a special
showtime for high school and college kids. Call for information.

The Improv was, and is, the trailblazer. In business for 30 years,
they've turned out some of the biggest names in show business.
The place is big and authentic. Meet the age requirements, put on
your old jeans, and go for it. On weekends the lines to get in go on
forever. The doors open 1 hour before the first show. You
absolutely must have advance reservations.

Stand-Up New York, 236 W. 78th St., New York, NY (tel.
595-0850)
Showtimes: Sunday through Thursday at 9pm, Friday at 9pm and
11:30pm, Saturday at 8pm, 10:15pm, 12:30am
Price: Cover and 2-drink minimum; Friday and Saturday $12
cover, Sunday through Thursday $7 cover
Credit Cards: AE, M, V

The under-16 crowd is welcome if they are with a parent or a
guardian. Ages 16 and over will be admitted alone if they have an
ID with a photograph. Three or four comics are showcased at

every performance. Usually the performers are very funny. Don't bother dressing. Reservations a must.

Blue Note Jazz Club, 131 W. 3rd St., off Sixth Avenue, New York, NY 10011 (tel. 475-8592 after 4pm)

Hours: Jazzy Brunch and matinee is held on Saturdays and Sundays from 2 to 6pm and the price is $12.50 per person. Regular Blue Note hours are Tuesday through Sunday from 7pm to 4am and Monday until 2am

Price: Cover and minimum. Cover charge varies depending on performance. Food and drink minimum is $5. Food prices range from $6.95 to $19.95.

Credit Cards: AE, M, V

Ages: Adult must accompany those under 16. All young people must bring ID with photograph

The Jazzy Brunch is great for kids who love jazz. Of course, the under-16 crowd will have to be accompanied by an adult. For jazz aficionados the top jazz artists appear nightly.

On Monday nights, after hours, the record companies showcase talent and the charge for being in the audience is $7.50. Tuesday through Saturday Ted Curson & Friends give late-night jazz performances. This is for older teenagers and you.

Jazzmobile, 154 W. 127th St., New York, NY 10027 (tel. 866-4900)

The best. In summer they do outdoor concerts, have free Saturday jazz workshops, and do a semiannual major concert hall series. Their aim is the preservation and propagation of jazz, "America's classical music." If you're in New York year round, call to see where they will be appearing. They have won an endless number of awards and serve a half-million people throughout the year with their programs.

South Street Seaport, Pier 17 Pavilion (tel. 669-9400)

There are free concerts given here at 6:30pm. Rock and folk music and all sorts of good things. These are programs scheduled for the mild weather months. They vary, so you will have to call for information or check the newspapers. They have the Summer Parliament Series of World Music for four consecutive Thursdays in July and August. Spring Rocks the Docks and Golden Sounds of

Fall are in guess what seasons? There are holiday celebrations on Memorial Day, July 4th, and Labor Day. As the street vendors say, "checkerout."

And Other Clubs

Mostly Magic, 55 Carmine St. at 6th Avenue and Bleecker Street, New York, NY 10014 (tel. 924-1472)
Hours: Saturday at 2pm
Admission: $7.50
Ages: 4 to 10
Reservations are suggested. Two magicians entertain for a 1-hour show. Some audience participation.

New Mother's Luncheon, Tony Roma's Restaurant, 400 E. 57th St., at First Avenue, New York, NY. For information call Ronnie Soled (tel. 744-3194).
Hours: Every Tuesday from 11am to 2pm
Price: $20
Credit Cards: All major cards accepted
Ages: Babies, newborn to age 1
Charming Joanne Mautone used to have this program at American Pie Restaurant. It is now in the hands of Ronnie Soled, a party planner and entertainer.

Group discussions, guest speakers, and very good food make up this package. The best part is you are with people who have the same problems and joys as you, a new baby.

If you are in New York with your baby this is a lovely way to spend 3 hours.

Rides for Children

BY BOAT

Boats are on the rise. More ferry boats are going from the Battery to Jersey City for commuters. There is a ferry from Roosevelt

Island to Wall Street. There is a 35-minute ride from the Atlantic Highlands in New Jersey to Wall Street.

Trivia Time. To locate a pier on the Hudson River, subtract 40 from the pier number and you'll get the correct cross street. For example, Pier 92 is on 52nd St. Impress the kids.

Boat schedules change from day to day and with the seasons. Check before you commit.

🍎 *Andrew Fletcher,* South Street Seaport, Pier 16 (East River and South Street), New York, NY 10038 (tel. 233-4800)
Hours: Sailing times change weekly. Call for information
Admission: $12 for adults, $6 for children under 12
Ages: All ages
Note: There are also evening cruises for adults only. You must be 21. They sail Thursday, Friday, and Saturday at 7pm and 9:30pm. The price is $18. Live musical entertainment. All good reasons to want to be 21. I can think of even better ones than a boat ride.

There are food concessions aboard for your stomach and tour guides for your brain.

The *Andrew Fletcher* is a replica of an old "sidewheeler" and it holds 400 passengers. The daytime cruise is a fun trip for your preteens and teenagers. Sometimes there is music.

The route is under the Brooklyn Bridge to Governor's Island, down the Hudson, and back to South Street Seaport. The cruise takes about 90 minutes. Buy your tickets at the Pilot House at the pier the day of the sail. It's wonderful, wonderful fun.

🍎 *Circle Line,* Pier 83, at W. 43rd St. and 12th Avenue, New York, NY 10036-1095 (tel. 563-3200)
Hours: 6:30pm boarding time; every Thursday evening, July and August only
Admission: $15
Credit cards: AE, M, V

For your music-loving teenagers, *Circle Line* offers "Rock Around the Dock," a 3-hour rock 'n' roll cruise. They get a good crowd so you might want to call Ticketmaster (tel. 307-7171) well in advance for your tickets, or buy them in advance at the *Circle Line* ticket booth. The boat docks at 10pm, so figure 3½ hours for this trip.

Circle Line also offers the "Harbor Lights Cruise" (from June to September, daily at 7pm), a 2½-hour cruise that leaves at twilight. It is magnificent. But you are the one who knows which kids will like this one, as well as what are the best ages for taking this outing. Reservations are not necessary.

The *Circle Line* trips around New York in the daylight hours are the best thing in town. For more details on *Circle Line* sightseeing cruises, see Chapter 7, "Touring the Town."

De Witt Clinton, South Street Seaport, Pier 16 (East River and South Street), New York, NY 10038 (tel. 233-4800)
Hours: Sailing times change weekly. Call for information. Evening cruises are Thursday, Saturday, and Sunday at 7pm and 8:30pm. They take 1 hour and the prices are the same as the daytime cruises
Admission: $12 for adults, $6 for children under 12
Ages: All ages

The *De Witt Clinton* is 150 feet long and 36 feet wide, and carries 600 passengers. Complete with steamboat whistle and all. Cruise the harbor. You can see it all from either the glass-enclosed dining room or the open decks.

The Seaport Line runs the *De Witt Clinton* and the *Andrew Fletcher.* They assure me their food is fresh and prepared by restaurants at the Seaport. There is a South Street Seaport guide on the *De Witt Clinton* voyages. He or she points out all the landmarks and interesting sights.

The ladies' room is redone and has a marble vanity that is a great spot to change a diaper. Strollers will be stowed for you.

Gondola in Central Park, (tel. 517-2233 for reservations)
Hours: 5:30 to 10:30pm (seasonal)
Admission: $20 for a half hour

It's on the lake, of course. It came from Venice, of course. Up to six people. Stand in line to board.

Petrel, Battery Park, New York, NY 10004 (tel. 825-1976)
Hours: Mid-April to October
Admission: $8 to $20 (depends on the cruise) per passenger—and your g.c. is a passenger
Ages: Every age, depending on the length of the trip

This 70-foot yawl is the fastest sailing ship in New York harbor. The schedule truly varies. Cruises are 45 minutes or 90 minutes on weekdays, or 2 hours on the weekends. To get an updated schedule, send a stamped, self-addressed envelope to Bring Sailing Back, c/o Petrel, Battery Park, NY 10004. Advance reservations are a must. Tickets are prepaid (no refunds, no transfers, and it's rain or shine). Also, you and your g.c. must wear sneakers to preserve the beauty of the deck. Despite the strictures, try not to miss this one.

Pioneer, South Street Seaport Museum, 207 Front St. (berth at Pier 16, East River and South Street), New York, NY 10038 (tel. 669-9400)
Hours: Sailing times vary, so call 669-9417 for up-to-date information
Admission: The 2-hour sail is $16 for adults, $13 for seniors and $8 for children, $11 for students with ID. The 3-hour sail is $22 for adults, $20 for seniors, and $16 for children.
Ages: 5 and up

My, she's yar. The *Pioneer* is 102 feet from the end of the bow to the end of the boom, 65 feet from stem to stern, and 22 feet wide. Built in 1885, she is a very stable craft. Because the winds chart the course, or alter it a bit, she holds only 40 passengers. Little kids could be a problem. Preteens and teenagers are sure to enjoy the Saturday evening sailings.

Reservations weeks in advance are best for passage on this schooner. Because the *Pioneer* is available for private charter, you must check the days and times in advance. Brown-bag this trip. And it gets cold, so wear warm clothes.

Spirit of New York, South Street Seaport, Pier 9, 2 blocks south of the Seaport (tel. 480-2970)
Hours: April to December 31st. Lunch cruise on Monday through Friday at noon to 2:30pm; brunch cruise on Saturday and Sunday from noon to 2:30pm; dinner cruise sails 7 nights a week from 7 to 10pm, board at 6:30pm
Admission: The lunch cruise is $25.35 per person. The weekend brunch cruise is $32.95. The dinner cruise on Monday, Tuesday, and Wednesday is also $32.95. Sunday and Thursday the dinner cruise is $46.95. Friday and Saturday the dinner cruise is $53.45.

These prices are the same for each young person aboard except for kids under 5; they are free on any and all cruises. These prices do not include gratuities

Credit Cards: AE, M, V

Note: There are moonlight sails for $20 per person. No menu, just a bar so you know it's for adults

This is a beautiful craft. And New York, viewed from the water, is a spectacular sight. The food is prepared aboard. Everything is fresh, tasty, and nicely served. The menu permits you a choice of beef, seafood, or chicken. And there is entertainment. A musical, a Salute to Broadway Review, is well performed by singing waiters and waitresses. Once a year they do a new production of the *Spirit of New York*.

The older kids would no doubt opt for the sophistication of an evening sail. It's a great outing. You only live once, and this is living!

The Staten Island Ferry, Battery Park and Whitehall Street, New York, NY 10004 (tel. 806-6940)

Hours: Daily, 24 hours a day—weekdays, every 20 minutes; on Saturday and Sunday, every 30 minutes to an hour; late at night, every hour

Admission: 50¢

Ages: All ages

The best buy in New York, with the most spectacular views, not from an aesthetic point, but because you know for sure on this trip that you're in a harbor and Manhattan is an island. The ferry itself is a blast from the past.

World Yacht Cruises, Pier 62 at W. 23rd Street and the Hudson River (tel. 929-7090)

Hours: Call for brochure and schedule

Admission: Buffet Lunch Cruise $24.75, $37.50 for adults and $24.50 for children under 12. Gratuities and beverages are extra

Credit Cards: AE, M, V

Ages: All ages

Note: Booster seats and "chair-adapters," no high chairs, diaper change possible, no strollers. Wheelchair access

Reservations are a must. The admission price for children under 12 means even a 2-year-old child.

The luncheon menu is always a hot and cold buffet with salads, chicken, pasta, seafood, and more. The dinner cruise features veal and fish and all sorts of specialties of the boat. Not buffet service. These boats are beautiful. To quote World Yacht Enterprises, which owns these boats, these are "the city's first and only luxury cruising restaurants." To sail around New York Harbor is lovely and luxurious. The cruise takes 2 hours. The *Duchess of New York* and the *Princess of New York* have been added to this fleet.

The Americana buffet luncheon is available if desired. Boarding time for the luncheon cruise is 11am.

A SKYRIDE

Roosevelt Island Tram, 60th Street and Second Avenue, New York, NY 10022 (tel. 718/330-1234)
Hours: 6am to 2am daily, every 15 minutes
Admission: One MTA token ($1.25); kids 6 and under ride free.

Now just don't skip this. The views are spectacular—choose a clear day. Avoid the rush hours (7 to 9am and 5 to 7pm). Don't even bother getting off to view the island. It's a shame it's such a short ride. It's swell.

HORSE-DRAWN CARRIAGES

Carriage Rides, on 59th Street (lined up from Fifth to Sixth Avenues)
Hours: All day and evening hours
Cost: $34 for the first half hour

Up to five people (kids are people). Ride in the park only. The law forbids these carriages on the streets. Discuss rates and time before you board. Check your watch with the driver's watch before you leave the starting gate. *Caveat emptor!*

Carriage Rentals, Château Stables, 608 W. 48th St., between 11th and 12th avenues, New York, NY 10036 (tel. 246-0520)
Château has more than 120 kinds of carriages—milk wagons, stagecoaches, hearses. Name it, they have it. This is the ultimate in unique. It's expensive, but if you have a group of kiddies you want to dazzle, visit Château. They will not disclose the prices on the telephone.

CHAPTER 11

Shopping for Clothing & Shoes

Note: If during any of your shopping ventures you find you cannot schlepp another thing, there is an alternative. Look in the *Yellow Pages* under "Mail Boxes." Located all over town, these little stores will pack, wrap, and ship for and to you. Now, back to work.

Shopping for Clothing

For any age or gender, don't overlook the department stores. Macy's, Lord & Taylors, and Saks have broad selections. You decide if you prefer the intimacy of a small shop to the anonymity of a department store.

When shopping the boutiques, be sure to inquire about the return policy. Will you get money back or a credit slip? This is especially important for visitors. Remember, our sales tax is an obscene 8¼% on every purchase.

Please be aware that the most skillful pickpockets operate in the finest shops and neighborhoods. You're armed with super information. Get out there and buy! buy! buy!

CLOTHES FOR CHILDREN

Barney's, Seventh Avenue and 17th Street (tel. 929-9000)
Hours: Monday through Thursday from 10am to 9pm, Friday to 8pm, Saturday to 7pm, and Sunday from noon to 6pm
Credit Cards: Barney's, AE, MC, V
This will be short. For the most exquisite, the most unusual, the most perfectly made, the most fashionable, and the most expensive clothes for sizes 0 through adult, go to Barney's. There are other shops with some items that may be more costly, but these are isolated examples. For consistent off-the-charts, out-of-sight, over-the-moon prices, go to Barney's.

Basic Youth, 49 Avenue A, between 3rd and 4th streets (tel. 995-5120)
Hours: Tuesday to Sunday from 10:30am to 6pm
Sizes: Infant through age 10 sizes
Credit Cards: All major cards accepted
Kids are free to move around, play with the toys provided for them, or read books while you peruse potential purchases. They specialize in 100% cotton clothing for all seasons and for boys as well as girls. The designs are comfortable. The clothes are colorful and reasonable, and the whole idea is relaxed shopping for clothes at the right price. It's good.

Ben's For Kids, Inc., 1380 Third Ave., between 78th and 79th streets (tel. 794-2330)
Hours: Monday through Friday from 10am until 5pm, Thursday till 8pm, Saturday from 11am to 5pm
Credit Cards: AE, M, V
This is a juvenile shop. They have strollers, car seats, and everything for the nursery. They have stock for layettes including 100% cotton diapers, which cost about $20 a dozen and are not easy to find. Ben's also has worthwhile toys for kids.

Bonpoint, 1269 Madison Ave., at 91st Street (tel. 722-7720)
Hours: Monday through Saturday from 10am to 6pm

Sizes: Infant through adult
Credit Cards: AE, MC, V

An authentic Paris boutique, with matching prices. For the specialty of la maison, see the famous smocked dresses. The prices are $175 to $500 for these future heirlooms.

They have lovely matching mother and daughter dresses. Bonpoint sells furniture as well as clothing—some very choice pieces. If you're looking for top-of-the-line clothing, *c'est ici.* The window displays are very special.

Boy Oh Boy, 18 E. 17th St., between Broadway and Fifth Avenue (tel. 463-8250)
Hours: Monday to Saturday from 11am to 5pm
Sizes: Infants to size 20
Credit Cards: AE, M, V

Upscale merchandise with matching service. They specialize in fitting your slim boy as well as your husky boy. They have dress clothes as well as casual clothes. If you feel the need of highly personalized attention, do not hesitate to call for an appointment.

For better clothing, the prices are in the upper range. There are some Italian and French imports. A good place to buy a blazer that will fit properly.

Cerutti, 807 Madison Ave., at 67th Street (tel. 737-7540)
Hours: Monday through Saturday from 9:15am to 5pm
Sizes: Infant to size 16, and preteen boys and girls
Credit Cards: AE, MC, V

They have everything. In depth. They even make clothes to order, should you need this service. Yes, it's pricey. Imported and American made. "Complete outfit—one stop." Elegant party frocks for your young ladies of all ages. Outerwear, underwear, school outfits, and play clothes. Cerutti's was a pioneer in the children's wear business on Madison Avenue. They know their customers. What they want, Cerutti has at the ready.

Chocolate Soup, 946 Madison Ave., between 74th and 75th streets (tel. 861-2210)
Hours: Monday through Saturday from 10am to 6pm
Sizes: Newborn to size 12, boys and girls
Credit Cards: AE, MC, V

An elegant little shop with lovely clothes for your little g.c. A tremendous amount of style in a small space. Decorated vests, painted overalls—why, even their umbrellas are too attractive for a rainy day. They have the best sales for any of the up-end kid's stores. Sale time at the Chocolate Soup is like playing sardines—how many people fit in a small space? It's always well worth the crush. They like kids, kids like their clothes—and it's one swell store.

Citykids, 130 Seventh Ave., at 18th Street (tel. 620-0906)
Hours: Monday through Saturday from 10am to 6pm
Sizes: Newborn to size 12, boys and girls
Credit Cards: AE, MC, V

Here is a shop that goes with the flow. They are focusing on science by including books and toys. What has this got to do with clothing? Everything, because they look at their little customers and understand them. And the clothing reflects this understanding.

They have exclusive designs done just for kids. They have clothing by Jean Bourget, among other names in the world of kids' designer clothes. They sell toys, educational, whimsical, and fun, just enough to keep the kids more than busy while you make brilliant selections.

They pride themselves on natural fabrics. They are devoted to 100% cotton. You'll find a pile of nifty things to buy. It's not inexpensive, although you get what you pay for. The prices are not off the charts. Personal, attentive, understanding, patient service is in this little shop. The clothing is very wearable. I like Citykids, because Citykids likes citykids. The emphasis here is on quality merchandise. Look at the shoes, 0 to size 2.

Elder Craftsman, 846 Lexington Ave., at 64th Street (tel. 535-8030)
Hours: Monday from 11am to 5:30pm, Tuesday through Friday from 10am to 5:30pm, and Saturday from 1pm to 5:30pm
Sizes: Infant to size 8, boys and girls
Credit Cards: M, V

There is no better place to find such a large collection of extremely well-executed handcrafts. Clothing, toys, quilts, sweaters, children's dresses, blankets, and dolls—and this is just a partial inventory.

There are lots of toys. The wood-carved barns with barnyard animals are unique because of extra-strong construction and charming animals. The paint is authentic barn red.

This shop is nonprofit and exists as the showcase for works by people 60 and older. The shop gets 35%; the elder craftsperson who made the item gets 65%. These craftsfolks are not working just for fun. Fixed incomes do not make for easy living.

They have lovely, dedicated volunteers to assist with your purchases. Not all the volunteers are in the shop; many of them are scooting around the Bronx and Brooklyn to pick up merchandise for the shop from the shut-in people who do the work.

The Elder Craftsman has doubled its former size, and for good reasons. Their collection of handcrafts is great and the prices are extremely reasonable.

You'll see many things you'll want to own, or send as gifts. Buy—don't dawdle. Many things I decided to "think about" were sold when I returned. And they were never to appear again.

GapKids, 215 Columbus Ave., between 69th and 70th streets (tel. 874-3740); 1164 Madison Ave., at 86th Street (tel. 517-5763); 123 E. 75th St., at Lexington Avenue (tel. 988-4460) *Note:* For further information on hours at these listed stores call the stores. For locations of other GapKids, and there are many, call (tel. 446-3889)
Sizes: 2 to 14, boys and girls
Credit Cards: All major cards accepted

For the best wearing clothes for kids at the best prices, the GapKids are numero uno. All sorts of stylish casual wear you could want. Chinos for boys and girls are $28, cotton turtlenecks are $16. There is always stuff on the sale rack. This is a great place to shop if you want to do the dressed alike number. And best of all, if you buy at GapKids in New York there is no problem returning the merchandise to any GapKids in any other city.

The name was derived from the phrase "generation gap."

These GapKids Stores feature babyGap: Sixth Avenue at Fourth Street (tel. 777-2420), West 34th Street (tel. 695-2521), West 57th Street at Broadway (tel. 956-3140), Madison Avenue at 54th Street (tel. 688-1260), Third Avenue at 85th Street (tel. 794-5791), 48th Street and Sixth Avenue (tel. 764-0285), and 75th Street and Lexington Avenue (tel. 988-4460).

BabyGap and GapKids are the best in clothing for young people. For durability, fashion, and perfect fit for any shape kid you can't do better than Gap for babies and kids.

Glad Rags, 1007 Madison Ave., between 77th and 78th streets (tel. 988-1880)
Hours: Monday through Friday from 9am to 6pm, and Saturday from 10am to 6pm
Sizes: Newborn to size 20, boys and girls
Credit Cards: AE, DC, MC, V

From underwear to outerwear all in one place—a very good shop to know. Not much icing on the cake, but if you need a robe, pajamas, and standard useful clothing, they do have those things.

Greenstones et Cie, 442 Columbus Ave., between 81st and 82nd streets (tel. 580-4322); 1184 Madison Ave., between 86th and 87th streets (tel. 427-1665)
Hours: Monday through Saturday from 11am to 7pm, and Sunday from noon to 6pm
Sizes: 3 months to 14 years, designer clothes to size 8
Credit Cards: AE, MC, V

"We cover it all," said the owner. They have designer clothes by Jean Bourget, Maugin, Petit Boy, and Monnalisa, among others. Merchandise for Greenstones et Cie is purchased from all over the world. Europe and Asia are regular sources of supply.

They have lots of pants outfits as well as great-looking dresses. A most prestigious place from which to send a gift. Lots of good choices. Everything in the shop looks expensive, because it is expensive. Travel isn't cheap.

Henri Bendel, Fifth Avenue between 55th and 56th streets (tel. 247-1100)
Hours: Monday to Saturday from 10am to 6:30pm, Thursday till 8pm, Sunday noon to 6pm
Sizes: 0 to 6, and teen-age girls sizes
Credit Cards: All major cards accepted

The children's department is very, very small. Not as small as the Bendel customers. If you have a slender young lady with upscale tastes, she will love Henri Bendel. This store has got to be seen to be believed. The Coty building has been restored to reveal the magnificent Lalique windows. It defies description, so you will just have to see it for yourself. Swell bathrooms, too.

Jacadi, 1281 Madison Ave., between 91st and 92nd streets (tel. 369-1616)
Hours: Monday through Wednesday and Friday from 10am to 6pm, Thursday and Saturday from 11am to 6pm, and Sunday from noon to 5pm
Sizes: Infant to size 16
Credit Cards: AE, MC, V
   This French boutique has very stylish clothing. The prices are high.

Kids Kids Kids, 44 Greenwich Ave., near Charles Street (tel. 366-0809)
Hours: Monday through Friday from 11am to 7pm, and Saturday 11am to 5pm
Sizes: Newborn to size 6X (some 7s and 8s)
Credit Cards: All major cards
   Accessories, clothing, and toys. That out of the way, now read about an idea whose time has come. Kids, ditto, ditto provides a shopping service for working parents who are encouraged to phone in their orders to save time and simplify life. This store prides itself on its great service and carries a wide range of merchandise, including a large selection of imports. They "want the children to grow with us"—I have a strong hunch they will. They have shoes and sneakers, sizes 4 to 12. Their prices range from moderate to expensive. They are in tune with today's busy parents and their kids.

Kinder Sport of Aspen, 1260 Madison Ave., between 90th and 91st streets (tel. 534-5600)
Hours: Monday through Friday from 10am to 6pm, Saturday 11am to 5pm
Sizes: 2 to 16
Credit Cards: MC, V
   This little shop changes stock with the seasons: ski wear for fall and winter, beach and swim wear in spring and summer—everything in perfect taste. They make it easy for you to be well dressed in Steamboat Springs or Southampton. Focus is on clothes for girls.

Lapin, 284 Columbus Ave., at 73rd Street (tel. 496-7317); 1023 Third Ave., at 60th Street (tel. 826-7159) and Madison Avenue at 65th Street (tel. 744-1914)

Hours: Monday through Saturday from 11am to 7:30pm, and Sunday from noon to 5pm
Sizes: Boys and girls, newborn to size 12
Credit Cards: AE, MC, V

Clothing made of French fabric, French design, manufactured in Greece.

Pants are elegant, lined in colorful fabric so they may be rolled up; they're trimmed in leather with lots of nice detail work. They run from $45 to $70. Dashing sweaters are $45 to $65. For outerwear Lapin has an oversize denim jumpsuit, with an industrial-size zipper closing for $95.

This clothing makes it through sister, brother, and six or seven cousins before it wears out or loses its panache.

Laura Ashley, 21 E. 57th St., between Fifth and Madison avenues (tel. 752-7300)

Hours: Monday through Saturday from 10am to 6pm, Thursday to 8pm
Sizes: Newborn to 12, girls
Credit Cards: AE, MC, V

Such a storybook look for little girls—this shop is lovely. The Laura Ashley shop on 63rd Street and Madison Avenue has no clothing.

Little Folks Shop, 123 E. 23rd St., between Park and Lexington avenues (tel. 982-9669)

Hours: Monday to Saturday 9:30am to 6:30pm, Sundays from noon to 5pm
Sizes: Infant to 14 years
Credit Cards: AE, DISC, M, V

Their slogan is "uptown service, downtown prices" and "all

MADISON AVENUE SHOPPING

MANHATTAN
Madison
Avenue
Shopping

Argosy Book Store ③③
Banana Republic ③④
Ben's for Kids, Inc. ⑮
Big City Kite Company ⑪
Blades ③
Capezio East ㉙
Cerutti ㉓
Chocolate Soup ⑳
E.A.T. Gifts ⑫
Eeyore's Books for
   Children ⑨
Elder Craftsman ㉕
FAO Schwarz ㉚
GapKids ①
Glad Rags ⑯
HMV ④
Infinity ⑩
Limited ㉗
Little Eric ⑰
Magic Windows ⑲
Mary Arnold Toys ㉑
New York Doll Hospital ㉖
New York Yankees
   Clubhouse ㉜
Off Campus ⑥
Second Act ⑬
Small Change ㉒
Storyland ⑭
Sweeteen ㉘
T-Shirt Gallery, Ltd. ㉔
Toy Park ②
Tru-Tred ⑧
Unique Card & Gift Shop ㉛
Wings ⑤
Youth at Play ⑦
Zitomer ⑱

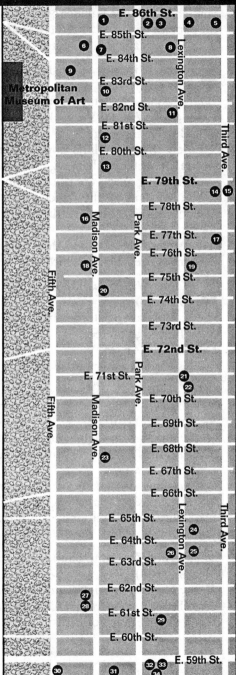

your children's needs under one roof." They come close, but I saw
no puppies or kittens. I did see clothing and furniture and toys.
This is a veritable discount supermarket for kids' stuff.

Magic Windows, 1046 Lexington Ave., at 75th Street (tel.
517-7271)
Hours: Monday to Saturday from 10am to 6pm
Credit Cards: AE, M, V
Sizes: Infants through 6X
Lovely things for little boys and girls. They will provide the
layette, the crib, the changing table, and other nursery necessities.
Christening gowns are priced from $80 to $400.
You will find all the basics in better children's wear. Magic
Windows specialize in party dresses for little girls and dress clothes
for little boys.
This is a neighborhood shop happy to provide all the lovely
custom-service amenities, including deliveries.

Magic Windows, 1186 Madison Ave., at 87th Street (tel.
289-0028)
Hours: Monday to Saturday from 10am to 6pm
Sizes: Infants to preteen
Credit Cards: AE, M, V
This branch caters to older kids. Dependable spot to buy
back-to-school clothing.

Maury's, 1184 Madison Ave., between 86th and 87th streets
(tel. 722-9510)
Hours: Monday through Saturday from 10am to 5:30pm
Sizes: All sizes for all ages, through teens
Credit Cards: MC, V
Everything one needs for a camper. And much, much more.
Attractive basics. A large selection of Oshkosh B'Gosh. Dependa-
ble Maury's has been around forever. They have it all. A good
place!

Melnikoff's Camp Shop, 1594 York Ave., at 84th Street (tel.
288-3644)
Hours: Monday through Saturday from 10am to 6pm
Sizes: For day campers and for sleepaway campers
Credit Cards: All major cards

Think 65 years is long enough to know the business? This is the place to buy everything for kids going to camp. If your kids wear uniforms, Melnikoff's has them. Even the trunk and duffle to put them in.

❧ Monkeys & Bears, 506 Amsterdam Ave., between 84th and 85th streets (tel. 873-2673)
Hours: Monday to Saturday from 11am to 7pm, Sunday noon to 6pm. Closed Sunday July and August
Sizes: Newborn to size 8, boys and girls
Credit Cards: AE, DC, M, V
The Upper West Side moms drop in here frequently and now I know why. This little bit of a shop is captivating. They sell some small size toys, a few well-chosen books, teddy bears, and clothing. Not a bunch of stuff, just choice selections. They have a label called Big Enough that does whimsically decorated shirts and beach suits. Designer Beth Schaeffer creates dresses for girls 6 months to 6 years that are suitable for framing as well as wearing. Whether it's the Winnie the Pooh painted area rug or the child-size wicker chaise, if it's here it has been selected with thought, care, and taste.

❧ Mouse 'N' Around, A & S Plaza, 33rd Street and Sixth Avenue (tel. 947-3954)
Hours: Monday, Thursday, and Friday from 9:45am to 8:30pm; Tuesday, Wednesday, and Saturday from 9:45am to 6:45pm; Sunday 11am to 6pm
Sizes: Newborn to size 16; boys, girls, and adults
Credit Cards: AE, DC, DISC, MC, V
For the infants, they have cotton jumpsuits decorated with you-know-who (about $32), and sleepers. For toddlers, they have T-shirts and sweatshirts with guess-what motif. For the older kids, and maybe for you, they have sweaters. Some of the sweatshirts are reversible. You do know the theme, on one side or the other. Let's all sing together: M-I-C, K-E-Y, M-O-U-S-E. They also have Looney Tune characters (Daffy Duck, Bugs Bunny, etc.) and Snoopy.
That's what this shop is all about, and it's mighty special. Not the Disneyland gift shop look, but a very trendy version and very stylish look is to be found here. And natural fibers.

Pamper Me, 322 First Ave., at 19th Street (tel. 677-0604)
Hours: Monday through Saturday from 10am to 6pm
Sizes: Newborn to size 14
Credit Cards: AE, MC, V; $20 minimum
   Easy, relaxed, pleasant personal shopping. A very nice, "unpricey" spot to get it together. Reasonably priced quality items. The emphasis is on style and comfort—in natural fibers. This shop bespeaks service. They will coordinate complete outfits and pamper you.

Peanut Butter and Jane, 617 Hudson St., between West 12th and Jane streets (tel. 620-7952), and 138 Duane Street, between Church and West Broadway (tel. 619-2324)
Hours: (Hudson Street) Monday through Saturday from 11am to 7pm, and Sunday from noon to 6pm. (Duane Street) Monday through Friday from 10am to 6pm, Saturday from 11am to 6pm
Sizes: Newborn to size 8, boys and girls
Credit Cards: All major cards
   The stock here consists of imports from France and Italy, plus a great many of Peanut Butter and Jane's own designs. They have divine hats. It might not be what you're seeking, but I defy you to resist these chapeaux. They have lots of hand-painted clothes, and hand-painted crafts as well, for both boys and girls. Their prices are moderate to high, and the shop is irresistible.

Pushbottom for Kids, 252 E. 62nd St., off Second Avenue (tel. 888-3336), and A. Peter Pushbottom, 1157 Second Ave., between 60th and 61st streets (tel. 879-2600)
Hours: Monday through Saturday from 11am to 7pm
Sizes: Newborn to about age 7
Credit Cards: AE, MC, V
   The same long-wearing cotton used in grown-up sweaters is

here for the kids. Imported designs—and more than just sweaters. Prices are fair for what you buy.

Robin's Nest, 1397 Second Ave., between 72nd and 73rd streets (tel. 737-2004)
Hours: Monday to Saturday from 11am to 6pm
Sizes: Newborn to size 14
Credit Cards: All major cards accepted
   Very special items for boys and girls; handmade sweaters and hand-painted T-shirts. They have a private label line of separates. The gift section for infants has a fine selection priced from $10 to $200. There are toys for your kids to play with while you shop.

Saks Fifth Avenue, 611 Fifth Ave., between 49th and 50th streets (tel. 940-4790)
Hours: Monday to Saturday from 10am to 6pm, Thursday till 8pm, Sunday from noon to 6pm
Sizes: Infants through adults
Credit Cards: All major cards accepted
   The eighth floor has it all. (In a little shop behind the infant's section you will find the maternity clothes.) Saks dresses kids of all ages. From layettes through size 6 and then move on to the K.I.D.S. section for girls sizes 7 to 14. Preteen clothes are in the same area. There are boys sizes 8 to 20 as well as a Polo Boys Club (whew).
   If you want a really tremendous selection of clothing at a price range so broad you'll not be shut out, shop at Saks Fifth Avenue. From underwear through outerwear they have it all. The lighting is revealing, the space is grand, the inventory is flawless, and the salespeople are attentive and knowledgeable. If you buy it at Saks in New York it can be exchanged at Saks in any other city. Pay special attention to those sales racks because Saks really slashes these items. They have everything for kids.

Shoofly, 506 Amsterdam Ave., between 84th and 85th streets (tel. 580-4390)
Hours: Monday to Saturday from 11am to 7pm, Sunday from noon to 5pm. Closed Sundays in July
Sizes: Shoes from 0 to a ladies size 10
Credit Cards: AE, M, V
   This little shop is unique. They sell socks, shoes, and hats. There are also ties and suspenders for little boys and sunglasses, jewelry, shoe clips, and earrings for girls. The children's hats are inspired, from straw hats decorated with horses and fences, a feathered Indian-style headdress, a patchwork poke bonnet to just romantic chapeaux that frame young faces; it's all delicious. The kids' socks are all high fashion and range in price from $3 to $17 a pair. The shoes, sandals, boots, and sneakers go on and on. They even have old unused Keds from the 1950s that were stockpiled in some warehouse. Small as the shop is, it has space for your stroller.

Small Change, 964 Lexington Ave., between 70th and 71st streets (tel. 772-6455)
Hours: Monday to Saturday from 10am to 6pm, July and August closed Saturdays
Sizes: Newborn to 14
Credit Cards: MC, V
   A small Upper East Side kids' shop with a devoted following. The reasons are the focused personalized attention and an owner with a keen sense of fashion. Realistic, easy styles with lots of pizzazz. Prices in keeping with the neighborhood uptown.

Space Kiddets, 46 E. 21st St., off Park Avenue (tel. 420-9878)
Hours: Monday through Friday from 10:30am to 6pm, Wednesday to 7pm, and Saturday from 11:30am to 5:30pm
Sizes: Newborn to size 10
Credit Cards: AE, MC, V
   The shop owners design at least half of their styles. They do overalls made by the usual manufacturers, but they don't settle for standard colors. They "overdye," which means they take the overalls and dye them—the result is unusual colors and a funky custom look.

They use mainly natural fibers. One of their most popular items is their T-shirt dress. You may buy them hand-painted for $36 or unpainted for $22. Also very popular are cotton leggings and T-shirts in bright colors.

If you want your youngster to look different from the other kids at a party, come to Space Kiddets. They carry some European lines. For boys, there are vintage (unworn) brocade jackets and black tuxedo jackets for $75, in sizes 2 to 12. They have lurex dresses with bubble-wrap inserts and lurex dresses that look as if UPS delivered from outer space. They sell classic velvet party dresses (name brands, in English velvet and Viyella) for $60 to $80—the same frocks were much more money at other places.

They employ five ladies who knit just for them—very special wool sweaters and hats. They have leather pants (from $70) and overalls and matching helmets ($36). They sell stuffed animals (World Wildlife), toys, books—nothing is run-of-the-mill.

If your youngster wears a school uniform and would like matching underpants, they dye them—just ask. They're 100% cotton for $4 a pair. They have cotton flannel shirts by Pepito ($22) and the best selection of cotton underwear with matching tops I ever did see. Underpants for $4 and tops for $7.50.

Your kids will like shopping here. Babies in carriages are welcome here. Nice little table and chairs, toys, and books, and they might even see a TV youngster in the store. They rent vintage clothing and costumes to all kids.

Do you get the picture? For unusual, distinctive, exciting, comfortable kids' clothing, go to Space Kiddets. You need not spend a fortune here to achieve a singular look.

Spring Flowers, 1710 First Ave., between 88th and 89th sts. (tel. 876-0469); 410 Columbus Ave., between 79th and 80th streets (tel. 721-2337)
Hours: (First Avenue) Monday through Sunday from 10am to 6pm; (Columbus Avenue) Monday through Sunday from 11am to 6pm
Sizes: Newborn to size 10, boys and girls
Credit Cards: AE, MC, V

Maria Flieger, the owner of Spring Flowers, has her fingers on the pulses of young people. This lady knows how girls want to look and she pulls it off—from shoes, stockings, hats, and coats, to go with that all-important special party frock. "How?" you ask.

Ms. Flieger travels all over Europe for these gems. She has located one or two on Seventh Avenue as well. There are very chic separates: luscious bathing suits with skirts and jackets. This lady knows how girls feel about their beach bodies, and she handles that, too.

The prices are not inexpensive, but they are not outrageous. Dresses run from $65 to $125. How much is your sanity worth to you? One stop at Spring Flowers, and your Cinderella is ready for the ball.

The shop is very small and the service is extremely personal.

Wicker Gardens Children, 1327 Madison Ave., between 93rd and 94th streets (tel. 410-7001)
Hours: Monday through Saturday from 10am to 5:30pm
Sizes: Newborn to size 6X, boys and girls
Credit Cards: AE, MC, V

Your first point of focus will be the white (and some natural) wicker furniture placed around and about. For sale? Of course—and charming.

They also have top-of-the-line manufacturers represented in depth. Florence Eiseman, Christian Dior, and others of this ilk. Elegant, traditional clothing. They carry playwear and partywear.

Zitomer, 969 Madison Ave., between 75th and 76th streets (tel. 737-4480)
Hours: 9am to 7:30pm daily
Sizes: Newborn on up, boys and girls
Credit Cards: AE, M, V

If you have the baby in a stroller or a carriage, no problem here; wheel it in.

Zitomer came to the Upper East Side 70 years ago as a neighborhood drug store. The rest is history. This is a 3-story small department store. The second floor has clothes, books, games, toys, jewelry, and everything for kids. You will find Miss Dior and other designer wear to age 10.

There is a big choice of videotapes, audiotapes, VCR tapes, and adhesive tape! Zitomer still stands as a complete pharmacy and can supply formula, diapers, prescriptions, medications, and first-aid kits.

If you have older kids, they can watch Zitomer's 35-inch TV while you shop.

CLOTHES FOR PRETEENS & TEENAGERS

If you want to shop for this age group, it would be a snap to go to Macy's and get the job done. This is not a true teenager's way of doing things, however, if he or she likes clothes.

This section includes unusual clothing, special places, and fun shopping. Because I'm aware of the disinterest this age group feels regarding boring shopping, I've given detailed reports on every place listed.

They will not be bored.

A&S Plaza, 6th Avenue and 33rd Street (tel. 465-0500)
Hours: Monday, Thursday, Friday from 9:45am to 8:30pm, Tuesday and Wednesday from 9:45am to 6:45pm, Saturday from 10am to 6:45pm, Sunday from 11am to 6pm
Credit Cards: All major cards accepted

A&S is a very nice department store. If you like malls, you'll like this one. It's recently renovated and it is good looking and functional. It is "nine levels tall" and has enough good shops to make this a worthwhile shopping expedition. You want names? The Children's Place, Mouse N Around 2, Kay Bee Toys, Jeans West, The Canary and The Elephant, and more.

On Level 7 is Taste of the Town Food Court. Ten counters offer their wares and there are places to sit and enjoy the views.

As I say, "if you like malls, go for it."

Au Coton, 755 Broadway, between 8th Street and Astor Place (tel. 529-9225); 533 World Trade Center (tel. 775-7147)
Hours: (Broadway) Monday through Saturday from 10am to 9pm and Sunday from noon to 8pm; (WTC) Monday through Friday from 8am to 6pm and Saturday from 10am to 5pm, closed Sunday
Sizes: Small, medium, large. They will fit your teenagers
Credit Cards: AE, MC, V

These sizes will fit your preteens, teenagers, and you. Au Coton proclaims their merchandise as "unisex"—not to moi. The buys are good. No price is over $34.99. This includes socks, tights, shirts, skirts, pants, sweatsuits, and jackets.

The colors are inspiring and there are lots of them. Mix, match, whatever. The styles are "fashionable and comfortable." The stuff washes beautifully in cold water. Well-organized inventory; easy to get an outfit together. Music, music, style, style, and 100% cotton, cotton.

Banana Republic, 130 E. 59th St., near Lexington Avenue (the flagship store) (tel. 751-5570); 205 Bleecker St., off Sixth Avenue (tel. 473-9570); 2376 Broadway, at 87th Street (tel. 874-3500); Pier 17 at the South Street Seaport (tel. 732-3090); and 215 Columbus Avenue (tel. 873-9048)

Hours: Monday through Saturday from 10am to 8pm; the Bleecker St. store to 9pm, and Sunday from noon to 6pm; the Seaport Monday to Saturday from 10am to 7pm, Sunday noon to 5pm

Sizes: Men's XS to XL, and waists 28″ to 40″; women's from 2 to 14

Credit Cards: All major cards

The 59th Street store is a visual jolt with its Disney World tree that covers the sidewalk. All the clothing is done in natural fabrics; they wear very well.

If you remember BR as the store of the great white hunter and jungle bungle, that's passé. The new image has shifted to bright colors, pastels, and a trip to the suburbs rather than Kenya. Still a good deal of black and white. It's very smart-looking clothing, still fun and casual. It's Gap owned.

They are opening new stores all over. Don't ask for the catalog; it's been discontinued. Don't ask for the travel book section; it's gone.

Canal Jean Co., Inc., 504 Broadway, between Spring and Broome streets (tel. 226-1130 for a recording, 226-0737 for a live person)

Hours: Sunday to Thursday from 11am to 7pm, Friday and Saturday from 10am to 8pm

Sizes: Teenage and up
Credit Cards: All major cards

A lot more than jeans—atmosphere! The kids love it and the neighborhood has that "in" feeling. They have all sorts of clothing: underwear, jackets, and even clothing to wear for a special date. They have "antique" clothing from the '40s, '50s, and '60s. They also have shoes and costume jewelry.

This is such an inexpensive place to shop (and has such trendy clothing) that I wanted to list it under discount shopping (take a look there, too). They have bins of sale stuff that really aren't worth the time or the trouble, because Canal Jeans is more than fair at the regular price.

Capezio Dance Theatre Shop, 1650 Broadway, at 51st Street between Broadway and Seventh Avenue (tel. 245-2130)
Hours: Monday through Saturday from 9:30am to 6:30pm, Thursdays till 7pm, Saturday until 6pm. Closed July and August
Sizes: Infants through adults
Credit Cards: AE, M, V

The address is Broadway, but the entrance is on 51st Street. If you have a child who is a dancer, or thinks she is, waltz her to Capezio. The shop is owned by Sommer and Terlizzi, and Terlizzi is a Capezio descendant. The shop is beautiful and huge. There are floor to ceiling windows on three sides. The west end has a postage stamp–size wooden floor that gives anyone who wishes "a chance to dance on Broadway." There is an area with a neon sign that reads, "Pete's (tel. 247-4850). Pete is the only theatrical shoe repair man in New York and has been the expert for 36 years.

Everything related to dance is here—shoes, tights, leotards, dance bags, leg warmers, and hair ornaments. If it's something a dancer will need, Capezio has it. The racks extend from Broadway to Seventh Avenue; we are talking heavy inventory. Do not overlook the glass case with baubles and gold charms that are $10 and irresistible. You may want the ballet shoe, the ballerina, or the charm that proclaims in block letters "My First Recital."

From the moment you exit the elevator and read "Capezio" in the terrazzo floor, you have a strong sense of the history of Broadway musicals. Don't let your dance students miss this.

There are two other Capezio stores on the west side; Steps at 2121 Broadway and 74th Street (tel. 799-7774) and Capezio at Ailey, 211 W. 61st St. But 1650 Broadway is the must-visit Capezio.

Capezio East, 136 E. 61st St., between Park and Lexington avenues (tel. 758-8833)

Hours: Monday through Friday from 10am to 6:30pm, Saturday from 11am to 6pm, and Sunday from noon to 5pm
Sizes: S, M, L, to fit preteens and teenagers
Credit Cards: AE, MC, V

Tights, socks, shoes, boots, warm-up suits, leotards, and more in this tiny shop. Everything one might need for exercise, dance, and civilian life.

The spandex in Capezio's tights is the best quality. If not here, then where? Lots of accessories.

The Cockpit, 595 Broadway, between Prince and Houston streets (tel. 925-5456)

Hours: Monday through Saturday from 11:30am to 7pm, and Sunday from 12:30 to 6pm
Sizes: Children's sizes 4 to 16; teenagers (jacket size 36 and up)
Credit Cards: AE, MC, V

The Red Baron flies again. Everything a boy could dream of to wear in an open cockpit—scarves, leather jackets, and insignia. If you have the fella, they have the flying look. Unique spot!

The Gap Stores, Inc. All Gap stores (19 AOTW) are listed in the Manhattan NYNEX directory; locations and telephone numbers as well. However, they are spreading like weeds.

Hours: Vary from store to store
Sizes: From extra small to extra large
Credit Cards: AE, DC, MC, V

For casual, fair-priced clothing that is stylish with a sense of the traditional, ladies and gentlemen, get thee to the Gap(s). The clothes are color coordinated for a mix and match effect, or do it all in one color: pants, shirts, sweaters, and socks. The natural fibers (mostly cottons) wear and wash forever and hold their shapes.

The stores are large, well lit, and easy to shop. Everything is on display. Very hard-wearing and very trendy clothing—all of it casual. For your younger than teenage kids, see the listing in the kids section: GapKids.

Infinity, 1116 Madison Ave., at the corner of 83rd Street (tel. 517-4232)

Hours: Monday to Saturday from 10am to 6pm
Sizes: Infants to adults
Credit Cards: AE, V

There are certain shops that are "in," "hip," or "hot," and Infinity is all of the above.

They specialize in preteen party and prom dresses, and dress outfits for boys. Now, these are not easy orders to fill because this group of consumers know what they want. Infinity also does custom-made clothes and accessories as well as alterations.

They have cruise wear and ski items. They put together packages to send to the kids at summer camp.

There is an assemblage of casual clothes—pants, T-shirts, sweatshirts, and so on.

Prices are less than department stores, the place has a very personal kind of feeling, and everything is up to the second.

No wonder discerning kids like Infinity. Ms. Morganroth, the owner, has excellent taste.

Betsey Johnson, 248 Columbus Ave., between 71st and 72nd streets (tel. 362-3364); 251 E. 60th St., between Second and Third avenues (tel. 319-7699); and 130 Thompson St., between Houston and Prince streets (tel. 420-0169)

Hours: Monday through Saturday from noon to 7pm, and Sunday from 1 to 7pm
Sizes: Petites and up (age 12 and up if she's tall)
Credit Cards: AE, MC, V

Betsey Johnson designs everything. She has skirts for $48–$96, and tops that range from about $50 to $80. Her dresses range from $70 to $150, with a few higher priced. Betsey also designs tight, sexy clothes made of cotton and Lycra.

There's a very special American look to the clothes. They are particularly good on slender, young bodies (and what isn't?). For a special occasion when your teenager doesn't want to look like frothy desserts, but needs something dressy, treat her to the BJ look.

The casual clothes here have a distinctive hallmark. Everything designed by Betsey Johnson has special chic. My girls and I have admired her from Betsey, Bunki, and Nini days—her work keeps improving with the years. If your girl really loves clothes, she will surely love these. They are known for their exceptional printed fabrics.

🍎 **Limited,** 691 Madison Ave., at 62nd Street (tel. 838-8787, ext. 753); Pier 17, South Street Seaport (tel. 693-0096); and 321-327 Columbus Ave. at 75th Street (tel. 580-5833)
Hours: (Madison Avenue) Monday through Friday from 10am to 7pm, Saturday to 6pm, and Sunday from noon to 5pm; (Pier 17) Monday through Saturday from 10am to 7pm, and Sunday from 11am to 7pm; (Columbus Avenue store) Monday through Saturday from 11am to 8pm, Sunday from noon to 7pm
Sizes: 1 to 13
Credit Cards: AE, MC, V

Before you enter the Madison Avenue store, pause to admire the building. It was designed by Robert A. M. Stern, and it's a knockout. Everything is fairly priced, of good value, and so much style that it makes one quite greedy. Good-looking, well-tailored khaki and denim pants. Heavy on accessories, socks, headbands, and much more.

Watch for the reduced items. It's done quietly, so keep your eyes wide open. The help is absolutely that—they help! Mostly their own labels. The look is "young contempo." Even the language here reeks of chic.

🍎 **LTD Express Stores,** 733 Third Ave., at 46th Street (tel. 949-9784); Lexington Ave., northwest corner of 58th Street (tel. 421-7305), A&S Plaza, 33rd Street and Sixth Avenue (tel. 629-6838)
Hours: (Third Avenue) Monday and Friday 10am to 7pm, Tuesday

to Thursday 10am to 8pm, Saturday and Sunday 10am to 6pm; (Lexington Avenue) Monday to Friday from 10am to 8pm, Saturday from 10am to 7pm, Sunday from noon to 6pm; (A&S Plaza) Monday to Saturday from 10am to 7pm, Thursday 10am to 8pm, Sunday from noon to 6pm

All part of Leslie Wexner's empire (The Limited, Bendels, to name but two). The LTD stores have terrific clothes. One thing that makes them terrific is when they feature a color they go all the way; pants, shirts, socks can all be matched, or mixed. Priced right and stylish. They do dresses with a young look that are made for young bodies.

Never a question if you wish to return unsatisfactory merchandise or if you just changed your mind.

Lonny's, 250 E. 60th St., between Second and Third avenues (tel. 688-8370); and 239 Columbus Ave., at 71st Street (tel. 496-2760)
Hours: (Columbus Avenue) Monday through Thursday from 11am to 8pm, Friday and Saturday to 9pm, and Sunday from noon to 7pm; (60th Street) Monday to Saturday from 10am to 7pm, Sunday noon to 5pm
Sizes: 4 to 12; the 60th Street store has selections for males with waists 24 to 32
Credit Cards: AE, DC, MC, V

The Columbus Avenue store has clothes by Esprit. It's casual clothing. The Columbus Avenue store is smaller and on one level with a broader size range.

Merry-Go-Round, Empire State Building at 350 Fifth Ave., at 34th Street (tel. 268-7082)
Hours: Monday to Saturday from 9am to 9pm, Sunday from 11am to 7pm
Sizes: Ladies from size 3 to 13, men from size 27 to 36
Credit Cards: All major cards accepted

This is worth your time when you're doing the Empire State Building and the Guinness Hall of Records, which are musts. There are two other branches of this store in New York but they don't look like this. The lower level in this shop has an 18-foot-high replica of the building's tower replete with Fay Wray and King Kong. Kong is under constant barrage from a plane. ". . . t'was beauty that killed the beast"; that was the last line in the movie. Oh, the store. Moderately priced and very up to the second, mostly for teenage girls and young women. This store is over 12,000 feet so you'll have lots of choices. They have a broad and well-priced selection of prom dresses.

Off Campus, 1137 Madison Ave., between 84th and 85th streets (tel. 879-4714)
Hours: Monday to Friday from 10am to 7pm, Saturday 10am to 6pm, Sunday from noon to 5pm
Sizes: Kid sizes 6 to 14, adult sizes S, M, L, and XL
Credit Cards: AE, M, V

They specialize in "mascot" apparel; mascot means wearing apparel with a school logo. They have hats, sweatshirts, T-shirts, boxer shorts, and even school pennants to decorate your walls at $3 a pop. Haven't seen those since the last Archie (comics) Annual. The kids sweatshirts are $21 or $40. Adult-size sweatshirts are $45. If your youngster wants to wear clothes emblazoned with a logo of the university of his or her choice, here's your place. They have some outerwear mascot styles as well.

Putumayo, 341 Columbus Ave., at 76th Street (tel. 595-3441); 857 Lexington Ave., at 65th Street (tel. 734-3111); and 147 Spring St., between West Broadway and Wooster Street (tel. 966-4459)
Hours: (Columbus Avenue) Monday through Saturday from 11am to 7pm, Sunday from noon to 6pm; (Lexington Avenue) Monday through Saturday from 11am to 7pm, Sunday from noon to 5pm; (Spring Street) Monday through Saturday from 11am to 7pm, Sunday from noon to 6pm
Sizes: Ladies' 4 and up, 12 years and older
Credit Cards: AE, MC, V

Putumayo has mainly their own brands, but carries Worlds Apart, Super-Crafts, and Sarah Arizona. They have very special embroidered sweaters in wool or cotton. The look is French country—romantic and functional. Everything they sell either matches or blends. They have embroidered cotton shirts, plus hats. They have printed rayon pants ($48) in very unusual, baggy shapes with tapered cuffs. These are available with matching or contrasting shirts.

Their oversize 100% cotton sweaters are about $38 to $48. They have dresses and jumpers in an American prairie style— shapeless, with buttons, 100% cotton and terrific on preteens and teenagers.

The staff is interested, and helpful. They love the stores and the merchandise they sell. There is good value here and the place was bulging with kids (Lexington Avenue) the day I was there. Their styles are timeless—none of this here-today, gone-tomorrow stuff.

RK Boutique, 2294 Broadway, near 83rd Street (tel. 362-9512)

Hours: Monday to Saturday from 10:30am to 6:15pm and two Sundays a month. Call for the dates
Sizes: 2 to adult
Credit Cards: All major cards accepted

A place to shop for "big event" dresses for ladies of all ages. Mother and daughter matching outfits come in sizes 3 to 22. Prom dresses and communion frocks. Flower girls, brides, and brides-maids can find their attire here.

They have romantic, dressy apparel with lots of details. The fabrics run from cotton to brocade. The prices vary; prom dresses start at $120 and party dresses, a bit more, at $150.

They sell Jessica McClintok clothes; a Missy line of party dresses in sizes 4 to 14. The Gunne Sax line is in junior sizes, 3 to 13. The McClintok clothes are stylish and well-made frocks.

When RK has a sale, it's serious slashing.

Reminiscence, 74 Fifth Ave., between 13th and 14th streets (tel. 243-2292)

Hours: Monday to Saturday from 11am to 8pm, Sunday from 1pm to 6pm
Sizes: Newborn to upper-teens, and adults
Credit Cards: AE, M, V

If you are familiar with the name, it's no surprise. Their labels are often found in department stores and specialty shops. Reminiscence was one of the first people to deal in gently used clothing, and old clothing that they discovered, unused, in storage. Their store decor reflects the time period most revered by Reminiscence; the '50s and '60s.

They have fabulous off-beat clothing and jewelry, games, and lots of stuff, stuff, stuff. Prices range from $3 on up and up. One-of-a-kind items, of course, cost more.

Reminiscence East, 109 Avenue B, at 7th Street (tel. 353-0626)
Hours: Monday to Saturday from noon to 8pm, Sunday from 1pm to 6pm
Price Range: $5 to $10, a few items are more
And
Reminiscence Garage, 175 Macdougal St., between 5th and 6th avenues, off 7th Street (tel. 979-9440)
Hours: Monday to Friday from noon to 8pm, Saturday from 11:30am to 8pm, Sunday from 1pm to 6pm
Price Range: Generally $5 and $10, some at $20 and $30
Credit Cards: None

Reminiscence East and Reminiscence Garage have about the same stock.

Reminiscence does its own manufacturing. If there is a label with its name in the garment it is new. But it sure looks old. The fabrics are very '50s. There are vintage clothes, too, very few are used, most have been dug out of warehouses and have never been worn. The clothes are terrific. For $18 you can have a biker's jacket; big with lots of strings so the jacket won't get caught in the wheels. Fritz, who works at the East store, pointed out the James Dean mannequin in the window. I was so busy with the 25¢ jewelry I had eyes for nothing else.

If you are into unusual clothes, a retro or funky look, head for these stores.

Screaming Mimi's, 22 E. 4th St., between Lafayette Street and Third Avenue (tel. 677-MIMI)
Hours: Monday to Friday from 11am to 8pm, Saturday from noon to 8pm, Sunday 1pm to 7pm

Sizes: Junior sizes that will fit preteen and teenage girls
Credit Cards: All major cards accepted
They have all sorts of styles from the '50s, '60s, and '70s. They have vintage clothing; some used, some unused as well as way out new stuff. Pocketbooks, jewelry, hats, collectibles as well as all sorts of wearable fun clothing. Katy-K is the lady who has the Western Boutique with the distinctive cowboy boots and belts.

If you're looking for really hip stuff in a cute, clean space, make it Mimi's. It's just east of Tower's Video Store.

Sweeteen, 675 Madison Ave., between 61st and 62nd streets (tel. 759-3872)
Hours: Monday to Saturday from 10am to 6pm
Sizes: Girls 12 years old to ladies sizes
Credit Cards: All major cards accepted
All the clothing here is imported from France except for "1% from the United States." These are primarily party frocks. A place to find that special dress for the wedding, bar mitzvah, sweet sixteen party, or what have you. Fabrics are luxurious. Prices range from $160 to $900. The casual clothing runs somewhat less. For very attentive personal service you will find Sweeteen one flight up at the above address.

Unique Clothing Company Warehouse, 726 Broadway, 2 blocks south of 8th Street (tel. 674-1767)
Hours: Monday through Thursday from 11am to 8pm, Friday and Saturday from 10am to 8pm, and Sunday from noon to 8pm
Sizes: Teens to adults
Credit Cards: All major cards
If anyone is responsible for awakening this NoHo area, the credit belongs to Unique. When these innovative folks introduced *in* clothing to this neighborhood, their focus was on '50s clothes, but they've gone beyond that concept. The clothes, the jewelry, even the sox reek of chic—adorable, young chic.

As we were preparing to go to press in early January 1992, we learned that Unique would be closing it's doors at the end of the month. Too bad! High rents have done in another of our favorite stores.

Urban Outfitters, 374 Sixth Ave., at Waverly Place (tel. 677-9350); 125 E. 59th St., between Park and Lexington avenues (tel. 688-1200)
Hours: Monday through Saturday from 10am to 10pm, and Sunday from noon to 8pm
Sizes: Older teens and up
Credit Cards: AE, MC, V

Let's confine ourselves to just the teenagers here. On the first level of this glitzy, hi-tech, and most attractive corner shop, you won't be able to overlook their wonderful housewares. Really funky, functional, attractive items for any youngster's room.

Downstairs is for men, and they have jackets. The underwear is teeny-bopper glamorous. Stretch pants, belts, hats, bags—all sorts of very stylish items.

The boys' outerwear, some by "Père Mar," is fine stuff. The interesting thing about Urban Outfitters, especially for the boys, is the style range. They have cotton pants in every imaginable wild color. The same pants are available in conservative khaki or gray. They have clothing that's a classic style—right next to wild broad-shouldered jackets.

Wings, 210 E. 86th St., at Third Avenue (tel. 879-2668); 666 Broadway, between Bleecker and Bond streets (tel. 254-9002); 2491 Broadway at 92nd Street (tel. 595-6662)
Hours: All stores have the same hours—Monday through Saturday from 9:30am to 9pm, Sunday from 10am to 8pm
Sizes: Infant through adult
Credit Cards: AE, MC, V.
Note: There are more Wings stores than these listed above. I gave you one downtown, one on the east side, and one on the west side. For more Wings outlets, look in your Manhattan telephone book. The 86th Street store has clothing, shoes, and sneakers for kids size 0 to size 16. Big selection and small sizes. Two doors north there is a Wings for older customers so the little ones and the big ones can fly together.

They have terrific casual clothing priced right. For the little ones there are overalls, shirts, jackets, and more. For older kids they have T-shirts and sweatshirts with unusual pictures and messages, all of which are very timely. They have a big selection of boxer shorts to be worn as outerwear. There is also jewelry, socks, bags, and a wide selection of jackets with baseball and football team logos. These are but a few of the items you'll find at Wings.

ARMY-NAVY STORES

Note: Army-navy stores now refer to themselves as A&N stores.

A&N Store, 1598 Second Ave., corner of 83rd Street (tel. 737-4661)
Hours: Monday to Saturday from 10am to 6:45pm, Thursday till 7:45pm, Sunday from noon to 5:45pm.

Chelsea A&N Store, 110 Eighth Ave., between 15th and 16th streets (tel. 645-7420)
Hours: Monday through Friday from 9am to 7pm, Saturday from 10am to 7pm, and Sunday from 1 to 6pm
Sizes: Ladies' sizes 4 and up; men's sizes S, M, L, and pants up to 50-inch waists
Credit Cards: AE, MC, V

59th Street A&N Store, 59th Street between Second and Third avenues (tel. 755-1855)
Hours: Monday and Thursday from 10am to 7:45pm; Tuesday, Wednesday, and Friday to 6:45pm; Saturday to 5:45pm; and Sunday from 1 to 6pm.

Village A&N Store, 328 Bleecker St., at Christopher Street (tel. 242-6665)
Hours: Monday through Wednesday from 10am to 7:45pm, Thursday through Saturday to 8:45pm, and Sunday from 1 to 5:45pm
The 59th Street branch store does not sell any housewares. The focus here is on clothing and they have two floors of the same merchandise as the downtown branch.
They bill their stores as "outfitters for the family" and I guess they are. Everything is unisex. However, if you're shopping for a

small-size child, call before you go to be sure they can fit your customer.

They have boots, sneakers, shoes, jeans, outerwear, underwear, socks, sweatshirts, T-shirts, gloves, earmuffs, scarves, duffel bags, backpacks, canteens, flashlights, and camping equipment.

Do I have to tell you about army-navy stores? These stores stock every name brand you know, and some you don't know. And if you're looking for thermal underwear you'll find it.

ANTIQUE CLOTHING, NEW WAVE CLOTHING, FUNKY CLOTHING & ACCESSORIES

The text will explain which is which and what's where. Here is where the generation gap bursts wide open. We're never too rigid to consider a new viewpoint, are we? If you were victimized by wearing an elder sibling's old clothing, you might have a smidgen of difficulty understanding this style. Give it a rum-go.

Alice Underground, 380 Columbus Ave., at 78th Street (tel. 724-6682); and 481 Broadway, between Broome and Grand streets (tel. 431-9067)
Hours: (Columbus Avenue) daily from 11am to 7pm; (Broadway) daily from 10am to 7pm
Sizes: Only a few children's sizes
Credit Cards: M, V.

Don't overlook Alice! It's terrific. Clean! Clean! Clean! Vintage used clothing. The stock changes minute to minute. They carry christening and communion dresses, small shirts for boys, and some infants' clothes. For your g.c. who has been yearning for a wool high school warm-up jacket complete with school name ($20), or an old letter sweater—they are here in depth. And a '50s prom dress is waiting.

Alice Underground is well lit, well stocked, well priced, and well—don't miss it. They have (lovely) quilts and linens.

Antique Boutique, 712–714 Broadway, between W. 4th Street and Washington Place (tel. 460-8830); and 227 E. 59th St., between Second and Third avenues (tel. 752-1680)
Hours: (59th Street) Monday through Saturday from 11am to

9pm, Sunday from noon to 7pm; (Broadway) Monday to Thursday from 11am to 9pm, Friday and Saturday till 10pm, Sunday from noon to 7pm
Sizes: Preteen and teenage
Credit Cards: AE, DC, MC, V

This clothing is used or unused and old. Lots of these clever dealers uncover warehouses full of clothing that was never sold in the '50s. There is an explanation for unused and old. Their slogan is "Largest & Best Vintage Clothing Store in the World." Now let's look at the positive side.

Your preteen and teenager will be smitten by the clothing from the '40s, '50s, and '60s. Leather jackets, prom dresses, Hawaiian shirts, and other lovelies that are teen dreams. Clean, very well organized. You'll like it. Not cheap—but you "get what you pay for," they say.

Cheap Jack's, 841 Broadway, between 13th and 14th streets (tel. 777-9564)
Hours: Monday through Thursday from 11am to 7:30pm, Friday and Saturday from 11am to 8pm, Sunday from 1pm to 7pm
Sizes: All sizes
Credit Cards: AE, MC, V

About 95% of the clothing is used, but it's all clean! They have two floors of clothing at the Broadway store. They have tailcoats, ball gowns, topcoats, West Point uniforms, costumes, old waitress outfits, nightshirts, and nightgowns. They have clothing from the '20s through the '60s and a huge supply of clothing from the '40s.

The young man working at the desk the day I visited kept saying, "not for teenagers." He was quite incorrect. There are loads of things for your kids—some looked so small it was hard to believe anyone could wear them.

I promise you it's all clean. I pressed my nose to each garment I picked up. The selection is huge. If vintage clothing is what you want, visit Cheap Jack's.

Alterations while you wait.

Love Saves the Day, 119 Second Ave., at 7th Street (tel. 228-3802)
Hours: Monday through Wednesday from noon to 10pm, Thurs-

day through Saturday from noon to midnight, and Sunday from 1
to 9pm

Sizes: Teenage and larger

Credit Cards: AE, MC, V

They carry costumes, masks, toys, '50s and '60s movie and TV
memorabilia, quilts, '50s and '60s bric-a-brac. They have antique
costumes, many of which shimmer like waterfalls. Some military-
motif outfits. There are old Barbie dolls, G. I. Joes, Elvis and
Marilyn memorabilia, and character watches. They have so much
highly affordable clothing, jewelry, accessories (need an ostrich-
feather fan?) that it's difficult to make a decision.

Their vintage clothing starts with the '30s and marches right
through the '60s. The true affection here in the jewelry stock lies
with the art deco pieces. If you're wondering whatever became of
Best and Company, don't look here.

Kids will love and appreciate the whole place. Not a very large
area, but the space is brimming with all that good stuff.

Trash & Vaudeville, 4 St. Marks Pl., between Second and
Third avenues (tel. 982-3590)

Hours: Monday through Thursday from noon to 8pm, Friday from
11:30am to 8pm, Saturday from 11:30am to 9pm, and Sunday
from 1 to 7:30pm

Sizes: Teenagers, if they are regular-size people

Credit Cards: AE, MC, V

All kinds of trash—right in the heart of it. What they lack in age
(clothing-wise) is compensated for in terrific styles. When I say
"terrific styles," I'm not suggesting that you might wear this to a
PTA meeting—I'm talking teens. There are two levels and two
separate entrances to Trash & Vaudeville; ease into this scene by
making Vaudeville your first stop.

They carry rock 'n' roll readywear. The look is very contemporary. There are vests that really look terrific on the young crowd.
They have all sorts of accessories—belts, ties, and gloves.

Downstairs is Trash. This is avant garde with a goodly amount
from the United Kingdom. It will give you good insight into the
War of Independence.

For the ladies (?) they have frocks of cotton/Lycra, leather, and
lace. They have belts, earrings, gauntlets, and the rhinestone-

studded leather bootstraps you've been looking for. For those of you who have led more sheltered lives, this is a leather strap encrusted with rhinestones one wears over a boot. It straps under the instep and adds a certain *Je ne sais quoi.* Could do wonders when worn with a school uniform.

Trash & Vaudeville requires a good sense of humor. Upstairs the clothing is really wearable fun. Downstairs is more of a sociological field trip. The merchandise looks old, but it's not. Everything is new.

Shopping for Shoes

East Side Kids, 1298 Madison Ave., at 92nd Street (tel. 360-5000)
Hours: Monday through Friday from 9:30am to 6pm, and Saturday from 9am to 6pm
Sizes: Infant to a big boy 6
Credit Cards: AE, MC, V

"We guarantee a perfect fit." I don't know if it includes your fit when you pay the prices. No reflection on East Side Kids, just the musings of a lady who raised her kids in the '50s and '60s.

They feature the finest in kids' shoes. And kids are brand buyers: Adidas, Amiana, Enzo, Keds, Bass, Oshkosh, Sebago, Right Step, Nike, Weebok, Le Arto, Ellesse, and Toddler University. They have them all. Plenty of sales help and lots of interest.

Harry's Shoes, 2299 Broadway, at 83rd Street (tel. 874-2035)
Hours: Monday and Thursday through Saturday from 10am to 6:45pm, Tuesday and Wednesday from 10:30am to 6:45pm; from mid-March to June 30 and from September to December 31 they are open Sunday from noon to 5:30pm
Sizes: All kids
Credit Cards: All major cards

Harry's Shoes may not fit your g.c. unless your g.c.'s foot is the same size as Harry's. A little joke. But there's no joke about Harry's inventory or their ability to fit kids properly. A good selection of footwear for your g.c. They are nice to the kids and do a good job fitting the little buggers.

Little Eric, 1331 Third Ave., between 76th and 77th streets (tel. 288-8987) and 590 Columbus Ave., between 88th and 89th streets (tel. 769-1610)
Hours at both stores: Monday to Saturday from 10am to 6pm, closed Sunday
Sizes: 0 through teenagers, ladies' sizes next door at Eric's
Credit Cards: AE, M, V

"If it covers the feet, we have it," to quote Robin of Little Eric. Socks, shoes, boots, sneakers. Tremendous selection in a small, comfortable shop. They have a horse to ride, a VCR for the kids to watch, a slide, and balloons. If the kids need shoes this is the painless way to shop.

My Shoes, 1712 First Ave., between 88th and 89th streets (tel. 410-2129)
Hours: Monday through Saturday from 10am to 7pm, and Sunday from 11am to 4pm
Sizes: All children's sizes
Credit Cards: All major cards

"The children's fashion footwear boutique" is a quote from the owner. The under-2-year-old crowd is easy. After 3 years old, they get very particular about what goes on their little tootsies. The boys want to look like all the other boys. The girls have an image of themselves that must be indulged—it's a cross between Barbie and Whitney Houston.

This store has a really stylish collection that is age-appropriate. They fit the kids' feet properly, and it's a good place for shoes.

Tru-Tred, 1241 Lexington Ave., at 84th Street (tel. 249-0551)
Hours: Monday through Wednesday from 9:30am to 5:45pm, Thursday and Friday to 7:45pm, Saturday to 5:45pm, and Sunday from noon to 4:45pm
Sizes: Toddlers and up
Credit Cards: All major cards

They claim to have the largest selection of children's shoes in the city. Their selection is as distinctive as their hours. Their shoes are in the moderate-to high-price range. Their concern is with fitting the child's feet properly. (Makes sense to me.)

They have imported shoes as well as those made in the United

States. What they have in depth is integrity. Tru-Tred will do the right thing for your g.c.'s feet. Not to worry.

Discount Stores & Resale Shops

There are buys to be found in the city that manufactures one-third of the kids clothes made in the United States. Two of the key buildings for baby and kids clothes are 112 W. 34th St. and 131 W. 33rd St. Once or twice a year they have fabulous sales in the showrooms; don't bring the kids because they are not welcome and you can't try the clothes on them. To find out when and where, you'll need a current copy of a publication called *Fashion Update*. To buy your copy, call their office as soon as you know when you'll be in New York (tel. 718/377-8873). Speak to Sarah Gardner.

Discount and off-price stores are usually rough going, crowded to the rafters, and lacking cachet. But saving money is fun (any fool can squander).

When it comes to clothes shopping, as a general suggestion, these shops are best done on your own prior to your g.c.'s arrival. This permits you time to return your purchases if he isn't pleased. Check return policies at off-price shops prior to parting with a buck—and hold onto those sales slips.

Used-clothing shops are a different matter. Take your g.c. with you; some provide toys while they are trying on—which makes your g.c. less trying. The prices are uneven.

CLOTHING

A & G Infants and Childrens, 261 Broome St., at Orchard Street (tel. 966-3775)
Hours: Sunday through Friday from 10:30am to 5:15pm
Sizes: Layette to size 14
Credit Cards: AE, M, V

Everything for children in clothing for 25% off the list prices and higher.

Albee's, 715 Amsterdam Ave., at 95th Street (tel. 662-5740 or 662-8902)

Hours: Monday through Saturday from 9am to 5:30pm
Credit Cards: AE, MC, V

Their prices are terrific on clothing and more. See Chapter 13 entry for further information.

Ben's Babyland, 81 Ave. A., between 5th and 6th streets (tel. 674-1353)
Hours: Monday through Friday from 10am to 6pm, Saturday and Sunday from 10am to 5pm
Credit Cards: AE, MC, V

Dependable discounters. See Chapter 13 entry for further information.

Canal Jean Co., Inc., 504 Broadway, between Spring and Broome streets (tel. 226-1130 for recorded information, or 226-0737 for a live person)
Hours: Sunday to Thursday from 11am to 7pm, Friday and Saturday from 10am to 8pm
Sizes: Teenage and up
Credit Cards: All major cards

A lot more than jeans—and they love the atmosphere, neighborhood, and *in* feeling. A must! (See page 221.)

Century 21, 22 Cortlandt St., west of Broadway (tel. 227-9092)
Hours: Monday to Friday from 7:45am to 7pm, Saturday from 10am to 6pm. Closed Sunday
Sizes: Infant to adult
Credit Cards: AE, M, V
Note: This is in the financial district, by subway the 1, E, or R to Cortlandt Street, or the 4 or 5 to Fulton Street.

This is a department store that is all discount. The best thing is each section of clothing has the manufacturer's name. For the boys, you will find clothes by B.U.M. Equipment, Adidas, Sahara Club, Bugle Boy, Wrangler, and others. From underwear to outerwear. The girls will find everything from Esprit and Trimfit tights to clothing by Crazy Horse, Little Topsy, Mexx, Yes Kids, Double Vision, and many more.

Shoes, sneakers, jewelry, belts, bathing suits, and robes are just a few of the items. They get lots of stuff in their three-story space.

The employees here are exceptionally nice. This is one discount store where you can take the kids in their strollers; plenty of room.

Louis Chock, 74 Orchard St., between Grand and Broome streets (tel. 473-1929)
Hours: Monday through Thursday and Sunday from 9am to 5pm, and Friday to 1pm
Credit Cards: MC, V

Think underwear, socks, and pajamas. This is their specialty from little, littles to adults and beyond. Ann says, "Some outerwear for children but only to two years." Stick with the specialty of the house—it's all here, discounted about 25%.

Conways, 1333–1345 Broadway, at 35th Street, and 225–247 W. 34th St. (tel. 560-9196 for the store; 695-8451 for the office for other store locations)
Hours: Monday through Saturday from 9:30am to 7pm, and Sunday from 11am to 6pm
Sizes: Infant to adult
Credit Cards: MC, V

Would I lie to you? I've only been to the Broadway complex—and the buys are super. Infant to preteen tights embossed with little hearts are $1.69. Name-brand tights (names off) are $1. My annual fall pilgrimage focuses on socks as well. Don't bring your g.c.—it's so crowded they'll despise it. Besides, for buys like these you need two hands.

The stock rotates like a revolving door—male and female. They also have a huge cosmetics-and-more department with the best buys in town. It's a mad house, but worth it if you love bargains.

Daffy's, 111 Fifth Ave., at 18th Street (tel. 529-4477); 335 Madison Ave., corner of 44th Street (tel. 557-4422)
Hours: Monday through Saturday from 10am to 10pm and Sunday from 11am to 6pm
Sizes: Infant through children, preteen to ladies, boys and girls; boys' clothing to size 20, narrow menswear for teenagers
Credit Cards: MC, V

Fifth Avenue Daffy's is huge! Take the kids on the elevator—it's an activity. The buyer assures me the discount is "40% off everything, all the time." I have no reason to doubt this information; I just can't verify it because most of the clothing is European Selection in junior and adult sizes.

☀ **Jack's Bargain Store,** 2 W. 14th St., at Fifth Avenue (tel. 924-5322) and 142 W. 34th St., between Sixth and Seventh avenues (tel. 947-4135)
Hours: Monday through Saturday from 9:30am to 7pm, Sunday from 11am to 6pm
Credit Cards: AE, DISC, V

It's madness so don't bring the kids. Some great buys with lots of stylish good clothing mixed in with all the junk. If you value time over money and don't mind foraging through the bad to find the good then here it is.

☀ **Kids Town,** 24 E. 14th St., at Fifth Avenue (tel. 243-1301)

If you're doing Jack's, do Kids Town. They are very close neighbors, and the contents are similar.

☀ **M. Kreinen & Co., Inc.,** 301 Grand St., at Allen Street (tel. 925-0239)
Hours: Sunday through Friday from 10am to 4pm
Sizes: Infant to preteen
Credit Cards: None

A very large selection of better children's clothing, and all top-of-the-line. Don't give up because the quarters are cramped. Hang in there and save a bundle.

☀ **Morris Bros.,** 2322 Broadway, at 84th Street (tel. 724-9000)
Hours: Monday through Saturday from 9:30am to 6:30pm, and Sunday from noon to 5:30pm
Sizes: Infant through adult (for men), to size 14 (for girls)
Credit Cards: All major cards

They have a huge seleciton of moderately priced, practical clothing. The stuff kids do wear. Oshkosh, Health-tex, and Carters always on hand. Petit Bateau (another indestructible line) is large on these premises. You know the brand names, so buy with two hands; the prices are so low.

☀ **Once Upon a Time,** 171 E. 92nd St, between Lexington and Third avenues (tel. 831-7619)

Hours: Monday through Saturday from 10am to 6pm; closed Saturday in July and August
Sizes: 0 to 14, boys and girls
Credit Cards: MC, V

All the merchandise in this used-clothing store is in perfect, pristine condition. Hand-smocked dresses are sold at such reasonable prices that I looked with disbelief at the tags several times. Girls wear these so seldom before they are outgrown that it is understandable. These have been laundered perfectly.

Lots of other merchandise, and it changes all the time. Ronnie Mann, president of this organization, has a most unusual policy for shops of this genre. You may return the merchandise if you are not delighted. Naturally, this must be done quickly, with the purchase in the same condition as when it was bought.

There is also a fabulous collection of new merchandise at unbelievable prices. Other 100% cotton, brand-name clothes are about half the price here. I promised not to name the brands. Loads of new infant clothes. Enormous bibs, in reversible cotton, from Belgium are $6.50 here, $12 other places. Terry cloth rompers, sweat suits, and a changing stock.

You'll feel as if you've struck gold when you visit Once Upon a Time. Friendly, concerned service. Once Upon a Time is a rare find.

Rice & Breskin, 323 Grand St., at Orchard Street (tel. 925-5515 or 925-5516)
Hours: Sunday through Friday from 9am to 5:30pm
Sizes: Infant to size 14
Credit Cards: MC, V

There are many handmade items; thus there are one-of-a-kind items. And if it's brands you're after, this must be the place. They are loaded with wonderful buys for your babies, toddlers, and kindergarteners.

Second Act, 1046 Madison Ave., between 79th and 80th streets (tel. 988-2440)
Hours: Tuesday through Saturday from 10am to 5pm
Sizes: Girls, infants up to size 14 and preteens; boys, infants to size 20
Credit Cards: None

If you need to get over your abhorrence of secondhand, this is a place to begin. Some of it is new but the majority is secondhand—everything is clean. You know the cost of winter coats and how little wear they get. It's worth a look.

Second Cousin, 142 Seventh Ave. South, between Charles and 10th streets (tel. 929-8048)
Hours: Monday through Saturday from 11am to 7pm
Sizes: Infants to size 14, used; infants to size 7, new
Credit Cards: All major cards
Everything is in perfect condition. The clothing is current and in style and priced right. They have only 450 square feet of selling space and they manage to stock all sizes, all kinds of merchandise, both new and used. They specialize in natural fibers.

CHAPTER 12

Shopping for Toys

Kids over 10 will enjoy electronics stores, places with select items, record shops, and sporting goods places. Some, even older, will like the funky stores. And some will opt for shopping for clothing.

For kids up to 4, find the cheapest items, hold one in each hand, and give them a choice. For kids from 4 to 6, give them time to look and consider; 6 through 7 need a price range and a prediscussion on types of selection: games, dolls, etc. You can't tell kids over 7 a damn thing. They know what they want. They usually understand price limits. It's all here. Read the chapter through before you decide where to go.

After the Rain, 149 Mercer St., between Houston and Prince streets (tel. 431-1044)

Hours: Monday to Saturday from noon to 7pm, Sunday till 6pm

Credit Cards: All major cards accepted

The decor of this shop is a medieval castle. Don't hardly see many like this. This is a place for the mature teenager (how's that for an oxymoron?) or the collector. A variety of handmade kaleidoscopes, optical toys, and musical instruments. There is good folk art done in wood, glass, and pottery. Charming place.

Mary Arnold Toys, 962 Lexington Ave., between 70th and 71st streets (tel. 744-8510)
Hours: Monday through Friday from 9am to 6pm, and Saturday from 10am to 5pm
Credit Cards: AE, MC, V

An adorable gimmick here. Your g.c. may leave his requests for birthdays, Chanukah, Christmas, etc., in the form of a "wish list." Little ones really like that.

The ages here are from infant to 15 years. They even have adult games. There are many European imports in the toy selections made here. You may be sure of one thing (among others) at Mary Arnold: If they sell a toy, it's a safe toy. If you need guidance with selections, it's provided here.

Big City Kite Company, 1201 Lexington Ave., between 81st and 82nd streets (tel. 472-2623)
Hours: Monday through Saturday from 10am to 6pm, Thursday to 7:30pm, and Sunday from noon to 5:45pm
Credit Cards: AE, DISC, MC, V; $15 minimum

Here's something your g.c. can fold up and carry home. They have animal kites, kites that look like comets and meteors, and those so-hard-to-locate, old-fashioned box kites. Every kite that ever was, $5 and up, up, up—just like a kite.

Children's Museum of Manhattan
Read about their shop in the "Museum" chapter.

Dinosaur Hill, 302 E. 9th St., between First and Second avenues (tel. 473-5850)
Hours: Daily from noon to 7pm
Credit Cards: AE, MC, V

This charming little shop majors in handmade, quality toys. So many of these verge on art forms that it's difficult to categorize for specific ages. There is clothing for sizes newborn to 5. The fabrics are exotic in design, natural in content. They are all definitely washable.

"Handmade wonderments" and "If we've got it, it's special" are quotes from the owner of Dinosaur Hill. To own a special shop, with little treasures, is like writing a guidebook: You get satisfaction and pleasure from your choices; you just don't make enough money.

🍎 **Doll House Antics,** 1343 Madison Ave, at 94th Street (tel. 876-2288)
Hours: Monday to Friday from 11am to 5:30pm, Saturday 11am to 5pm. Closed July and August
Credit Cards: AE, M, V
What we have here are dollhouses and everything one might dream of to furnish a dream house. Furniture, wallpaper, accessories, linens, and electrical equipment to light the lamps. Of course there are the doll families ready to move in. Everything at this shop is on a 1-inch scale.

Please bring children of any age to appreciate and understand, and you'll have a wonderful experience. You will be unable to leave empty handed.

Collectors come from all over to visit Doll House Antics.

🍎 **E.A.T. Gifts,** 1062 Madison Ave., between 80th and 81st streets (tel. 861-2544)
Hours: Monday through Saturday from 10am to 6pm, and Sunday from noon to 5pm
Credit Card: AE
Large selection of little items, from bags of chocolate sneakers to unusual novelty items to big stuff. They have nursery furniture, the entire world of Babar the Elephant, and baby gift items in depth. Mickey, Minnie, Donald, decorated shirts, pens, etc.

This is the kind of store where kids can spend hours making a selection because there is so much stuff. Stop here only if you have time to waste.

If you are planning to get a bite at the E.A.T. restaurant next door, do read the menu posted in the window. An egg salad sandwich is $14. Not a typo; an egg salad sandwich is $14.

🍎 **Enchanted Forest,** 85 Mercer St., between Spring and Broome streets (tel. 925-6677)
Hours: Monday to Saturday from 11am to 7pm, Sunday from noon to 6pm
Credit Cards: All major cards
This SoHo shop is, well, enchanting. The owner's description is

comprehensive reporting: "A gallery of beasts, books, and hand-made toys celebrating the spirit of the animals, the old stories, and the child within." Nice. And so is the store.

Forbidden Planet, 821 Broadway, at 12th Street (tel. 473-1576); and 227 E. 59th St., between Second and Third avenues (tel. 751-4386)
Hours: (Broadway) Monday, Tuesday, Wednesday, and Saturday from 10am to 7pm, Thursday and Friday till 7:30pm, Sunday from noon to 7pm; (59th Street) Monday to Saturday from 11:30am to 8:30pm, Sunday from noon to 7pm
Credit Cards: All major cards

Don't miss this! They deal in science fiction and fantasy so there are things of interest for all ages. Grimm's fairy tales and Walt Disney come under the head of fantasy.

They have stuffed animals of the sci-fi genre. Comic books and collectibles, some not too pricey. The 59th Street store has original art on the first floor.

Hersheys Stationers, 48 Clinton St., at Rivington Street (tel. 473-6391)
Hours: Monday through Friday and Sunday from 10am to 5:30pm
Credit Cards: None; check with ID

This is a discount store. Toys and school supplies and office supplies, if your g.c. is planning to open an office. Fifty years in one place. "We have everything."

Iris Brown's Victorian Doll and Miniature Shop, 253 E. 57th St., between Second and Third avenues (tel. 593-2882)
Hours: Monday through Friday from 11am to 6pm, Saturdays from 12:30 to 5:30pm

For your older girl who is a serious doll collector, or for you, go see the Doll Lady, a/k/a Iris Brown. This is her shop and she sells only antique dolls. Her specialty, Victorian dolls. She is most famous for her repairs and the dressing of period dolls in period clothing.

Last Wound Up, 889 Broadway, at 19th Street (tel. 529-4197)
Hours: Monday to Thursday from 10am to 6pm, Friday and Saturday to 8pm, Sunday noon to 6pm
Credit Cards: AE, MC, V; $15 minimum

Just the way it reads—a little shop full of tin (and plastic) windup toys. Some old, some new, all fun. Music boxes, too. From 50¢ to big numbers.

Lionel Kiddie City, 35 W. 34th St. (tel. 629-3070 or 629-3089); Broadway and 79th Street (tel. 877-4252 or 877-4331); Union Square at 14th Street (tel. 353-0215 or 353-0258)
Hours: Tuesday, Wednesday, and Saturday from 9am to 8pm, Monday, Thursday, and Friday from 9am to 9pm, Sunday from 10am to 6pm
Credit Cards: AE, MC, V

These stores are expanding and they seem to be doing everything right. They are well lit, well stocked, and well priced.

There is a wide selection to choose from in their electronics department with Nintendo, Master System, etc. with all the current releases and accessories.

They have bikes, car seats, and cars the kids can drive. The board games are on the shelves in alphabetical order, which is a terrific time-saver when you're looking for whatever. All the famous brand-name toys are among the 18,000 items in the stores. They claim their discount is 20% off on everything. Pay attention when you are in the stores and look for the red-tag items; these are slashed to the bone.

The stores are well run and well staffed. Except for Christmas time, you rarely wait to check out.

If Kiddie City stores would arrange for UPS, it would be easy to buy large items. The way things are, it is just too difficult. Nice stores, just keep your purchases few in number and small in size.

R. H. Macy and Company, 34th Street at Herald Square, Broadway and Seventh Avenue (tel. 695-4400)
Hours: Monday, Thursday, and Friday from 9:45am to 8:30pm; Tuesday, Wednesday, and Saturday to 6:45pm, and Sunday from 10am to 6pm
Credit Cards: AE, MC, V, Macy's; checks with ID

This department of the "World's Largest Store" is enchanting. Their toy displays in the glass cases as you enter this department are very pretty. For Christmas and Easter, they have Santa Claus and the Easter Bunny, respectively. They also have puppet shows at Christmas time.

The merchandise is endless. They have the standard toy items at regular prices (except for sales and special purchases).

Mythology, 370 Columbus Ave., between 77th and 78th streets (tel. 874-0774)
Hours: Monday through Saturday from 11am to 11pm, and Sunday from 11am to 6pm
Credit Cards: AE, MC, V

Sophisticated stuff for adults; kids get the Mythology message instantly. There's 1950s TV stuff; wild fruits, vegetables, and fish; fun jewelry, posters, inflatables, and science projects. A selection of books, gardening and architecture included, antique toys, and little Lucite boxes stocked with inexpensive little things to make your kids happy. The stock changes constantly. This is a very special place; for the kids over 8 it's a natural.

New York Doll Hospital, 787 Lexington Ave., at 62nd Street (tel. 838-7527) one flight up
Hours: Monday through Saturday from 10am to 6pm
Credit Cards: None

Ah, the things they have done for Barbie and Ken! But that's a piece of cake. This old shop (second floor) can do miracles on the finest antiques. There are dolls for sale, but only for collectors. Do take your g.c. to see the place. They also repair teddy bears and other stuffed animals.

Penny Whistle Toys, 448 Columbus Ave., at 82nd Street (tel. 873-9090); 1283 Madison Ave., at 91st Street (tel. 369-3868); and 132 Spring St., between Wooster and Greene streets (tel. 925-2088)
Hours: (Columbus Avenue) Sunday and Monday from 11am to 6pm, Tuesday and Wednesday 10am to 6pm, Thursday 10am to 8pm, Friday and Saturday 10am to 7pm; (Madison Avenue) Monday to Friday from 9:30am to 5:30pm, Saturday 10am to 6pm, Sunday noon to 5pm; (Spring Street) Monday to Friday from 10:30am to 6pm, Thursday and Friday till 7pm, Saturday 11am to 7pm, Sunday 11:30am to 6pm
Credit Cards: All major cards accepted; $25 minimum

These are excellent stores in which to shop. The stock is distinctive and special. Items from little prices (so no child has to leave empty handed) to off-the-charts. The help is knowledgeable, the shops are attractive, and they are full-service toy stores.

Look for the bubble-blowing teddy bears out front—you should be able to spot them from a block away if the wind is up.

Polks, 314 Fifth Ave., at 32nd Street (tel. 279-9034)
Hours: Monday to Saturday from 9:30am to 5:30pm. Closed Sunday. Polks has been in business for fifty-nine years!
Credit Cards: AE, MC, V; $25 minimum

"The only difference between men and boys is the price of their toys." Not that I'm suggesting this is pricey—it's more than fair. Model makers who require kits for planes, cars, and boats don't fit into an age category. For your older boy and girl g.c., this place is heaven. Everything for the scientific mind. The most extensive collection of radio-controlled toys I have encountered—and large-scale model trains. They also have racing sets that your younger g.c. will love as well, but your older g.c. will understand the workings and be enthralled.

Red Caboose, 16 W. 45th St., 4th floor, between 5th and 6th avenues (tel. 575-0155)
Hours: Monday to Friday from 10:15am to 7pm, Saturday till 5pm
Credit Cards: AE, MC, V

Everything for kids who love electric trains. All the different model trains and railroad equipment. They also have boats and cars, but trains are the big item. They discount everything. Generously.

The Train Shop, 23 W. 45th St., between Fifth and Sixth avenues (tel. 730-0409)
Hours: Monday to Friday from 10am to 6pm, Saturday till 5pm
Credit Cards: All major cards accepted

Walk down one short flight and you will find a tidy freight yard. The trains are arranged by size; N's to HO's, to the old Lionel monsters. All with matching equipment. The employees know their subject and will help you fill in a car or two or start from scratch.

FAO Schwarz, 767 Fifth Ave., between 58th and 59th streets (tel. 644-9400)

Hours: Monday through Saturday from 10am to 6pm, Thursday to 8pm, and Sunday from noon to 5pm
Credit Cards: AE, MC, V

This is a "must see" place. As you enter you will be greeted by the revolving clock. Because it is so stupendous, I shall not ruin the impact by description. Allow at least 15 minutes to take it in.

The first floor is occupied by stuffed animals. What a menagerie. The second floor sells blocks by the pound, toys, games, dolls, trains, trucks, some clothing . . . why try? There are 100 boutiques in FAO.

The aim of management is "personal service to the customer." To aid management, Teddy Ruxpin is in charge of the store directory at the escalators. He is as much fun as the real live mimes and jugglers who are there to entertain.

You cannot visit New York and not visit FAO. If you enter on Fifth, exit on Madison or you will miss a little part of the store that is quite charming.

Second Childhood, 283 Bleecker St., 1 block south of Sheridan Square (tel. 989-6140)
Hours: Monday through Saturday from 11am to 6pm
Credit Cards: AE, MC, V

You will adore it. Let your g.c. wander a while and he or she will get the message. None of the abundance of Toys-Я-Us. This is the other end completely. You'll find wicker doll carriages, scooters, china dolls, and more. It's small and lovingly run. The prices range from under $1 to four figures. All the romance of toys is in this shop. They even gave me a button with a picture of an old-fashioned boy and girl. Do see this! From 1820 to 1950. Gotcha, huh?

Tiny Doll House, 231 E. 53rd St., between Second and Third avenues (tel. 752-3082)
Hours: Monday through Saturday from 11am to 5pm
Credit Cards: AE, MC, V

Don't blink or you'll miss the shop. If your g.c. is feeling dwarfed by New York, this is a perfect opportunity to show her there are teeny-weeny things, even smaller than she is. Doll furnishings in every style—Victorian, log cabin, contemporary—right down to dishes. Reassuring.

 Toy Park, 112 E. 86th St., between Lexington and Park avenues (tel. 427-6611)

Hours: Monday from 10am to 6pm, Tuesday and Wednesday from 10am to 7pm, Thursday from 10am to 8pm, Friday and Saturday from 10am to 7pm, and Sunday from noon to 5pm

Credit Cards: MC, V; $10 minimum

The entrance to Toy Park is submerged, so to enter you go down a few steps. When you get inside, you'll know it was well worth the descent. The front of the store on the west side has dolls, doll carriages, doll clothes, and stuffed animals.

The boys will head for the middle of the store. They know intuitively that on the wall are all those wonderful/hideous creatures they so admire. Thank you Steven Spielberg et al.

In the middle of the store there is an indented area where there are many challenging crafts (big Lego sets and such) and mind bogglers for older kids. They have an enormous selection of games and everything else.

If you don't see what you want, don't hesitate to ask. Their salespeople seem to be able to locate all sorts of things "in the back," as they say.

This store is not really as large in area as I make it seem. It's just well organized with a large inventory—a bigger-than-average New York toy store. And they deliver anything above a $10 purchase from 59th Street to 96th Street, East Side; 59th Street to 110th Street, West Side.

 Toys-Я-Us, 1293 Broadway, Herald Square at 33rd Street (tel. 594-8697)

Hours: Monday, Thursday, and Friday from 9am to 9pm, Tuesday, Wednesday, and Saturday from 9am to 8pm, Sunday from 10am to 6pm

Credit Cards: AE, MC, V

I have long been a steadfast Toys-Я-Us customer. The stock is huge. They are willing to take back a dead horse if the customer finds it an unsatisfactory purchase. This store tested my loyalty and flunked. It's on two floors. You have a choice of escalator or elevator, which is important if you are pushing a stroller. That's the good part. Here are the bad parts. To find a board game is impossible; they are stacked in a disorderly manner. There is not a soul on either floor to answer a question, and the checkout is a waiting ordeal if there are as many as two customers. I asked at the service desk if the computer could tell me if Jr. Scrabble was in stock. The answer? "If you know the store's code number on this item, we'll check." Huh?

I am sensitive to attitude—who isn't?—and it's not good here. Could be the people who work here find the clumsy space as oppressive as I did. Not to worry, Kiddie City is in the same neighborhood.

They also have clothing at Kids-Я-Us.

West Side Kids, 498 Amsterdam Ave., corner of 84th Street (tel. 496-7282)
Hours: Monday through Saturday from 10am to 6:30pm, Thursday till 7pm, and Sunday from noon to 5pm
Credit Cards: AE, MC, V

"Classic toys that just don't lose it," says Sam, manager of this wonderful shop. They have Tinkertoys, Lego, Brio, Playmobile, Fisher Price, and the T. C. Timber wooden train sets. But this stuff is far from all of their inventory; they also have special educational toys. Lovely personal service and guidance in selections for those in need.

Youth at Play, 1120 Madison Ave., at 84th Street (tel. 737-5036)
Hours: Monday through Saturday from 10am to 6pm
Credit Cards: AE, $10 minimum; MC, V, $50 minimum

Inventory forever! And what a selection. Having a party? They have everything you'll require (except the cake). Sports equipment and all kinds of games, records, dolls, puzzles, costumes, etc. An absolutely remarkable assemblage for any age g.c., and if he or she can't find it here, you have a problem.

CHAPTER 13

General Stores & Classified Material

The heading, General Stores, doesn't begin to disclose the treasures awaiting you in these shops. If you like kitsch, collectibles, tricks, souvenirs, unusual accessories, and just plain fun stuff, this is your chapter.

General Stores

Architectural Salvage Warehouse, 337 Berry St., between 4th and 5th streets, Brooklyn (tel. 718/388-4527), for more information call Richard at 212/553-1100

Hours: Monday, Thursday, and Friday afternoons till 6pm and by appointment only; write or call in advance

Credit Cards: None; payment by check only if drawn on a New York bank

Note: This warehouse is for New York City residents only (I bet you have a friend)

City-owned buildings scheduled for demolition are a primary source of inventory supply. Doors, mantels, grills, and plaques. Iron fences, lamp posts, and sewer covers. Finials, trims, and pillars from old buildings. Cast-iron pieces and lots more stuff. Years ago I bought subway fans and old cane trolley-car seats.

If you want the real thing, the authentic thing, a piece of New York at absolute bargain prices, then make the appointment and go with your New York friends. Your competition will be the antique dealers, but this is not an auction. Merchandise is sold as marked.

If you are willing to settle for an authorized, authentic reproduction, see Citybooks listed below and in Chapter 15, Shopping for Books. Citybooks is not connected with Architectural Salvage Warehouse.

Broadway Gifts, One Shubert Alley, from 44th to 45th streets, between Broadway and Eighth Avenue (tel. 944-4133)
Hours: Monday through Saturday from 9:30am to 11:30pm, and Sunday from noon to 7pm
Credit Cards: AE, MC, V

Everything here is Broadway theater: T-shirts, with logos of current shows; sweatshirts; posters; programs; tapes; and CDs. A big seller is a key chain adorned with a brass theater ticket, $9.95. They also have the Phantom's mask. There is a wonderful jewelry selection, and it's not expensive.

They also have mail and phone order. Call for a catalog toll free 800/223-1320. If you live in New York, call 586-7610. You will be put on the free catalog mailing list that has "selected items." I know I told you not to wander in this area. However, Shubert Alley is a private street, well lit, and well patrolled.

Citybooks, Municipal Building, 1 Centre St., at Chambers Street (tel. 669-8245)
Hours: Monday through Friday from 9am to 5pm
Credit Cards: None
Note: For a catalog, write to Citybooks, New York City Department of General Services, 2223 Municipal Building, New York, NY 10007

If you're wondering why this isn't included in the chapter on books, it is. It's here because it's far more than just books. If you don't have time to visit Citybooks, write for their free catalog. It's as good as a visit to the store.

For authentic, city-approved, New York artifacts and approved reproductions, this is your place. Stick pins made from subway tokens are $3. A Lucite-mounted Staten Island ferry token is $6. Posters, T-shirts, jewelry, ties, teddy bears, and of course, books.

Dapy, 232 Columbus Ave., between 70th and 71st streets (tel. 877-4710); and 431 West Broadway, between Spring and Prince streets (tel. 925-5082)
Hours: (Columbus Avenue) 11am to 10pm daily; (West Broadway) 11am to 7pm daily
Credit Cards: AE, MC, V
For kids with a sense of humor, Dapy has outrageous things: pens with frog feet holding a ball, $10. Back packs, animal slippers, and lots of wild things. The price range is very broad. I, for one, yearn for the mini-pool table. An absolutely bizarre collection of stuff at Dapy.

The Funny Store, 1481 Broadway (in Times Square), between 42nd and 43rd streets (tel. 730-9582)
Hours: Daily from 9am to 9pm
Credit Cards: No, no
All of this wonderful junk is an American art form. For the budding collector, this place is a bit of heaven. Whoopee cushions, jokes, magic, replicas of city landmarks such as the Statue of Liberty and the Empire State Building.

Don't just glance—study. The assemblage is what consumes you, if you go with the flow. It's all so tacky, and so New York. Some of it is a bit raunchy, but if you're a junk junkie, it's part of the game.

Hudson Street Papers, 581 Hudson St., between 11th and Bank streets (tel. 243-4221)
Hours: Monday through Saturday from 10am to 8pm, Sunday noon to 6pm
Credit Cards: AE, MC, V
A shining example of how not to spend a fortune to delight a

youngster. Lots of little toys, sidewalk chalk, paper products from France and Italy, nice jewelry, and lots of inexpensive fun things. So nice to find a store with a stylish inventory.

Jeremy's Place, 322 E. 81st St., between First and Second avenues (tel. 628-1414)
Hours: Daily 11:30am to 6:30pm
Credit Cards: None

This is a party store with lots of good buys. Jeremy guarantees his prices as the lowest in town. Well, stickers that cost 25¢ in other places are 9¢ at Jeremy's; blow-up dinosaurs are 59¢; 91% of the items sell for 91¢ or less. When was the last time you had change from a dollar spent? For $2.95 a bag, with a six-bag minimum, your kids may fill each bag with $4 worth of goodies. They're called "party bags to go." Either have a party, or pig out.

Little Rickie, 49½ First Ave., at 3rd Street (tel. 505-6467)
Hours: Monday through Thursday and Saturday from 11am to 8pm, Friday from noon to 9pm, Sunday from noon to 8pm
Credit Cards: AE, M, V

It is called Little Rickie in honor of *I Love Lucy*'s baby boy.

You must be over 18 to be admitted on your own, younger folk must be accompanied by an adult. Not because the inventory is blue, but because there is lots of one-of-a-kind stuff that must be handled with care. Take your kids over 10; they are going to love it.

There is a booth where you step inside and for $2 have your photograph taken. This photo-booth is one of the few remaining machines of this kind. They used to be in every 5 and 10 store in the 1940s.

There is also a Lucky Charm machine. For 50¢ you punch in up to 32 letters on a medallion. Remember these?

They have old, toy, Davy Crockett watches still affixed to the original cardboard holders for $2.95. How about a huge plaster of Paris, original Elvis lamp complete with shade? Or an Elvis guitar clock, also *original* and in working condition for $55. These are the same items that bring at least double the price in shops that deal in antiques or memorabilia. An original Davy Crockett belt sells here for about $20. I saw the very same belt priced at $80 in a shop on Melrose in Los Angeles. The prices here are better than fair.

There are T-shirts, boxer shorts, jewelry, musical instruments, and everything singular and special. Things priced for as little as $1 and up to a $1,000 for folk art pieces.

Phillip Retzky, the delightful guy who owns Little Rickie's says, "My shop is the cathedral of kitsch," and "If we don't have it, you don't need it. I just can't imagine what we don't have. . . ."

If you see something you like, want, and can afford, buy it. These items come and go and may never surface again.

Did I mention the Lava Lamps? The originals, from the '60s, are $65. The same lamps, just as ugly, continue to be manufactured by the same factory and are $55. You may buy with confidence because Phillip will explain these differences.

Little Rickie's is a winner.

Mythology, 370 Columbus Ave., between 77th and 78th streets (tel. 874-0774)
Hours: Monday through Friday 11:30am to 6:30pm, Saturday and Sunday from 11am to 6pm
Credit Cards: AE, MC, V

The price range varies greatly. They have a vast collection of unusual stuff. Mythology is well worth a visit because you will see things not to be found anyplace else. See Chapter 12.

The Paper House, 269 Amsterdam Ave., between 72nd and 73rd streets (tel. 724-8085); 1020 Third Ave., between 60th and 61st streets (tel. 223-3774); 180 E. 86th St., between Lexington and Third avenues (410-7950); 1370 Third Ave., corner 78th Street (tel. 879-2973); 2235 Broadway between 79th and 80th streets (tel. 595-5656); and 18 Greenwich Ave., corner of 10th Street (tel. 741-1569)
Hours: Monday to Saturday from 9:30am to 10pm, Sunday from 11am to 8pm. These hours vary so call the store you plan to visit
Credit Cards: M, V; a $15 minimum

The first three listings above are the largest of the Paper Houses. They have everything. Cards, gifts, masks, party goods of all sorts, party favors, gift boxes and wrap, toys, games, and some books.

I think you have the general idea. These are well-stocked stores with new things coming in all the time. I neglected to mention the large selection of unusual pens and pencils.

P.S. I Love You, 1242 Madison Ave., between 89th and 90th streets (tel. 722-6272)
Hours: Monday through Saturday from 10am to 6pm, and Sunday from 11am to 5pm
Credit Cards: AE, MC, V

A super spot for inexpensive, great-looking jewelry for very little girls who yearn to bedeck themselves, and their older sisters. Nothing vulgar, all in perfect taste—T-shirts, sweatshirts, teddy bears, pens for coloring. Just mercifully priced. What a find!

Rubinstein's & Son Merchandise, Inc., 874 Broadway, at 18th Street (tel. 254-0162)
Hours: Monday through Friday from 9am to 6pm, and Saturday to 2:30pm
Credit Cards: MC, V

Everything you buy here will cost you less than you pay uptown. They have all the things needed for a party: cups, plates, and favors. Best of all, they have the makeup to do a make-your-own-monster face. Top this with a selection from the masks, and your kids are ready for anything. The masks are terrific, and very fairly priced. There are several good novelty stores still left in this upscale neighborhood from 19th Street down to Union Square.

Tah-Poozie, 332 Bleecker St., between Christopher and 10th streets (tel. 242-2715)
Hours: noon to 7pm daily
Credit Cards: MC, V

It's a tiny shop and every item has been selected with care. The owner, Shmuel Kerhaus, is really involved with everything in the store and will give you all the help you need. Whether it's a $2.98 trick or a koosh ball with a face, it's different. There are flip-books, mobiles, handmade jewelry, embroidered hats, folk art, special toys, and things you will find no place else.

What attracts parents is there is nothing violent or vulgar or sexy about any of the offerings found in Tah-Poozie.

That's New York, 843 Seventh Ave., corner of 54th Street (tel. 582-7072)
Hours: 8:30am to 11:30pm daily
Credit Cards: All major cards accepted

Distinctive souvenirs that are a large cut above the usual tacky stuff one finds on Broadway. They have watches, videos of New York, postcards, maps, sweatshirts, warm-ups, and jewelry. They do custom silk-screening while you wait. This is a very clean, attractive, reliable shop. If this is the merchandise you want, try this shop if you are in the neighborhood.

Think Big, 390 West Broadway, between Spring and Broome streets (tel. 925-7300)
Hours: Monday to Saturday from 11am to 7pm
Credit Cards: AE, M, V

Everything here is larger than life and suitable for hanging. A 56-inch Crayola crayon is $40, a huge paintbrush that is anatomically perfect is far more money, a giant Prince tennis ball is $35, and an oversize racket is $225. They also have "little stuff." The tiny tennis ball is $4, the mini-racket is $10, and the teeny baseball bats are $7.50.

Perfect gift pickings for the person who has everything.

Unique Card & Gift Shop, 52 E. 59th St., between Madison and Park avenues (tel. 688-4211); and 133 W. 50th St., between Sixth and Seventh avenues (tel. 265-0628)
Hours: Monday to Friday from 8:30am to 7pm, Saturday from 10:30am to 6:30pm
Credit Cards: AE, M, V

Leave yourself lots of time. Everything in these stores has a funny twist. From cards and buttons, soft-cover books, slippers, dolls, to items you may never have seen before. The 59th Street store is tremendous, a good opportunity to stock up on greeting cards; lots of funny ones.

If this is the kind of stuff you like (and who doesn't?) you have found two homes.

Classified Material

Shhhhh. This is the classified material.

ARTS AND CRAFTS

Arthur Brown and Brothers, Inc., 2 W. 46th St., between Fifth and Sixth avenues (tel. 575-5555)
Hours: Monday through Friday from 9am to 6:30pm, and Saturday from 11am to 10pm
Credit Cards: All major cards

Let the other ladies go to Cartier. This place intensifies personal greed. Paints, crayons, pens, and paper (even sold by the pound). Scissors shaped like animals—and they work. Your mini Jasper Johns will love it. You will vow to change your life-style and clean up your desk when you see their supplies. Don't, because you won't. (That means don't buy it, because you and your desk won't change.)

M & J Trimmings, 1008 Sixth Ave., between 37th and 38th streets (tel. 391-9072)
Hours: Monday through Friday from 9am to 6pm, and Saturday from 10am to 5pm
Credit Cards: All major cards; checks accepted with ID

Wouldn't your child like a hand gadget to put stones on T-shirts? Get it here, along with all the rhinestones, sequins, and trimming for your g.c. to make collages, pictures, etc. Stop in and stock up on beads and patches, or maybe you need a crown or two. Not usual guidebook advice, but great stuff for a rainy day and it costs less than little packets of junk you find in the dime store.

Sheru, 49 W. 38th St., between Fifth and Sixth avenues (tel. 730-0766)
Hours: Monday through Friday from 9am to 6pm, and Saturday from 9:30am to 5pm
Credit Cards: AE, MC, V; $25 minimum

The largest bead store in New York. Ribbons, shells, and all the makings for your g.c.'s jewelry. (They'll show you how if it's not busy.) These purchases are ideal for a rainy afternoon.

BASEBALL CARDS

❧ **Card Collectors Co.,** 105 W. 77th St., a few steps west of
Columbus Ave. (tel. 873-6999)
Hours: Daily from noon to 7pm
Credit Cards: AE, MC, V

This is the place for the serious baseball card collector. Mr.
Pasternack, the shop owner, buys baseball cards and sells them. He
also operates a wholesale and retail business here. Don't overlook
the sports memorabilia.

This is a well-organized, spotless, baseball card treasure house.
Leave the sticky-fingered little kids elsewhere. If you have a real
aficionado, he or she will choke at Card Collectors Co.

❧ **Collector's Stadium,** 214 Sullivan St., between Bleecker and
W. 3rd streets (tel. 353-1531)
Hours: Daily from 11am to 7pm
Credit Cards: AE, MC, V

For your older kids who are interested in sports memorabilia.
Get it? Collector's Stadium. They have baseball cards and collect-
ing supplies (albums and mounts, etc.), posters, prints, and all the
stuff for which baseball buffs willingly empty their banks to own.
Other sports are covered nicely at the Stadium.

❧ **New York Mets Clubhouse Shop,** 575 Fifth Ave., corner of
47th Street (tel. 986-4887)
Hours: Monday to Friday 9am to 6pm, Saturday 10am to 6pm,
Sunday noon to 5pm
Sizes: Toddler 2 to adult sizes
Credit Cards: AE, DISC, MC, V

Everything with the official Mets logo. All the pro jerseys of the
current teams. What is most unusual is their "Cooperstown
Collection," replicas of the uniforms of leagues of yesterday that
are long gone. Extensive research has gone into this project and
the results are startling. A company in Pennsylvania produces the
uniforms in the actual fabrics used decades ago with the identical
logos. The "Negro Leagues" are heavily represented. Aside from
finding terrific things you want to buy, you will get a history of
baseball under idyllic circumstances.

They have all the items the Yankee Clubhouse has, so read on.

New York Yankees Clubhouse, 110 E. 59th St., between Park and Lexington avenues (tel. 758-7844)
Hours: Monday to Friday 9:30am to 7pm, Saturday till 6pm, Sunday from noon to 5pm
Sizes: Toddler 2 to adult sizes
Credit Cards: AE, DISC, MC, V

Robert McDonald of the Clubhouse said, "This is a playland for kids . . . and for bigger kids."

The official Yankee logo is on watches, sport bags, warm-ups, shirts, and caps ($5.95 for kids). A dress for a toddler at $24.95 replete with logo is a hit. This shop is very proud of its collection of memorabilia, including baseball cards, garnered directly from the New York Yankees. There are bats, shirts, caps and even mitts. All of these belonged to former Yankee players.

Other teams are represented in sweatshirts at $29.99 and T-shirts that start at $13.99.

This is a Ticketron outlet and you may buy tickets for the baseball games at $1 above the price.

If you and the kids like baseball, the Mets Clubhouse and the Yankees Clubhouse could be your sports picks.

COMIC BOOKS

Comic Art Gallery, 231 E. 53rd St., between Second and Third avenues (tel. 759-6255); and 227 Sullivan St., between Bleecker and W. 3rd streets (tel. 777-2770)
Hours: (53rd Street) Monday through Saturday from 11am to 7pm. (Sullivan Street) Monday through Wednesday from 11am to 8pm, Thursday through Saturday from noon to 10pm, and Sunday from noon to 6pm
Credit Cards: MC, V

Both shops have current comic books as well as older comics for the collector. They have posters, too, and much reading material.

Funny Business, 656 Amsterdam Ave., corner of 92nd Street (tel. 799-9477)
Hours: Monday through Thursday from 1 to 5pm, Friday from 1 to 6pm, and Saturday and Sunday from noon to 5pm
Credit Cards: MC, V

Here is one of those special places that buy and sell all sorts of comic books. G.c. over 8 years old love these places. Teenagers and adults are filled with awe and respect.

There's a fine line of children's comic books here. If you don't consider comic books to be fine, in any sense of the word, you must be getting older. Look again at the Marvel and D.C. comic books. New issues and back issues. They are for kids. Hot items are Archie and Batman.

Village Comics, 227 Sullivan St., between Bleecker and W. 3rd streets (tel. 777-2770)
Hours: Monday to Saturday from noon to 6pm, closed Sunday
Credit Cards: MC, V

They have Marvel comics in depth. This is the store for mark-downs, closeouts, and bargains. Even the new comics, which arrive every Thursday, are sold at discount prices.

For regular customers, as purchases of $5 and over reach $250, the reward is a $25 credit at Village Comics.

Village Comics, 163 Bleecker St., between Sullivan and Thompson streets (tel. 777-2770)
Hours: Monday through Wednesday from 10am to 8:30pm, Thursday through Saturday from 10am to 9:30pm, and Sunday from 11:30am to 7:30pm
Credit Cards: MC, V

The merchandise is much the same, the bigger price savings are on the merchandise at the other store. For science fiction posters you are in the right place. If you are a comic book aficionado, you are in one of the right places, the other is around the corner.

West Side Comics, 107 W. 86th St., between Amsterdam and Columbus avenues (tel. 724-0432)
Hours: Monday through Wednesday from noon to 8pm, Thursday through Saturday from 11am to 9pm, and Sunday from noon to 7pm
Credit Cards: AE, MC, V

This was a tough source to locate. There are lots of spots to buy comic books if you are a collector; this is not one of them. The comic books here are hot off the presses and new as tomorrow.

The biggest collection around makes it a good place to know. They have lots of rental videos and none for sale. Perfect!

CHESS

Village Chess Shop, 230 Thompson St., between Bleecker and W. 3rd streets (tel. 475-9580)

Hours: Daily from noon to midnight
Credit Cards: MC, V

This is a shop for your older kids who like chess and chess sets. They have backgammon, checkers, cribbage, dominoes, and mah-jongg here as well. If you happen to be in the market for a wonderful gift for your chess-loving child, this is the place.

I did ask the owner about replacing a lost piece to any of the above games. He said, "Possible, bring a piece to me, I'll see." I did like his attitude. I'm not missing any pieces (well, it's questionable). I want my readers to have sources for everything.

COSTUMES AND MASKS

Abracadabra, 10 Christopher St., between Gay Street and Greenwich Avenue (tel. 627-5745)

Hours: Monday to Saturday from 11am to 9pm, closed Sunday
Credit Cards: DC, MC, V
Note: If you go to Abracadabra, you are 2 or 3 blocks from Tah-Poozie and T-Shirt Museum. If the day is nice, it's fun to walk this most charming section of the Village

They bill themselves as "Halloween Headquarters." They are that and way beyond. You can choose from masks of rubber that cover the head and depict every politico, vampire, and horror character ever known and many unknown. There are lion suits, tiger suits, and clown suits with oversize shoes to match. The costumes come in enough styles to take care of any body's fantasy. They even have flesh and blood rubber body decorations (ugh). There is also an outlandish collection of off-the-wall items from gum ball machines to a light that is a color-changing shell.

A bizarre collection is to be found at Abracadabra. It is, of course, for kids over 8 or 9 with an interest in the macabre and the outrageous. An absolutely one-of-a-kind store. My grandsons Ben and Daniel Fisher (14 and 9) consider this an "awesome place."

MAGIC

Flosso-Hornmann Magic Co., 45 W. 34th St., between Fifth and Sixth avenues (6th Floor, Room 607) (tel. 279-6079)
Hours: Monday through Friday from 10am to 5:30pm and Saturday to 4pm
Credit Cards: MC, V

Would you and yours like to see a handkerchief turn into a ghost? Bet your sweet bippy you would. They have handkerchiefs that turn color (no, it's not a linen store with all those handkerchiefs—they're necessary staples in the magician's inventory), magic coloring books, magic wands, appearing and vanishing egg tricks.

Museum of Magic tours are offered in August; at other times you are able to look through the museum on your own. This is the oldest magic shop in the United States, and it's not to disappear before your eyes see it. Take the kids—those 3 and over should be mystified.

Tannen Magic Co., 6 W. 32nd St., between Fifth Avenue and Broadway (4th floor) (tel. 239-8383)
Hours: Monday through Friday from 9am to 5:30pm, and Saturday from 9am to 4pm
Credit Cards: AE, MC, V

This is the world's largest magic store! If this information doesn't reach you, then you just are not interested in magic and illusions. They have lots of things for the kids. They are very gracious at Tannen, and I suggest a visit.

MUSIC

Sam Ash, 160 W. 48th St., between Sixth and Seventh avenues (tel. 719-2625, or 516/485-2122 for the main office)
Hours: Monday through Saturday from 10am to 6pm

If your budding musician is in need of a microphone or an amplifier, this is your best bet. Because they supply the "pros," they know every place to rent or to buy new or used musical instruments. They also have, or will guide you to, all the state-of-the-art electronic devices used to make those noises. This information is a public service.

NATURE'S TREASURES

Astro Minerals Ltd., 155 E. 34th St., between Lexington and Third avenues (tel. 889-9000)
Hours: Monday through Saturday from 10am to 6pm, Thursday till 8pm, and Sunday from 11am to 6pm
Credit Cards: AE, MC, V

Guess what they have? Minerals from all over the world. Drawers that are just your g.c.'s height and available for foraging. Beautiful bits of geological treasures, and for $1 he can take it home. Fun time.

NOVELTIES

Gordon Novelties, 933 Broadway, between 21st and 22nd streets (tel. 254-8616)
Hours: Monday through Friday from 9am to 4:30pm
Credit Cards: Cash only

Do not be put off by the sign on the door that reads "To the Trade." I was assured that my readers will be welcomed. "Cash only, and we're not a playground." That's fair.

If you want a cone head, complete costumes, masks, capes, crowns, scepters, and even the makeup for a complete transformation, come to Gordon's. Lots of choices. But prices are pretty steep.

Jimsons Novelties Inc., 30 E. 18th St., east of Broadway (tel. 477-3386 or 477-3692)
Hours: Monday through Friday from 9:30am to 5:15pm, and Saturday from 10am to 3pm
Credit Cards: Cash only

This small store is so stuffed with wonderful things, you can't see them all. Study the window display before you go in. They have dynel wigs: $15 elsewhere, $5 here. They have novelties, toys, party favors, costume jewelry, and lots of crazy, wild stuff. I bought miniature cars, which cost $2 to $3 each all around town, for $6 for 12 cars here.

This store is "to the trade." I was assured that if we were prepared to pay in cash and make quick decisions, we would be more than welcome. What an opportunity to stock up on gifts, party favors and prizes, and Halloween supplies for years to come.

Jimsons is opposite Rubinstein's & Son (see below). Do a complete party for very little money in no time. It will be original, creative, and easy. Two great sources; use them to your best advantage.

Rubinstein's & Son Merchandise, Inc., 874 Broadway, at 18th Street (tel. 254-0162)
Hours: Monday through Friday from 9am to 6pm, and Saturday from 9am to 2:30pm
Credit Cards: MC, V
    See page 258, "General Stores" section in this chapter.

POSTERS

Memory Shop, 109 E. 12th St., between Third and Fourth avenues (tel. 473-2404)
Hours: Monday to Saturday from 10am to 6pm
Credit Cards: None accepted and no personal checks
Note: Mail-order address: Memory Shop, Box 36, Cooper Station, New York NY 10003

It may not be the most beautiful place in town, but the compensations are enormous. They have thousands of posters, lobby cards, and press books. Their movie material specializes in horror, serial, westerns, and classics of the screen. Their Rock and Roll collection is vast. This is not a place for browsing because the space is small and the inventory immense. The prices are very fair.

If you are coming to New York, you would do well to write or telephone in advance for their free listing. If you are looking for something specific, call and they will tell you if they have it.

🍎 **Triton Theatre Posters,** 323 W. 45th St., between Eighth and Ninth avenues (tel. 765-2472)
Hours: Monday through Saturday from 10am to 6pm
Credit Cards: AE, MC, V

Triton not only has the current theater posters but lots of golden oldies. The prices are reasonable. The people are nice. The inventory is complete and deep.

If your kids are into these, try to stop here. If you run out of time, send 50¢ to the above address and you'll be able to order from the full-color brochure you'll have in your hot little hands.

T-SHIRTS & SWEATSHIRTS

🍎 **T-Shirt Gallery, Ltd.,** 154 E. 64th St., corner of Lexington Avenue (tel. 838-1212)
Hours: Monday through Saturday from 11am to 6pm
Credit Cards: AE, MC, V

They will airbrush or print the shirt you select. They have regular-size T's and sweatshirts and oversize. They even have cotton dresses. If you want something special, bring in a photograph and they'll put it on a shirt while you wait for $15 plus the cost of the shirt. They will also print any message. You can have your shirt the same day or while you wait. If it's a complicated order it could take a bit longer.

Nice people and they've been at this spot for a long time. Just walk up that flight of stairs on 64th Street.

🍎 **T-Shirt Museum,** 333 Bleecker St., between Christopher and 10th streets (tel. 645-2441)
Hours: Daily from "11ish" am to 11pm
Sizes: 4 years and up

"A whole world of printed sportswear." You can purchase decorated sweatshirts for kids from $15.99, T's in this size are less. There is a very special collection of shirts decorated with cartoons. They also do silk-screening and there are posters and postcards for sale. The store is as neat as a little pin and it's full of stuff you and the kids will want.

SHOPPING FOR CHILDREN'S FURNITURE & ACCESSORIES

When shopping for furniture, rugs, and smaller items, don't overlook Lord & Taylor and Macy's. If you're doing a nursery, you're a pigeon if you fall for the duck and chicken decor; kids outgrow these motifs in about 15 minutes. Be brave.

ABC, 888 Broadway, at 19th Street (tel. 473-3000)
   Hours: Monday through Friday from 10am to 7pm (on Monday and Thursday to 8pm), Saturday from 10am to 6pm, and Sunday from 11am to 6pm
Credit Cards: AE, DC, MC, V
   They specialize in the country look for kids. Rag rugs of cotton are reversible, hypoallergenic, and easy to clean—dhurries with sheep and bunnies and teddy bears. The furniture is country pine from armoires to rockers. If you want to do a knockout room for any age youngster for the right price, learn ABC.

Albee's, 715 Amsterdam Ave., at 95th Street (tel. 662-5740 or 662-8902)
Hours: Monday through Saturday from 9am to 5:30pm
Credit Cards: AE, MC, V
   They have two phones for a reason. Their prices are terrific and they have everything. Furniture for children, layettes, clothing, strollers, cribs, high chairs, and everything else for little people. Discount prices all the way. And do watch for their special sales. Things at Albee's go from better to best when you want quality for the lowest prices. A discount store.

Bellini, 473 Columbus Ave., between 82nd and 83rd streets (tel. 362-3700)
Hours: Monday through Saturday from 10am to 6pm (Thursday to 8pm), and Sunday from noon to 5pm
Credit Cards: MC, V
   They also have accessories for children's rooms—clothing, gift items, playpens, and strollers. Let's talk about the furniture. It's nice. They will custom-make.

Ben's Babyland, 81 Avenue A, between 5th and 6th streets (tel. 674-1353)

Hours: Monday through Friday from 10am to 6pm, Saturday and Sunday from 10am to 5pm
Credit Cards: AE, MC, V

Just call, don't even bother going if you know what you want. They're dependable, and they discount car seats, carriages, strollers, furniture, sheets, blankets—all of it. They even have the Port-a-crib. Ben's was the only place (outside the U.K.) I could locate the Silver Cross stroller, a sturdy little bugger. A discount store.

Rug Tower, 399 Lafayette St., at the corner of E. Fourth Street (tel. 677-2525)
Hours: Monday through Friday from 10am to 8pm, Saturday from 10am to 6:30pm, and Sunday from 11am to 6pm
Credit Cards: AE, MC, V

If you are in search of area rugs for the nursery or the children's rooms, try the Rug Tower. A grand collection. They also have rugs for your living room.

RT's owners are honest and they know their business, from wall to wall. Prices range from modest to what you expect to pay for the finest-quality, handmade, museum-quality merchandise. Prices are good, and service is attentive. You'll see top-name decorators buying here.

Wicker Gardens Children, 1327 Madison Ave., between 93rd and 94th streets (tel. 410-7000)
Hours: Monday through Saturday from 10am to 5:30pm
Sizes: Newborn and up
Credit Cards: AE, MC, V

Your first point of focus will be the white (and some natural) wicker furniture placed around and about. For sale? Of course—and charming. Also incredible antiques. Clothes include playwear, partywear, shoes, and socks. They have hand-painted children's furniture.

SHOPPING: THE MUSEUM MELANGE

A large assemblage of things creates the museum shops' melding pots.

American Museum of the Moving Image, 35th Avenue, at 36th Street, Astoria, Queens (tel. 718/784-4520)
Hours: Tuesday through Friday from noon to 4pm, Saturday and Sunday noon to 6pm
Credit Cards: AE, MC, V
They have many film-related souvenirs. Also lunch boxes, color forms, and picture viewers. The viewer is $9 and the cassette is $4.

American Museum of Natural History, Central Park West and 79th Street (tel. 769-5100)
Hours: Sunday, Monday, Tuesday, Thursday from 10am to 5:45pm; Wednesday, Friday, Saturday from 10am to 9pm
Credit Cards: AE, MC, V
They have almost as many shops as they have exhibits. Books, dinosaurs, and everything else. You will not leave this building without some souvenir.

Brooklyn Museum, 200 Eastern Pkwy., Brooklyn, NY 11238 (tel. 718/638-5000)
Hours: Wednesday through Sunday from 10:30am to 5:30pm, closed Monday and Tuesday
Credit Cards: AE, MC, V
They have a separate ARTSMART Section with a great selection of educational and creative toys. There are packs of beautifully colored origami papers, the *Anti-Coloring Book,* and old-fashioned hobbyhorses. Plus, you'll find minitote bags and T-shirts with paints.

Children's Museum of Manhattan, 212 W. 83rd St. (741-1234)
Hours: Gift shop is open when the museum is open
This shop is small in space, but big in selections, such as the pocket-size toys that are quite humorous. You will find books that are worth browsing through and toys that are related to the exhibits on display.

Cloisters, Fort Tryon Park (tel. 923-3700)
Hours: Tuesday through Sunday from 9:30am to 4:30pm. Closed Sunday
Credit Cards: AE, DISC, MC, V

Castle sets from $8.95 to $39.95. These are not easy to find and the price can't be beat. Toy knights and their ladies and more.

Museum of the City of New York, Fifth Avenue and 103rd Street (tel. 534-1672)
Hours: Wednesday through Saturday from 10am to 5pm, Sunday 1pm to 5pm Closed Monday and Tuesday
Credit Cards: AE, MC, V with a $20 minimum purchase
They specialize in reproductions of the Old New York scene. Common street toys from the 1920s to the 1940s in kit form. Dolls in appropriate costumes are about $20. Pop-up books are about $5 and are a constant source of pleasure for children.

Museum of Holography, 11 Mercer St. (tel. 925-0581)
Hours: Monday through Sunday from 11am to 6pm
Credit Cards: AE, MC, V
They have laser specs, lasers, and glow star, as well as books about holography. The best thing about a gift from this shop is the possibility that you will come to understand the how and the why of holographs. Some child not old enough to cross the street by himself will explain it to you.

Moving hologram stickers at $1. A space scene, in sticker or puzzle form, has comets, planets, and satellites for $5. Hold the scene to the light and it appears to move.

Museum of Modern Art, 44 West 53rd St. (tel. 767-1050)
Hours: Friday through Tuesday from 11am to 6pm, Thursday until 9pm, Saturday and Sunday from 11am to 6pm. Closed Wednesday.
Credit Cards: AE, MC, V
One shop is in the building; the other is a few doors west. The shop in the main building is for you. Bauhaus blocks are $47.50 for the set, and what is better than lots of blocks? Not a large selection of things for kids but what they have is choice stuff. The designs are flawless and the wooden items are extremely well constructed.

CHAPTER 14

Shopping for Sporting Goods & Electronic Equipment

Sporting Goods

For sporting goods, I have included only one small shop. The larger stores that specialize in goods for all sports make life a whole lot easier.

🍎 **Blades,** 105 W. 72nd St. (tel. 787-3911); and 160 E. 86th St. (tel. 996-1644)

Hours: Monday to Friday from 11am to 7pm, Saturday and Sunday till 6pm

Credit Cards: All major cards accepted

This is the spot to rent your rollerblades; $15 for 2 hours, $25 for the day. You can also buy skateboards, assembled for $155. They carry On-Line skates, rollerblade skates, ice skates, snowboards, and all sorts of accessories. You can also purchase socks and gloves.

Blades is a professional sporting goods store. If you require the best in knowledgeable guidance when buying protective gear, this is the place to go. It is a reliable place to buy a foot bed; your older skaters know this is a molded plastic insole to use as an innersole in a skate or a shoe. They cost $65, or $50 if you buy your skates at the same time. Allow 24 hours, these are custom made.

G & S Sporting Goods, 43 Essex St., between Grand and Hester streets (tel. 777-7590)
Hours: Monday through Friday and Sunday from 9:30am to 6pm; closed Saturday
Credit Cards: MC, V; check with ID
They specialize in sporting goods and sneakers. This is a discount store.

Herman's World of Sporting Goods, 39 W. 34th St., off Fifth Avenue (tel. 279-8900)
Hours: Monday through Friday from 9am to 7pm, Saturday to 6:30pm, Sunday noon to 5pm
Credit Cards: All major cards accepted
This is the only Herman's that has children's things and not too much of that. There are other Herman's all over town. For other locations call tel. 201/541-1550.

R. H. Macy and Co., 34th Street, at Herald Square (Broadway and Seventh Avenue) (tel. 695-4400)
Hours: Monday through Friday from 9:45am to 8:30pm (on Tuesday, Wednesday and Saturday to 6:45pm), and Sunday from 10am to 6pm
Credit Cards: AE, Macy's, MC, V; check with ID
Whether it's for boys or for girls, for preteens or teenagers, for sports apparel or equipment, Macy's has a vast selection. I can never believe the depth of their stock for each activity. The clothing supply, too, is endless. Go for the whole enchilada in Macy's stadium.

Paragon Sporting Goods, 867 Broadway, at 18th Street (tel. 255-8036)
Hours: Monday through Friday from 10am to 8pm, Saturday from 10am to 6pm, and Sunday from 11am to 6pm
Credit Cards: All major cards

They have every piece of equipment needed for 18 different sports: hockey, skiing, baseball, basketball, tennis (in depth), skating, squash—keep going. They also have the necessary clothing for each activity: warm-up suits, jackets, ski parkas, baseball jackets.

They have an extremely wide selection of name brands if your youngster has a special loyalty to a particular manufacturer. This is the world's largest sporting goods store. Their prices are fair and their summer sales are sensational.

Prepare to spend lots of time here. The store is vast and the merchandise covers three floors. If your child is very small, call before you head for Paragon to avoid a wasted trip and a downcast youngster. This is not to negate the aforementioned praise. It's just better to be safe than sorry—and cranky.

SoHo Skateboards Etc., 19 E. 7th St., between Second and Third avenues (tel. 477-7590)
Hours: Monday through Thursday from noon to 7pm, Friday and Saturday from 11am to 8pm, Sunday from noon to 5pm
Credit Cards: AE, MC, V

This shop sells skateboards and clothing for young adults; kids over 16 are "young adults." For kids who know how to use these boards and have a place to exercise these skills, SoHo has all the necessary paraphernalia.

Audio & Video Equipment, Cameras, Computers & Typewriters

Prices for these items are highly competitive. Any one of these places is well in the ballpark as far as costs of the listed items. Be sure to see the ads in the Tuesday edition of *The New York Times* for very special buys. Don't miss 47th Street Photo; it's an experience you shouldn't miss. Tower Records on 4th Street and Broadway is a positively "must see."

🍎 **47th Street Photo, Inc.,** 67 W. 47th St., between Fifth and Sixth avenues, second floor (tel. 398-1410); 115 W. 45th St., between Sixth and Seventh avenues (tel. 398-1410); and 116 Nassau St., between Beekman and Ann streets (tel. 608-6934)
Hours: Monday through Thursday from 9am to 6pm; Friday to 2pm, and Sunday from 10am to 5pm
Credit Cards: AE, MC, V, 47th Street credit card; checks with ID

No matter on what street they're located, it's still 47th Street Photo—cameras, electronics, audio, video, computers, darkroom accessories. There's no place that sells for less so consistently. No tricks, no nonsense. And no nonsense on your part, please. It's not for browsers, because it's crowded and intense. Make no mistake—when it's your turn, you get full attention. The 45th Street store is easier shopping because it's less crowded, but all of life is a trade-off. It lacks the 47th Street high drama that accompanies a group of hunters loaded for bear.

My g.c. (over 8) find the place "awesome." So do I. It's owned and operated by Orthodox Jews who close early on Friday and don't open on Saturday for religious reasons.

🍎 **Uncle Steve's,** 343 Canal St., between Greene and Wooster streets (tel. 226-4010)
Hours: Monday through Saturday from 9:30am to 6:30pm, and Sunday from 11am to 5:30pm
Credit Cards: Cash only; no checks

Everything in electronics. And I mean everything! The owner told me, and I quote, "We will beat anybody's price." To do this, I was told, "1. First shop someplace else. 2. Call with the exact model number on any item. 3. Then come here—we'll beat 'em."

My intelligent friend, I.F., who accompanies me on trips to the nether world of audio, stereo, video, and computers, said he had "never seen a better price on Casio synthesizers." Well, that's good enough for me. I don't know what a Casio synthesizer is, or what it does, but if it's good enough for my I.F., it's got to be good.

Uncle Steve sells only brand names. I saw familiar things, consulted my notebook, and I must admit, he will beat anybody's price.

Willoughby's, 110 W. 32nd St., between Sixth and Seventh avenues (tel. 564-1600)
Hours: Monday through Friday from 9am to 7pm, Saturday from 9am to 6:30pm, and Sunday from 10:30am to 5:30pm
Credit Cards: All major cards
   They have cameras of all sorts, computers, audio and video equipment, projectors. The intelligent friend who accompanied me on this outing thought the prices were terrific. He also explained that this area is "camera row" and is highly competitive in price.

The Wiz, 6th Avenue at Eighth Street; 17 Union Square at 15th Street; 31st Street and Sixth Avenue; 33rd Street and Fifth Avenue; 12 W. 45th Street, between Fifth and Sixth avenues; 97th Street and Broadway; Third Avenue between 86th and 87th streets. For information call 289-8800
Hours: (6th Avenue) Monday to Friday from 10am to 10pm, Saturday from 10am to 9pm, Sunday from noon to 7pm; (Union Square) Monday to Saturday from 10am to 8pm, Sunday from 11am to 7pm; (31st Street) Monday to Friday from 10am to 9pm, Saturday from 10am to 8pm, Sunday from noon to 7pm; (33rd and 45th street stores) Monday to Saturday from 10am to 7pm, Sunday from noon to 7pm; (97th Street and Third Avenue stores) Monday to Friday 10am to 10pm, Saturday 10am to 9pm, Sunday 11am to 7pm.
Credit Cards: All major credit cards
   "Nobody beats the Wiz" is their claim. You have 30 days to spot a competitor's ad with a lower price than you paid and you will get the difference back with an additional 10%. There's a bunch of small print in this claim . . . so bring your reading glasses.
   These are "Home Entertainment Centers" so they sell walkmen, TVs, CDs, radios, cameras, Fax machines, computers, camcorders, Nintendo and cartridges, microwave ovens (hey! watch that broccoli defrost, that's entertainment), audio cassettes, and record albums of "yesterday" and today. Oh, they sell video cassettes, too.

CDs, Tapes, Videos & Records

There are teenagers and adults who come to New York with a plan to enlarge their music libraries. Because I have been asked "where?" by so many people I've included the following list:

Bleecker Bob's, 118 W. Third St. (tel. 475-9677)
Dayton's, 799 Broadway, at 11th Street (tel. 254-5084)
Golden Disk, 239 Bleecker St. (tel. 255-7899)
House of Oldies, 35 Carmine St. (tel. 243-0500)
It's Only Rock n' Roll, 49 W. Eighth St. (tel. 777-7090)
Jazz Record Center, 135 W. 29th St., 12th floor (tel. 594-9880)
Revolver Records, 43 W. Eighth St. (tel. 982-6760)
Rocks in Your Head, 157 Prince St. (tel. 475-6729)
Second Coming, 235 Sullivan St. (tel. 228-1313)
Vinylmania, 41, 60, and 43 Carmine St. (tel. 463-7120)

These are the places with 45s, records of all kinds, and albums you thought were lost forever.

For video's, **Blockbuster** is all over town. But we all know the closest rental center is the best.

Colony Record and Tape Center, 1619 Broadway, at 49th Street (tel. 265-2050)
Hours: Monday through Friday from 9:30am to 2am, Saturday from 10am to 1am, Sunday from noon to midnight
Credit Cards: All major cards

The specialties at Colony are their Golden Oldies records and their sheet music. They've been in business for 45 years. This place is, and always has been, frequented by the professional musicians. Must be that sheet music. They also sell audio tapes, CDs, and current records.

Sam Goody, 51 W. 51st St., at Sixth Avenue (tel. 246-8730), and 666 Third Ave., at 43rd Street (tel. 986-8480)
Hours: (51st Street) Monday through Friday from 9am to 9pm, Saturday from 10am to 6pm, and Sunday from noon to 5pm; (Third Avenue) Monday to Friday from 9am to 8pm, Saturday from 10am to 7pm, Sunday from noon to 5pm
Credit Cards: AE, MC, V

Videotapes, sheet music, records, cassettes, accessories, and compact discs. In depth—that's for sure.

HMV, 86th Street and Lexington Avenue (tel. 348-0800), and 72nd Street and Broadway (tel. 751-5900)
Hours: Monday to Thursday from 10am to 10pm, Friday and Saturday till midnight, Sunday from 11am to 7pm
Credit Cards: All major cards accepted
HMV is the British firm His Master's Voice. They are here to knock the socks off Tower. Space-wise the 86th Street store with its 40,000 square feet claims to have pulled this off. It has high-tech decor, wide aisles, and an escalator. There are listening spots for classical music, and booths and headphones in the pop-music area. HMV also employs an on-premise DJ. Big selection of everything.

The 72nd Street store is smaller in size than 86th Street but still plenty big.

Prices at HMV and Tower are neck-and-neck. Visit both HMV and Tower and select your top pick.

Tower Records and **Tower Video,** 692 Broadway, at 4th Street (tel. 505-1500 for general information; no video rentals or video sales at this store); 1965 Broadway, at 67th Street (tel. 799-2500 for general information; no video rentals or video sales at this store); 383 Lafayette St., at 4th Street (tel. 505-1166; video rentals only at this store); 1977 Broadway, at 67th Street (tel. 496-2500) (sales and rentals only at this store); 215 E. 86th St., between Second and Third avenues (tel. 369-2500; video sales and rentals only at this store)
Note: Hours are the same at all Tower locations, from 9am to midnight 365 days a year. Rental prices are uniform as well: $2.50 for 24 hours. For your first rental, bring a major credit card
As you can see from the addresses, the video stores and the record stores are cheek by jowl. The exception is the E. 86th Street store. This listing should give you an idea of their huge selections in videos (sales and rentals), records, CDs, tapes, and all other musical accoutrements. For further information, here are some telephone numbers: classical music, call 505-1500; cassettes, call 505-1333; videos, call 505-1166; tickets, call 505-1444. The store at 692 Broadway, at 4th Street, has a special department for sales of kids' videos and kids' books. At 383 Lafayette St. are the

cut-rate records and tapes (tel. 505-1500). The bookstore is in the "Shopping for Books" chapter.

Tower has its own publication, *Video Collector*. It includes a section on kids' videos and books. Ask to get on the mailing list. This publication and newspaper ads will announce special buys. Look in these publications for store appearances of rock performers. The big action is at the downtown Broadway store where they have an average of 35,000 customers daily. Ask for your free copy of *Pulse*.

My teenagers consider Tower Records downtown a happening. It is an absolute "must visit" and is followed in popularity only by 47th Street Photo, Inc. (see "Audio and Video Equipment" section in this chapter). Well, we can't all opt for the Metropolitan Museum of Art as a first choice.

CHAPTER 15

Shopping for Books

You can rent books or you can buy books—as long as you have them. Do not, however, lend or borrow *New York City with Kids*. It will turn to ashes.

Hints on Selecting Children's Books

To take the confusion out of selecting children's books: I recommend that you buy *Choosing Books for Children: A Commonsense Guide* by Betsy Hearne, published by Delacorte. The paperback costs $9.95. It has been a most reliable source for 10 years.

Bookstores for Children of All Ages

Argosy Book Store, 116 E. 59th St., between Park and Lexington avenues (tel. 753-4455)
Hours: Monday through Friday from 9am to 6pm (on Saturday from 10am to 5pm, October to April)
Credit Cards: MC, V; $25 minimum

Argosy is for older readers, 8 and up. They have several thousand out-of-print children's books. This will be an experience for your g.c. who has never been exposed to the romance of an old bookstore. There are six floors of books. There are used books. There are bins of prints that range from 25¢ to $10. Give your g.c. time to browse. Encourage him or her to peruse. Remember how your public library smelled when you were a kid? That's Argosy.

Barnes and Noble, 600 Fifth Ave., at 48th Street (tel. 765-0590 for recorded information), general information (tel. 633-3300); 105 Fifth Ave., at 18th Street (tel. 807-0099); and the Sale Annex at 128 Fifth Ave., at 18th Street (tel. 807-0099)
Hours: All stores Monday through Friday from 9:30am to 7:45pm, Saturday 9:30am to 6:15pm, Sunday 11am to 5:45pm
Credit Cards: AE, MC, V
Note: The store at 105 Fifth Ave. has textbooks only—no children's materials

The discounts at Barnes and Noble are no secret. The 48th Street store is loaded with well-priced games, records, tapes, pocketbooks, etc. They have dollar books and broken books, too.

If your g.c. is really into books, go to the Sale Annex at 128 Fifth Ave. They have 3,000,000 new and used books and give as much as a 90% discount.

If your kids are over 8, the Jr. Sales Annex has been created for you. It is at 120 Fifth Ave., at 18th Street. The hours are Monday through Friday from 9:30am to 8pm, Saturday until 6:30pm, and Sunday from 11am to 6pm. All of the books for kids 8 to 14 (depending on reading skills, of course) are in one area. This makes life so simple . . . book life, that is. Big selection, low prices, all one would expect of the "world's largest bookstore."

Books of Wonder, 464 Hudson St., at Barrow Street (tel. 645-8006); and 132 Seventh Ave., at 17th and 18th streets (tel. 989-3270)
Hours: Monday through Saturday from 11am to 7pm, and Sunday from noon to 6pm
Credit Cards: AE, DISC, MC, V

The Hudson Street store is cozy and comfortable. Kids feel very at home here. There are well-chosen books and a well-chosen staff to help you make your selections.

The Seventh Avenue store is the largest children's book store on this island. The size is not intimidating, which is remarkable considering the main floor is 1,650 square feet and there are 5,000 books—out-of-print bargains as well as new books. It's done so well. Be sure to get on the mailing list.

The owners, Peter Glassman and James Carey, genuinely care about books and children. The inevitable result is the nicest place in New York to take the kids for books. Why, you might want to go just to amble down memory lane. Many old books and drawings.

Corner Bookstore, 1313 Madison Ave., at 93rd Street (tel. 831-3554)
Hours: Monday through Friday from 10am to 8pm, Saturday from 11am to 6pm, and Sunday from noon to 6pm
Credit Cards: None; cash, checks with ID, and house charge only

A carefully selected stock. This is a fine choice if you want to buy children's books for any age. You'll have no trouble because there are so many books. One third of the books are devoted to kids of all ages.

Personal and friendly service. It's a neighborhood bookstore with a warm feeling. They have lots of happenings here.

B. Dalton, 666 Fifth Ave., at 52nd Street (tel. 247-1740); 396 Sixth Ave., at 8th Street (tel. 674-8780)
Hours: (Fifth Avenue) Monday through Friday from 8:30am to 7pm, Saturday from 9:30am to 6:30pm, and Sunday from noon to 5pm; (Sixth Avenue) Monday through Saturday from 9:30am to midnight; Sunday from 11am to 8pm; (Broadway) Monday through Friday from 8am to 6pm
Credit Cards: AE, DISC, MC, V

The Fifth Avenue Dalton is on two very attractive levels. The children's books are on the lower level. They are mercifully divided into categories: humor, books and cassettes, bedtime stories, and such for the younger children. The older children who are interested in *The Hobbit, Tom Sawyer,* or the Hardy Boys will find their age selections with no difficulty.

The aisles are nice and wide for browsing in comfort, and the overhead lighting is so good that it encourages perusing the contents of the volume in hand.

Doubleday Book Stores, 724 Fifth Ave., at 56th Street (tel. 397-0550 for the children's department); 777 Third Ave., at 49th Street (tel. 888-5590); Citicorp Center, at Lexington Avenue and 53rd Street (tel. 223-3301); and at the South Street Seaport, Fulton Market Building, Fulton and Front streets, second floor (tel. 571-1284)

Hours: (Fifth Avenue) Monday through Saturday from 9am to midnight and Sunday from noon to 5pm; (Third Avenue) Monday through Friday 8:30am to 7pm, Saturday 11am to 6pm, Sunday noon to 5pm; (Citicorp) Monday through Friday from 8am to 9pm, Saturday 11am to 7pm, Sunday noon to 6pm; (Seaport) Monday through Saturday from 10am to 7pm, Sunday 11am to 6pm
Credit Cards: AE, DISC, MC, V

There are four floors of books and records at the 724 Fifth Ave. store. The lighting is good, displays are well organized, and there are lots of children's books. One must feel deep respect for a bookstore that stays open until midnight. That way you buy a book when you know you and your older kids can't sleep.

Eeyore's Books for Children, 25 E. 83rd St., between Fifth and Madison avenues (tel. 988-3404); and 2212 Broadway, between 78th and 79th streets (tel. 362-0634)

Hours: (East Side) Monday through Saturday from 10am to 6pm; Sunday from noon to 5pm; (West Side) Tuesday, Wednesday, Friday, and Saturday from 10am to 6pm, Monday and Thursday till 8pm, and Sunday from 10:30am to 5pm
Credit Cards: AE, MC, V

Eeyore's specializes in children's books, posters, and stuffed animals. This is a bookshop exclusively for children. Oh, there are some books on "parenting," but heaven knows that's child-related.

Keep in touch with Eeyore's for story hours. On Sunday (September through May) they have storytelling hours from 11am to 12:30pm, but you must call to confirm.

Twice a year Eeyore's puts out a calendar of events for children. Call to be put on their mailing list.

Endicott Booksellers, 450 Columbus Ave., at 81st Street (tel. 787-6300)

Hours: Tuesday through Saturday from 10am to 9pm, and Sunday and Monday from noon to 8pm
Credit Cards: AE, MC, V
  A large selection of children's books that "spur the imagination"—classics, fairy tales, mythology, and more. If your g.c. has never been exposed to the sight of a signed first edition, introduce him or her to Endicott.

  Forbidden Planet, 227 E. 59th St., between Second and Third avenues (tel. 751-4386); and 821 Broadway, at 12th Street (tel. 473-1576)
Hours: (59th Street) 11:30am to 8:30pm daily; and (Broadway) Monday through Saturday from 10am to 7pm, Sunday from noon to 7pm
Credit Cards: All major cards
  Science-fiction book specialists. Fairy tales, mythology, the classics, too. They have comic books from the 1930s until tomorrow. Original illustrations that have to be seen to be believed. You'll love it, and so will the kids. Action figures, robots, Gobots, Masters of the Universe abound. As was said by Claude Rains in *Casablanca,* "round up the usual suspects" and take them to Forbidden Planet. No time whistle on browsing time prior to purchase—or nonpurchase. Nice people at Forbidden Planet.

  Rand-McNally Map Store, 150 E. 52nd St., between Lexington and Third avenues (tel. 758-7488)
Hours: Monday through Friday from 9am to 6pm, and Saturday from 11am to 4pm
Credit Cards: AE, MC, V
  They publish their own children's books, and sell books of other publishers as well. These books are map related.
  This is a sight to see. This beautiful store must have every map known to man. And an intense collection of guidebooks as well. Please look up. There's a globe hanging from the ceiling that's beyond impressive.

  Science Fiction Bookshop, 163 Bleecker St., between Sullivan and Thompson streets, second floor (tel. 473-3010)

Hours: Monday through Saturday from 11:30am to 6:45pm, and Sunday from noon to 6pm
Credit Cards: MC, V

Again, a place for the older g.c. who is really a SF aficionado. A super selection of books on the subject. They also have fantasy books.

Shakespeare & Co., 2259 Broadway, at 81st Street (tel. 580-7800); and 716 Broadway, at Washington Place (tel. 529-1330)
Hours: (2259 Broadway) Monday to Thursday and Sunday from 10am to 11:30pm, Friday and Saturday till 12:30am; (716 Broadway) Monday to Thursday and Sunday from 10am to 11pm, Friday and Saturday till midnight
Credit Cards: AE, MC, V; $25 minimum

I have not been to Shakespeare & Co. downtown. Let me tell you about the uptown store where I am a frequent customer. This place has every book for which you've been searching; 60,000 volumes last count. The first floor has a children's section that is stuffed to overflowing. The store has an old-world charm enhanced by ladders that roll so that some helpful salesperson can reach the top shelves.

This is a wonderful bookstore and it has lots of space upstairs and downstairs. They have a section for resource books on every phase of parenting that is excellent. Shakespeare uptown is terrific.

Storyland, 1369 Third Ave., at 78th Street (tel. 517-6951); and 379 Amsterdam Ave., at 78th Street (tel. 769-2665)
Hours: (Third Avenue) Monday through Saturday from 10am to 6pm, and Sunday from 11am to 6pm; (Amsterdam Avenue) Monday and Wednesday to Saturday from 11am to 7pm, Tuesday to 8pm, Sunday to 6pm
Credit Cards: AE, MC, V

This is a well-stocked, small bookstore. They also have videos and cassettes that are blessedly age-appropriate and tasteful. Kids like the intimacy of the space as well as the inventory. I like their helpful, patient attitude.

Every Sunday they have a story hour; 12:30pm at the Amsterdam Avenue store and 1pm at the Third Avenue store.

The Strand Bookstore, Inc., 828 Broadway, at 12th Street (tel. 473-1452)

Hours: Monday through Friday from 9:30am to 9:20pm, Saturday from 9:30am to 6:20pm, and Sunday from 11am to 6pm

Credit Cards: AE, DISC, MC, V

There are two valid reasons to visit the Strand Bookstore with your teenagers. First, this is the largest store for used books in the entire world. It has used books for all ages. Second, it remains in the area of New York City that was the original center for book publishing. The Strand is a very exciting, wonderful place that seethes with New York history. The selection is unending and the prices are super. (I almost forgot to tell you!)

Tower Books, 4th and Lafayette streets, above Tower Video (tel. 228-5100)

Hours: 365 days a year, from 9am to midnight

Credit Cards: AE, MC, V

30% off all bestsellers (that usually means one *Waldo* or another), 20% off all hardbacks, 10% off all paperbacks. The children's section is one of the best organized I've ever seen; all series books, The Hardy Boys, for example, are together.

The lighting in this store is terrific. The inventory is deep. The displays are faultless. Chances are excellent they will have the books you are looking for at the right price. However, if you need assistance in making a selection because you don't know too much about kids books, you had better head over to Books of Wonder.

Traveller's Bookstore, 22 W. 52nd St. (75 Rockefeller Plaza) (tel. 664-0995)

Hours: Monday through Friday from 9am to 6pm, Saturday from 11am to 5pm

Credit Cards: AE, MC, V

This is not a shop for kids; they simply reap the benefits of all you learn from Traveller's. "For travellers who read and readers who travel" is the statement of the charming owners of this highly specialized shop. However obscure the place you plan to visit, they have the perfect book. They have fiction and nonfiction relating to each country. Good books for planning family travel. These books have been read by the owners, who will give you a fast review of every book. They also stock small and practical travel accessories.

If you are a serious traveler who knows the importance of a good guidebook, visit the Traveller's Bookstore or write for their elegant catalog. An astounding collection of books in a small shop. The service here is not personal—it's downright intimate.

Waldenbooks, 57 Broadway (tel. 269-1139); 931 Lexington Ave. (tel. 249-1327); 270 Park Ave. (tel. 370-3758); and 55 Water St. (tel. 425-6055); 600 Columbus Ave. (tel. 874-5090)

The locations are all at strategic points. Because there are so many stores, please call for the hours—they differ.

Waldenbooks, the largest national chain, has a tremendous selection. It also has the 60 Plus Book Club. If you know someone in this age group, write c/o Waldenbooks, 201 High Ridge Rd., Stamford, Connecticut 06904, for free membership. On Tuesday or Wednesday, the holder of the membership card saves 10% to 15% on any purchase at Waldenbooks. There are 1,200 stores nationwide.

Not Just a Bookstore

Citybooks, Municipal Building, 1 Centre St., at Chambers Street (tel. 669-8245)

Hours: Monday through Friday from 9am to 5pm
Credit Cards: None
Note: For a catalog, write to Citybooks, New York City Department of General Services, 2223 Municipal Building, New York, NY 10007

A very special place for an authentic souvenir of New York. For those old enough to understand the meaning of "authentic," this is the place to buy a special something to remember New York.

The word *book* belies what's really found on the 22nd floor of this building. Every book ever printed about every phase of the City of New York—from the charter through a directory of women's organizations—is here. For us? Great maps. A walking-tour guide. A guide to city landmarks.

And it only gets better. Cast-iron city seals from the West Side Hwy. (circa 1937) weigh in at 65 pounds. Songs of New York, T-shirts, notes, totes, and obsolete tokens. And what kid wouldn't love a New York City traffic sign? Aluminum or cardboard, $35 and $15, respectively.

For those kids who understand authentic and abhor the words *unauthorized reproduction*, you're home.

Note: See the listing in Chapter 13.

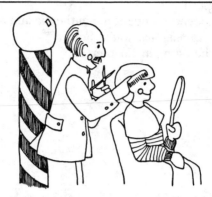

CHAPTER 16

Haircuts for Boys and Girls of All Ages

If you think your g.c. looks, well, unkempt and you think he needs new clothes, look again. He or she might need a haircut and not a new wardrobe!

Astor Place Hair Designers, 2 Astor Pl., between Broadway and Lafayette Street (tel. 475-9854)

Hours: Monday through Saturday from 8am to 8pm, and Sunday from 9am to 6pm

Prices: Adults and kids pay the same prices, $10 for boys $12 for girls

My tongue is firmly planted in my cheek. If your g.c. is old enough to consider going "punk" or really needs an outrageous "Bart Simpson"—you're on a roll. The lines are forever. The price is right. The work is skilled.

Here's a perk. You can buy spray-on hair colors at Unique Clothing Company, a few doors south, on Broadway. It washes out with a shampoo. You'd better get a written note from home before you take your g.c. on this junket. The perfect way never to speak to his or her parents again. Think about it! Be sure you look in the window for one of the great Off-Broadway shows.

Michael's Children's Haircutting Salon, 1263 Madison Ave., between 90th and 91st streets (tel. 289-9612)
Hours: Monday through Saturday from 9am to 5pm
Prices: $20 for kids and adults (no shampoos)

They accept appointments, but these are not necessary. This is the kind of place you thought no longer existed. They have little horses and cars for the kids to sit in while being shorn.

Shooting Star Hair Parlour at FAO Schwarz, 767 Fifth Ave., between 58th and 59th streets (tel. 758-4344)
Hours: Tuesday through Saturday from 10am to 5:30pm, and Sunday from noon to 5pm
Prices: $20 and up
Note: Prices include a shampoo and conditioner

Good luck on your walk through the store to get to Shooting Star. You'd better leave extra time for this stroll. Appointments are a must.

Short Cuts, 104 W. 83rd St., between Amsterdam and Columbus avenues (tel. 877-2277)
Hours: Tuesday through Saturday from 10am to 6pm
Prices: Children, $8.70; child and one parent, $34.50

"Kids are our specialty," to quote the owner. It sure looks it! There is a play area complete with TV, VCRs, and a bunch of things to play with. They also sell boys' and girls' sportswear, sizes 4 to 6X. If you have nothing to do while your youngster is getting trimmed, you can buy something from the hair accessory line.

Not only do they give great cuts but the kids will look forward to them. Appointments are advisable. Unless you have the urge to socialize, avoid Saturday mornings because it's the busiest time slot.

CHAPTER 17

Eating All Around New York, But Not Around a Table

Many of the following listings do not have hours or cross streets because they are not destinations, but places to bump into along the way. These are hints.

Bagel Bonanza

Should you pass any place that begins with the word *bagel* and you and your youngster require a little something to keep body and soul intact before or after you eat, go in and sample the offerings, or try one of the following places, or any of the hundreds of others for a nosh-to-go. You may also sit and eat in some of these bagel boutiques.

🍎 **Ess-A-Bagel,** 359 First Ave., at 21st Street

🍎 **Bagels & Everything,** 51 Spring St., at Mulberry Street

🍎 **Bagels on the Square,** 7 Carmine St., at Bleecker Street

🍎 **The Bagel Place,** 55 West 56th Street, near Sixth Avenue

Eating on the Street—from Pushcarts

This is so New York—your g.c. will have to have a go. When the weather is fair to good, you'll find food carts in ready position on 48th Street and the west side of Sixth Avenue.

There are roughly 9,000 licensed food vendors in the five boroughs. You'll have a chance to sample Italian sausage, Chinese noodles, Jewish knishes, Mexican tacos, German bratwurst, Indian samosas, Philadelphia cheese steaks, Japanese tempura, Caribbean roti, Argentinean empanadas, and New York cheesecake. You'll find carts all over town. Let me recommend the steak-on-a-stick sold on the corner of 62nd Street and Madison Avenue in the heart of the high-rent district.

Ice Cream on the Move

🍎 **Ben and Jerry's Homemade Ice Cream Inc.,** 41 Third Ave., at 30th Street (tel. 995-0109), 327 Sixth Ave. at 4th Street (tel. 929-9175), 187 Columbus Ave., between 68th and 69th streets (tel. 787-0265).
Hours: Daily from 11am to 12:30am. 2323 Broadway at 84th Street (tel. 874-4556). *Hours:* Daily from 11am to 12:30am, Friday and Saturday till 1am.

If undecided, try the Heath bar chocolate mixture made by these two great guys from Vermont.

🍎 **Häagen-Daz Ice Cream Shop,** 313A Columbus Ave., between 72nd and 73rd streets (tel. 877-3200)
Hours: Daily from 11:30am to 11:30pm

Need I describe the richest ice cream around? Frozen yogurt, too. For H-D addicts, see the NYNEX white pages for shop locations.

Le Glacier, 1022 Madison Ave., between 78th and 79th streets

Hours: Monday through Saturday from 11am to 7pm, and Sunday from noon to 7pm

After doing the Museum Mile, a good spot for a cool-down ice cream. There's also yogurt to drip down your face while looking in the shop windows on Madison Avenue.

Lexington Candy Shop, 1226 Lexington Ave., at 83rd Street (tel. 288-0057)

They've been in business for 67 years and the shop is still owned by the same family. It has a real ice cream soda fountain and booths. What they dish up are absolutely the best ice cream sodas and sundaes. You're gonna love it.

Original Chinatown Ice Cream Factory, 65 Bayard St., near Elizabeth Street

If you like almond cookies, try the matching ice cream. Litchi, ginger, green tea, red bean, coconut, to name but a few of the exotic flavors. You can't go wrong at this factory.

Tofutti Shop, 336 Columbus Ave., at 76th Street (tel. 874-1564)

Hours: Sunday through Thursday from 8am to 11pm, and Friday through Sunday from 11am to midnight

Pick it up, and slurp away.

Knishes to Nosh

Yonah Schimmel Knishery, 137 E. Houston St., between First and Second avenues (tel. 477-2858)

Hours: 8am to "about" 6pm daily

If you're on the Lower East Side, don't miss the opportunity to sample the ultimate in walking and eating pleasure. A knish from Yonah Schimmel is an experience. Potato, kasha, whatever.

If you don't know what a knish is, if you don't know what kasha is, if you don't know what Yonah Schimmel is—you've never been to New York.

All Around New York—Candy, Candy

🍎 **Economy Candy Market,** Rivington Street, between Essex and Ludlow streets (tel. 254-1531)
Hours: Sunday through Friday from 8am to 6pm, Saturday till 5pm
Credit Cards: MC, V; $25 minimum

From a nickel (do you remember a nickel?) on up. This place opened in 1937 with the same owners for more than 50 years. They call this a "nosher's paradise, everything and anything."

What they have are all the old-time candies. I would elucidate, but the pages would get wet from saliva. Candy, nuts, dried fruits, health foods.

This is the place for "gourmet gluttons." Everything is discount priced—even the name-brand boxes of chocolates. Economy Candy also features homemade dietetic chocolates.

If your g.c. opts for the caviar instead of the dried fruits, you've come to the right place. Pâtés, fruit baskets, jams, and jellies. They mail around the world. A far cry from penny candy. Economy Candy—is a chunk of heaven for anyone with a sweet tooth.

If the Lower East Side is off your beat, you're missing some of the best shopping in New York. However, you can call for their mail-order catalog. The prices are better than correct. Everything is fresh. It's a wonderful place to list in your address book. Keep candy under "E" for emergency.

🍎 **Mutual Dried Fruit Co.,** 127 Ludlow St., between Rivington and Delancey streets (tel. 673-3489)
Hours: Sunday through Friday from 8:30am to 5:30pm
Credit Cards: None; personal checks accepted with ID

Dried fruit indeed. They also have nuts and candies in depth. It's hard to decide what is most satisfying, the products or the prices. Everything is as fresh as tomorrow. Unbelievable buys.

🍎 **Sweet Temptation,** 1070 Madison Ave., at 81st Street (tel. 734-6082)
Hours: Monday through Sunday from 10am to 6pm
Credit Cards: AE, MC, V

They have candies that are wrapped in pretty foil papers and shaped to look like all sorts of things other than candy. They have imported candy and chocolate for the tutored tooth.

And a Convenient Cookie

Mrs. Field's Cookies, 30 Lincoln Plaza, Broadway, between 62nd and 63rd streets (tel. 262-6340)
Hours: Daily from 11am to 9pm
   While wandering around the Lincoln Center neighborhood, a few cookies not only provide a sugar rush but are a nice, cheap bribe for kids. There are many more branches around town. Check the phone book.

Hamburger Eating All Around New York

Burger King
   If you're heading for a neighborhood—and not sure where to eat—check the classifieds for the reliable backup. With this and McDonald's, no child is ever disappointed. Why, it's like having a meal with an old friend.

McDonald's
   Shall I describe the ambience? The cuisine? Will you settle for a bit of trivia? McDonald's has created more millionaires than any other company in America. How do you like that nugget, chicken? With kids not old enough to have discovered "dining"—it's sure-fire. Let your fingers do the walking for the nearest, dearest McD.
   Do note the branch at 47 W. 57th St., between Fifth and Sixth avenues. State-of-the-arch McDonald's. Had you not been alerted, you'd never recognize this as McD's. Two floors of bathed-in-blue glamour, punctuated with red neon. To live in this neighborhood, you'd better be chic. McDonald's pulled it off.

Hot Dog!

If you're a New Yorker, you call them "frankfuhtas." Remember the street vendors. Don't even think about the ingredients—just bite into the real taste of New York.

Papaya King, 179 E. 86th St., at Third Avenue.
Hours: Monday through Thursday from 8am to 1am, Friday and Saturday till 3am, Sunday from 9am till 1am

This is nothing more than a hot dog place with a counter and no chairs. They serve the best frankfuhtas in New York. You can have 'em topped with chili, onions, oh—lots of stuff ($1 apiece). Try a papaya drink with this mess (80¢ and up).

On the West Side, try:

Gray's Papaya, 2090 Broadway, corner of 72nd Street
Hours: Monday through Saturday from 8am to 1am or later, Sunday till 11pm

For 50¢, your g.c. can have an all-beef hot dog with all the trimmings; for $1.95, two frankfuhtas *and* a fruit drink.

Pizza Eating All Around New York

Goldberg's Pizzeria, 996 Second Ave., at 52nd Street (tel. 593-2172)
Hours: Daily from noon to 11pm

Everything on these but the old kitchen sink. But I'm sure if you asked, they'd do their best.

John's Pizzeria, 278 Bleecker St., at Jones Street (tel. 243-1680); and 408 E. 64th St., off First Avenue (tel. 935-2895)
Hours: Daily from 11:30am to 11:30pm

John's is the best pizza in New York City. Everyone knows that! You can't buy just a slice, and you won't want to. Divide it on the street if you must keep moving, but both John's have places to sit down and eat.

🍎 **Little Vincent,** 1399 Second Ave., at 73rd Street (tel. 249-0120)

Hours: Daily from 11am on

My young friend Jake Schlang says ". . . all the kids from Wagner Junior High patronize this place because you get a slice and a soda for $1 and it's great pizza." What age group could critique pizza better?

🍎 **Ray's Pizza,** 465 Sixth Ave., at 11th Street (tel. 243-2253)

Hours: Daily from 11am to 2am

There's no way I'm getting into which is the original Ray's. This one is great—and you may buy by the slice.

🍎 **Ray's Pizza of Greenwich Village,** 53 W. 72nd St., on Columbus Avenue (tel. 877-4405)

Hours: Daily from 11am to 2am

The implication is "original" because it says Greenwich Village. You know better. But it is good pizza. A plain large pie (8 slices) costs $11. There are a few tiny tables and stools.

🍎 **Ray's Pizza,** 1330 Third Ave., at 77th Street (tel. 988-3337)

Hours: 10:30am to 3am

And this is good, good pizza, too—8 slices for $11.75. These are but a few. No problem locating more—ask the roundest person you see.

CHAPTER 18

Eating in Restaurants

You will be greeted with joy by any restaurant in town. They are all suffering in this economy. You will see restaurant ads in *The New York Times* and other papers announcing special offers to attract your business—for example. ". . . 12 years and younger eat free . . . one per family." Many restaurants continue to drop their prices and many others close their doors, so call before you go.

This is the complete compilation of New York City restaurants that *welcome* children. There is a large difference between "tolerate" and "welcome." You are genuinely wanted at any place listed here.

I know you hate to read, so I'll make this brief. If you want to just get meals over with quickly and on the cheap, duck into Food Courts. Look for the green-and-white-checked awnings. They house Roy Rogers, Del Taco, Nathan's, and Dunkin' Donuts. There are 28 in New York. Here are a few locations: 41st Street and 46th Street on Fifth Avenue, Broadway at 50th Street.

There are also the Pepsico Inc. Kentucky Fried Chicken, Pizza

Hut, and Taco Bell combos all over town. Same genre as the Food Courts.

You don't need me to alert you to McDonald's. They are listed in the NYNEX white pages.

A very good bet are the Ottomanelli Cafés. There are 17 of them around town. More information later in this chapter. For locations of Ottomanelli Cafés, call 772-8427.

If you're doing Macy's, the Empire State Building, or Kiddie City, you will be at or near Herald Square. Go to the A&S Plaza at 6th Avenue and 33rd Street. The Eat at the Top spot on the seventh floor has 10 terrific fast-food stalls where you can purchase lunch items and lots of places to sit and eat and enjoy the view. It's fast, cheap, and good.

Another good place to know is Dallas BBQ. You'll find them at key locations: 1265 Third Ave., off 73rd Street (tel. 772-9393); 27 W. 72nd St., off Central Park West (tel. 873-2004); 21 University Place, at 8th Street (tel. 674-4450); and 132 Second Ave., at St. Mark's Place (tel. 777-5574).

They take all major credit cards and they give lots of good eating for little money. The early-bird special costs $7.95 *for two people,* for which you get soup, cornbread, fries, and half a roasted chicken. Two people can't eat at home for that. Everything at the BBQ is good eating.

Tony Roma's is another great place to take the kids. You'll find TRs at the following locations: 26 E. 42nd St., between Fifth and Sixth avenues (tel. 557-7427); 450 Sixth Ave., between 10th and 11th streets (tel. 777-7427); 395 W. Broadway in SoHo (tel. 226-7427); 565 Third Ave., between 37th and 38th streets (tel. 661-7406); 400 E. 57th St., at First Avenue (tel. 421-7427); and Ribs to Go, 1600 Broadway, at 48th Street (tel. 582-3722). See the Tony Roma listing in this chapter for specifics. The hours are different at each branch so you will have to call.

If you have a yen for Japanese food, try Dosanko. This is a chain operation, and the noodles and soups—which the kids like—are cheap. There are about 15 Dosankos, so I'll list just a few; the rest you'll find in the NYNEX white pages. Strategic branches will be found at: 123 West 49th St., between Sixth and Seventh avenues (tel. 245-4090); 24 W. 56th St., between Fifth and Sixth avenues (tel. 757-4339); and 19 Murray St., between Broadway and Church Street (tel. 964-9696). Just stools, bare-bones attractive.

So much for stuffing face, not dining, heaven knows.

For memorable dining experiences take every-age youngsters to the Tavern on the Green, and Saturday or Sunday brunch at Windows on the World. Take 7 and older to Mickey Mantle's and Ed Debevic's. For a sweet repast, take the toddlers to age 5 to Rumplemayer's, and age 4 to forever to Serendipity. Ten years and older find the Hard Rock Café awesome. If you're in the Broadway theater district, all-age kids do well at Hamburger Harry's, a reliable pit stop. These and other fine suggestions are listed later in this chapter.

Every restaurant in town is yearning for you and your kids over 12. Check upscale bistros like Tavern on the Green for pre-theater dinners; these are far less expensive than the same meals served later in the evening. Management will not ask to see your tickets (smile).

If you are going to a restaurant with little kids, tuck some crackers and carrot sticks in your bag before you leave home. If they are impatient at the table, present these for their first appearance. Snacks used earlier in the day have lost their novelty. Waiting for rolls and butter is tough on kids. A pad, crayons, and little toys help bridge the waiting time nicely.

Now on to the main listings. I visited, tasted, and talked with owners or managers at each of the following places. I always asked the same question: "Do you want children to come here?" If the answer was "yes," I pushed. "I don't mean will you tolerate kids. I mean will you welcome kids?" With two "yes" answers and considered reflection on the food and the prices, I made these choices.

For attentive restaurant service, avoid peak hours.

Lower Manhattan

Lower Manhattan includes (from south to north) the Financial District, Chinatown, Tribeca, the Lower East Side, Little Italy,

SoHo, NoHo, Greenwich Village, and the East Village. This is a general description—very general.

Bayamo, 704 Broadway, north of 4th Street (tel. 475-5151)
Hours: Daily from 11:30am to midnight
Credit Cards: All major cards
Price Range: $8.95 to $16.95
Children's Services: Booster seats available, diaper change possible

This is the "home of Chino-Latino" cuisine. It sounds good and it tastes good. Big, softly lit, nice murals, full of music and great-looking young people. You can't go wrong here. And they like kids!

If you want to do it on the cheap, you can have rice and beans. The food is excellent. There are 200 items on the menu to choose from and they change this list every three weeks.

Because it's big, it's noisy, it's glitzy, and it swings; your kids over 7 will like it; teenagers will love it. At dinner the din will be a bit intimidating for little ones.

The Corner Bistro, 331 W. 4th St., at Jane Street (tel. 242-9502)
Hours: Daily from noon to 4am
Credit Cards: None
Price Range: Very cheap
Children's Services: No booster seats, diaper change available

This is the best of g.c. fare. Only hamburgers, fries, and chili. It's very good lunchtime eating. Open seven days a week until 4am. Nighttime there's a different crowd due to a swingin' bar.

The Cottonwood Café, 415 Bleecker St., between Bank and W. 11th streets (tel. 924-6271)
Hours: Monday through Friday from 11am to 3pm and 5 to 11:45pm, Saturday from 10am to 4pm and 5 to 11:45pm, and Sunday from 10am to 4pm and 5:30 to 11pm
Credit Cards: None
Price Range: Lunch from $5 to $7; dinner from $9 to $14
Children's Services: Booster seats available, no diaper change

Famous for frozen margaritas for the over-21 crowd (us). Southwestern cuisine and chicken-fried steaks are fine eatin'. There are pancakes for your less adventurous eater. Come here for brunch—and come early to avoid a wait. The evening country music is a bit loud for these old ears, and the management is not looking for kids in the evening. Brunch Saturday and Sunday only.

Cowgirl Hall of Fame, 519 Hudson St., corner of 10th Street (tel. 633-1133)

Hours: Daily for lunch from noon to 4pm, for dinner from 5pm to midnight; brunch on Saturday and Sunday from 11:30am to 3:45pm

Price Range: Lunch entrees from $3 to $8.95 for kids, from $5 to $9 for regular portions; dinner from $10 to $16

Credit Cards: AE

Children's Services: High chairs, booster seats, diaper change possible

The kids can order wooden-nickel pancakes with a wooden nickel on top on the Sunday brunch special for $4.50. You or the bigger kids may prefer fried chicken or chicken-fried steak with mashed potatoes for $6.95. The regular children's menu is huge, and the kids get crayons and such to keep them busy while they're waiting.

The theme and the look is Wild West. Leather saddles, antelope chandeliers, cowboy memorabilia. The Cowgirl Hall of Fame is a find.

Delmonico's, 56 Beaver St., near William Street, 2 blocks south of Wall Street (tel. 422-4747)

Hours: Monday through Friday from 7am to 9pm

Price Range: $15 to $30 for entrees

Credit Cards: All major cards

Children's Services: No booster seats or high chairs, no diaper changes

This 152-year-old restaurant is for kids 8 and older. The youngsters, and you, will get a fabulous tour with your dinner. See the secret panels in the kitchen, see where Charles Dickens ate his dinners. This is the restaurant where Baked Alaska and Lobster Newburgh were created. The food, I might add, is as fabulous as the history.

When you make your reservations, you must tell Jackie—or whoever answers the phone—that you want to go on the kitchen tour.

🍎 **Ed Debevic's,** 661 Broadway, between Bleecker and Bond streets (tel. 982-6000)

Hours: Opens all days at noon, closes Monday through Thursday at midnight, Friday and Saturday at 1am, and Sunday at 10pm.

Credit Cards: MC, V

Price Range: $5.95 to $7.95 for entrees, about $10 for dinner

Note: The humor of this restaurant is lost on the high-chair and diaper crowd, and the inevitable wait is tedious with babies; it's for kids 7 and up

Ed's place is pronounced DUH-buh-vick's. Ed himself is a mythical, beer drinking, one-night-a-week bowler who likes stick-to-the-ribs food and a good time. If you're from Chicago, Phoenix, L.A., or Osaka you're already familiar with Ed's. If this is your first visit, you are in for a big treat.

This is a Fifties' diner decorated with lots of neon, smart sayings, posters, lava lamps, and pins for you and the kids. The well-trained waiter/actors are costumed in period garb and each is a distinct character. Not one of them ever breaks stride, or does or says anything not consistent with his or her role. All are perfect in their parts and super-fast in getting the food to your booth, where they often sit and dish with you.

The food is great, with lots of menu items from the steam-table at your old high-school cafeteria. They call it meat loaf here, but you've never tasted it this good before. The chicken and ribs are terrific, the salad bar is huge and stocked with only the fresh-est and crispiest greens. Best of all are the desserts—brownies, cakes, and the world's smallest sundae (it's three bites and costs 49¢).

There is seating for 475 people and the tables turn over about every 45 minutes. Needless to say, the lines move fast and the crowds remain cheerful due to the ambience.

The place is an absolute hoot!

🍎 **Elephant and Castle,** 68 Greenwich Ave., at 11th Street and Seventh Avenue (tel. 243-1400)

Hours: Monday through Thursday from 8:30am to midnight, Friday and Saturday from 10am to 1am, and Sunday from 11am to midnight

Credit Cards: All major cards

Price Range: lunch entrees $7; dinner $8 to $12
Children's Services: Booster seats available; no diaper change (no space—do it on the floor for this place)

The food is fine—superb burgers and divine omelets. The kids will get lots of attention—management likes them. A happy, hip spot. I promise that you'll end up comfortable and well fed, too. There's an Elephant and Castle in SoHo, too, at 183 Prince St. between MacDougal and Sullivan streets.

Ferrara's, 195 Grand St., between Mulberry and Mott streets (tel. 226-6150)
Hours: Daily from 8am to midnight
Credit Cards: None
Price Range: Moderate
Children's Services: Booster seats available, diaper change possible

This institution in Little Italy has been here forever! Gelati, cannoli, and dozens of different pastries are the only foods served here. Coffee for us, a cold drink for the kids—what could be better? Old European atmosphere, conversations in many languages, groceries, and the sound of the cash register. Relax, shift your gear into low, and all of you will feel ready to start walking with a quickened step.

Fraunces Tavern Restaurant, 54 Pearl St., at Broad Street (tel. 269-0144)
Hours: Monday through Friday from 7:30 to 10:15am, 11:30am to 4pm, and 5 to 9:15pm
Credit Cards: All major cards
Price Range: $25 to $30 at dinner
Children's Services: No booster seats, diaper change possible

Let's be clear. They welcome children in the morning and afternoon. Forget dinner. This is the "oldest continuously operated restaurant in New York." And they're proud of it. It seethes with history. It's a scant 2-block walk to the ferry that will take you to the Statue of Liberty. Is all this damning with faint praise? Not meant to be. Your comfort is my desire.

Breakfast and lunch are, as the kids say, "cool" (but a tad pricey). The food is regional American with specialties like Carpetbagger Steak and Baked Chicken à la Washington (this is where he gave his Farewell Address). Wonder what he ate with wooden teeth.

Hee Seung Fung (a/k/a HSF), 46 Bowery, south of Canal Street (tel. 374-1319)
Hours: Daily from 7:30am to midnight
Credit Cards: None
Price Range: Inexpensive to moderate
Children's Services: Booster seats available, diaper change difficult but possible
The perfect spot for tasty dim sum. There are less expensive places—but HSF is good, reliable, and clean. And not that much more expensive. All ages.

Katz's Delicatessen, 205 E. Houston St., at the corner of Ludlow Street (tel. 254-2246)
Hours: Daily from 7am to 11pm
Price Range: Inexpensive
Credit Cards: AE (on orders of $50 or more only)
Children's Services: High chairs, no booster seats, no diaper change possible
I had to include this place because it's part of history. At the same spot since the early 1940s and still attracting crowds. During World War II they sent "a salami to your boy in the army"—and they will still ship their deli items anywhere.
Sandwiches as thick as your fist, hot dogs (with or without sauerkraut), and all the standard deli fare. If you're into neatness (salt and pepper shakers on every table, filled napkin holders, and tidy sandwiches), this place is not for you, but if you want great pastrami and Lower East Side ambience you'll love Katz's. If you're doing this part of town, why not?
When I asked about a place to change a diaper, the answer was "With all these tables, you gotta ask?" That's only one of the reasons I am devoted to Katz's. It's earthy, it's real, the food is good, and it's cheap.

Manhattan Chili Company, 302 Bleecker St., between Barrow and Grove streets, just off Seventh Avenue (tel. 206-7163)
Hours: Sunday through Thursday from 11:30am to midnight, Friday and Saturday till 1am
Price Range: $5.95 to $8.95 for entrees
Credit Cards: MC, V
Children's Services: No high chairs, booster seats, diaper change

It's a chili parlor with Santa Fe decor. You know—armadillos, deserts, etc. They have a special children's menu that feature such daily offerings as chili with three toppings, grilled hot dogs, fried potatoes, a crunchy vegetable plate, or margarita pie; dessert could be a chocolate banana or tortilla cake—all for (brace yourself) $3.95!. And they have alcohol-free piña coladas. Hamburgers and pastas are on the menu as well. In the clement months (as opposed to inclement months), you may eat in their garden.

Good, cheap eats.

Minter's, Battery Park City, 4 World Financial Center, 250 Vesey St. (tel. 945-4455)
Hours: Monday through Friday from 6am to about 9pm, and Saturday and Sunday from 9am to about 8:30pm
Credit Cards: None
Price Range: Moderate
Children's Services: No boosters or high chairs; wheel the stroller to the table; diaper change in ladies' lounge, same level

Located in the courtyard, it is self-service. There are chairs and tables. "Oh, we really love to have children here, really," said the charming young woman in charge. The menu affirms her statement. Waffles, plain, with fruit, or with an ice cream sundae topping are from $2 to $5. The health bar has yogurt, fruit, and fruit juices. The cones are encrusted with chocolate. The cones are not friends of mine—they are the receptacles to hold the ice cream.

Minter's menu reads "fun food & drink." The food is very good; the menu is mercifully limited. The fun is to sit in this magnificent courtyard, admire the marble floors in designs and earth colors, look up at the glass roof, and feel like royalty.

NoHo Star, 330 Lafayette St., at Bleecker Street (tel. 925-0070)
Hours: Monday through Friday from 8am to midnight, Saturday from 10:30am to 12:30am, and Sunday from 11am to 11pm
Credit Cards: All major cards
Price Range: $7 to $15
Children's Services: No booster seats, diaper change possible

They are famous for their unique, eclectic menu. It's large in scope. In the daytime there are hamburgers and omelets. At night they feature many Chinese specialties because they have a Chinese chef—evenings only. A high recommendation from *moi* and assorted kids. "This is such a cool place!"

Oriental Pearl Restaurant, 103–105 Mott St., between Canal and Hester streets (tel. 219-8388)
Hours: Monday through Friday from 8am to 3pm, Saturday and Sunday till 4pm
Price Range: Inexpensive (about $10 for an adult)
Credit Cards: None

For the dim sum experience—and why not?—this is a good choice. The place is good for kids because there are tanks with frogs and fish and turtles. They will love the dim sum because the courses are frequent and small. Attentive waiters will keep wheeling them to your table, and the kids will "eat up good." The staff is kindly.

Why not Chinatown while it's still light? There are absolutely delightful little, little shops with lots of funny things kids like—tiny slippers, tricks, wind chimes, and lots of other stuff.

Ottomanelli's Café, 62 Reade St., between Church Street and Broadway (tel. 349-3430)
Hours: Daily from 10:30am to 8:30pm
Credit Cards: AE
Price Range: $5 to $9 for entrees; 10-inch pizzas cost $5.95
Children's Services: High chairs and space to change a diaper

I am very enthusiastic about all the Ottomanelli Cafés because the quality of their food is high and their prices are low. These little restaurants are super-clean. Attitude—a 1990s word—is very positive here.

Bryan Miller, restaurant critic of *The New York Times,* gave their hamburger four stars. It is $4.95 and is served with cross-hatch fries, lettuce, tomato, and pickle. The menu also features chicken, pasta, ribs, Buffalo chicken wings, and other good stuff.

Phoenix Garden, 46 Bowery, at Elizabeth Street—this is in an arcade, you have to look for it (tel. 962-8934)
Hours: Daily from 11:30am to 10:30pm
Credit Cards: None
Price Range: Moderate; $5.25 and up for entrees

Children's Services: No booster seats, high chairs, or place for a diaper change

This is sure-fire, consistent, Chinatown Cantonese. The food is so good Phoenix Garden attracts crowds. Mostly families.

Nora Chu, the manager, is delightful. She assured me "nursing mothers are welcome," and "we could find a spot to change a diaper."

Pizza Piazza, 785 Broadway, at 10th Street (tel. 505-0977)
Hours: Monday through Thursday and Sunday from 11:45am to 11:30pm, and Friday and Saturday from 11:45am to 12:30am
Credit Cards: AE, MC, V
Price Range: Moderate
Children's Services: High chairs, booster seats, diaper change possible; stroller storage available

Pizzas come in 6 inches, 9 inches, and 12 inches; the 12-inch deep-dish pizza serves four people. The prices range from $5.95 to $18.95. They use only "natural ingredients" in Pizza Piazza pizzas. They also serve hamburgers, salads, pastas, rich desserts, and lots of other stuff.

From Monday through Friday from 11:45am to 3pm they serve a special $6.50 lunch. On Saturday and Sunday they have special brunch from $8.95 and up.

It's attractive, clean, and cheerful. A few blocks away are Union Square, Forbidden Planet, Strand Bookstore, and jumpin' tacky Eighth Street. Good food.

Pizzeria Uno, 55 Third Ave., between 10th and 11th streets (tel. 995-9668); other locations are: 432 Columbus Ave., at 81st Street (tel. 595-4700); 391 Sixth Ave., between 8th Street and Waverly Place (tel. 242-5230); 1 Herald Square, 34th Street and Sixth Avenue (tel. 239-6633)
Hours: Monday through Thursday from 11:30am to 1am, Friday and Saturday from 11:30am to 2am, and Sunday from noon to 1am
Credit Cards: AE, MC, V
Price Range: Inexpensive
Children's Services: Booster seats and high chairs

Deep-dish pizza is the specialty. Heavy, sloppy to eat, and absolutely delicious. If your kids are expecting pizza, you'd better prepare them for the Chicago style served here. A "Watch-a-Ma-Call-It" is a 6-inch pie with anchovies, olives, and tomatoes ($5). This is the only place where I've found pizza skins. They are $4.25 and are lined with potatoes, bacon, and cheese. Nonpizza addicts—if there are any—may choose a hamburger or a cheeseburger, about $4. Buffalo wings for $4.50 are a good choice. A Big Frankie at $3.25 is just that (why do New Yorkers call them "frankfuhtas" and the rest of America calls them hot dogs?).

The kids will not be able to resist a dessert titled Dumb Monkey; it's a banana split for $2.75. The Works is ice cream with fudge, strawberries, and a cookie for $2.65. I know the kids will like Uno because soda is served in pitchers. Cheerful, fun, informal, terrific food, happy service, and cheap.

Ratner's, 138 Delancey St., near Norfolk Street (tel. 677-5588)

Hours: Sunday through Friday from 6am to 10pm, Friday they close at 3pm and reopen Saturday at sundown

Credit Cards: All major cards

Price Range: $3.50 to $14

Children's Services: Booster seats available, diaper change possible

For the prices listed, you can eat your way into oblivion. The trick is not to fill up on bread and rolls. A great place for vegetarians. The blintzes are poetry. The fish is as fresh as tomorrow.

If you want to take your g.c. to the one restaurant that gives the full flavor of New York Jewish cooking, this is the place. It's a dairy restaurant—the food is tahka good. The rolls and bread are beyond words, and there's a bakery counter. Buy before you eat. After you eat you'll never want to see food again. If you're too old to remember the Tip Toe Inn and the C & L, fill up on nostalgia at Ratner's. Don't let the lines scare you away—they flow like chicken fat. Every age will enjoy.

The Royal Canadian Pancake House, 145 Hudson St., between Beach and Hubert streets, 4 blocks south of Canal Street (tel. 219-3038)

Hours: Daily from 7am to 7pm

Credit Cards: None

Price Range: Inexpensive to moderate

Children's Services: Booster seats, sassy seats, place to change a diaper

Breakfast is served here all day long and what a breakfast! Waffles, pancakes, eggs, ham, bacon, and "womelettes"—this is a combination of pancake and omelet, filled with your choice of stuffing stuffs. There are salads, sandwiches, and entrees as well.

The breakfast selections are very, very good. Never tasted the others. The portions are large enough to serve two hungry adults. Share. A full breakfast with bacon and the rest of the trimmings will run about $9.

RCPH attracts a big, friendly crowd of patrons.

Sammy's Famous Roumanian Restaurant, 157 Chrystie St., at Delancey Street (tel. 673-0330 or 673-5526)
Hours: Daily from 3pm to "whenever"
Credit Cards: AE, MC
Price Range: Dining about $40
Children's Services: Booster seats available, diaper change possible, reservations necessary

For an ethnic experience with your older kids, try Sammy's. There is so much food, and so many courses (most unfamiliar), little ones won't have the patience.

In the middle of the table is the seltzer bottle, the U-Bet chocolate syrup, and the milk to make your own—egg creams, of course. Tile floor, friendly waiters, all-size groups, lots of fun. Pitcha (calves' foot jelly), gribenes (what's left after chicken fat is rendered), Roumanian rib steaks, eggplant salad, and on and on.

This is a true Jewish/Roumanian experience. The food is superb eating—standing up afterward is the hard job.

The Second Avenue Kosher Delicatessen, 156 Second Ave., at 10th Street (tel. 677-0606)
Hours: Sunday through Thursday from 11am to midnight, and Friday and Saturday from 11am to 2am
Credit Cards: None
Price Range: $7 to $15
Children's Services: Booster seats available, diaper change possible

You won't be hungry when you leave here—chopped liver, chicken-in-the-pot, corned beef. Maybe the best corned beef in New York. The rye bread is poetry; the mushroom barley soup a symphony. Abe, the owner of the Second Avenue Deli, caters in your home. Why, he has been summoned all over the United States to do big parties for ex–New Yorkers who salivate at the mention of his pastrami. One of the few authentic such establishments in town. Eat here. You and the kids won't be sorry.

The Silver Palace, 50 Bowery, at Canal Street (tel. 964-1204)
Hours: Daily from 8am to 11pm (dim sum and lunch from 8am to 4pm, dinner from 4 to 11pm)
Credit Cards: All major cards for dinner; none for lunch
Price Range: Inexpensive to moderate
Children's Services: Booster seats and high chairs available, diaper change possible
The only Chinese restaurant this side of Hong Kong with an escalator, making you aware of the high quality of the Asian cuisine. They can handle a large crowd or a small crowd—everybody will have a fortunate evening.

Tony Roma's of Greenwich Village, 450 Sixth Ave., between 10th and 11th streets (tel. 777-7427)
Hours: Sunday through Thursday from 11:30am to 10pm, Friday and Saturday from 11:30am to midnight
Credit Cards: AE, DC, MC, V
Price Range: Moderate
Children's Services: Booster seats available, diaper change possible
These Tony Roma's (there are more around town—check the NYNEX white pages) are great for the kids because they serve kids' food—chicken, ribs, and the best mountain of fried onion rings (a whole loaf actually) you've ever wrapped your mouth around. Casual, attentive service—good for us.

Windows on the World, 1 World Trade Center (107th floor) (tel. 938-1111)
Hours: Monday through Saturday from 5 to 10pm for dinner, Saturday from noon to 2:30pm for buffet, and Sunday from noon to 7pm
Credit Cards: All major cards
Price Range: Expensive; $25.50 for buffet
Children's Services: No high chairs or booster seats
The weekend buffet costs $25.50 per person, and kids are

people. Management describes the buffet as "a food festival," and "families are more than welcome." The buffet table is glorious. Bring a camera. The variety and the presentation of the food enhances the taste.

The room is exquisite. The setting is breathtaking. The views one enjoys from the WTC observation deck take on a new dimension when viewed from these lush surroundings. Everything about Windows on the World is first cabin. Book your buffet reservations as early as possible and when you are sure of a clear day.

Dinner runs about $45 and up per person. Luncheon during the week is served to members only. The weekend buffets are the only options for our crowd to dine at Windows on the World.

14th Street to 59th Street—East Side

America, 9 E. 18th St., between Fifth Avenue and Broadway (tel. 505-2110)
Hours: Sunday through Thursday from 11:30am to midnight, and Friday and Saturday from 11:30am to 1am
Credit Cards: All major cards (except DC)
Price Range: $12.95 to $22.95
Children's Services: Booster seats available, diaper change difficult—no changing area but the coat room is possible

A great, big kid's heaven. The food is unusual (lots of funny things) and good eating—even peanut butter and jelly. The specialty is charcoal-grilled meats, and the menu has five times as many listings as there are states in the union. If you want to make an evening of it with your preteen or teenager, America is typical of the big, big social restaurants.

Benihana of Tokyo, 120 E. 56th St., between Park and Lexington avenues (tel. 593-1627); and 47 W. 56th St., between Fifth and Sixth avenues (tel. 581-0930)
Hours: Monday through Friday from noon to 2:30pm for lunch, Monday through Saturday from 5:30 to 10:30pm for dinner, and Sunday from 5 to 10pm for dinner

Credit Cards: All major cards
Price Range: $13.50 to $38.50 per person; prices are the same for lunch as for dinner
Children's Services: Booster seats available, no diaper change

If your children are old enough to sit on a high stool unaided and you want to take them out to dinner, Benihana is a treat. Kids are captivated by the whole business of eating in the round and watching the chef cut, mince, chop, cook, and perform. Sitting with strangers (and you of course) absolutely enthralls the over-5-year-old crowd. Of course it's for tourists—but that's not the mayor with you, it's your g.c. And the food is good. Not cheap.

Broadway Diner, 590 Lexington Ave., at 52nd Street (tel. 486-8838)
Hours: Monday through Friday from 7am to 11pm, Saturday from 8am to 11pm, Sunday brunch from 11am to 4pm
Credit Cards: None; traveler's checks and personal checks with proper ID only
Price Range: $8.95 to $13.95 for entrees, sandwiches $3.50 to $6.50
Children's Services: Booster seats but no high chairs, diaper change possible

It's a diner that is a throwback in time. The walls are tile, the signs are neon, the clock is violet, and the mirrors are blue. Now guess what time period.

Diner-style food to go with the decor. Did they grill fish in diners? They do in this one, and chicken, too.

Cafe Iguana, 235 Park Ave. South, at 19th Street (tel. 529-4770)
Hours: Monday through Friday from 11:30am to 4am, Saturday and Sunday from noon to 4am
Credit Cards: All major cards
Price Range: $7.95 to $21 for entrees, dinner will cost $25 to $35; Kid's Special, $5.95, for kids under 12.
Children's Services: Booster seats, high chairs, space for a diaper change; strollers are fine

The Kid's Special offers a choice—mini-tacos, a burger, a hot dog, or a grilled cheese sandwich and a beverage; dessert is a brownie or ice cream. Well, you can't beat that for $5.95.

The food has a South-of-the-border influence—burritos and enchiladas, for instance. But fish, poultry, grilled meats, and the like are also on the menu.

The place is stunning. The decor was inspired by the movie *Night of the Iguana,* and those Mexican lizards are all over the place. There are terrific murals. Upstairs is the Cancún Room, which features a tropical bar and a stage-set veranda.

El Rio Grande, 160 E. 38th St., between Lexington and Third avenues (tel. 867-0922)
Hours: Daily from noon to 12:30am, Saturday and Sunday brunch from noon to 3:30pm
Credit Cards: All major cards
Price Range: $8.95 to $19.50 for entrees
Children's Services: Booster seats available, no changing facilities

All ages are welcome and reservations are recommended. There is a lovely whimsical quality to this restaurant; the passway through the kitchen that connects this two-room restaurant is called the Rio Grande. The decor is Tex-Mex and so is the food. Tortillas, queso fundido, and fajitas are some of the staples. The food is *muy bueno* and the service is *simpático.*

Forty-First Precinct, 24 E. 41st St., between Fifth and Madison avenues (tel. 679-3565)
Hours: Monday through Friday from 11:30am to 8:30pm
Credit Cards: All major cards
Price Range: $8.95 to $14.50
Note: They don't want little ones! This is strictly for 15 years and older

The name is authentic. This building formerly housed a police station. The waiters wear police-type outfits. The burgers are as great as the place is adorable. You'll find this place arresting.

Friend of a Farmer, 77 Irving Place, between 18th and 19th streets (tel. 477-2188)
Hours: Tuesday through Friday for lunch from 11am and dinner

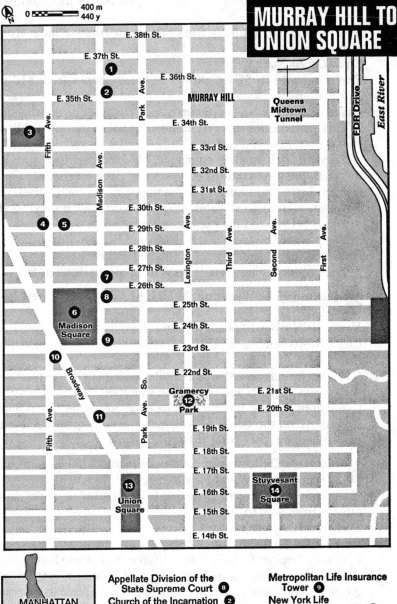

400 m
0
440 y

E. 38th St.
E. 37th St. ①
E. 36th St.
E. 35th St. ②
MURRAY HILL
Queens
Midtown
Tunnel
E. 34th St.
③ E. 33rd St.
E. 32nd St.
E. 31st St.
E. 30th St.
④ ⑤ E. 29th St.
E. 28th St.
⑦ E. 27th St.
⑧ E. 26th St.
⑥ E. 25th St.
Madison
Square E. 24th St.
⑨ E. 23rd St.
⑩ E. 22nd St.
Gramercy E. 21st St.
⑫ Park E. 20th St.
⑪ E. 19th St.
E. 18th St.
E. 17th St.
⑬ E. 16th St. Stuyvesant
Union E. 15th St. ⑭ Square
Square E. 14th St.

Fifth Ave.
Madison Ave.
Park Ave.
Lexington Ave.
Third Ave.
Second Ave.
First Ave.
Broadway
Fifth Ave.
Park Ave. So.

FDR Drive
East River

MANHATTAN
Murray Hill to
Union Square

Appellate Division of the
State Supreme Court ⑧
Church of the Incarnation ②
Church of the Transfiguration ⑤
Empire State Building ③
Flatiron Building ⑩
Gramercy Park ⑫
Madison Square ⑥
Marble Collegiate Church ④

Metropolitan Life Insurance
Tower ⑨
New York Life
Insurance Building ⑦
Pierpont Morgan Library ①
Stuyvesant Square ⑭
Theodore Roosevelt
Birthplace ⑪
Union Square ⑬

from 5 to 10pm, Saturday from 8:30am to 10pm, Sunday from 10am to 3:30pm
Credit Cards: None
Price Range: $6 to $7 for entrees at lunch; dinner from $10 to $14
Children's Services: No booster seats, high chairs, or diaper changes

This is a bakeshop and restaurant. The bakeshop opens at 8am for take-out cake and coffee.

They pride themselves on simple, old-fashioned food such as meatloaf, pot pies, sandwiches, pasta, and duck for dinner. They have no liquor, no smoking, no hamburgers, no french fries, no hot dogs, and no kids' plates. What they do have is good food, modestly priced, and lines until tomorrow.

The place itself is very pretty, enhanced by bountiful baskets of fruits and veggies which are "not to be touched."

The outside dining space is open from spring through fall.

Jackson Hole Wyoming, 531 Third Ave., at 35th Street (tel. 679-3264)
Hours: Daily from 10:30am to 1am
Credit Cards: None
Price Range: $5 to $9
Children's Services: Booster seats available, diaper change possible; they prefer 14 years and older at this location only

You aren't seeing triple (other locations are at 64th and 83rd streets). All on the East Side—all have the same great hamburgers. Grilled, but they cover them while cooking. Juicy!

Kaplan's Delicatessen (at the Delmonico), 59 E. 59th St., between Madison and Park avenues (tel. 755-5959)
Hours: Monday through Saturday from 7:30am to 10pm, and Sunday from 9am to 10pm
Credit Cards: All major cards
Price Range: $9 to $16 for entrees
Children's Services: Booster seats available, no diaper change

This is one of my favorite delis. A favored brunch spot for my g.c. of all ages. (And you thought the Plaza was a place to brunch.) The people are swell and the food is great. Try off-hours to avoid the crowd if you opt for a normal lunch or dinner or late snack hour. The place is large and the line goes fast.

S. Kinder, Fresh Bagel Restaurant, 200 Park Ave. South, between 17th and 18th streets (tel. 982-1767)

Hours: Daily from 7am to 9pm
Credit Cards: None
Price Range: Very inexpensive
Children's Services: Booster seats available

This bakery/restaurant is shiny clean. The neon signs proclaim "take-out"; it's too scrubbed to leave. The room is small, with both table seating and counter service.

The Kinder Kids menu offers a variety of choices. Challah french toast, grilled cheese on bagelettes, two Kinderburgers on bagelettes, and more. One of the above, a beverage, and cookies costs $2.25. That's not a typo—$2.25.

Soups, salads, chicken, and pasta are available at similarly inexpensive prices. Of course there are desserts. It's all good, it's all cheap, and it's all yours. Not fancy, but with kids what is?

If you visit Union Square on a Wednesday or Saturday for the Greenmarket and kids' activities (tel. 860-1811 or 408-0204), this is a good bet.

Oyster Bar and Restaurant, Grand Central Station (lower level), 42nd Street, between Vanderbilt and Lexington avenues (tel. 490-6650)

Hours: Monday through Friday from 11:30am to 9:30pm
Credit Cards: All major cards
Price Range: $8.95 to $25.95; less at the counter
Children's Services: Booster seats available, no diaper change

It's over 70 years old and seems to improve with age. If your g.c. enjoys fish or seafood, may I present the freshest in New York? When you see all the people in and out you'll know why. It moves! The bouillabaisse is outstanding and authentic. Pan-roasted shellfish or any other fish will make you wish you were a commuter to Grand Central. You'd never make it home for dinner. And the desserts—fresh fruit, pies (apple), and cakes are a big treat. There is a huge vaulted ceiling and twinkling lights.

Dining room reservations are a must. Don't turn up your nose at the counter seating. A perk—sit near the chefs and you'll see them prepare the food. If you want more comfortable seating, make your reservation for the tavern, but settle for the main room.

An extra treat for your g.c.: Right in front of the Oyster Bar is a vaulted ceiling where three corridors join together. Have your g.c. stand at one corner of the intersection. You go to the diagonally opposite corner, turn your face to the wall, and speak in a normal voice. Your g.c. will hear every word you say. The explanation? This is known as the Whispering Gallery Effect. Sound waves glance off a curved surface and keep on bouncing across arcs of the surface. They can travel as far as 200 feet.

Rascals Restaurant & Club, 12 E. 22nd St., between Broadway and Park Avenue South (tel. 420-1777)
Hours: Monday through Friday from 11:30am to 1am, open for dinner only on Saturday, closed all day Sunday
Price Range: $12 to $15 for entrees
Credit Cards: AE, DC, MC, V.
Children's Services: Booster seats, diaper change possible
    The kids can play basketball or pool while waiting for their dinner to arrive. The menu is simple American fare which can be mixed and matched in smaller portions for kids. Rascals prides itself on its huge menu selection. Everything from sandwiches and burgers to gourmet dining. It's a fun place.

Roy Rogers Restaurant, 677 Lexington Ave., corner of 56th Street
    Hours: Monday through Friday from 7am to 10pm, Saturday and Sunday from 6am to 10pm (hours may vary at other Roy Rogers locations)
Credit Cards: None
Price Range: Inexpensive
Children's Services: Booster seats available, diaper change difficult but possible
    The reason I list the 56th Street restaurant is because this is the AT&T, IBM, Trump Tower neighborhood, and inexpensive eating places where the kids will feel at home and enjoy the vittles are few and far between.
    Kids' special plate (drumstick, french fries, and a drink) is $2.53. Normal-size burgers are $1.95. Don't overlook the Hot Topped Potatoes, $1.25 to $2.49. The price depends on the stuffin', pardner.

This spread has a Del Taco Mexican Café and upstairs a Houlihan's Restaurant: one of many in this moderate-price restaurant chain.

Roy has the best fried chicken east of the Pecos (the what?). There are many, many locations and they are "growing weekly," as an exec with Reese, the parent company, explained.

Saks Fifth Avenue, Cafe S.F.A. N.Y.C., 8th floor, 611 Fifth Ave., between 49th and 50th streets (tel. 940-4790)
Hours: Open during store hours Monday through Saturday from 10am to 6pm, Thursday till 8pm
Price Range: Special children's meals, none more than $6, sandwiches about $6, salads $8 to $12
Credit Cards: All major cards
Children's Services: High chairs and diaper change possible

If you're shopping the store or doing Rockefeller Center you might opt for lunch here. The menu for "children of all ages" has a Double Dare for $5 (hamburgers and chips), "Rover the Dog" for $4.50 (guess), and "Sesame Street" for $6 (cup of soup, half a turkey and cheese sandwich, and fresh vegetable slices). With each meal you get a minibag of chocolate chip cookies. For the best Cobb salad ever, this is the spot. The breads are fresh and varied and would be a meal in themselves. The "breadless sandwich" is great, but so is everything else they dish up here. The room is handsome and quiet. If you get there early, you'll get a table with a view of Rockefeller Center. If you're in a mad hurry, sit at the counter. You'll enjoy some of the best food in all New York.

Tony Roma's "A Place for Ribs," 400 E. 57th St., between First Avenue and Sutton Place (tel. 421-7427)
Hours: Monday through Thursday from 11:30am to 10pm, Friday from 11:30am to midnight, Saturday from 3pm to midnight, Sunday from 11am to 10pm, and Sunday brunch from 11am to 3pm
Credit Cards: All major cards
Price Range: $9.95 to $22.50 for entrees
Children's Services: Booster seats available

They have a children's menu and take-out. The ribs (beef and pork), chicken, steak, and fish are all super. Get that onion loaf!

Huge restaurant, good food, interested management—and they love kids. Nicely priced. A good spot for baby back ribs and barbecued chicken. And kids, kids, kids!

Wylie's Ribs, 891 First Ave., at 50th Street (tel. 751-0700)
Hours: 11:30am to 1am daily
Credit Cards: All major cards
Price Range: $12 to $18
Children's Services: Booster seats available, diaper change possible
   Very informal. Good spot for kids who like chicken, ribs, and french fries. Go early to avoid the crowds.

60th Street and Up—East Side

Atomic Wings, 1644 Third Ave., at 92nd Street (tel. 410-3800), and 206 Avenue A, at 13th Street (tel. 477-1700)
Hours: Monday through Friday from 11:30am to midnight, Friday and Saturday till 3am
Credit Cards: None
Price Range: Cheap! No dinner over $12
Children's Services: No boosters, high chairs, or diaper changes. This place is for older kids, even if Adam Lippon, the creative owner dispenses free rubber frogs to little ones.
   Atomic Wings advises "parent's discretion." Your almost-teenagers and teenagers are gonna love it here. Sawdust on the floor, pinball machines and other games, Animal House ambience—what's better than that? They have sensational buffalo wings for $4.95, a good chicken sandwich platter (their most expensive item) for $5.95, plus burgers, fries, and all sorts of sandwiches. And everything's great.
   People forever! If you can buck the well-deserved crowds, do it.

Brother Jimmy's Bar-B-Que, 1461 First Ave., at 76th Street (tel. 288-0999)
Hours: Daily from 5pm to midnight
Credit Cards: AE ($25 minimum)
Price Range: $7.95 to $12.95 for entrees, less for sandwiches
   As the name proclaims, it's barbecue. For the less adventurous, there are also hamburgers, chicken, and hot dogs. AOTW

Jimmy's has a special gimmick—weekdays meals are free for kids 9 and younger; two kids' meals maximum for each adult meal. Children who clean their plates also get ice cream for dessert. Check before you go to see if the special deal is still available.

Contrapunto, 200 East 60th St., between Second and Third avenues (tel. 751-8616)
Hours: Daily from noon to midnight
Credit Cards: AE, DC, IGT, MC, V, Air Plus
Price Range: $12 to $21 for dinner entrees
Children's Services: No boosters, high chairs, changing facilities; banquette seating for kids who need to stretch out
   Pasta, pasta, pasta. Plus sinful desserts and gelati. All-age kids are welcome. It's a second-floor eatery. Lots of windows, lots of people, lots of noise; it's Bloomingdale's country. No reservations accepted.

Fuddrucker's Restaurant, 1619 Third Ave., at 91st Street (tel. 876-3833)
Hours: Daily from 11:30am to midnight
Price Range: $3.95 to $7.95 for entrees
Credit Cards: AE, MC, V
Children's Services: Booster seats and high chairs available, diaper change possible
   The kids get a hamburger, hot dog, or taco with french fries, soda and a cookie all for $3.95. Not to worry, they have more choices for you. They have lots of terrific salads, chicken done in good, simple style. What this place has going for it is a happy atmosphere. As the night goes on, the bar makes things happier but it's still a good spot for us.

Greener Pastures, 117 E. 60th St., between Park and Lexington avenues (tel. 832-3212)
Hours: Monday through Thursday from 11:30am to 9pm, Friday to 8:30pm, Saturday to 10pm, and Sunday from noon to 8:30pm
Credit Cards: None
Price Range: Inexpensive to moderate
Children's Services: Booster seats available, diaper change possible
   A vegetarian restaurant and very good. There's a lovely glass-roofed section where your child may enjoy a "Doll Salad" for $7. It

has a face like Raggedy Ann, made of carrots, sprouts, tuna, and eggs, so they say. Like all good restaurants, I'm sure they forgot to tell me about some key ingredient.

🍎 **Jackson Hole Wyoming,** 232 E. 64th St., between Second and Third avenues (tel. 371-7187); and 83rd Street at Second Avenue (tel. 737-8788)
Hours: (64th Street) Monday through Saturday from 10am to 1am, and Sunday from noon to midnight; (83rd Street) Monday through Thursday from 10am to 1am, Friday and Saturday from 10am to 4am, and Sunday from 11am to 11:30pm
Credit Cards: None
Price Range: $5.50 to $10
Children's Services: No booster seats, no diaper change

They have super-duper hamburgers. And perfect for all-age kids because these are such low-key, anything-goes places. The biggest burger you ever saw for $4.50 (AOTW); think about splitting one with your g.c., for starters.

The best hamburger you can eat in the smallest area—this place serves as a fine example of how to utilize every inch of space.

🍎 **Ottomanelli's Cafés,** 1370 York Ave., at 73rd Street (tel. 794-9696); 413 E. 71st St., at York Avenue (tel. 517-8365); 439 E. 82nd St., at York Avenue (tel. 737-1888); 1626 York Ave., at 86th Street (tel. 772-7722); and 1518 First Ave., at 79th Street (tel. 734-5544); and there are more!
Hours: Daily from noon to 9:45pm
Credit Cards: Cash only
Price Range: Inexpensive
Children's Services: Booster seats available

The Ottomanelli brothers are butchers and "they know beef." They also know "cheap." A sirloin steakburger, lettuce, tomato, pickle, on a sesame bun with cross-hatch fries, all for $4.95. Bryan Miller, the restaurant columnist for *The New York Times,* gave this burger four stars and calls it the "World's Greatest Burger."

They also have great grilled chicken (my review, not Bryan's) for $8.95, and all sorts of pastas with garlic bread—they're Angelica Ottomanelli's recipes. And of course all the Ottomanellis serve pizzas.

There are more of these restaurants all over town. For good reasons. They are casual, family style, friendly, anxious to please, shamefully inexpensive (tsk, tsk, and oh goody, goody!), and the food is great. Did I tell you about clean? Yup. That, too.

For six or more people they will do an indoor Australian barbecue. You have to book that one in advance. My only worry with Ottomanellis is, who's watching the stores while they're watching the restaurants? All of my g.c. are crazy for these places, even the baby without teeth.

Pig Heaven, 1540 Second Ave., at 80th Street (tel. 744-4333)
Hours: Monday through Thursday from noon to 11:30pm, Friday and Saturday from noon to 12:30am, Sunday from noon to 11pm
Credit Cards: AE, DC
Price Range: $10 to $20 for entrees
Children's Services: No booster seats, high chairs, or changing facilities; reservations are accepted and recommended

Despite the lack of children's services, Pig Heaven is first rate for kids 3 and older. Why, they even have children's parties in the afternoon so "kids can run around to their hearts' delight." The decor proves it. A giant pig holds a menu, and little pigs dance around the room. It might make the kids skip the spareribs, but it's mighty attractive. The decor is frivolous, but the food is very serious. The dim sum (dumplings) come steamed or pan fried, and children love them. Fish or chicken are both good choices. The dessert menu separates East from West. Definitely U.S. style, and so rich it should be served in a trough.

If you're on the Upper East Side, be sure to eat at Pig Heaven. If you're in some other part of town, it's well worth the trip.

Sarabeth's Kitchen, 1295 Madison Ave., between 92nd and 93rd streets (tel. 410-7335)
Hours: Monday through Friday breakfast is served from 8am to 11am, lunch from 11am to 3:30pm, tea from 3:30 to 5pm, dinner from 6 to 10:30pm; Saturday and Sunday brunch only is served from 9am to 4pm
Price Range: About $13 for luncheon entrees, $14.25 to $19.50 for dinner entrees
Credit Cards: AE, DC, MC, V

Children's Services: Booster and sassy seats are available

There's a branch of Sarabeth's on the West Side (Amsterdam Avenue) and one here; when you're good, you multiply. The fare is simple but first rate, and the place is very pretty. Brunch is so well attended that you'll be lucky to get seated in less than a half hour. The high tea is a treat, and a lovely way to recover from a hard day. All the food at Sarabeth's Kitchen is just wonderful. The breads and muffins are light as air. For more information, read about Sarabeth's on the West Side later in this chapter.

Serendipity, 225 E. 60th St., between Second and Third avenues (tel. 838-3531)
Hours: Monday through Thursday from 11:30am to 12:30am, Friday to 1am, Saturday to 2am, and Sunday from 11:30am to midnight
Credit Cards: All major cards
Price Range: $6 to $13
Children's Services: Booster seats available, no diaper change

Go, go, go! If it's your only ice cream, lunch, tea, or dinner stop, you just can't miss this. Don't even try on a Saturday—it's jammed. Do go for an early dinner, a late lunch, or a 3 or 4 o'clock indulgence. But not Saturday.

The ice cream whatevers defy description. Salads and sandwiches are great. Have the chocolate slush, $4.50. No one ever comments (but I will) that they have one of the best hamburgers in New York and 12-inch hot dogs, frozen hot chocolate, and pizza. All ages love Serendipity; they have for more than 30 years.

14th Street to 59th Street— West Side

American Festival Café, Rockefeller Center at 20 W. 50th St., between Fifth and Sixth avenues (tel. 246-6699)
Hours: Monday through Friday from 7:30 to 11am for breakfast, 11:30am to 3:30pm for lunch, 3:30 to 4pm for coffee and desserts;

the pre-theater dinner is served from 4 to 6pm; after 6pm service is
à la carte until closing
Credit Cards: All major cards
Price Range: $7 to $10 for breakfast, $13 to $20 for entrees
Children's Services: Booster seats available

Monday through Friday from 5pm to 9pm is Skate-A-Date. For
$23.50, you have dinner, admission to the skating rink, and skate
rental. Saturday and Sunday days they offer the Skaters' Special
for $21.95. You may have breakfast or lunch. Admission to the
rink is $7 to $10 and skate rentals are $4, so the package is really a
good deal. Reservations are a must.

This is a very pretty spot, especially when the ice skaters are
performing. You will find the escalator on 49th Street to take you
down to the American Festival Café. The kids think this is a swell
way to enter a restaurant. When you make your reservations
request a rink-side table. In addition to the ambience, all will enjoy
the good food.

J.J. Applebaum's Deli Co., "Sandwiched between 33rd and
34th streets on Seventh Avenue" (tel. 563-6200)
Hours: Monday through Friday from 7:30am to 8pm and Saturday
and Sunday from 8am to 8pm
Credit Cards: AE
Price Range: $5 to $15
Children's Services: Booster seats available, no diaper change

They start out with puns in the address and get wilder from
there. Don't miss this, especially if you're going to Madison Square
Garden (right in the neighborhood). The food is great. This
three-floor restaurant/deli is very attractive.

Cabana Carioca, 123 W. 45th St., between Sixth and Seventh
avenues (tel. 581-8088)
Hours: Daily from noon to 11pm
Credit Cards: All major cards
Price Range: $9 to $16
Children's Services: Booster seats available, diaper change possible

For an ethnic experience while around the Times Square area.
Brazilian food—shrimp, oysters, and "national Brazilian dishes."
Lovely people. Friendly service. Clean—I mean *limpia!*

W. 59th St.
W. 58th St.
W. 57th St.
W. 56th St.
W. 55th St.
W. 54th St.
W. 53rd St.
W. 52nd St.
W. 51st St.
W. 50th St.
W. 49th St.
W. 48th St.
W. 47th St.
W. 46th St.
W. 45th St.
W. 44th St.
W. 43rd St.
W. 42nd St.
W. 41st St.
W. 40th St.
W. 39th St.
W. 38th St.

Columbus Circle

Broadway

THEATER DISTRICT

Seventh Ave.

Eighth Ave.

Ninth Ave.

Tenth Ave.

Eleventh Ave.

Avenue of the Americas

(6th Ave.)

Rockefeller Center

Port Authority Bus Terminal

Broadway

Bryant Park

500 m
550 y

MANHATTAN

Midtown

Algonquin Hotel 26
American Craft Museum 9
AT&T World Headquarters 18
Bryant Park 24
Chrysler Building 29
Daily News Building 30
Duffy Square 23
Exxon Building 7
Ford Foundation Building 31

General Motors Building 16
Grand Central Terminal 28
IBM Building 17
International Building 1
ICP Midtown 25
Lever House 19
Lower Plaza, Rockefeller Center
McGraw-Hill Building 6
Museum of Broadcasting 11

MIDTOWN MANHATTAN

E. 59th St.
E. 58th St.
E. 57th St.
E. 56th St.
E. 55th St.
E. 54th St.
E. 53rd St.
E. 52nd St.
E. 51st St.
E. 50th St.
E. 49th St.
E. 48th St.
E. 47th St.
E. 46th St.
E. 45th St.
E. 44th St.
E. 43rd St.
E. 42nd St.
E. 41st St.
E. 40th St.
E. 39th St.
E. 38th St.

TURTLE BAY

Sutton Pl.
Sutton Pl. So.
Beekman Pl.
Mitchell St.
FDR Drive
East River

Fifth Ave.
Madison Ave.
Vanderbilt Ave.
Park Ave.
Lexington Ave.
Third Ave.
Second Ave.
First Ave.
Tudor City Pl.

Museum of Modern Art 10
New York Public Library 27
The Plaza 15
Radio City Music Hall 4
RCA Building 3
St. Bartholomew's Church 21
St. Patrick's Cathedral 12
St. Thomas's Church 13
Seagram Building 20

Simon & Schuster Building 5
Time-Life Building 8
Times Square 22
Trump Tower 14
United Nations Headquarters 32

Carnegie Delicatessen, 854 Seventh Ave., between 54th and 55th streets (tel. 757-2245)
Hours: Daily from 6:30am to 3:30am
Credit Cards: None
Price Range: $10 and up for sandwiches, $12 and up for entrees
Children's Services: Booster seats available

Please plan to share a sandwich or the blintzes. They pickle their own pastrami and corned beef here, and all baking is done on the premises. One corned beef on rye could feed a family of six for a week. And is it good! So is everything else. They're very nice to children. There is always a long wait here.

Century Café, 132 W. 43rd St., between Sixth Avenue and Broadway (tel. 398-1988)
Hours: Monday through Saturday from 11:30am to 11:30pm, and Sunday from noon to 9pm
Credit Cards: All major cards
Price Range: $9 to $16
Children's Services: No booster seats, diaper change possible, reservations advisable (go early, it gets crowded)

The specialty is chicken with mustard sauce. For lesser gourmets they have pizzettas (small pizzas to you). A great, big, and lively place and a good spot for older g.c. (8 or 9 and up) before or after a show. It's priced right—and there's plenty going on! TV screens reflect huge pictures on the walls.

Hamburger Harry's, 145 W. 45th St., between Sixth and Seventh avenues (tel. 840-0566)
Hours: Daily from 11:30am to midnight, and Sunday from noon to 11pm
Credit Cards: AE, MC, V; $10 minimum
Price Range: $8 to $14
Children's Services: Booster seats available, diaper change possible

They cater to children, especially on weekends. Children are allowed to sit at their own tables with other children. They are given games and creative crafts to do. Balloons, puzzles, chalkboards, and (get ready) crowns for their little noggins. "Watch that they don't eat the craft materials instead of the food" is the management's quote. All this and free french fries. What better spot when you're in the Times Square area? It's a four-star selection.

🍎 **Hard Rock Café,** 221 W. 57th St., between Broadway and Seventh Avenue (tel. 489-6565)
Hours: Sunday through Thursday from 11:30am to 2pm, Friday and Saturday from 11:30am to 4am; long lines all the time—go at 11am or an off-hour
Credit Cards: AE, MC, V
Price Range: $17 for average meal
Children's Services: Booster seats available, diaper change possible
    The preteens' and teenagers' "must go" place. Above the entrance is a car crashing into the building. It's spectacular looking, a lot of fun. Good food. Burgers and American food, and the memorabilia decorating the place is worth the trip. Kids 11 and over will consider it the high spot of their visit. They give kids balloons and buttons. Music is nice and loud! Go, go, go. There is a shop with Hard Rock T-shirts, hats, etc., where you can buy, buy, buy (open at 10am daily).

🍎 **Lox Around the Clock,** 676 Sixth Ave., corner of 21st Street (tel. 691-3535)
Hours: Monday through Wednesday from 8am to 3am, and Thursday through Sunday, 24 hours a day
Credit Cards: AE; $15 minimum
Price Range: $7.95 to $11.75 for entrees
Children's Services: Booster seats available
    A let-it-all-hang-out kind of spot that makes kids feel comfortable. Everybody here from the waiters to the customers are out for a good time. The food is swell, or maybe it just tastes better in these happy surroundings. Of course bagels and lox. Lots of other choices for kids who don't know what's good. Let me amend that—for kids with less ethnic cravings.

🍎 **Mamma Leone's Ristorante,** 261 W. 44th St., between Seventh and Eighth avenues (tel. 586-5151)
Hours: Daily from 7 to 10am for breakfast, Monday through Saturday from 11:30am to 2:30pm for lunch, and 4 to 11:30pm for dinner, and Sunday from 2 to 9pm
Credit Cards: All major cards

Price Range: $21.50 to $37.50 for dinner, a six-course fixed-price meal
Children's Services: Booster seats and high chairs available, diaper change possible; reservations are a good idea, but don't be afraid to chance it

I was told at Mamma Leone's by the management person, "Tell your people if they come for dinner, don't eat all day." The MP's not kidding. For party atmosphere, complete with balloons and endless attention to the bambinos, see Mamma.

There is a reason or two they've been doing business here forever (since 1906, anyway). Nothing is too much trouble for their staff. The food is good. No group is too large for them to handle.

The ambience is pure fiesta. Make a big evening out of this for the younger kids especially. They do fuss over the 10-years-and-under crowd. The one item not on the menu is what they serve in the largest quantities: friendliness.

Manganaro's Hero-Boy, 492 Ninth Ave., between 37th and 38th streets (tel. 947-7325)
Hours: Monday through Saturday from 6am to 8pm, in summer open at 7:30am
Credit Cards: AE; $15 minimum
Price Range: $6 to $8
Children's Services: No booster seats, no diaper change

The specialty of the house, or one of their claims to fame, is the "mile-high hero sandwich" stuffed for block after block with assorted cold cuts, tomatoes, and spices on wonderful crunchy Italian bread.

There is some seating, lots of Italian goodies (provolone, sausage, and such), and if you want to have a teenage party, let Manganaro's make you a hero, or a heroine.

Mickey Mantle's, 42 Central Park South, between Fifth and Sixth avenues (tel. 688-7777)
Hours: Monday through Saturday from noon to 1am, Sunday from noon to midnight
Credit Cards: All major cards
Price Range: $7.25 to $8.50 for kids, $10.95 to $19.95 for entrees

Reservations are a must. There is the Little League menu,

children's portions, from $6.75 for a burger to $10. Your older sports fans (over 8) are going to be swept away with this one. They'll see high-profile sportscasters doing a daily radio program that'll knock their baseball socks off. There are eight TV sets turned to all the major sporting events. There's a good chance of seeing Mickey himself. This place is a homer for Himmm with his little slugger.

Old Fashioned Mr. Jennings Ice Cream Parlor, 12 W. 55th St., between Fifth and Sixth avenues (tel. 397-2625)
Hours: Monday through Saturday from 7am to 5pm
Credit Cards: AE
Price Range: Moderate
Children's Services: No booster seats, no diaper change
   If you're in the neighborhood, this is a good spot for ice cream, sodas, and sundaes. Sandwiches, salads, and the inevitable hamburgers.

O'Neal's, 60 W. 57th St., at 6th Avenue (tel. 399-2361)
Hours: Daily from 11:30am to midnight
Credit Cards: All major cards
Price Range: $11 to $20 for entrees
Children's Services: Booster seats available, diaper change possible
   A swell spot for kids. The food is good and uncomplicated. The staff is usually pleasant to children, and everybody else. Casual ambience with reliable steaks, hamburgers, and stick-to-the-ribs (not to the fork) fare.

Palazzo, 1 Rockefeller Plaza, on 50th Street west of Fifth Avenue (tel. 757-6575)
Hours: Daily from 7am to 4:30pm
Credit Cards: None
Price Range: Inexpensive
Children's Services: No booster seats, no diaper change
   You'll see a small glass enclosure on the south side of 49th Street just off Fifth Avenue. It houses the elevator that will take you down one floor. Prepare yourself for new splendors. The interior of this building at the skating-rink level has been refurbished—marble, brass, and hanging plants. Palazzo serves breakfast from 7am to 11am. From noon to 2pm you can have pizza for one or for two.

They do Chicago-style pizza, too (that's the deep-dish version with tons of cheese), and burgers and salads. The pastry, gelato, and sorbeto are yummy. There's a $3.50 minimum per person at lunch (rent ain't cheap at Rockefeller Center). The place is small so try for an off-hour. On the same level is a free exhibit of the history and building of Rockefeller Center.

There are two other restaurants here: Sea Grill, expensive, formal, and not for us; and Savories, open from 7:30am to 7pm for breakfast, lunch, afternoon tea, and take-out. They are all pretty, but Palazzo is appropriate for us.

To find a place to eat with children in this area is not easy. Most are expensive and cater to business lunches. Palazzo does the job if you're in the neighborhood.

Tony Roma's, 1600 Broadway at 48th Street (tel. 956-7427)
Hours: Daily from 11:30am to midnight
Credit Cards: All major cards
Price Range: Moderate
Children's Services: Booster seats available, diaper change possible
It's nice when in the Times Square area to find a familiar place to eat that you know is dependable. This was the third Tony Roma's in Manhattan. The food formula and the attitude is the same in all TRs (goody!). Ribs, chicken, and of course, the golden mountain loaf of fried onions. Try to remember when you start on them that you ordered them for the kids. All ages are very welcome.

Rumpelmayer's, 50 Central Park South, at Sixth Avenue (tel. 755-5800)
Hours: Daily from 7am to 1am
Credit Cards: All major cards
Price Range: See text
Children's Services: Booster seats available, no diaper change
There are very few places in New York, unlike Vienna, where you may go to have just dessert and coffee—Rumpelmayer's is one of these rare birds. The price of this repast depends, of course, on what you choose from the menu. The ball (of ice cream?) is in your court. With restraint, dessert and a beverage for you and one child will run about $18. A sandwich at lunch costs about $10. Enough of this vulgar discussion of money. Is this not the best guidebook

you have ever read? I want you to have a good time, no matter what it costs you. Go for the sweets.

Rumpelmayer's has been located in the St. Moritz Hotel forever. It is a joy to see the faces of the children when they enter this village of stuffed teddy bears. After you overdo Central Park, this is pleasurable. Everything is so continental.

Stage Delicatessen, 834 Seventh Ave., at 53rd Street (tel. 245-7850)
Hours: Daily from 6:30am to 2am
Credit Cards: None
Price Range: $5.95 to $16.75 for sandwiches, add $2 if you share; $7.45 to $13.75 for entrees
Children's Services: No boosters, high chairs, or diaper changes
"Fifty-four years of service" and all by very funny waiters and waitresses. Stage is famous for their corned beef and pastrami, not to mention their chopped liver. Let's lift our seltzer glasses and make a toast. The sandwiches can feed a family of four. Share.

60th Street and Up—West Side

The Alameda Restaurant, 2160 Broadway, on the northeast corner of 76th Street (tel. 873-1500)
Hours: Daily from noon to midnight
Price Range: $8.95 to $13.50 for dinner entrees
Credit Cards: All major cards
Children's Services: Booster seats available, diaper change possible
They offer kids' special quesadillas for just $1.50. If your g.c. like grilled cheese sandwiches, they'll like these. The cuisine is authentic Mexican and *me gusto mucho.* Hamburgers? Of course they have hamburgers because they like having kids at the Alameda.

American Restaurant, 2020 Broadway, at 69th Street (tel. 724-4000)
Hours: 24 hours every day
Credit Cards: AE
Price Range: Moderate
Children's Services: No booster seats, high chairs, or diaper changes

If you suffer a knot in the stomach when you have to select a place to eat near Lincoln Center, you have my respect. Most places are overpriced and understaffed. I hasten to add, not all; there are many good ones in this book.

The American is an overendowed coffeeshop. The food is good. They have full-course meals as well as sandwiches and all the foods kids like. They have booth seating, which is comfortable and cozy for you and the kids. This place is clean, large, comfortable, and has very nice owners and most accommodating help.

Bahama Mamma, 2628 Broadway, between 99th and 100th streets, one flight up (tel. 866-7760)
Hours: Daily from 5pm on
Price Range: Inexpensive; entrees about $8 to $10
Credit Cards: None
Children's Services: Booster seats and diaper change possible

Ask a 5-year-old to decorate a restaurant and she might come up with Bahama Mamma, where Christmas tree lights, plastic pelicans, a hula dancer mural, and samba music make for a party ambience as spirited as the menu. Lots of spice here, but they'll tame down the entrees for children. Crayons available. A great place for kids of all ages and the eats are good.

Bimini Twist, 345–347 Amsterdam Ave., between 73rd and 74th streets (tel. 362-1260)
Hours: Daily from 6pm on
Credit Cards: MC, V
Price Range: Moderate, dinner entrees from $9.75 to $12
Children's Services: Sassy seats, diaper change possible

The owner of this restaurant is the same gentleman who owns Marvin Gardens. He likes kids and wants them in both restaurants. It's our kind of ambience—booths and wooden tables and floors. A most attractive restaurant. Don't let the name fool you.

The cuisine is American. Lots of gourmet fare on the menu: Crab cakes are $6.75, pastas $9.25 to $13, and Moroccan veal shanks, $14. The food is excellent. Please save room for dessert. Even if you don't order the sweet potato cheesecake with caramel pecan sauce, $6, you'll find something great.

Border Cafe, 2637 Broadway, at 100th Street (tel. 749-8888)
Hours: Sunday to Thursday from noon to 2am, Friday and Saturday from noon to 4am
Price Range: $7.95 to $8.95 for lunch entrees, $7.95 to $12.95 for dinner entrees; kid's menu entrees start at $5.95
Credit Cards: AE, MC, V
Children's Services: High chairs, boosters, and diaper change possible

Crayons, balloons, video monitors, and a grazing bar where the kids can see what ingredients go into what dishes. Miniburgers, monster nachos, barbecued ribs and chicken. Soda is served in pitchers. Piña coladas without the booze are a popular drink with my kids.

The theme and the look is American Southwest. The best look at the Border Cafe is the smile with which you're greeted when you come with the kids. The Sunday Brunch attracts a very young crowd. Oh, I forgot, the food is very tasty.

Boulevard Café, Broadway, at the corner of 88th Street (tel. 874-7400)
Hours: Daily from noon to midnight
Credit Cards: AE, MC, V
Price Range: Moderate
Children's Services: Booster seats available, diaper change possible

The tablecloths are made of paper and the management provides the crayons. A nice opening touch.

My kids loved the pizza on tortilla bread; their tastes are so exotic. They have Mexican food that is *muy bueno*. The buffalo chicken wings are a crowd pleaser. If you like fish, you will find it fresh and prepared well at Boulevard. Whatever the kids order, you will find the check is small. Good food and inexpensive prices make the Boulevard a winner.

You will notice there is no street number listed because they are in the Montana. This is an apartment building you can't miss because there is a very tall, round clock planted in the street directly in front of the building.

Caramba III, 2567 Broadway, at 96th Street (tel. 749-5055)
Hours: Daily from noon to midnight
Credit Cards: All major cards except Discover
Price Range: Moderate. $5.75 to $11.95 for dinner entrees
Children's Services: Sassy Seats and diaper changes possible

Sassy Seats on the premises indicate how "with it" the Caramba crowd is. And balloons for each child. You know how you are wanted.

The menu consists of simple Mexican food. The fajitas and the burritos are no better in Mexico City. If the kids do not like Mexican food, they will serve you uncomplicated chicken in one form or another.

A charming place. *Muy simpático* . . . and it tastes good, too, at Caramba Tres.

Diane's Uptown, 249 Columbus Ave., between 71st and 72nd streets (tel. 799-6750)
Hours: Daily from 11am to 2am
Credit Cards: None
Price Range: Very inexpensive
Children's Services: No booster seats, high chairs, or diaper change

For a sensational 7-ounce hamburger on a toasted sesame bun do Diane's. The burger is $4.50; the fries are $1.60 and are just the way we like them. A revelation. Really good food on the cheap. Warm, friendly service. About 25 tables, but quick turnover. This little watering hole is a find for both its quality and its prices. Diane's Ice Cream Bar is on the premises. Get your dessert to go or pick up an ice cream while sauntering by.

E.J.'s Luncheonette, 433 Amsterdam Ave., at 81st Street (tel. 873-3444)

Hours: Monday to Thursday from 8am to 11pm, Friday from 8am to midnight, Saturday from 9am to midnight, Sunday from 9am to 11pm
Price Range: Sensible neighborhood prices
Credit Cards: None
Children's Services: Booster seats, no high chairs, no diaper change

They serve old-fashioned blue-plate specials priced from $7 to $10. They have very tasty pancakes with all kinds of trimmings. The soups are superb. The sandwiches are inspired; they use challah or seven grain bread on request. The desserts include, among other tummy-treats, real banana splits.

This is a neighborhood place, and what a great kids neighborhood this is. The Children's Museum and the Museum of Natural History could not be closer.

The interior of E.J.'s is great looking. The walls have 1950s photos and lots of shadow boxes. There are chrome-rimmed counter stools. It's what we call the fifties look, but it never looked this good.

Ernie's, 2150 Broadway between 75th and 76th streets (tel. 496-1588)
Hours: noon to midnight
Price Range: $6.95 to $18.95 for entrees
Credit Cards: AE, MC, V
Children's Services: Booster seats, high chairs, diaper change possible

This is a good place to take the kids when grown-up food is important, too. Good seafoods, salads, and pastas. It's a tiled restaurant where the noise level is high enough to drown out fussy babies and just about anything else. The size of the servings of this Italian cuisine are enormous so think about sharing.

Fine and Shapiro, 138 W. 72nd St., between Broadway and Columbus Avenue (tel. 877-2874)

Hours: Daily from 11am to 11pm, on Friday to 9pm
Credit Cards: AE
Price Range: $12.95 to $18 for a complete dinner
Children's Services: Booster seats available, diaper change possible

For years *New York* magazine has rated the chicken-in-the-pot here the best in New York. They opened in 1927—if they haven't gotten that soup right by now, when? Don't overlook the stuffed cabbage. According to these third-generation owners, "Our reputation speaks for itself." That's a good trick, but at the risk of echoing the reputation that's speaking, it's mighty good eating. You can't go wrong at Fine and Shapiro's.

This West Side standby is not too far from Lincoln Center, so keep it in mind if you and the g.c.s are headed there.

Fiorello's, 1900 Broadway, between 63rd and 64th streets (tel. 595-5330)

Credit Cards: All major cards
Price Range: Moderate to expensive; $12 and up for entrees
Children's Services: Booster seats available

Reservations are a must. An Italian menu with English translations. The $12 entree is an individual pizza. The place is lovely and the food is good. There is seasonal outside dining. Fiorello's is for kids over 10, for sure.

Good Enough to Eat, 483 Amsterdam Ave., between 83rd and 84th streets (tel. 496-0163)

Hours: Monday through Friday from 8am to 4pm for breakfast and

lunch, 6pm to 10pm for dinner; Saturday and Sunday brunch from 9am to 4pm, no lunch served. Saturday dinner from 6pm to 11pm, Sunday dinner from 5:30pm to 10pm
Credit Cards: AE, M, V
Price Range: About $15 for lunch with dessert, $7.50 to $17 for dinner entrees
Children's Services: Booster seats, no high chairs, no diaper change, no strollers allowed

Antique quilts, old brick walls, lots of copper and barn wood provide a fitting background for the "home-style America" grub. Shepherd's pie, meat loaf, turkey, and the kids' favorite, macaroni and cheese. The desserts are off the charts.

The only problem here is the wait. It's close to the Museum of Natural History and the Children's Museum of Manhattan so try for an off-hour. It really is good.

Houlihan's, 1900 Broadway, between 63rd and 64th streets (tel. 362-1340)
Hours: Daily from 11:30am to midnight
Credit Cards: All major cards
Price Range: Moderate and up
Children's Services: Booster seats available

Houlihan's is a rapidly expanding chain of restaurants. The decor is college rathskeller, and it's attractive. For $7.25 you may bite into a hamburger. If your companion is overburgered, the Cajun chicken breast is $9.75.

Realistic prices in the Lincoln Center area; a reservation is a splendid idea, as sometimes the music, theater, and circus crowds arrive in droves.

La Caridad, 2199 Broadway, at 78th Street (tel. 874-2780)
Hours: Monday through Saturday 11:30am to 1am, Sunday 11:30am to 10:30
Credit Cards: None
Price Range: Very inexpensive
Children's Services: High chairs

You've done the Children's Museum of Manhattan on 83rd Street or you're heading for the Planetarium on CPW & 82nd Street and you've spent enough money. Try this restaurant. It's Chinese-Cuban but not exotic food. How exotic can a bean get? It's always crowded because it's good and mercifully cheap. Try to get in at an off time.

Lucy's Retired Surfers, 503 Columbus Ave., at 84th Street (tel. 787-3009)
Hours: Sunday through Thursday noon to 10pm, Friday and Saturday noon to 11pm
Price Range: About $7 for entrees, very inexpensive
Credit Cards: AE, MC, V
Children's Services: Boosters, high chairs, diaper change possible

Good Southern California–Mexican fare including vegetarian specials. It's noisy and it's fun, and they are very nice to kids. It's in the hot neighborhood of the Museum of Natural History and the Children's Museum of Manhattan. You need choices in this part of town.

It is inexpensive. As if that were not enough, on Sundays KIDS EAT FREE! Can you believe?

Marvin Gardens, Broadway, between 81st and 82nd streets (tel. 799-0578)
Hours: Daily Monday to Friday 7:30am on. Saturday and Sunday from 9am till 2am
Credit Cards: MC, V
Price Range: $10.50 and up for dinner entrees
Children's Services: Sassy seats available, diaper changes on a counter in the ladies' room

The owner has kids and wants more—yours. With a location 1 block from the Children's Museum of Manhattan, and three meals a day, he can have us.

They have waffles, oatmeal, and eggs (even eggs Benedict) for breakfast. For lunch and dinner the owner explains, "The menu has nothing exotic." Well, it may not be exotic, but it's very, very good. Is this owner our kind of people? You betcha! Is this restaurant our kind of restaurant? You know it!

Museum Café, 366 Columbus Ave., between 77th and 78th streets (tel. 799-0150)

Hours: Daily from 11:30am to 5pm for lunch, and from 5pm to 1am for dinner

Credit Cards: AE, V

Price Range: Moderate

Children's Services: Booster seats available

You may dine on individual pizzas for $5.95 to $7.50. A hamburger is $6.95. Everything tasted fine to my gourmets. The place is typical of West Side restaurants. Ask to be seated next to a window. Good people-watching.

Ollie's, 2315 Broadway corner of 84th Street (tel. 362-3111 or 362-3712)

Hours: Daily from 11:30am to midnight, Saturday until 1am

Credit Cards: AE, M, V

Price Range: Inexpensive; entrees from $7 to $15

This is a noodle shop and grille across the street from the Loews 84th Street Sixplex. There are 25 people (I counted them) working behind the counter. I am told there is a second kitchen downstairs. Do not be put off by the waiting crowds: they turn the tables quickly. Nobody will rush you, the waitstaff couldn't be nicer. The place has a luncheonette look. This is the best Chinese food in town for the least amount of money. The Cantonese Wonton Soup at $2.50 could feed a couple of people. The egg roll at $1.10 is a kid pleaser, as are the 8 steamed dumplings for $3.75. This is a real family place. If you are heading for the Upper West Side and like Chinese food, why not try Ollie's? No room for high chairs, but everyone seems to manage.

Pertutti Cafe, 2852 Broadway, between 111th and 112th streets (tel. 864-1143)

Hours: Monday through Saturday from 10am to 1am, Sunday from noon to midnight

Price Range: Inexpensive; entrees are $6.95 for chicken to $10 for veal
Credit Cards: None
Children's Services: Booster seats, diaper change possible

Great pastas, enormous fresh salads, and decaffeinated cappuccinos, which are a big plus for nursing moms and the babies being nursed. Kids of all ages couldn't be more welcome here. The owner suggests "mix and match" on different sauces for your crowd. They are all homemade and he is proud of them for very good reason.

Popover Cafe, 551 Amsterdam Ave., between 86th and 87th streets (tel. 595-8555)
Hours: Monday through Friday from 8:30am to 11pm, Saturday 9:30am to 11pm, Sunday till 10pm
Credit Cards: M, V
Price Range: $8 to $9 for lunch entrees, $10.95 to $17.95 for dinner entrees, which include popovers and salad
Children's Services: Booster seats and diaper change possible, no high chairs. Okay for strollers and wheelchairs

We are talking "c'mon everybody." The eclectic decor—that means no tablecloths but lots of cushions and some booths—is great for kids. There is a collection of stuffed bears because the owner is Carol Baer. You can even take a bear to dinner, but not Carol because she's working.

The food is American. And innovative. A house specialty is the slopover, a combination crêpe and pancake filled with fruits and topped with a dollop of sour cream. It is possible to dollop *sour* cream. They feature a burger that is half veal and half beef. Ms. Baer suggests a cup of soup and a popover for lunch or a peanut butter and jelly sandwich. The soups are homemade. Many other good things on the menu: meat loaf, fish, and lots more.

Saturday and Sunday they dish up a terrific brunch at Popover.

My g.c. and I were very happy at the Popover Cafe. A friendly, hospitable spot makes this a favorite with museum goers and neighborhood people.

Ruppert's, 269 Columbus Ave., between 72nd and 73rd streets (tel. 873-9400)
Hours: Monday through Friday from 11am to 4am, Saturday and

Sunday from 10:30am to 4am. Lunch is to 4:30pm. Dinner is from 5pm on.
Credit Cards: All major cards
Price Range: Moderate
Children's Services: Booster seats available

Don't be misled by the sophisticated hours. The only way you'll see 4am is if your baby is teething. What a great idea! If the little one can't sleep, boogie over to Ruppert's. They say they like kids. It's test time.

Pasta is $7.95 to $10.95; an omelet is $5.95. How's that for reasonable? The actor who is waiting tables will do a resonant reading of the specials of the day. Ruppert's seats about 150 people; the food is good, and they'll be glad to see you.

The Saloon, 1920 Broadway, at 64th Street (tel. 874-1500)
Hours: Daily from 11:30am to 2:30am
Credit Cards: All major cards
Price Range: $6.95 to $17.95 for entrees; average is $12 to $13
Children's Services: Booster seats available, diaper change possible

Italian, Mexican, Japanese, burgers—there are well over 200 items on one menu. Will you believe me if I tell you they're all pretty good? And some are plain superb?

Okay, how do you feel about seeing waiters and waitresses carrying trays while wearing roller skates? The room is huge and they need them.

It's always crowded, but it moves. If you're going between 6 and 8pm, you'd better make a reservation. You'll wait anyway, but it's right across from Lincoln Center as well, you know. Your kids will like this very much, but don't go in the busy, busy hours. Avoid before a matinee, unless you get in about noon.

Sarabeth's Kitchen, 423 Amsterdam Ave., between 80th and 81st streets (tel. 496-6280)
Hours: Monday through Friday—breakfast from 8 to 11am, lunch 11am to 3:30pm, high tea from 3:30 to 5pm, dinner from 6 to 10pm; Saturday and Sunday brunch only is served from 9am to 4pm
Price Range: From $4 for soup to $13 for lunch entrees, $14.25 to $19.50 for dinner entrees
Credit Cards: All major cards except Discover

346 **EATING IN RESTAURANTS**

Children's Services: Boosters and sassy seats

This is such a fluffy, pretty place you just feel happy as soon as you enter. There is a special seating area set aside for people with children, a considerate policy for everyone. Great omelets, breads, muffins, and desserts. The Saturday and Sunday brunch is terrific, but it is just about impossible to get in; it's that crowded. The tea is a delight; tea is $2, cappuccino is $3, and scones and muffins are $2 each. Sarabeth's is a charming place and does she keep her kitchen clean!

🍎 **Tavern on the Green,** Central Park West and 67th Street (tel. 873-3200)
Hours: Daily from 11am to 3:30pm for lunch, 5:30 to 11:30pm for dinner
Credit Cards: All major cards except Discover
Price Range: $8 to $31 for dinner entrees. The pretheater dinner special at $19.50 per person is the best buy in New York

Tavern on the Green looks as if it had been created by the Brothers Grimm. It has the quality of a beautiful fantasy. Compliments to Mr. LeRoy. The beauty of the Tavern begins with the approach. The trees laden with little lights twinkle you to enter. Do take a moment to admire the courtyard. Try to imagine this through the eyes of your little girl and boy. If the weather is warm, request a table in the garden. If you prefer indoors, ask for the Crystal Room. Just be sure to see it all.

The menu is full of tempting choices. They taste even better than they read. The service is focused and attentive. If you are celebrating a special day, the staff will serenade you. If yours is a daytime outing, you could rent peddle bikes in the parking lot after lunch. If you're going for dinner, arrive in a horse-drawn carriage for an extra $34.

Tavern on the Green is an experience the children will remember. They should be 6 or over for full appreciation of the event. Reservations are a must.

🍎 **Victor's Café,** 240 Columbus Ave., at 71st Street (tel. 595-8599); and 236 W. 52nd St., between Broadway and Eighth Avenue (tel. 586-7714)

Hours: Daily from 11am to 1am
Credit Cards: All major cards
Price Range: $8.95 to $20.95 for entrees
Children's Services: Booster seats available, diaper change possible, reservations advised for more than three

This is a family-type place. The food is Cuban and international. Black-bean soup, wild rice, you know. The ambience is pleasant. They love kids and the food is superb.

World Yacht Cruises, Pier 62 at W. 23rd Street on the Hudson River (tel. 929-7090)

Hours: Call for brochure, schedule, or general information. Sailing times change with the seasons
Credit Cards: AE, MC, V
Price Range: $24.75 per person for the lunch cruise, and a 2-year-old is a person. $37.50 for adults and $24.50 for children under 12 for the Sunday cruise. Gratuities and beverages are extra on all cruises
Ages: All ages
Children's Services: Booster seats, chair adapters, and diaper change possible. No strollers.
Note: Wheelchair access. Reservations are a must

The food served on these cruises is quite good and it is displayed in an eye-pleasing fashion. The lunch menu is always a buffet. Hot and cold buffet with seafood, pasta, salads, chicken, and more. The dinner cruise is beautifully served and is not buffet style. There are specialties of the World Yacht Cruises, for example, veal and fish.

The cruises and the dining take 2 hours. You must call for specifics because there are late-night cruises, special cruises, and some "no cruises" because of private parties.

The boats are glorious and the views are sensational. It all makes for a memorable meal and a very special outing.

CHAPTER 19

Family Hotels in New York

The average price for a room in a first-class hotel is an obscene $250 a night. Here are some hints on how to beat the system and information on what's best for you and the kids.

Hints on Beating the System

Call or write to the New York Convention and Visitors Bureau, 2 Columbus Circle, New York, NY 10019 (tel. 397-8222). Have them send you their New York City Tour Package Directory. (Ask them to throw in a copy of "A Child's New York" and their latest calendar of free events while they're at it.)

Watch the Sunday *New York Times* for special deals. Ask hotels about family discounts; they do not volunteer this information. When a hotel quotes a room price, ask if they have any for less. Hang in there.

Weekends and holiday times are when you will get the best rates because businesspeople, the mainstay of the hotel business, stay home. If you bring your car, parking is much, much less expensive in garages on the streets farthest west or east. Read the posted signs carefully. Prices quoted are starting prices for a one-night stay.

Hotels with Pools

INDOOR

There are no great buys, unless there's a reason. For reduced rates, read the introduction. An indoor pool is a very special amenity when you're in New York with your kids.

Holiday Inn Crowne Plaza, Broadway at 49th Street, New York, NY 10019 (tel. toll free 800/465-4329 or 977-4000)
Rates: $159 to $169 for a double on the weekend, $195 to $205 midweek, free for children under 16

I like this chain because they maintain high standards of cleanliness. This hotel is in the heart of the theater district, a neighborhood being upgraded. Health club and the only Olympic-size hotel pool in New York City.

Le Parker Meridien, 118 W. 57th St. (between 6th and 7th avenues), New York, NY 10019 (tel. toll free 800/543-4300 or 245-5000)
Rates: $240 for a double with a city or park view, $260 for a junior suite with a king-size bed and a sleep sofa in the living room, $300 and up for suites, free for children under 12, $25 per older child

A rooftop swimming pool, running track, squash courts, and racquetball. This facility is a "members only" health club as well as a spot for hotel guests.

The rooms are quite small but nicely decorated. Le Patio Restaurant is informal and appropriate for kids; this neighborhood has lots of restaurant choices. A central neighborhood that is as safe as you get in New York. The hotel has a garage for which you will pay dearly. (AOTW, $28 per day.) But peace of mind is priceless, right? Car entrance is at 119 W. 56th St.

Peninsula New York Hotel, 700 Fifth Ave., New York, NY 10019 (tel. toll free 800/262-9467 or 247-2200)

Rates: $250 for low-floor double, $270 for high-floor double, $345 for low-floor double with Fifth Avenue view, $385 for high-floor double with Fifth Avenue view, free for children under 12, $20 per child over 12

This is expensive and it's a beauty. A new 17 × 42-foot pool and health club cover the top three floors. Neighborhoods don't get much better than this one.

Travel Lodge Hotel, Skyline Manhattan, 725 10th Ave. (between 49th and 50th streets), New York, NY 10019 (tel. toll free 800/433-1982 or 586-3400)

Rates: $115 for a double, free for children under 12, $10 per child over 12

Here are the pluses: the price, the pool, the exercise equipment, the sauna, and the free parking with an in-and-out charge of $2. The minus is the neighborhood. It is not safe for strolling, and it's about 4 long blocks too far west. The crosstown bus on 50th Street is a compensation for the distance.

U.N. Plaza Park Hyatt, 1 United Nations Plaza (between 44th and 45th streets), New York, NY 10017 (tel. toll free 800/223-1234 or 355-3400)

Rates: $205 for a queen-size bed, $225 for a king-size bed, free for children under 18 but only two children per room

There is a pool, health club, and 24-hour indoor tennis court. The Greenhouse Restaurant is in the hotel. The UN Plaza Hotel provides free limo service to Wall Street. This is an elegant, if removed, neighborhood. Fairly well patrolled because it's in UN country. Very well patrolled when political demonstrations are underway.

Vista International, 3 World Trade Center, New York, NY 10048 (tel. toll free 800/258-2505 or 938-9100)

Rates: $215 to $290 for a double; some rooms face west toward the Hudson River.

A deluxe hotel at the World Trade Center. If you're coming to New York in warm weather, the South Street Seaport, the Statue of Liberty, and the World Financial Center are in the area. It gets cold here in winter. A 50-foot pool, racquetball court, fitness center, and jogging track are all in the hotel.

OUTDOOR

🍎 **Travel Inn,** 515 W. 42nd St., between 10th and 11th avenues, New York, NY 10036 (tel. toll free 800/223-1900 or 695-7171)

Rates: $105 for a double with two queen-size beds, free for children under 16

On the plus side we have an outdoor pool, rooftop sun deck, solarium, exercise equipment, pleasant rooms, and if you so request, a room with a terrace overlooking the pool; they will "arrange for tennis and racquetball at a nearby club," you may park your car free, eat in the coffee shop, and not faint at checkout time. You are 2 blocks from the Javits Convention Center. The desk will call for taxis for you.

The minuses are the neighborhood, neighborhood, neighborhood. Even with a police station across the street, these streets are not for you and yours. The taxi service is because this area is isolated, and it is not safe to stand on the street at night in hopes of finding a cab. The halls are tacky, but rooms are pleasant.

For summer visitors this hotel offers a great deal for a small price. Now you know why. Forewarned is forearmed. So much of living is involved in trade-offs.

For Your Consideration

Hotel suites are sensible solutions when traveling with kids. A fully equipped kitchen and the extra space of a living room make for gracious living, especially for long stays in New York. So many delis and restaurants deliver: You stock the corn flakes and milk.

Manhattan East Suite Hotels represents a group of nine hotels. They are all in acceptable neighborhoods; the Surrey Hotel is in the best neighborhood. Suites are consistently clean, despite an occasional worn sofa here and there. Hotel staffs are friendly and cooperative. Savvy European travelers are frequent patrons.

They may read expensive, but money is saved on restaurants. These work well for families here for extended visits.

🍎 **Manhattan East Suite Hotels** (tel. toll free 800/ME-SUITE
Rates: From $150 to $235 for junior suite with living room, kitchen, and separate sleeping area, three-person maximum, weekends $125; $185 to $355 for one-bedroom suite with living room, dining area, kitchen, and bedroom, four-person maximum, weekends $145; $350 to $550 for two-bedroom suite, six-person maximum, weekends $245 (their maximums aren't written in stone; they are flexible with kids)

Monthly rates are available. Hotels represented in the Manhattan East Hotel Suites are as follows: **Beekman Towers,** 49th Street and First Avenue, **Dumont Plaza,** at 34th Street and Lexington Avenue; **Eastgate Tower,** 39th Street, between Second and Third avenues; **Lyden Gardens,** 64th Street between Second and Third avenues; **Lyden House,** 53rd Street, between First and Second avenues; **Plaza 50,** 50th Street and Third Avenue; **Shelburne Murray Hill,** Lexington Avenue at 37th Street; **Surrey Hotel,** 76th St. and Madison Avenue. The only location on the West Side is **Southgate Tower** at 31st Street and Seventh Avenue.

Friends of the Family

These hostelries, some little known, are as perfect as it gets. Price range, amenities, staff attitudes, and locations have all been considered. Each of these hotels has had high praise from families who enjoyed long stays. That some are not well known will no longer be true a week after *New York City with Kids* hits the bookstores. Book as early as possible.

🍎 **Excelsior Hotel,** 45 W. 81st St. (between Central Park West and Columbus Avenue), New York, NY 10024 (tel. 362-9200)
Rates: $99 for a spacious suite with kitchenette

The best section of the young, vibrant, upscale Upper West Side. The American Museum of Natural History is a neighbor. Central Park is the backyard.

Not fancy, spotlessly clean, in the midst of the restaurants and shops. Request a room with a view of the park. This is the perfect place for you and your family.

🌿 **Grand Hyatt,** Park Avenue at Grand Central Station (and 42nd Street), New York, NY 10017 (tel. 883-1234 or toll free 800/233-1234).

Rates: $250 for a double, weekend specials from $119; Regency Club rooms go for $280 with continental breakfast, but no discounts

The Kids' Frequent Stay Program includes an award of a Camp Hyatt carry pack after four stays. Kids stay free in their parent(s)' room, and, when available, are offered a second room at half price. Children's menus are available at the hotel's restaurants as well as through room service (a bargain at $3 for breakfast and $5 for lunch or dinner). At check-in, kids will receive a free cap and other goodies and can borrow games from the concierge. The location is central, although not the most attractive area of the city.

🌿 **Hotel Wales,** 1295 Madison Ave., between 92nd and 93rd streets, New York, NY 10028 (tel. 876-6000)

Rates: $95 to $125 for a double with either one queen-size bed or two twins; $145 for a junior suite with pull-out couch in living room

This newly renovated Upper East Side hotel is just 1 block from Central Park and within walking distance of the Metropolitan Museum, the Whitney, and the Museum of the City of New York (which has a superb collection of antique dollhouses). The neighborhood is residential and upscale. A good choice if you think your family might enjoy a break from the zaniness of midtown.

🌿 **Leo House: A Catholic Hospice,** 332 W. 23rd St., between 8th and 9th avenues, New York, NY 10011 (tel. 929-1010)

Rates: $55 for double room with half-bath; $63 for double room with full bath; $80 to $140 for family rooms (up to 6 people)

No, you don't have to be Catholic to stay here. This clean, pleasant hotel isn't fancy (a step up from a Y), but for budget-minded families, there is probably no better (or safer) place at these prices. The family rooms (one overlooks a garden) contain two double beds and miles of room for cots. Homemade feasts are served on lace-covered tables in the breakfast room: oven-baked breads, eggs the way you like them, freshly made waffles. The staff (mostly nuns) is friendly and helpful. There are phones in each room, but the only TV is in the lounge. (Did I hear a cheer?) While the price is reminiscent of another era, so is the atmosphere. Doors are locked at midnight and no couple with different last names can stay without producing a marriage certificate.

Mayflower Hotel, 15 Central Park West, at 63rd Street, New York, NY 10023 (tel. toll free 800/223-4164 or 265-0060)
Rates: $160 for a double, $180 for a double with a view of the park; weekend rates include breakfast and a park view for $120; free for children under 16, surcharge of $15 for each child 16 and over

Marvelous location. Walking distance to Broadway theaters, Fifth Avenue, Lincoln Center, and you're right at Central Park. Restaurants and shopping—you have it all at this friendly, older hotel. Rooms with park views are hard to get, but they are perfect for Thanksgiving Day Parade viewing. One can only request. With or without a view, this is a good, good choice.

Salisbury Hotel, 123 W. 57th St., between Sixth and Seventh avenues, New York, NY 10019 (tel. toll free 800/223-0680 or 246-1300)
Rates: $135 to $165 for a double, weekends $90; $195 for a suite, weekends $139; free for children under 12

This is a very family-friendly hotel. The location is most convenient with all public transportation at the doorstep. Walking distance to Fifth Avenue, Broadway theaters, Central Park, and FAO Schwarz. The suites and the double rooms are very spacious in this grand old dame. Request the renovated accommodations. Don't be put off by the dark exterior; this is an excellent place to stay. The weekend rooms at $90 are hard to book. If you reserve well in advance, your chances are improved.

Bed-and-Breakfast

If yours is a prolonged stay, or if you want to try SoHo loft living, a Greenwich Village walk-up, an East Side brownstone, or a West Side condo, here's the information.

For those of you who are afraid of heights, it's an alternative. The prices are comparable to hotel suites, but some are a real bargain. You are responsible for the housekeeping. They supply the cleaning items and the sheets. Hosted B & Bs that welcome kids are scarce. Unhosted are easier. These groups require big deposits. When you are traveling with kids, life is always "iffy." Check the refund policy of each before you commit.

Aaah! Bed & Breakfast #1 Ltd., P.O. Box 200, New York, NY 10108 (tel. 246-4000, toll free 800/776-4001, Fax 265-4346)

Rates: $60 single, $80 double, and $120 and up for luxury suites

Wonderful prices from this eager and friendly bunch. Call them 24 hours a day, seven days a week, or drop in at their new office at 342 W. 46th St. and check out some photos before you select your abode.

City Lights B & B, Ltd., P.O. Box 20355, Cherokee Station, New York, NY 10028 (tel. 737-7049, Fax 535-2755)

Rates: $75 to $300 per night based on location and size of accommodations

They have hosted and unattended apartments for families. Ms. Nielsen will be happy to assist with locations. As a deposit, 25% of your bill is required when you make reservations.

New World Bed and Breakfast, 150 Fifth Ave., New York, NY 10011 (tel. toll free 800/443-3800 or 675-5600)

Rates: $120 for a studio apartment, $200 for a one-bedroom apartment

The director of this operation is Kathleen Kruger. She has "many unhosted apartments for families." A deposit of 25% of the total amount due is required when making reservations.

Urban Ventures, 306 W. 38th St., 6th Floor, New York, NY 10018 (tel. 594-5650)

Rates: $75 per night and up

This is the largest and oldest B & B organization in New York. They have 700 listings spread throughout the five boroughs. These are all unhosted apartments, only for families. A major credit card as security is a must when you make reservations.

CHAPTER 20

For Lucky Kids Who Live in New York

New York is a nice place to visit, and the best place to live. This is New York for New Yorkers. So what, you may ask, makes this chapter different from the rest of this book? This section includes programs of longer duration than a tourist may require. An oversimplification. New York parents, a group I know quite well, have one thing in common: a desire to take advantage of everything that the city offers. The shared obstacle is limited time to research and commit to various programs.

The single greatest joy of maturity (in years) is free time. Hard to imagine for you pressured, overextended parents. And since I am now living in a different world from you burning-at-both-ends parents, I brought in a relief pitcher to make this book even more valuable (though that's hard to imagine).

Much of this chapter was written by Helen Klein Ross.

She's the mother of two lucky kids, Margaret, age 4, and Katherine, age 2. She is far closer to the subject of Lucky Kids Who Live in New York than I am. Helen did this fabulous section.

Publications

In addition to *The New York Times* (look for their "For Children" section on Fridays), *New York* magazine, and the *Village Voice* (see Chapter 3), the following publications are also very helpful.

🍎 *Big Apple Parents' Paper,* 928 Broadway, Suite 709, New York, NY 10010 (tel. 533-2277)
Price: $25 for 12 issues ($18 if you don't mind delayed delivery by bulk-rate mail)

A newspaper for parents by parents that provides a good scoop on what's happening around town each month for kids. There's a pull-out calendar of daily events and annual updates on parenting programs, birthing options, schools, and more.

🍎 *Family Travel Times,* Travel With Your Children (TWYCH), 80 Eighth Ave., New York, NY 10011 (tel. 206-0688)
Price: $35 for 10 issues a year (for a sample, send $1 to the above address)

Stupendous is the only word for this newsletter. It provides information that is light-years ahead of old pap like, "Take crayons on the plane." Every bit of minutia to make travel with the kids fun and easy is included. There are reviews of the latest family travel guides, and books for travel-bound kids. Also city-by-city listings of special events. They have answers to questions that have not crossed your mind. Like how to childproof a hotel room or where to visit a 30-acre village built entirely out of Lego blocks. (In Legoland, of course, located in Denmark.)

If you are a newsletter subscriber, you can get back articles on wherever you're planning to visit. If TWYCH hasn't published a piece yet on that spot, you can get the information you need by phone. Subscribers are invited to call Tuesdays and Thursdays (10am to noon) for free advice from *the* expert in family travel, Dorothy Jordon, who also publishes *Skiing with Children* and *Cruising with Children.*

🍎 *Green Book,* City Books, 2223 Municipal Building, New York, NY 10007 (tel. 669-8245)
Price: $12.58

This book is a must. It lists all services provided by every relevant city, state, and federal agency from the obvious to the obscure. You'll find out where you can file noise complaints, patent your idea for a new toy, or attend a board of education public meeting. Mail a check for $12.58 to the above address, or save yourself $2.75 by picking one up in person at Citybooks, 61 Chambers St., between Centre Street and Broadway. There, it's only $10.83.

🍎 *Green Pages,* Department of Parks and Recreation, 16 W. 61st St. (off Broadway), 6th Floor, New York, NY 10023 (tel. 397-3100)

A handy pocket-size guide to the Department of Parks and Recreation's incredibly diverse services and activities, from archery, badminton, and bird-watching to chess and checkers, skating, and kite flying—all for free and so is the guide. No phone orders, but you can pick one up in person from 9am to 5pm, Monday through Friday.

🍎 *Kids' Culture Catalog,* Alliance for the Arts, 330 W. 42nd St., Suite 1701, New York, NY 10036 (tel. 947-6340)
Price: $11.45 (includes postage)

The good news is, the writers have done their best to list any and every cultural resource for children in New York. The not-so-good news is that it hasn't been updated since the summer of 1987 so call before you leap. To help solve the problem, they publish *Kids' Culture Calendar* every September and January; it lists cultural events throughout the (school) year. To receive the latest edition, send $3.50 to the above address.

🍎 **Metropolitan Transportation Authority,** 370 J St., Brooklyn, NY 11201 (tel. 718/330-8754)
Price: Free

The MTA *does* do some things right—one of them is to provide subway and bus maps that are blessedly easy to read and include tips on the best public transportation routes to museums and zoos.

Go to any subway token booth or contact the above. If you're mapless and in need of information, call their Travel Hotline at 718/330-1234. Agents are on line from 6am to 9pm seven days a week to help you get anywhere in the five boroughs.

🍎 *New York Family Magazine,* 420 E. 79th St., Suite 9E, New York, NY 10021 (tel. 744-0309)
Price: $30 (12 issues)

This magazine is packed with items of interest for New York families: a daily calendar of events, entertainment highlights, reviews of kids' videos and handy info on urban-parent issues like "Nannies and the Law." Their coverage is extensive, and they cover it well.

🍎 *ParentGuide News,* 2 Park Ave., Suite 2012, New York, NY 10016 (tel. 213-8840)
Price: $14.90 annual subscription

This monthly newspaper is the only one that offers regular listings of calendar events not only by category ("Museums," "Zoos and Stuff," "Sports Fun," you get the idea) but by borough. They'll also keep you up on what's happening in Long Island, New Jersey, and Connecticut. (You'd be surprised!) A must for any parent who recognizes that life exists beyond a 212 area code.

🍎 *Parents & Kids Directory,* P.O. Box 1717, Dover, NJ 07802-1717 (tel. 473-3348 . . . note that it's not a NJ area code)
Price: $16.95 annual subscription (6 issues)

No parent in or near Manhattan should be without this gem. It lists every event at museums, children's theaters, libraries, parks, you name it. What's more, the listings are coded to let you know which spots provide facilities for diaper-changing or breast-feeding and "if there's a rest area where kids can work off energy while parents can regain some." When you join the Children's Museum of Manhattan, you'll get a free subscription.

🍎 *Walks and Workshops,* Manhattan Urban Park Rangers, 1234 Fifth Ave., Room 113, New York, NY 10029 (tel. 427-4040)
Price: Free

This is a bimonthly bulletin of free weekend programs sponsored by the Urban Park Rangers. No matter what your 8-or-over is interested in—astronomy? history? kite making? photography?—it's bound to be the subject of one of these family programs offered every weekend of the year throughout the city. Call to get on their mailing list.

🍎 *Whole Y Catalog*, 92nd Street Y, 1395 Lexington Ave., at 92nd Street, New York, NY 10128 (tel. 427-6000, main number, or 996-1100 for a catalog)
Price: Free

There is no charge for the Y catalog. You will be astounded by all the programs offered: classes, tours, workshops, theater, lectures, symphony, summer camp, and more. They are very parent-friendly here, proven by the fact that they have over 200 children's programs which are listed not only alphabetically but by age. You can order tickets and sign up for classes and special events by phone. Do so as quickly as possible. Plenty of parents are probably interested in the same things you are.

A Publication and an Organization

🍎 **Parents League of New York,** 115 E. 82nd St., between Park and Lexington avenues, New York, NY 10028 (tel. 737-7385)
Price: $35 annual membership

This is a nonprofit organization with intelligent parents who are devoted to their volunteer work. Members can use their resources to choose a school, find a summer camp, land a baby-sitter, organize a birthday party, even plan a family vacation. Membership includes the *Parents League Review* with articles like "Acne and the Ecstasy" (some titles stick in one's mind). You'll also get a copy of their flawless calendar of events for children, a newsletter, and invitations to parenting seminars. You'll be glad you joined. Plan on spending time at the office to dive into the files.

An Organization

Your branch library, your favorite museum, your chosen gym, of course. Here is another goody.

The Children's Book Council, Inc. 568 Broadway, at Prince Street, Room 404, New York, NY 10003 (tel. 966-1990)
Price: See text

This association is the official sponsor of and headquarters for National Children's Book Week in November. They are open weekdays to the public from 9:30am to 5pm. Drop in to see what's new in children's books.

If you want information on the council's work and activities, there is a one-time charge of $45 for which you will receive *CBC Features*—a newsletter which tells you of publishers who will be happy to send you great postcards, bookmarks, and posters *free*. You will also receive a *Book Week* brochure and information on other special council activities.

Send your check and a stamped, self-addressed no. 10 envelope to Children's Book Council, Order Center, 350 Scotland Rd., Orange, NJ 07050.

Resources for New York City Parents

Raising kids is always challenging, but even more so in New York. Here's a sampling of what's out there to help. Courses and costs change, so call to check.

Bank Street College of Education, Office of New Perspectives, 610 W. 112th St., between Broadway and Riverside Drive, New York, NY 10025 (tel. 222-6700, ext. 249)
Price: $30 one parent, $10 second parent

Saturday workshops on parenting include topics such as how to communicate effectively with your child and strategies for choosing the right school. Childcare is provided for $10 during these adults-only workshops (reservations are a must). I especially like the weekend parent/child workshops where families share creative activities like art, improvisation, weaving, and songs. (My 2-year-old had a ball discovering flour-play in "Art With Toddlers.") Fee for one parent/child couple ranges from $15 to $35; additional family members may attend for $5 each.

Early Care Center, 69 E. 89th St., between Park and Madison avenues, New York, NY 10128 (tel. 427-1818)

Price: $325 for a year's worth of tapings and family conferences. This fee also includes two home visits by an early childhood specialist

Dr. Sirgay Sanger will assess your parenting skills, even before you give birth! Parents are encouraged to come as often as every 3 months for videotapings with their child up to age 3. Tapes are played back at family consultation sessions without the child. The goal is to improve the child's emotional, cognitive, and social development.

Early Childhood Resource and Information Center, 66 Leroy St., at Seventh Avenue South, New York, NY 10014 (tel. 929-0815)

The New York Public Library has a whole floor of materials on resources for parents of children to age 5. The Family Room, with sliding gym, playpens, blocks, etc., provides a learning environment for parent and child. They also offer a series of lectures by childhood experts. Don't lose this number. And it's all free.

Educational Alliance West, 80 Fifth Ave., between 13th and 14th streets, New York, NY 10011 (tel. 675-5560)
Price: $85 annual family membership plus course fee

Robin Bernstein heads the Parenting Center at this lower Manhattan community center for families with newborns to age 3. Here you'll find new mother groups, weekly parenting sessions, a "Pops & Tots" class, drop-in play groups, single parent groups, adoptive parent groups, and a "minisummer camp" for kids from 18 months to 3 years. Membership includes free workshops and a 10% discount on courses, but you don't have to be a member to sign up for classes. They run between $180 to $505 for 15 weeks, depending on the subject. (For course listings, see "The Arts" section in this chapter.)

Elizabeth Bing Center for Parents, 164 W. 79th St., between Columbus and Amsterdam avenues, New York, NY 10024 (tel. 362-5304)
Price: Varies—please call

For parents-to-be, the center offers Lamaze, breast-feeding courses, and more. For parents-already, there are exercise classes (with baby-sitting), infant massage, parenting sessions, and the 92nd Street Y-affiliated "Rock 'n' Roll with Baby."

Family Focus, Inc., 210 E. 86th St., between Second and Third avenues, New York, NY 10028 (tel. 517-7160)
Price: Courses for expectant and new parents include Lamaze classes ($195 for 5 sessions), evening seminars on childcare ($30 per person/$50 per couple), infant massage (5 classes for $75), baby exercise (12 sessions for $180), and "Baby and Life Infant CPR and First Aid" ($45 per person for a 3-hour course)
They also offer other goodies like custom birth announcements and toys for infants and preschoolers.

Hospitals
Many New York hospitals offer pre- and postnatal workshops and parenting courses. Columbia-Presbyterian, Lenox Hill Hospital, New York Hospital, Mt. Sinai Medical Center, St. Luke's–Roosevelt Hospital and St. Vincent's Medical Center to name a few.

Jewish Board of Family and Children's Services, 120 W. 57th St., between Sixth and Seventh avenues, New York, NY 10019 (tel. 582-9100)
This is the largest voluntary social service and mental health agency in the United States, offering help for families and children, Jewish or not, with minor or major problems of all kinds via counseling, therapy, and consultation services with more than 100 programs throughout the metropolitan area. The quality and vast range of services offered by the JBFCS is to be commended.

Kindred Spirits, 92nd Street Y, 1395 Lexington Ave., New York, NY 10128 (tel. 427-6000)
Price: $60 for a yearly membership, but nonmembers can also participate
This dynamic organization was formed to make life easier for separated, divorced, or widowed parents. Here, you'll find a wealth of opportunities to share the experience of single parenthood in a supportive atmosphere. Seminars led by mental health professionals address topics such as the impact of divorce on kids, single-parent burn-out, and dealing with the death of a spouse. "Family

Fundays" include children in activities like miniature golf parties, ski trips, a Mets baseball game, brunches, picnics, and travel packages.

Adult social events are offered, too: cocktail cruises, comedy nights, wine-tastings, and more.

Lenox Hill Neighborhood Association, 331 E. 70th St., between First and Second avenues, New York, NY 10021 (tel. 744-5022)

In addition to the multitude of after-school, weekend, and summer activities for children (see "Burn-Off" section), the association has a single-parents' group, seminars for single women (ages 25 to 40), a walk-in tenants' rights service, a concert series, and much more.

Lower East Side Family Resource Center, 137 E. Second St., between First Avenue and Avenue A, New York, NY 10009 (tel. 677-6602)

This community center provides families with child-care information and referral, play groups, information on drug and alcohol abuse, a support group for single parents, parent counseling, even a thrift shop (kids' clothing, furniture, toys). They also publish a parent newsletter.

Mommy Made and Daddy Care, 453 8th St., Brooklyn, NY 11215 (tel. 718/832-2411)
Price: $75 to $90 are the course fees

This family-run company was selling fresh and natural baby foods long before Diane Keaton did it in *Baby Boom.* They share their recipes for healthy, home-cooked baby and toddler food in cooking classes at several locations in Manhattan. They also provide "Cooking with Kids" workshops for you and your child.

NYU School of Continuing Education (tel. 998-7080)
Price: $35 for some Saturday morning one-shot workshops; $120 for 6-week ongoing sessions

The Center for Career and Life Planning provides parenting workshops for both parents and about-to-be-parents. AOTW offerings include "Finding Affordable Quality Child Care" and "Making the Decision to Adopt." Call for a catalog.

🍎 **92nd Street Y,** 1395 Lexington Ave., New York, NY 10128 (tel. 427-6000, ext. 611)

The Parenting Center is nothing less than fantastic, offering an extraordinary choice of classes on parenting, from courses for parents-to-be to those for parents of teens ("Sex, Lies, and MTV") and everything in between. Courses are also listed for single parents, adoptive parents, working-outside-the-home parents, and stepparents.

🍎 **Parent Guidance Workshops,** 180 Riverside Dr., New York, NY 10024 (tel. 787-8883)

Price: Varies—call for information

Nancy Samalin, author of *Love and Anger: The Parental Dilemma* (Viking Books), runs these no-nonsense, down-to-earth workshops and seminars. She teaches parents how to communicate more effectively with their children, with topics like "What to Do When Your Child Drives You Up a Wall" and "Positive Discipline: Alternatives to Yelling, Nagging, Bribing, and Threatening." She's helped multitudes of parents get through the challenge of raising kids.

🍎 **Parents Resource Network,** P.O. Box 3054, Skokie, IL 60076 (tel. 708/675-3555)

Price: See text

If you don't have time or energy to attend parenting classes and seminars in the city, you can still hear it from the experts (like Dr. Burton White, Betty Weeks, Nancy Samalin) by ordering audiocassettes for $9.95 each, and if you're really zealous, you can get all 24 cassettes in the series for $179. Topics cover sibling rivalry, overprogramming children, sleep disorders, and much more.

🍎 **Parents Resources, Inc.,** P.O. Box 107, New York, NY 10024 (tel. 873-0609)

Price: $15 for membership

This nonprofit, volunteer organization provides peer support groups for new parents.

🍎 **Programs for Education, Inc.,** Gesell Institute Programs, Box 167, Rosemont, NJ 08556 (tel. 686-3830 in New York)

According to Dr. Louise Bates Ames, cofounder of the Gesell

Institute, the most important contribution that a parent can make to a child's education is "to be sure that the child starts school on the basis of his developmental age, not his age in years."

Although most of the materials from Programs for Education, Inc. are for professionals, they provide invaluable tools for parents as well. Write for the catalog, *Films and Books for Professionals and Parents.*

They have videos you can rent for 2 weeks, and fun-to-take tests that will help you evaluate your child's readiness for kindergarten. There is also a wealth of reading materials for parents. These are fragile years for you and your child. The more you know, the better.

Skhool for Parents, 1 Lincoln Plaza, Suite 34-P, New York, NY 10023 (tel. 877-8700)
Price: See text

Director Dr. William Koch, consultant to many publications, including *Working Parents and Mothers Today,* believes that "great parents aren't born, they develop." The basic "Easier Parenting" 5-session course covers discipline, independence, sexual development, aggressive behavior, communication, and relating ($150 for the series.) "Living with Your Adolescent" costs $90 for 3 sessions. Both are held at 20 W. 64th St. Advanced courses and support groups are also available. Believe it or not, tuition is refunded in full if you're not satisfied with the courses.

Stepfamily Foundation, 333 West End Ave., New York, NY 10023 (tel. 877-3244)
Price: $50 for annual membership

If you've stepped into a stepfamily situation, then this organization will be of great help. They issue a most informative quarterly newsletter, hold workshops, and offer counseling (from $40 to $130 per hour).

Sutton Place Synagogue, 225 E. 51st St. (between Second and Third avenues, New York, NY 10022 (tel. 593-3300)

The Parenting Center here has everything: play groups, Funworks, parenting forums, a Couples Club. They also have parties to celebrate the Jewish holidays and family dinners every Friday evening.

Resources . . . Sometimes

Drug Abuse Hotline (tel. toll free 800/522-5353)
Also known as the Substance Abuse Hotline. They're available 24 hours, bless them.

Parent Help Line (tel. 925-8002)
Hours: Monday through Friday from 8am to 8pm, except holidays
This is the mayor's Parent and Child Abuse Help Line run by the Family Services Office (Human Resources Administration) for questions about drugs and child abuse. Even if you call after hours, the recording is helpful and in Spanish, too. We hope you won't need it, but here it is if you do.

REACH (Recreation, Education, Athletics, and Creative Arts for the Handicapped) (tel. 718/699-4213)
The Department of Parks and Recreation runs worthwhile programs of all kinds.

Resources for Children with Special Needs, Inc., 200 Park Ave. South, New York, NY 10003 (tel. 677-4650)
This nonprofit organization provides information, referral, and support for parents of children (newborn to age 21) with learning, developmental, emotional, or physical disabilities. They can be instrumental in helping parents get the services they need (and are entitled to) from the board of education.

SKIP (Sick Kids need Involved People), 990 Second Ave., Apt. 2, New York, NY 10022 (tel. 421-9160)
This is an advocacy group for families of children who must depend permanently on medical technology or must rely on home care.

After-School, Weekend & Summer Activities

How could a child possibly get bored in a city with more than 854 playgrounds, 150 museums, 400 galleries, 25,000 restaurants, 250 theaters . . . the choices are endless. Those we've listed cover various parts of the city area and are well run. This does not suggest that because something is not listed, it's not worthwhile. It would not be possible to list them all.

The Parents' League (tel. 737-7385) has a gold mine of information on activities for kids year round, including feedback from parents and a free counseling service for members (see "A Publication and an Organization," earlier in this chapter).

As heat rises, so do costs. Always check first, as well as hours, addresses, courses offered, etc. AOTW, they were correct. Take advantage of all that this vibrant city has to offer.

Special Places & Things

This is a short and sweet section. Just a few unusual listings.

🍎 **Children's Express,** 245 Seventh Ave., between 24th and 25th streets, New York, NY 10001-7302 (tel. 620-0098)
Price: Free
Ages: 8 to 18

For any child who expresses an interest in journalism, this is an extraordinary opportunity to get firsthand experience in reporting and editing. The kids publish a newsletter and a nationally syndicated column that appears weekly in newspapers around the country. Half-day training workshops are led by the kids themselves to train new "reporters" (age 8 to 13) and "editors" (age 14 to 18). These are held on Saturdays, about five times a year. Publishing the paper is an after-school activity. This not-for-profit organization, funded by major corporations and private groups nationwide, was featured on *60 Minutes* and has been around for more than 16 years.

🍎 **French Workshop for Children,** mailing address: 516 Fifth Ave., New York, NY 10036 (tel. 221-6864)
Hours: Monday through Saturday year round
Price: $300 to $400 for a 12-week session
Ages: One year to adult

French classes start as early as age 1 with "French for Tots" (ages 1 to 3) with a parent (just guess who has more trouble). Siblings age 3 to 15 are offered "French for Children" classes after school and on Saturdays as well as a summer day camp program. Director Francois Thibault will be happy to tell you about his well-run programs, held at locations on both the Upper East Side and the Upper West Side.

Kids Computer News, 619 W. 114th St., between Broadway and Riverside Drive, New York, NY 10025 (tel. 932-1987)
Hours: First Wednesday of each month during the school year
Price: $10 per year
Ages: High school

This club is for high school students who have an interest in computers. The club meets on the first Wednesday of each month from 7 to 9:30pm at St. Hilda's and St. Hugh's School. To receive their newsletter, send $10 to the above address. (Members get the newsletter free.)

Parties

New York City is a party town! Great places for kids to let off a little steam are parties at such gyms and exercise clubs as Alzerreca's, Jodi's Gym, Jump for Joy Diskorobics (with swimming!), Playorena, Richard Chun Tae Kwon Do Center, and Sutton Gym (see individual listings). Many museums, such as the Children's Museum of Manhattan, the Brooklyn Children's Museum, and South Street Seaport Museum, to name a few, organize parties that are both fun and educational. All the skating rinks and bowling centers we list host parties as well as many schools, theaters, and "Ys" (swimming parties for West Side Y members are popular). The Parents League has an extensive file on party ideas and services; check out their list if you're a member. Here are others:

Auntie L, 249-A E. 82nd St., New York, NY 10028 (tel. 988-8445)
Price: $250 to $500

Auntie L is actually the effervescent Vivian-Lorraine Bruton, creator of "Party in a Box" (a portable party with all the trimmings) and "Picnic in a String Bag" (just like the ones Mom used to pack, complete with homemade cookies). Her favorite creations are children's parties, though. When we spoke, she was in the midst of scouting for miniatures to add the finishing touches to a Birthday Tea Party for a 4-year-old girl.

Her party will cater completely to the whims and personality of your child. She's very flexible about location—she's done kite parties in the park, for instance.

Big Apple Circus Clowns (tel. 226-5077 and ask for Laine Barton)
Price: $195 for 1½ hours in Manhattan

Yes, the Big Apple Circus clowns do parties! They make the rounds of children's hospital wards during the week, but are available for private events on weekends. Aside from classic clowns, you can request bubble magicians, puppeteers or other specialists.

John Colligan, Storyteller, 130 W. 71st St., Apt. 1, New York, NY 10023 (tel. 580-1650)
Price: $100 to $125

John Colligan, a former Montessori teacher from Ohio, is a professional storyteller (and you thought *you* had a good job). He'll come to your house and enchant a living room full of partygoers with a special tale tailored to the interests of the Birthday Child. His stories last about 40 minutes (which is all a celebrant can sit still for, anyway). He'll do something as charming as Winnie the Pooh, as literary as "The Odyssey," or a tale that's never been told before. When he's not entertaining 3- to 10-year-olds, he teaches after-school programs and sits on the board of directors of the New York City Storytelling Center.

Federal Rent-a-TV, 1588 York Ave. (between 83rd and 84th streets), New York, NY 10128 (tel. 734-5777)
Price: $200 including delivery and pickup (the movie rental is $5 extra)

If you're brave (or crazy) enough to have a party at your place, you might consider renting a 40-inch movie screen TV with a video player.

Foolish Mortal Productions, 133 E. 7th St., #4A, New York, NY 10009 (tel. 979-9669)
Price: $200 per hour

You can hire a professional cameraman/comic director to mesmerize your TV-generation child and peers with a "videofilmmaking" party. Director Matt works out plot ideas with the Birthday Person, and introduces kids to the fine points of interviewing, scene-creating, and editing while he films them. The kids will love it and you'll end up with a wonderful record of the day.

Incredible Merlin (tel. 982-1751 or 914/783-7568)
Price: $300 and up (performs in your home)
Jack Adams and Rani Mandel have been entertaining kids and their families for the past 30 years and perform worldwide, including NYC at Lincoln Center and the Children's Museum of Manhattan. It's a great magic show with plenty of participation, but most especially, they have the ability of relating to people of any age—"two to toothless."

Jeremy's Place, 322 E. 81st St., between First and Second avenues, New York, NY 10028 (tel. 628-1414)
Hours: 11:30am to 6:30pm, daily
Price: See text
Ages: 4 to 11
A fantasyland with wind tunnels, electric trains (eight sets), puppets, games, light shows, robots, and a magic show. The magic show is Jeremy, who claims to have been a failure as a magician. But the kids love him. Jeremy hasn't missed a show in 27 years.

The price is $399 for the "place" and $6.95 per child, with a minimum of 12, maximum of 30. (You're only charged for the kids who show up.) "Party Bags to Go" are $2.95 (six-bag minimum). His "disco parties" are a big hit with the 9- to 11-year-old crowd.

Maurice the Bear (tel. 582-4240)
Price: $150 per ½ hour
He's a droll, human-size teddy who will breeze into a party of tots, hug them, dance with them, or simply schmooze. He'll greet your guests as they arrive, or make his entrance midparty with the cake. He's quite an "event," as regulars of some of the poshest children's parties in town will tell you. The man inside Maurice is actor David Robinson who does nine other children's characters, too.

McDonald's, 1499 Third Ave., at 85th Street, New York, NY (tel. 628-8100)
Price: $2.50 per child, which includes invitations, party hats, a

birthday cake, party bags, and a gift for the birthday child; $3.86 per child, all the above and Happy Meals, too (which means hamburger, french fries, and soda)

This is by far the best-looking McDonald's in New York. The party group is seated in a special room closed off to regular customers. Be prepared to entertain the kids. The hostess will be too busy getting the food.

Mostly Magic, 55 Carmine St., between Bleecker Street and Sixth Avenue, New York, NY 10014 (tel. 924-1472)
Price: See text
Ages: 4 to 11

If you want a private party with light lunch, beverages, balloons, birthday cake, hats, noisemakers, and your very own magician, here it is. For $300 you'll have a magic show and party time for 20 people (including adults). For $15 per person, you may have a few extra attend. The whole shebang takes about 2 hours, including an hour of entertainment.

Want to check it out first? Drop in to see their magic show on any Saturday at 2pm. Admission is $10 per person and it's open to the public.

The children will love it. You'll love it. And your home remains intact.

Patchiddy Players (tel. 496-1839)
Price: See text

Trisha Gray and Anne Pasquale are mothers of preschoolers who went into business to become the "party people we couldn't find to do our own children's parties." Hire them, and all you'll have to do on The Big Day is open the door. They provide 1½ hours of theater games, paper crafts, face painting, and a 45-minute storybook musical starring your child in which every celebrant gets a part! (My daughter loved donning a crown to play the queen in a party performance of "Snow White Bites the Big Apple.") $150 gets you one Patchiddy Player, $215 for the two.

13th Street Repertory, 50 W. 13th St., between Fifth and Sixth avenues, New York, NY 10011 (tel. 675-6677)
Price: $10 reservation fee; $4 per child
Ages: 4 and up (no minimum number of kids; 35 maximum)

This popular children's theater offers performances usually about an hour long. Partygoers will get to meet and mingle with the actors and enjoy refreshments (you must bring them) in the large, homey lobby after the performance.

Tip to Toe, 162 Third Ave., corner of 16th Street, New York, NY 10003 (tel. 995-5572)
Price: See text

This is a neighborhood beauty salon where little girls as young as 3 can celebrate the big day with their friends by getting "the works." Owner Sheila Hymowitz offers two party packages: For $12 per child, kids get a manicure ("complete with rhinestone nail") in any of the latest shades including green and purple, plus stick-on earrings, a "makeover," and a makeup-kit. For $20 per child, they also get their hair done and can choose any hair accessory in the store. Parties are held during the week only. BYO cake, pizza, whatever. Some parents may be horrified at the political-incorrectness of this one, but little-to-preteen girls adore it.

Burn-Off

This section includes "sign-up" activities, bowling, permits for tennis and golf, gym programs, and swimming pools.

INDOOR BALL

Bowlmor Lanes, 110 University Pl., between 12th and 13th streets, New York, NY 10003 (tel. 255-8188)
Hours: Sunday through Thursday from 10am to 1am, and Friday and Saturday from 10am to 4am (no kids after 5pm Monday-Friday, and after 7pm Saturday and Sunday)
Price: $3 per person per game; 75¢ for shoe rental
Ages: 8 years and older
Credit Cards: None
Note: Strollers welcome; food available at snack bar except in the summer when you must BYO pizza, etc

By far the most family-friendly bowling alley in town though they have a "no-kids" policy at night, due to league play-offs. They do birthday parties, too. (A friend's son has enjoyed several here, including a smashing bash with 23 celebrants!) Facilities are well run and spacious—44 lanes! Fun for the family . . . just as it was in the '50s.

Hackers, Hitters & Hoops, 123 W. 18th Street, between 6th and 7th avenues, New York, NY 10011 (tel. 929-7482)

Hours: Monday through Thursday from 11am to 11pm, Friday from 11am to 1am, Saturday from 10am to 1am, Sunday from 10am to 6pm

Price: tokens are $1.50/each or 10 for $10

Here, there's something for everyone: golf, miniature golf, computerized driving ranges, basketball hoops for all ages, Ping-Pong, and batting cages for both baseball and softball practice ($23 per ½ hr., $35 per hour). For less ambitious sports fans, there's a snack bar and a large TV screen in the lounge. When you (or your downstairs neighbors) are fed up with "hallway hoops," this is the place to bring aspiring Michael Jordans. Three large rooms are available for birthday parties.

TENNIS

CATS (Children's Athletic Training School), 593 Park Ave., at 64th Street, New York, NY 10021 (tel. 751-4876)

Ages: 1½ to adult

Price: from $335 for 10 weeks

This program teaches kids more than tennis basics like how to grip a racket; it's designed to give city kids the fundamentals they often miss out on by not being able to walk out the door and play a game of catch: hand-eye, eye-foot coordination body stability, motor skills, and body confidence.

"Kiddie Cats" is for ages 1½ to 3½ accompanied by adult. "Cats Basics" for ages 3½ to 6 emphasizes coordination skills in a noncompetitive environment. "Cats Sports" for ages 6 to 12 teaches tennis, soccer, and basketball. Classes are given at the above location, and also on the west side and on Randall's Island. They also offer a Tennis Summer Camp for 6 to 9 year olds.

City of New York Parks and Recreation, Tennis Programming, Olmsted Center, Flushing Meadow–Corona Park, Corona, NY 11368 (tel. 718/699-4233)

Price: Free
Ages: 8 to 18

Free youth tennis lessons are provided throughout the city year round, including use of racquets and balls. Summer Youth Tennis clinics are held twice a week from early July to August 12 at 38 sites in the five boroughs, including Central Park. About 10,000 kids take advantage of these programs run by Michael Silverman, who's done a tremendous job in the city of democratizing this sport. The Reebok Urban Youth Tennis Academy provides a scholarship program that offers advanced training for 50 talented kids age 8 to 18 (tryouts are held each May). Other programs include the Penn Junior Tournament Series for kids 16 and under and nationwide U.S. Youth Games for top tennis players, with a chance to compete in England.

Eve Ellis' School of Tennis, 41 W. 83rd St., New York, NY 10024 (tel. 289-3133)

Price: $20 registration fee and $139 for 8-week sessions (50-minutes each)
Ages: 3 and up

Tennis classes for kids in several Manhattan locations, including Central Park at the Tennis House at 96th Street and Central Park West (no permit required). Beansprout Tennis for children ages 3 to 7 uses foam balls and small racquets on small courts with little nets. There's a junior pre- and postcamp tennis program, a junior tennis plus sports camp in July and August, as well as after-school and weekend clinics.

Jeff Nerenberg's Tennis Academy, Manhattan Plaza Racquet Club, 450 W. 43rd St., New York, NY 10036 (tel. 549-9391)

Price: $450 plus $150 for transportation, if required, for 13 1½-hour sessions
Ages: 6 to 18

Jeff Nerenberg, the affable coach of Manhattan College's tennis team and a member of the Prince National Advisory Board, runs

Developmental Tennis Programs at the location above and also at the Mt. Vernon Tennis Center in Mt. Vernon, N.Y. Classes run from September through June.

Stadium Tennis, 11 E. 162 St., Bronx, NY 10452 (tel. 293-2386)
Price: See text

Tennis programs year round for kids 7 and up. You can sign your kids up for 1-hour lessons ($300 1-hour classes for 12 weeks, transportation is extra). In the summer, Skip Hartman's Junior Tennis Camp for ages 9 to 14 is held mid-June to the beginning of September, with weekly sessions from 9am to 4pm on 10 outdoor courts in a country setting at the Horace Mann School in Riverdale, including swimming. Transportation is extra. The cost is $330 for 1 week, $640 for 2 weeks, and $930 for 3 weeks.

Sutton East Tennis Club, 488 E. 60th St., at York Avenue, New York, NY 10022 (tel. 751-3452)
Price: See text

Tennis programs for children ages 5 to 18 in the spring and fall. Two 12-week sessions (2 hours weekly) cost $550 per session. All courses are conducted Monday through Thursday from 4 to 6pm, Fridays from 3 to 5pm and 5 to 7pm, and weekends from 9am to 5pm.

Tennis Courts in Central Park, permits available at the Arsenal, Central Park, 64th and Fifth Avenue, New York, NY 10021 (tel. 360-8133)
Price: See text

There are 26 clay courts and 4 all-weather courts in Central Park at 96th Street and Central Park West, open from April to November from 7am to 8pm. Throughout the five boroughs, there are 509 public tennis courts. Bring proof of residence and an ID photo (a photo machine is thoughtfully provided.) The seasonal permit is $50 for adults and $10 for kids 17 and under. Cash or personal check with two pieces of ID. If you're not planning on playing a lot of tennis, you can pay an hourly rate of $4, but one player still needs a permit. Registration is open from April through November from 9am to 4pm on weekdays (also Saturday mornings from 9am to 12pm from April through June).

BURN-OFF 377

HORSEBACK RIDING

🐴 **Claremont Riding Academy,** 175 W. 89th St., New York, NY 10024 (tel. 724-5100)

Hours: Monday through Friday from 6:30am to 10pm, and Saturday and Sunday from 6:30am to 5pm (these hours are for instruction)

Price: $32 for ½ hour

Ages: Private lessons start at age 6 and group lessons start at age 8, if not a complete novice. Those under 16 must ride with an adult, and those under 18 must have a note from their parents

For everything else you'll need to know, call Claremont. Yes, they have a ring for training riders. Although the instructors are not what you would call child fans, it's the best we can do in Manhattan, and the kids seem to enjoy it.

🐴 **Pelham Bit Stables,** 9 Shore Road, Bronx, in Pelham Bay Park (tel. 885-0551)

Price: See text

Ages: 8 and up

Director Jim Martin has pony rides for younger kids while brother or sister (over age 8) take a riding lesson ($25 per hour). Trail riding without a lesson for ages 13 and up is $15 per hour. Pony rides are $1.

PERMITS AND PROGRAMS OFFERED BY THE DEPARTMENT OF PARKS AND RECREATION

What's available is phenomenal. Parks and Recreation has everything. Get a free copy of the *Green Pages* with all the phone numbers you'll need at 16 W. 61st St. 6th Floor. They're open weekdays from 9am to 5pm (call 397-3100 before you go just to make sure). Here's a sampling:

🍎 **After-School Programs and Summer Day Camps** Manhattan (tel. 408-0204); Bronx (tel. 430-1824); Brooklyn (tel. 718/965-8939) Queens (tel. 718/520-5366); Staten Island (tel. 718/816-6172)

🍎 **Aquatics** (tel. 718/699-4219)

🍎 **Baseball and Softball Permits** (tel. 408-0209)

🍎 **Croquet Permits** (tel. 360-8133) at the Arsenal, $30 (May through November). The croquet lawn is located in Central Park near Sheep Meadow (67th Street near West Drive).

🍎 **Tennis Permits** (tel. 360-8133) at the Arsenal, $50 adults, $10 kids under 18 (April through November). See "Tennis" section.

🍎 **Tennis Programs** (tel. 718/699-4233) See "Tennis" section.

🍎 **REACH** (Recreation, Education, Athletics, and Creative Arts for the Handicapped) (tel. 718/699-4213)

🍎 **Urban Park Rangers** (tel. 427-4040)

GYMNASTICS, SPORTS & EXERCISE PROGRAMS

This city has practically more exercise programs and gyms than it does kids! So get your couch potatoes out and moving. In addition to the Ys listed separately, here are a few places to check out . . . there are many more. Let word of mouth be your best judge.

🍎 **After-School Workshop,** 122 E. 83rd St., between Park and Lexington avenues, New York, NY 10028 (tel. 734-7620)
Price: See text
Ages: 5 to 12
   This gem is open when schools are closed. After-school and holiday activities include touch football in the park, computer classes, reading and math tutoring, ballet, sewing, cooking, and woodworking.
   Open September 1 through June 30. Fees are $20 for 3 hours; each additional hour, $6; weekly rate is $85 from 3 to 6pm. They're open on school holidays from 8 to 6pm for $48; school holiday programs are also available for $25 from 8:30am to 12:30pm or from 1 to 5pm.

🍎 **Alzerreca's Sport Program,** 210 E. 23rd St., between Second and Third avenues, New York, NY 10010 (tel. 683-1703)

Price: See text
Ages: 1 to 17

Classes are from $50 to $225 (10 to 18 weeks), depending on the activity (see below). Gymnast Jorge Alzerreca and his wife, Kim, formerly with the New York City Ballet, run programs from basic sports skills to competitive gymnastics. Gymnastics is offered at 3:30 and 4:30pm each semester on Tuesdays, Thursdays, and Fridays and costs $225 for an 18-week session. They have soccer for kids ages 6 to 13 on Wednesdays from 4 to 5:30pm (16 weeks is $160). Teenaerobics and jazz dance is a hit with kids 6 to 16 as is "Aerobikata," a combination of aerobics and karate; $50 is the price for a 10-week session of Teenaerobics or Aerobikata. Summer courses are held Tuesday and Thursday mornings for ages 1 to 17 for 8 weeks (once a week, $80; twice weekly, $150). A good place to have a birthday party, too.

Asphalt Green, 555 E. 90th St., between York and East End avenues, New York, NY 10128 (tel. 369-8890)
Price: See text
Ages: 1 to 16

With two gyms, a theater, art studios, and an outdoor all-purpose AstroTurf field, there's lots to do, starting with gymnastics (from $210 to $400 for a 19-week session); to fitness for teens ($10 per individual class); to a summer day camp for 5- to 15-year-olds ($1,600 for 8 weeks, scholarships available). Family memberships are $250 for single-parent families and $450 for couples and family; these include free use of indoor facilities and 50% off all program fees except for the summer camp. Word is that an Olympic-size swimming pool is in the works, ready by the summer of 1993, we all hope.

Astros Sports Club, 838 West End Ave., between 100th and 101st, New York, NY 10025 (tel. 749-7202)
Price: See text
Ages: 5 to 14

The cost is $30 from 3 to 6pm; $45 on Saturdays from 9am to 4pm. Peter and Mark Meyer have after-school sports with school pickup and home drop-off, including baseball, floor hockey, football, and soccer. They also have a summer program sleep-away camp.

Billdave Sports Club, 206 E. 85th St., between Second and Third avenues, New York, NY 10028 (tel. 535-7151)
Price: $25 on weekdays from 2 to 5pm: $40 on Saturdays and holidays. Transportation is extra
Ages: 3 to 12

This is one of New York's most popular sports programs for boys and girls after school and Saturdays as well as summer (see "Day Camps" section). Sports include soccer, baseball, ice and roller skating, basketball, bicycling, foot hockey, and touch football, to name a few. Directors Bill Axelrod and Ed Lasky and staff genuinely like kids. One-dayers are welcome, if there's space.

CATS (Children's Athletic Training School), 593 Park Ave., at 64th Street, New York, NY 10021 (tel. 751-4876)
Price: From $335 for a 50-minute weekly session for 17 weeks during the school year
Ages: 3 to 7

Director Butch Seewagen runs sports skills programs, introducing children to tennis, basketball, baseball, soccer, and hockey. The goal is "to promote a child's confidence and positive self-image in a relaxed and supportive environment." They also offer tennis programs for kids 6 to 12 (see "Tennis" section).

Champions Sports Club, 248 E. 117th St., between Second and Third avenues, New York, NY 10035 (tel. 427-3800)
Price: See text
Ages: 4 to 14

Champions are champions in their fields with every sport possible, including skiing, tennis, swimming, basketball, hockey, soccer, skating, and football. Directors Thomas Fitzpatrick and Warren and Oscar Schwartz offer programs after school, Saturdays, and school holidays as well as a summer day camp program and a late August program (when schools and camps are out).

Team sports are played outdoors, weather permitting, at Randalls Island or in indoor gyms if weather is bad.

The cost is $275 to $500 for 2 hours after school for 10 sessions, depending on the activity (tennis is naturally the most); this includes transportation. Saturdays and holidays are $50 to $60. Ski trips are $400 to $1,200 depending on location and length of stay.

If you're still not convinced, you can sign up for a trial day for $30 (maximum two).

Richard Chun Tae Kwon Do Center, Inc., 220 E. 86th St. between Second and Third avenues, New York, NY 10028 (tel. 772-3700)
Price: $80 to $120 per month (1 or 2 hourly classes per week) on Monday through Saturday
Ages: 3 to adult

Tae Kwon Do is a Ninja Turtle–style approach to fitness. Author Dr. Richard Chun holds nine Dan Black Belts and teaches Karate Tae Kwon Do (the Korean art of self defense) to kids as young as 3. Classes are divided into age groups: 3 to 8, 9 to 12, and teenagers. Kids, be patient—it usually takes 2 to 3 years to get the black belt. Private classes are offered, too. Plus—cowagunga!—birthday parties.

Discovery Programs (tel. 749-8717, west side locations or 348-5371, east side locations)
Ages: 9 months to 16 years

Olympic gymnastics for tots and nots. Worth the call for information. They also have many, many other programs of interest (see "Multi-Arts Programs" section).

Gymboree (tel. 308-6353)
Price: $15 for a trial class
Ages: 3 months to 4 years

There are Gymborees worldwide and five locations in Manhattan. Each 45-minute class involves music, songs, colors, bubbles, games. Parent or care giver participation is required.

Both you and your child wear socks, no sneakers. Your attire need not be a leotard (did I hear you say "Thank God"?). Loose clothing in which you can bend and lift easily will do the job.

Classes are for infants (3 to 5 months), babies (6 to 11 months), walkers (12 to 14 months), (14 to 22 months), plus a class for 2 to 2½ years, big children's games and activities group (2½ years), and gym grad class (2½ years and up).

They have 40 pieces of colorful equipment and wonderful supervision. They do birthday parties. Get ready for an absolute winner!

Jodi's Gym, 244 E. 84th St., between Second and Third avenues, New York, NY 10028 (tel. 772-7633)
Price: See text
Ages: 13 months to 12 years

Weekly classes (40 minutes to 1 hour) are $295 for 17 weeks. Classes held Mondays through Saturdays are small and extremely well supervised. Boys and girls use bars, balance beams, ladders, ropes, tumbling mats, and trapeze bars. Classes include Mommy (or Daddy or Nanny) and Me (12 months to 3 years), Tumbling Tots (3 to 5), Beginning Gymnast (5 to 6), and Intermediate and Senior Gymnasts (10 to 12). Yes, Virginia, there is a Jodi. She's gymnast Jodi Rosenwasser-Levine, certified by the U.S. Gymnastics Safety Association and with an M.A. in psychology. Parental participation is required for children under 2½. With 10,000 square feet of gym space, more than 1,000 kids, and 20 instructors, it's a winner. A birthday party here goes for $275 for 10 kids, and $12 for each extra child. You can even shop at Jodi's: She carries dancewear, activewear, and gymwear for sizes 2 to 14 (cute accessories, too).

Jump for Joy Diskorobics (tel. 535-8916)
Price: $150 for 10 weeks during the school year
Ages: 5 to 11

Barbara Cramer, an elementary schoolteacher who saw that city kids needed more of an outlet for their energy than gym class provided, created a program that is "most definitely not a scaled-down version of an adult exercise program." Hour-long sessions include creative dancing, rock 'n' rolling, ingenious games, lots of enthusiasm, giggles, and fun. Classes are held at several Manhattan locations. Jump for Joy birthday parties are available for ages 5 to 11—one party package includes swimming!

Lenox Hill Creative Center, 331 E. 70th St., between First and Second avenues, New York, NY 10021 (tel. 744-5022)
Price: See text
Ages: 3 to 18

Here, kids can swim, dance, take drama and arts and crafts classes, cook, and lots more. Snacks, dinner, and full-day programs during school holidays are among the services that this commendable association offers. The cost ranges from $5 to $40 per week depending on income and family size. Free pickup service from local schools is available. They also provide fun programs for teens and a summer camp that families of all incomes and backgrounds can afford.

New York Road Runner's Club Youth Program, 9 E. 89th St., between Madison and Fifth avenues, New York, NY 10128 (tel. 860-4455 for general club info, 737-7480 for youth program details)
Price: $10 annual registration fee
Ages: 2 to 18
   This club isn't just a hangout for marathoners—it's a community service organization devoted to keeping the whole family fit. They offer noncompetitive PeeWee Runs for kids 2 to 6, Junior Runs for ages 6 to 18. They also sponsor an annual Junior Marathon for 5- to 12-year-olds, a week before The Big One where kids get to cross the "real" Marathon Finish Line and everyone gets a medal.
   They also sponsor City-Sports-For-Kids, a year-round program that gives 5- to 12-year-olds a chance to build fitness (and self-esteem) with basketball, track and field, and cross-country competitions.

Playorena, mailing address: 125 Mineola Ave., Roslyn Heights, NY 11577 (tel. toll free 800/645-PLAY)
Price: $164.50 for 12 weekly sessions of 45 minutes on Monday through Saturday; siblings or the same child in a second class costs $110
Ages: 3 months to 4 years
   Directors Michael and Susan Astor have opened more than 80 branches across the country, with five Manhattan locations and 12 more in the other boroughs. Exercise programs for little people (similar to Gymboree's) with adult participation required. They do birthday parties, too.

School for Creative Movement, mailing address: 98 Riverside Drive, Suite 1A, New York, NY 10024 (tel. 724-2044)
Price: $165 for 12 1-hour sessions
Ages: 3 to 7
   What is creative movement? Jack Weiner, founder and director

since 1962, defines it as exercises that "encourage a child's imagination and help kids invent their own movements." Dance classes as well as workouts on the trapeze and rings are held Saturdays at 37 West 21st St.

Sutton Gymnastics & Fitness Center, 440 Lafayette St., at E. 8th Street, New York, NY 10003 (tel. 533-9390)
Price: See text
Ages: 18 months to 18 years (and then to age 80)
   Sutton Gym's attractive 12,000-square-foot gym is equipped with Olympic gymnastic apparatus, including a full-size trampoline. Programs include Baby Gym (18 to 36 months), Kinder Gym (3 to 5 years), Jr. Gym (6 to 9 years), and Pro Gym (age 10 plus). Classes cost $305 for a 16-week session. The popular KinderCamp for ages 3 to 5 is held in the summer (mid-June through July or end of July through mid-August) and costs $700 for 5 weeks (3-hour classes, twice a week.) Two-week sessions range from $375 to $400. You can sign up on a weekly basis, too. This is also a fun place for a gymnastics birthday party ($250 for 10 kids minimum, $15 for each additional child).

SWIMMING

New York City is great but lacks decent swimming pools that are open to the public on a drop-in basis. I was appalled by a public pool on E. 54th Street. Filthy, dismal, depressing. Some NYC hotels like the Holiday Inn Crowne Plaza will allow you to come for a swim on a drop-in basis, at quite a price; check our list of hotels with pools, but call first. Unless you live in a building with a pool or are a member of a club, your child will have to take classes. Here are some ideas:

Aerobics West, 131 W. 86th St., between Columbus and Amsterdam avenues, New York, NY 10024 (tel. 787-3356)
Price: $200 for 12 weekly ½-hour lessons
Ages: 6 months to 9 years
   Three wonderful children's swim programs are available: Swim for Tots for kids 6 months to 3½ years (parental participation required); Swim Magic for kids 3½ to 7 years; and Pre-Competitive Swim for kids 7 to 9 years. The pool is 40 feet long,

which is just the right size to make kids feel comfortable in water and learn to love swimming.

Aquatics, City of New York Parks & Recreation, mailing address: Passerelle Building, Flushing Meadow Park, Corona, NY 11368 (tel. 718/699-4219)
Price: Free
Ages: 1 to 18
Director John Hutchins has done a wonderful job of running free programs in all five boroughs for kids of all ages, starting with Tiny Tots (5 and under), to competitive swimming (if you qualify, try out for the NYC Swim Team!) for advanced swimmers 18 and under; everything in between is available and gives everyone in the city a chance to learn to swim year round.

Asphalt Green, 555 E. 90th St., between York and East End avenues, New York, NY 10128 (tel. 369-8890)
An Olympic-size pool is to be built by the summer of 1993. Let's hope this project is completed; this city desperately needs decent pools for its residents.

Lenox Hill Neighborhood Assn., 331 E. 70th St., between First and Second avenues, New York, NY 10021 (tel. 744-5022)
Price: $215 for a family membership
Ages: Any child who's toilet trained and has medical approval
Drop-in Family Swims are on Friday evenings from 7 to 8pm and Saturday afternoons from 3 to 4:40pm. Free for members, but nonmembers are welcome, too, for a fee of $10 per family. BYO towels and locker lock.

Marymount Manhattan College, 221 E. 71 St., between Second and Third avenues, New York, NY 10021 (tel. 517-0564)
Price: See text
Anyone who signs up for lessons gets free swim time Saturdays from 3:30 to 5pm or Tuesdays from 1 to 2pm. Others must register for Recreational Swim. The cost for a 3-month membership is $135 per person, $77.50 for each additional family member. Hours are weekdays (except Thursdays) from 2:15 to 3:30pm, Saturdays from 1 to 2pm, Sundays from 11am to 12pm.

Granted, their "swimmable" hours are limited, but their 20 × 60 foot beautiful pool (with wheelchair access to boot!) is a good resource for NYC families.

McBurney YMCA, 215 W. 23rd St., between Seventh and Eighth avenues, New York, NY 10011 (741-9210)
Price: See text
Ages: 6 months and up

They are open after school and on weekends as well as summer. Prices vary; for example, 6 classes for ages 6 to 8 months is $65; annual fee, $25; family swims are free on weekends; $663 for adult membership.

92nd Street Y, 1395 Lexington Ave., New York, NY 10128 (tel. 427-6000)
Price: $25 per ½-hour private lesson; $180 for 15 group lessons (½ hour); $180 for annual membership for children 7 to 14; $160 for children 5 or 6 (younger children sign up for individual courses)
Ages: 6 months to adult

For all you polliwogs, guppies, minnows, and turtles out there, the 92nd Street Y has the right class for you in their 75-foot indoor pool. Members receive substantial discounts on class fees.

Trinity School, 101 W, 91 St., New York, NY 10024 (tel. 873-1650, ask for the Facilities Office)
Price: Annual family membership is $650 for four, $50 for each additional family member
Ages: All ages welcome, but children must be accompanied by parents

The Trinity Swim Club is open year round, except for a month from mid-August through mid-September. Pool hours are Mondays through Thursdays 7 to 9:30pm, Saturdays and Sundays 1:30 to 5pm. Closed Fridays. BYO towels.

Vanderbilt YMCA, 224 E. 47th St., between Second and Third avenues, New York, NY 10017 (tel. 755-2410)
Price: Membership is $50 per year for ages 6 months to 13 years; $75 per year for ages 14 to 17
Ages: 18 months and up

Membership entitles kids up to 13 years to free swims on

Mondays through Fridays from 4 to 6pm and on Saturdays from 1 to 4pm. On Saturdays, parents may swim with children for a $1 fee.

A swim program for beginners ("Guppies") to Advanced ("Sharks") is available to members for $40. There's also a Preschool Swim for members age 18 months to 4 years with an adult, $25 for seven ½-hour sessions.

West Side YMCA, 5 W. 63rd St., at Central Park West, New York, NY 10023 (tel. 787-4400)
Price: Weekly sessions range from $80 to $133 per 10 or 13 week term
Ages: 3 months to teens

The names of the courses are catchy: Pikes, Perch, Eels, Shrimp, Starfish, Kipper, Polliwog, Shark, and Porpoise Club! You can also opt for a family membership—$160 for two parents and as many kids as you have. This entitles you to recreational swims on Fridays, Saturdays, and Sundays.

YWCA, 610 Lexington Ave., at 53rd Street (tel. 755-4500)
Price: $90 for 10 ½-hour sessions

They have a program for infants ("H$_2$O Babies"), provided the infant has a note from a pediatrician. Ages 2 to 4 can participate in "Toddlers Swim" that teaches basic swimming skills. Ages 3 to 5 ("Sprites") are given instruction in blowing bubbles, kicking, and floating. Ages 5 to 14 are classified according to swimming skills. Children under 5 must wear plastic panties in the pool, available for purchase from the locker room receptionist.

The Arts

THEATER

The entertainment chapter of this book (Chapter 10) covers this topic. If you live here, however—and you do—seriously consider subscriptions.

Please use Chapter 10, "That's Entertainment" for more information.

New York Shakespeare Festival, Public Theatre, 425 Lafayette St., off 8th Street and Astor Place, New York, NY 10003 (tel. 598-7100)
Price: $30 for individual tickets; subscription rates can bring down the cost to as low as $12
Ages: Any age, whenst ready for Shakespeare

For NYC students, their families, and teachers. In the Fall of 1988, the festival began a "Shakespeare Marathon," a 6-year program to present 36 Shakespeare plays. The late Joseph Papp presented Shakespeare plays for free at the Delacorte Theatre (W. 81st Street in Central Park) and the traditional will go on. As he put it: "We count our achievements by the faces we've lit, by the young minds we've opened and by the generations of theatre-goers we've helped create."

Open Eye: New Stagings, 270 W. 89th St., between Broadway and West End Avenue, New York, NY 10024 (tel. 769-4141)
Price: $125 for a family membership
Ages: 5 and up

Productions throughout the year are of high educational value, with such recent plays as Homer's *Odyssey,* Dickens's *Cricket on the Hearth,* and a multicultural presentation with drama, song, and movement. Family memberships are a terrific value: for $125, you get four season passes to all events (except benefits), four half-price guest tickets to events you attend, and a poster or T-shirt.

Theatreworks, 890 Broadway, New York, NY 10003 (tel. 677-5959)
Price: $125 for 10 shows
Ages: 5 to 14; children under 5 are not admitted

The plays are entertaining, creative, and a delight for adults as well as children. Past performances have included *Harold and the Purple Crayon* and *The Velveteen Rabbit.* Performances are at the

Promenade Theatre on Broadway and 76th Street. The "no-commitment" subscription for $125 includes 10 admissions to shows. In July, tickets are free! Line up at the box office starting at 10am to receive free tickets to that day's performances. They're available on a first-come, first-served basis.

Triplex Theatre, 199 Chambers St., between Greenwich Street and West Side Highway, New York, NY 10007 (tel. 618-1980)
Price: $40 for 10 shows
Ages: 3 and up
   The Triplex offers a 10-pass children's series for only $40 that you can use all at once for a birthday party or any time you wish. Even if you buy individual tickets at only $6, you can hardly afford not to go. This past season has included two contemporary dance companies, a special Christmas performance of *Nutcracker,* and eight classic children's tales. Kids love it. The Triplex is located at the Borough of Manhattan Community College.

ACTING CLASSES

Stage Struck, mailing address: 313 W. 80th St., New York, NY 10024. Classes are held at 162 W. 83rd St. (tel. 787-1044)
Price: $300 to $425 for 15-week sessions
Ages: 6 to 16
   W.C. Fields once advised those in the theater never to work with children, but that hasn't deterred Nancy Hillman, a former actress who starred in Broadway's *Bye Bye Birdie.* She teaches hundreds of kids how to put on productions like *Hello, Dolly, Oliver,* or *A Chorus Line* in once-a-week after-school classes. "I've never met a child who couldn't sing," she claims. "You just have to give them confidence." Bravo!

Weist-Barron, 35 W. 45th St., New York, NY 10036 (tel. 840-7025)
Price: $280 for 8 weekly 2-hour classes
Ages: 4 through teens

The "Kids Love Acting" program here instructs kids in scene study, improvisation, and commercial acting. But the *real* reason many parents love it is that director (and exprofessional actress) Sharon Richardson also builds confidence, enhances creativity, and even increases reading levels. Classes are divided into 4- to 6-year-olds, 7- to 12-year-olds, and teens.

DANCE CLASSES

Ballet Academy East, 1651 Third Ave., between 92nd and 93rd streets, 3rd Floor, New York, NY 10128 (tel. 410-9140)
Prices: $280 for 4 months of weekly 45-minute sessions; $385 for twice-weekly sessions; many other options available
Ages: 2 to adult

My daughters live for their time spent here! The studios are renovated and spotless. The instructors are excellent with children—the little ones seem convinced that these chiffon-clad creatures (Miss Candice, Miss Lola, no Ms.'s here) are fairy princesses in real life. "Mother (or Father or Nanny) and Child" classes introduce 2-year-olds to the joy of moving to music. Pre-Ballet offers 3- to 5-year-olds a noncritical approach to dance, encouraging a musical sense and a healthy dose of fantasy. From 6 up, children learn ballet the traditional way, gradually learning more structure and less improvisation. The ambience here is somewhat more "serious" than many studios around town (even the 2-year-olds require leotards and slippers!). Parents and camcorders are invited to recitals twice a year.

Dance Theatre Workshop, 219 W. 19 St., between Seventh and Eighth avenues, New York, NY 10012 (tel. 254-0286)
Price: $150 per 15-week semester (1½-hour classes)
Ages: 5 to 18

Ellen Robbins teaches children modern dance technique, improvisation, and composition so that kids learn "dance as an art form right from the start."

Dance with Ms. Piver, 1459 Third Ave., between 82nd and 83rd streets, New York, NY 10028 (tel. 517-9436)
Price: $185 for 45-minute to 1-hour class once a week for 15 weeks
Ages: 2½ to teen

Creative Dance, Ballet Foundation, and Jazz Dance are offered at many times during the week. For the youngest, the studio becomes a make-believe garden where sculptures come to life accompanied by voice, guitar, and percussion instruments. For teens, it's a jazz studio where they learn improvisational and technical skills. Whatever the age of your child, it's a good place to learn dance in a low-key, creative atmosphere.

Martha Graham School of Contemporary Dance, 316 E. 63rd St., between First and Second avenues, New York, NY 10021 (tel. 838-5886)

There are modern dance classes for the next generation of dancers for ages 8 to 16. The preteen class is introduced to the Martha Graham method; teens learn repertory and basic dance composition in addition to technique, which is the primary focus. The "Parent and Child Plan" lets the parent participate simultaneously in an adult beginner class. Call for prices and hours.

MUSIC CLASSES

Bloomingdale House of Music, 323 W. 108th St., at Broadway, New York, NY 10025 (tel. 663-6021)
Price: See text
Ages: 2 to adult

Musical instruction for students of all backgrounds. Ages 3½ and up learn the legendary Suzuki method by which toddlers learn to play simple melodies on the violin, viola, and cello before they learn to read music. Parental involvement is encouraged, so they can help the child at home. The cost for 18 1-hour classes is $10 per session (plus a $35 registration fee per family). Private piano lessons for children 5½ and up are only $13. Music theory is taught to children over 8 for $6 a session. Lots of other courses are offered, including a Tumbling Tots program (ages 2 to 3) and Creative Movement (3 to 5). During the month of July, about 35 lucky children in grades 2 through 7 attend "camp" with opera, dance, visual arts, and field trips.

Dalcroze School of Music, 161 E. 73rd St., between Lexington and Third avenues, New York, NY 10021 (tel. 879-0316)
Price: $200 and up
Ages: 3 and up
Dr. Hilda M. Schuster and her staff teach the Dalcroze Method: an approach to music education involving rhythmic movement, ear training, sight reading, dictation, and improvisation at the piano. Both private and group lessons are available.

Jazzmobile, mailing address: 154 W. 127th St., New York, NY 10027 (tel. 866-4900)
Price: Free
Ages: 8 and up
Children and adults of all ages can learn about and play jazz at Saturday workshops held at I.S. 201 on 127th Street between Park and Madison avenues. (Not the safest part of town, so cab it.) Workshops are held from October through April from 10am to 5pm. Jazzmobile also goes on the road, offering jazz demonstrations in schools as well as 80 free summer concerts in the parks and on the streets.

Juilliard School, Pre-College Division, Lincoln Center, 144 W. 66 St., (at Broadway), New York, NY 10023 (tel. 799-5000)
Price: About $3,000 for 1-hour private music lesson, 1-hour solfège, 1-hour theory, and membership to an orchestra and/or chamber music group from mid-September through mid-May
Ages: 8 to 18
For very talented young people, this is the best in instrumental classical instruction. If the above is not enough, your child can learn a second instrument, at an additional cost.

LINCOLN CENTER

Growing Up with Opera (tel. 769-7000)
Price: $35 per person, including kids
Ages: 5 and up

To rid kids (and adults) of the notion that it's more fun to go to the dentist than to the opera, The Metropolitan Opera Guild offers a membership program filled with appealing events. You'll be treated to a behind-the-scenes glimpse of an opera production; live opera performances created especially for children; invitations to a cast party where you can mingle with the singers; and an "Introduction to Opera" home activity kit.

Little Orchestra Society, Administration: 220 W. 42nd St., 18th Floor, New York, NY 10036-7202 (tel. 704-2100)
Price: $84 for three concerts, Lolli-Pops series; $64 to $119 for five Happy Concerts for Young People, depending on seating
Ages: 3 to 12

My 4-year-old was enchanted by "A Musical Toy Store," one of the series of concerts directed by Maestro Dino Amognost to introduce preschoolers to orchestra. (The jolly cast of Giant Stuffed Animals gave the audience not only a taste of Haydn, but toy clarinets!) Fifty-minute shows on Saturdays and Sundays have relocated from Lincoln Center to Florence Gould Hall, French Institute/Alliance Francaise, 55 E. 59th St.

For the 6- to 12-year-old set, there are "Happy Concerts for Young People" performed at Lincoln Center's Avery Fisher Hall on Saturdays only. Early ticket-getters can make reservations for a postshow "Maestro Club" lunch where families can dine with the maestro himself.

New York Philharmonic (tel. 580-8700)
Price: $5, all seats unreserved

Open rehearsals at Lincoln Center's Avery Fisher Hall are held on selected weekdays (except Mondays) at 9:45am. Organize this on a parent-teacher conference day when the kids are off but the rest of the world isn't.

MUSEUM MEMBERSHIPS AND PROGRAMS FOR CHILDREN AND FAMILIES

The following provides details for NYC families on memberships and workshops (for members and nonmembers) at several museums. It's worthwhile to be a member: Not only do you support the museum (it's tax deductible) but you get unlimited admission, newsletters, discounts on workshops and the museums' shops, and other special privileges. See Chapter 8 on Museums for general information on hours, admission prices, accesses, and so on.

🍎 **American Craft Museum,** 40 W. 53rd St., between Fifth and Sixth avenues, New York, NY 10019 (tel. 956-3535)
Family ("Dual") Membership: $65 (2 adults, children under 12)
Members get two invitations to members openings, a subscription to *American Craft* magazine, a 10% discount at the Museum Sales Desk, and special invitations and discounts on educational workshops, lectures, films, and symposia. Also two free admissions to craft fairs across the country.

🍎 **American Museum of Natural History,** Central Park West at 79th Street, New York, NY 10024 (tel. 769-5000)
Members are offered behind-the-scene tours, evening and weekend family programs, a 25% discount on admission to the Hayden Planetarium, 40% off Naturemax films (up to six people) and party privileges. Members also receive a monthly newsletter, a museum calendar of events, and a subscription to *Natural History* magazine.

🍎 **American Museum of the Moving Image,** 35th Avenue at 36th Street, Astoria, NY 11106 (tel. 718/784-0077 for information; tel. 718/784-4520 for reservations)
Family ("Dual") Membership: $45 (2 adults, children to 18)
In addition to unlimited admission, members have reservation privileges for screenings and celebrity appearances in the Riklis Theater. The museum is best for your preteens and up.

🍎 **Brooklyn Children's Museum,** 145 Brooklyn Ave., Brooklyn, NY 11213 (tel. 718/735-4400)
Family Membership: $35 (2 adults, children under 16)
A host of films, special events on weekends, after-school and weekend workshops in a participatory learning environment. Also a museum calendar, newsletter, party privileges and invitations for two to openings, receptions, and members-only events.

🍎 **Children's Museum of Manhattan,** 212 W. 83rd St., between Broadway and Amsterdam Avenue, New York, NY 10024 (tel. 721-1234)

Family Membership: $30 per person, or $50 for a family of four or less, $5 for every additional child

Membership includes admission and a free subscription to the *Parents & Kids Directory* (see "Publications" section). Programs for members AOTW include the Parent-Toddler Program ($345 for 15 sessions, bring lunch) for ages 18 to 36 months with music and movement and hands-on activities. Art programs for kids 3 to 8 years cost $150 on Wednesdays for 10 sessions. Summer programs are also available. Birthday parties cost $175 for 15 children, uncatered, or $250 catered.

The Cloisters, Fort Tryon Park (Fort Washington Avenue near 190th Street), New York, NY 10040 (tel. 923-3700)
Family ("Dual") Membership: $125 (2 adults and children)

There are special gallery workshops for families (for children ages 5 to 12), free with admission to the museum (includes materials). Meets at 1pm in the Main Hall on the first Saturday of each month. There are also week-long programs during Christmas and Easter vacations with enticing topics, such as "Beasts, Monsters, and Pets," and "Poison and Other Medieval Brews."

Hayden Planetarium, 81st Street at Central Park West, New York, NY 10024 (tel. 769-5920)
Family Membership: None, but 25% admission discount for members of the American Museum of Natural History (see above)

They have programs for kids on various Saturdays throughout the year. AOTW programs include the Wonderful Sky with Sesame Street Muppets for ages 3 to 6 and the Secret of Cardboard Rocket for ages 6 to 9 (book 2 to 3 months in advance). There are also sky show performances, laser light shows, and parent/child astronomy courses.

InfoQuest, 550 Madison Ave., at 56th Street, New York, NY 10022 (tel. 605-5555)
Family Membership: Free

There are special programs throughout the summer, call for information.

International Center of Photography, 1130 Fifth Ave., at 94th Street, New York, NY 10128 (tel. 860-1777)

Family ("Supporting Patron") Membership: $100 (2 adults, up to 4 children)

For your future photographers, summer workshops are offered for ages 11 to 18, including photo printing (lab fee is $40; registration is $20). There are also weekend family workshops for kids of any age.

🍎 **Lower East Side Tenement Museum,** 97 Orchard St., between Broome and Delancey streets, New York, NY 10002 (tel. 431-0233)

Family Membership: $35 (2 adults, children under 18)

Members get a 10% discount on all museum gift items, advance notice of programs, invitations to preview performances, and a subscription to *Tenement Times,* a newsletter filled with stories, games, articles, recipes, and more.

🍎 **Metropolitan Museum of Art,** Fifth Avenue at 82nd Street, New York, NY 10028 (tel. 535-7710)

Family (Dual) Membership: $125 (2 adults, children under 16)

Membership includes admission to the Met and the Cloisters and member workshops (at a nominal fee). Whether you're a member or not, there are many outstanding programs (free with admission) for children and families, including the Charles H. Tally Lecture Series for parents and kids ages 6 to 12 on Fridays from 7 to 8pm. On weekends, families with children ages 6 to 12 explore art together at the Uris Center for Education on Fifth Avenue at 81st Street. On Saturdays short films are shown at 12:30 and 2pm. Students ages 10 to 15 can sketch and participate in other art activities. There are workshops for families with developmentally disabled members of all ages as well as free programs for high school students throughout the year.

🍎 **Museum of Holography,** 11 Mercer St., New York, NY 10013 (tel. 925-0581)

Family Membership: $70 (2 adults, children under 18)

Members receive invitations to exhibition previews, lectures, and special events (an invitation I received was a hologram that kept my 2-year-old mesmerized for 15 minutes!) as well as a 10% discount at the museum's gift shop and a subscription to *Holosphere* magazine.

✿ **Museum of Modern Art,** 11 W. 53rd St., New York, NY 10019 (tel. 708-9795)
Family Membership: $90 (2 adults, children under 18)
   The Parent/Child Workshops (ages 5 to 10) at MOMA aim at demystifying museums with different techniques for enhancing the gallery-going experience. On Saturday mornings, children 5 to 10 and their parents can tour the collections before the museum opens to the public. Meet at 10am at the 18 W. 54th St. entrance. The museum also provides a weekend Family Film Series: classic film shorts ranging in subjects from documentary to fantasy provide temporary relief from a common case of TV blahs. Membership also includes admission to the Members Dining Room, a calendar of events and discounts on museum books, reproductions, and gift items.

✿ **Museum of Television and Radio** (formerly the Museum of Broadcasting), 25 W. 52nd St., between Fifth and Sixth avenues, New York, NY 10019 (tel. 888-2525 for membership hotline)
Family Membership: $50 (two adults and children under 16)
   Membership includes unlimited admission to daily programs in the museum's theater and videotheques, use of the library's card catalog, and use of a radio/TV console to view your favorite selections from over 25,000 radio and TV tapes dating back to the 1920's, discounts on lectures and seminars (past speakers have included Alan Alda, Eric Sevareid and writers from *Sesame Street*). On Saturdays at 10am, kids age 8 to 13 can attend a "Re-creating Radio" workshop, where they actually reproduce an old-time radio show themselves. At 12:30pm, there are special film screenings for kids ages 3 to 10. (Past offerings: *The Secret Garden, The Cat in the Hat, The Elephant's Child.*)

✿ **Museum of the City of New York,** Fifth Avenue at 103rd Street, New York, NY 10029 (tel. 534-1672)
Family Membership: $50 (for everyone in the family)
   Special programs, performances, and hands-on workshops are held for families throughout the year on certain Sundays from 1 to 5pm as well as during Christmas and Easter holidays.

🍎 **New-York Historical Society,** 170 Central Park West, between 76th and 77th streets, New York, NY 10024 (tel. 873-3400)
Family ("Dual") Membership: $60 (2 adults, children age 18 and under)

    This is New York State's oldest museum, where members will be invited to special events and to view the Tiffany lamps, Audubon prints, Hudson River paintings, and Early American Founding Father exhibits. (A good way to make American History more palatable to young students.) The staff members are most cooperative and eager to participate in the development of young minds.

🍎 **South Street Seaport Museum,** 207 Front Street, New York, NY 10038 (tel. 669-9400)
Family Membership: $50 (2 adults, children under 18)

    In addition to super family workshops held throughout the year, kids and parents can help raise the sails of the *Pioneer* from late spring to fall for 2- or 3-hour sailings at the Pilothouse on Pier 16 or take 90-minute cruises on the *De Witt Clinton* steamboat. The Children's Center, the 1800s Print Shop, and the Maritime Crafts Center are other popular family choices.

🍎 **Staten Island Children's Museum,** 1000 Richmond Terr., Staten Island, NY (tel. 718/273-2060)
Family Membership: $35 (2 adults, children under 18)

    Interactive exhibits, arts and crafts workshops, films, children's concerts, and a theater in New York's only indoor/outdoor youth museum. It's surrounded by an 84-acre cultural park perfect for picnics and running around.

ART CLASSES

In addition to the many programs for kids at the museums here are a few of the many excellent art schools in the city:

🍎 **Art Students' League,** 215 W. 57th St., between Seventh Avenue and Broadway, New York, NY 10019 (tel. 247-4510)
Price: $40 for ½ day per week for a month, $70 for 1 full day per week for a month

Ages: 8 to 12

Children will learn to paint and draw in classes given on Saturdays only.

Studio in a School Association, 596 Broadway, Suite 701, New York, NY 10012 (tel. 431-6300)

This is a wonderful program that places artists in the public schools to work with children. While the artists expose students to art worlds they would otherwise miss, they also train teachers in art instruction.

The children's work is shown at various places throughout the year—City Gallery, Federal Hall, Paine Webber, subway stations, etc. This program benefits both local artists and schoolchildren. Call to see if it's in your school.

MULTI-ARTS PROGRAMS

ACT Program, Cathedral of St. John the Divine, 1047 Amsterdam Ave., between 110th and 111th streets, New York, NY 10025 (tel. 316-7530)

Price: Call; they vary greatly

Ages: Kindergarten to age 15

The after-school program for kindergarteners to grade 7 and the multi-arts summer program for young people ages 8 to 15 is popular, so book early. You have to sign up far in advance. The summer program runs for 3 weeks in August from 9:30am to 4pm (extended hours available) with workshops in dance, art, music, theater, and video. Located on 13 acres on the west side with two large indoor gyms for rainy days, 80% of the activities in the summer are held outside and include swimming, art, sports, camping, gardening, water games, music, drama, and dance.

Discovery Programs, 251 W. 100th St., at West End Avenue, New York, NY 10025 (tel. 749-8717 or 348-5371 for east side locations)

Price: See text

Ages: 9 months to 14 years

Four Manhattan locations hold Discovery Programs, including the Toddler Center (9 to 36 months) with Gym for Tots, Music, Dance, and Storytime, and art (fees start at $275 for 1 class per week for the fall or spring term of 16 weeks). Classes for ages 3 to 5 include Young Artists and Science Wonders ($275) for 1 class per week. Theater is offered for children 7 to 14 ($325). Dance classes start at age 3, ballet at age 7, and jazz dance is for ages 9 to 14 ($275 for once a week; $450 for twice weekly). An Olympic gymnastics course is also offered (from $325 for once a week). The summer camp is held from mid-June to the end of August.

Educational Alliance West Parenting Center, 80 Fifth Ave., between 13th and 14th streets, New York, NY 10011 (tel. 675-5560)
Price: $180 to $505, depending on the course
This parenting center offers toddler art (called Messy Play), music, dance, gymnastics for ages 20 months to 36 months, and parent discussion groups and workshops, including 6-week summer programs. See "Resources for New York City Parents" section.

Elaine Kaufman Cultural Center (formerly the Hebrew Arts School), Abraham Goodman House, 129 W. 67th St., off Broadway, New York, NY 10023 (tel. 362-8060)
Price: Call; they vary greatly
Ages: 2 to 18
An impressive list of music, dance, art, and theater programs are available, including Dalcroze, piano, violin, and all other instruments. Ballet, jazz dance, tap dance, and theater dance are taught throughout the year as well as many kinds of art classes. Theater classes include creative dramatics, playwriting, and acting.

Funworks for Kids, Sutton Place Synagogue, 225 E. 51st St., New York, NY 10022 (tel. 734-7523)
Price: $325 for once weekly per semester, $595 for twice weekly
Ages: 1 to 4
Funworks programs in three Manhattan locations (also 339 E. 84th St. and 120 W. 76th St.) focus on music, art, and movement. The 90-minute classes include music, coloring, painting, collages, and movement exercises using balls, beanbag hoops, and blocks. A popular sanity-saver for city parents is their "Unstructured Playtimes" which allow you and your child to "just hang out" at

their supervised indoor playground facilities. The cost for this is $100 for 10 2-hour sessions, or $15 on a drop-in basis.

Henry Street Settlement, Louis Abrons Arts Center, 466 Grand St., New York, NY 10002 (tel. 598-0400)
Dance: They offer dance for children and teens (ages 4 to 16), 16 classes for $90.
Music: The music school gives private instruction as well as group lessons. Private sessions for a neighborhood student cost $13 for 40 minutes; for a nonneighborhood student it's $14. Group classes hold 6 students per class. The session is for 34 weeks.
Drama: For ages 14 to 19, classes of 15 to 25 students present a full-length production at the end of the workshop.
Visual Arts: They offer pottery, mask making, parent-toddler art, and experimental art for all different age groups, from ages 2 to 16. This is to whet your appetite for all that is offered at the Henry Street Settlement.

Write or call for your brochure, which includes directions by bus and subway to Grand and Allen streets. Princess Di made a point of coming here on her New York trip. You should, too.

Rhythm and Glues, 1393 York Ave., at 74th Street, New York, NY 10021 (tel. 737-2988)
Ages: 1 to 3
AOTW, classes your 1- to 3-year-olds will like include baking a cake, making pizza, playing in the band, planting flowers, and dramatic play. Children must be accompanied by an adult. Call for hours and prices.

Mini-Trips

The following is a listing of places for outings. If you're in the mood for a day trip, look into these. Call them ahead of time to see what exactly is going on.

THE BRONX

Bronx River Art Center and Gallery, 1087 E. Tremont Ave., Bronx, NY 10460 (tel. 589-5819)

Hours: Wednesday through Saturday from 1 to 6pm
Admission: Free
This is the location of the Sound Garden. There are outdoor installations and gallery works. Call—the exhibits change. It is also the site of festival and art workshops throughout the year.

Wave Hill, 675 W. 252nd St., at Independence Avenue, Bronx (Riverdale), NY 10471 (tel. 549-3200)
Access: Subway and bus—1 or 9 to 231st St.; at the northwest corner of Broadway and 231st Street take 7 bus to 252nd Street and then walk across the Parkway Bridge to Wave Hill (about 90 minutes from Manhattan). Car—Henry Hudson Parkway to 245th Street/250th Street exit; continue north to 252nd Street and follow the signs to Wave Hill (about ½ hour).
Hours: Every day from 10am to 4:30pm
Admission: Free Monday through Friday; on Saturday, Sunday, and holidays, $2 for adults, $1 for students, and free for under 6 (sometimes a charge for craft materials or performance—$2 to $3)
Ages: All ages
Note: Strollers permitted, no food, diaper change difficult. This is open in good weather, so call and check.
For nature-starved New Yorkers, a 28-acre estate. They have a 19th-century mansion and three greenhouses all open to the public. (That's us.) Photography workshops for the family, garden walks, walks in the woods, special performances, and a unique nature program for under-2-year-olds. Of course, you must check to see what's happening before you go, and ask about their special events for kids.

BROOKLYN

Brooklyn Center for the Urban Environment, Tennis House, Prospect Park, Brooklyn, NY 11215 (tel. 718/788-8500)
They have lots of workshops, programs, seminars, and events for families. They also sponsor after-school programs in the parks and various public schools.

QUEENS

🍎 **Alley Pond Environmental Center (APEC)**, 228-06 Northern Blvd., Douglaston, NY 11363 (tel. 718/229-4000)
They have regular preschool programs with seasonal themes. School-age programs, too, and family walks and events.

🍎 **Jamaica Bay Wildlife Refuge**, Cross Bay Boulevard, Broad Channel, NY 11693 (tel. 718/474-0613)
Access: Subway—A to Broad Channel, then a ½-mile walk (takes about 50 minutes from Manhattan, including the walk). Car—Belt Parkway to Exit 17 South, follow Cross Bay Boulevard about 3 miles over the North Channel Bridge (about ½ hour)
Hours: Open all year, Monday through Friday from 8:30am to 5pm, and Saturday and Sunday to 6pm (summer hours)
Admission: Free
Ages: Best for 10 and over, but every age is welcome
Note: Strollers okay (but gravel trails make for rough going), no food available (brown-bag it), diaper change possible but not easy
This is a 9,155-acre preserve that boasts more than 300 species of birds. There is a spectacular view of the New York skyline. It's not all woods—there are salt marshes, fresh water ponds, and gardens.
When you get to the Jamaica Bay Wildlife Refuge, stop at the Visitors Center for a free day permit and printed trail guide ($1) that will tell you what's flying.

🍎 **New York Hall of Science**, 47-01 111th St., Corona, NY 11368 (tel. 718/699-0005)
Family Membership: $40 for all family members (including Grandma)
Most of the exhibits are hands-on. You and yours will find plenty to crank, pedal, and manipulate. Don't lose a second. I have never, never had anything this splendid to provide me with a visual understanding of science. (See Chapter 8 on museums.)

🍎 **Playground for All Children**, Flushing Meadow–Corona Park, 111-01 Corona Ave., Flushing, NY 11368 (tel. 718/699-8283)

This is definitely for your little ones. It's a playground for both able-bodied and disabled children. They have craft workshops as well as free programs that introduce able-bodied children to the world of the disabled.

Queens County Farm Museum, 73-50 Little Neck Parkway, Floral Park, NY 11004 (tel. 718/347-3276)
Hours: Saturday and Sunday from noon to 5pm
Admission: Free

The only place in New York City where kids can take a hayride, a ponyride, and feed farm animals. They also have quilting classes, Native American Indian festivals and craft fairs throughout the year at this 47-acre farm that was in operation before the Revolutionary War.

STATEN ISLAND

Staten Island Institute of Arts and Sciences, 75 Stuyvesant Pl., Staten Island, NY 10301 (tel. 718/727-1135)
Family Membership: $30 (one adult and all children under 18)

The education department has great weekend creative work-shops for kids ages 4 and up, and nifty summer day camp programs for kids ages 6 to 13. (With environmentally correct names like Earth Camp, Young Naturalists, and Museum on the Go.) They're famous for their Dinosaur Parties: 2 hours of prehistoric fun costs $35 plus $7 per child (15 kids minimum; BYO cake and other munchies).

Staten Island Zoo Olympics

This is a 1-day annual event in mid-July (call for the date). Kids learn to do things that any bird is able to do (like build a nest), plus unusual races and games. It's from 1 to 3pm. Bring your toddlers and your teenagers. It's unusual. The ferry ride from Battery Park to Staten Island is part of the fun. With your extra hours, view the zoo—all for $2 per person. The zoo is at 614 Broadway, Staten Island; for more information, call 718/442-3174. For travel information, call 718/442-3100.

BEACHES

There are public (city- or state-operated) beaches at Coney Island, Brighton Beach, Manhattan Beach, Orchard Beach, and Rockaway Beach. None of these has bathhouse facilities, so if you're still interested and wish further information, call the Department of Recreation (tel. 408-0219). The following beaches have bathhouses, snack bars, lifeguards, and rest rooms.

Jones Beach State Park, Wantagh, Long Island, NY (tel. 516/785-1600)

Access: Long Island Railroad—schedules change, so call 718/217-5477 for information to your Wantagh destination

Hours: 8am to 7pm, daily in season

Admission: Free; bathhouse, $3 includes locker (small parking fee)

If you choose to bypass the ocean for pool swimming, there is a charge. There is also a fee if you wish to play miniature golf or paddle tennis. There is a boardwalk and there are playgrounds for the kids.

Besides snack bars, there is a genuine sit-down restaurant. The sand is white and fine. Because this is a state park, it's well cared for and supervised (AOTW). The fees mentioned for recreation are nominal for the same reason.

If you're driving, try West End 2, the farthest and largest beach; it's gorgeous, and not crowded if you don't mind walking. Jones Beach organizes fishing contests, deep-sea fishing trips, a yearly children's activity day, and much more.

Orchard Beach, Pelham Bay Park, Bronx (tel. 885-2275)

Access: Subway and bus—6 to Pelham Bay, then the Bx12 bus to Orchard Beach

Admission: Free; no charge for storage lockers, but BYO lock. End of May to the beginning of September, 7am to 7pm

There is a picnic area if you choose to brown-bag it, snack bars, and a cafeteria if you don't want to shlep. The beach is huge. They have play areas for the kids.

Jacob Riis Park, Beach 149th Street to Beach 169th Street, Queens (tel. 718/474-4600)

Access: Subway and bus—A or C to Rockaway Park–116th Street, then the Q22 bus to Jacob Riis Park
Hours: 6am to midnight
Admission: Free

   This beach is wide, white, and beautiful. There is a boardwalk to stroll and playgrounds in which the kids may play. AOTW, they were closing the bathhouses temporarily, so call to check.

Wolfes Pond Park, Hylan Boulevard and Cornelia Avenue, Staten Island (tel. 718/984-8266)
Access: Ferry and bus—Staten Island Ferry to St. George, then the No. 78 bus to Wolfes Pond; this takes 90 minutes because the bus ride is a full hour, but not unpleasant
Hours: 10am to 6pm, daily in season
Admission: Free
Note: Strollers permitted, brown-bag your food for the picnic area, diaper change possible

   This is beach in the country. You may swim at the beach or there's a freshwater pond. There are birds, a picnic area, a playground, and a lovely day to be had by all.

Excursions Outside the City

State travel bureaus are an often overlooked but terrific source of information on events, places to stay, adventure trips, and are always free! Here's how to contact them in our neighboring states.

CONNECTICUT

Connecticut Tourism, 865 Brook St., Rocky Hill, CT 06067 (tel. 203/258-4290 or toll free 800/CT-BOUND)
   New England's beauty starts in Connecticut: endless things to do with kids, including the **Norwalk Aquarium** (tel. 203/853-7477) and superb beaches (many are public). **Mystic Seaport** with 19th-century ships as well as a Children's Museum makes for a lovely weekend (about 3 hours from New York City) with great beaches nearby (tel. 203/572-0711).

Between May 1st and October 15th, take your kids on an **Out O'Mystic Schooner Cruise** (tel. toll free 800/243-0416). Ride a steamship up the Connecticut River (tel. 203/345-4507).

NEW JERSEY

New Jersey Division of Travel and Tourism, C.N. 826, Trenton, NJ 08625 (tel. 609/292-2470)

Swimming on the Jersey shore, skiing, apple picking in the fall, biking in gorgeous countryside. Call for a free vacation kit.

Action Park, Rte. 94, Vernon, NJ 07462 (tel. 201/827-2000)

Access: Bus—Lincoln Tunnel to Rte. 3, then west to 46 west to 23 north to 94 north (takes about 1 hour)

Hours: Seasonal; Monday through Thursday from 10am to 9pm, and Friday and Saturday to 10pm

Admission: $24.95 for adults, $17.95 for children 6 through 8 years, free for under 6

Ages: Toddlers and up

This is the world's largest water park. There are rides, water slides, and all sorts of good activities. For the younger crowd there are three shows daily and rides for the very young. Bring a bathing suit and a change of clothing. One never knows. Everyone will have a swell time. Wintertime they have great skiing.

NEW YORK STATE

I Love New York, New York State Department of Economic Development, One Commerce Plaza, Albany, NY 12245 (tel. toll free 800/CALL-NYS)

You'll find literature such as *I Love New York Trips by Car, I Love New York State Travel and Adventure Guide,* and *I Love New York Skiing and Winter Adventures* most useful. Here are specific ideas: **Strawberry picking** in June at the Greig Farm, Red Hook, NY (tel. 914/758-5762) (2 hours north of Manhattan). **Whale watching** in the summer on the Okeanos Whale Watch Cruises, Montauk, NY (tel. 516/728-4522). **Artpark,** Lewiston, NY (tel.

716/745-3377 or 716/754-9001) with daily children's productions, overlooking Niagara Gorge. **Long Island Game Farm,** Manorville, NY (tel. 516/878-6644), 300 acres with Bambiland, Old MacDonald's Farm, rides (mid-April to mid-October). **Kayaking** through the Nissequoque River on Long Island's North Shore (tel. 516/979-8244). **Sleepy Hollow** is fun to visit around Halloween: This is the home of the headless horseman (tel. 914/631-8200).

PENNSYLVANIA

Pennsylvania Department of Commerce, Bureau of Travel Marketing, 230 S. Broad St., 5th Floor, Philadelphia, PA 19102-3826 (tel. toll free 800/VISIT-PA). Visit the Amish country, ski in the Poconos, go on fishing trips and camping vacations, enjoy Hershey chocolate country, and the ultimate treat for kids: Sesame Place. So close to home, and so beautiful.

Hawk Mountain Sanctuary, Kempton, PA (tel. 215/756-6961).
If your kids love bird-watching, then take a long weekend. They're open every day of the year. It's 4 hours from NYC.

Point Pleasant Canoe and Tube, P.O. Box 6, Point Pleasant, PA 18950 (tel. 215/297-TUBE)
Hours: Seasonal, 8am to 6pm
Ages: All ages
Admission: $12 for adults, $10 for children under 12 for a 1- to 4-hour tubing, canoeing, or rafting trip
Access: Bus—It's less than a 2-hour ride from the Port Authority Bus Terminal; call 564-8484 for schedule and prices. Car—From the Lincoln Tunnel, take U.S. 22 West to U.S. 202 South to N.J. 12 West to Pa. 32 (Frenchtown), then 7 miles south to Point Pleasant; it takes about 90 minutes
Note: There is a Point Pleasant, New Jersey, as well. You want Point Pleasant, *Pennsylvania.* Let us avoid an error
President Marie McBrier welcomes families who come from around the world and will be happy to accommodate anyone with special needs, too.
There is no park like this and none better. It's absolutely the

most fun you could possibly imagine. You and the kids will have the time of your lives. Pick a really warm day—it's all on or in the crystal-clear water. Don't forget suits and towels.

Sesame Place, Langhorne, PA 19047 (tel. 215/757-1100 for recorded information, 215/752-7070 for a person)
Hours: May through September
Credit Cards: M, V; for admission and merchandise only
Access: Unfortunately, AOTW there is no access by public transportation. By Car, it's 95 miles from New York; take the tunnel or bridge to the New Jersey Turnpike, then Interstate 95 to the Oxford Valley or Levittown exit

Here you'll find 40 outdoor activities, Sesame Street characters working the crowds, a replica of the famous Sesame Street neighborhood, daily shows, and almost 100 Sesame Street computer video games. (Be warned, admission does not include video game tokens—you need $1 for 3.) If you've got small children (or very short adults) you should know that there are height restrictions for some activities. Pack swimwear; it will definitely be needed for many of the rides. It's a terrific outing for younger kids. They say 3 to 13 years (I say 2 to 10 years), but the adults will love it. It's fun, it's safe, and it's clean.

BIKE TRIPS OUTSIDE THE CITY

Country Cycling and Hiking Tours, 140 W. 83rd St., New York, NY 10024 (tel. 874-5151)
This is lots of fun for family outings. The best trips they organize with kids are strawberry-picking tours along the back roads of eastern Long Island in June and apple picking in the fall.
For longer trips consider the following:

Travel with Your Children (TWYCH), 80 Eighth Ave., New York, NY 10011 (tel. 206-0688)
Price: $35 annual fee
This travel information resource organization is headed by Dorothy Jordan, Travel Editor of *Family Circle* and consultant to several other publications. She provides skiing, cruising, or any kind of vacation info for families. She has the most up-to-date

travel info and publishes *Family Travel Times* (see "Publications" section in this chapter).

Summer in the City

Summer programs are offered by the museums, the Ys, the zoo, the parks, and the libraries. Here are but a few. Please note that all costs, activities, and dates of summer camps and summer programs are subject to change.

THE YS

Emanu-El, YM-YWHA Midtown, 344 E. 14th St., between First and Second avenues, New York, NY 10003 (tel. 674-7200)
Ages: 6 to 12
They have 4-week sessions, 6-week sessions, and all sorts of programs.

McBurney YMCA, 215 W. 23rd St., between Seventh and Eighth avenues, New York, NY 10011 (tel. 741-9210)
Ages: 2½ to 16
They have programs by the week from 9am to 5pm and programs with extended hours. Call for current information.

92nd Street YM-YWHA, 1395 Lexington Ave., need I add at 92nd St?, New York, NY 10128 (tel. 996-1100)
Ages: 3 to 18
Programs forever. New York residents could spend their entire life attending programs at the 92nd Street Y, and they would still come up with something new. What a place! Call for a free brochure. Membership is required. The single best investment you may make.

West Side YMCA, 5 W. 63rd St., off Central Park West, New York, NY 10023 (tel. 787-4400, ext. 128)
Ages: 3 to 15
They have 2-week sessions, which you may extend. Call for current information.

THE BRONX ZOO

🍎 **New York Zoological Society,** 185th Street and Southern Boulevard, Bronx, NY 10460 (tel. 220-5114)

Ages: 5 to 12

Prices are lower for Zoological Society members. The Zoo camp programs are given on a weekly basis and are absolutely wonderful for your animal-loving kids. They can even stay overnight at the zoo! Call well in advance for information and reservations.

PARKS

🍎 **Sports and Recreation in Central Park,** North Meadow (tel. 348-4867)

Ages: 3 to 6 and 8 to 13

Programs are for 3-day periods during July and August.

🍎 **Summer Programs,** City of New York (tel. 360-8111)

These are also run by the New York City Parks and Recreation Department.

LIBRARIES

The New York Public Library offers more services of the highest quality than one may imagine. It would seem to me that if these administrators took over the subway system, it would operate like silk off a spool.

Pick up your copy of *Events for Children,* available free of charge at all branches of the New York Public Library. Program inquiries may be made by calling 340-0849 for telephone references or 340-0906 for children's services.

Film Classics

🍎 **The Children's Room,** New York Public Library at Lincoln Center, 111 Amsterdam Ave., between 64th and 65th streets, New York, NY 10023 (tel. 870-1633)

Hours: 2 to 5:45pm Mondays, Wednesdays, Thursdays, and Fridays; Saturdays 1 to 4:45pm; closed Sundays and Tuesdays

Admission: Free
Ages: 2 to 14

One mother of a 3-year-old claims this is her favorite place in New York. There are wonderful programs here: sing-alongs, storytelling, puppet shows. Rumor has it that they are moving across the street to the Riverside Branch Library.

🍎 **Donnell Library Center,** Central Children's Room, 20 W. 53rd St., between Fifth and Sixth avenues, New York, NY 10019 (tel. 621-0636)
Hours: Year round, including summer. Closed Fridays
Admission: Free
Ages: Vary with subjects; check

This program is made up of fine feature films: *Willie Wonka, Tom Thumb,* and others of this ilk.

Other Programs

There are dance programs for parents and children from ages 3 to 5 years, as well as a wealth of other programs for all ages of kids—reading clubs, craft programs, etc. Preregistration is required for most. Library program space is limited and admission is on a first-come, first-served basis.

All programs are subject to last-minute change and cancellation.

These two branches also have music and theater productions in the summer. Check for schedules.

Sailing

🍎 **Offshore Sailing School,** 459 City Island Ave., City Island, NY (tel. 885-3200 or toll free 800/221-4326)
Price: See text
Ages: 12 and up

The 3- and 4-day courses (offered from mid-April to mid-October) cost $415 and $425 during the week and $425 on weekends and holidays, from 8:30am to 1:30pm or from 11am to 6pm. Two hours are spent in the classroom and 5 hours on their

27-foot racing sloop, the *Soling*. The fees include 8 additional hours of sailing. Bus transportation is available for $10 round-trip from Manhattan. They also have courses on Captiva Island, Cape Cod, and in Florida and the Caribbean. They're now connected with Moorings if you'd like to charter a vessel for the family.

Day Camps

Summertime, and the living is easier for the kids and you if your youngster is committed to a structured program. Call the number below for a complete New York City Day Camp Directory of all the day camps licensed by the Department of Health. They're all in Manhattan.

Department of Health, 65 Worth St., Second Floor, Bureau for Day Camps and Recreation, New York, NY 10013 (tel. 334-7735)

The list you receive will be according to zip codes. If you wish to have information on camps in other boroughs, or camps listed, don't hesitate to call the above number. They also have camps for children with special needs.

American Camping Assn., New York Section, 12 W. 31st St., New York, NY 10010 (tel. 268-7822 or toll free 800/777-CAMP)

The ACA provides parents with guidance in selecting an accredited ACA summer camp meeting their health, safety, quality programming, and staff standards. The Camp Referral Service is free and hosts two camp fairs in the winter at the 92nd Street Y. The ACA has more than 5,200 individual members and 2,400 affiliated camps in the United States.

If you're considering a day camp out of the city, find out how long the trip is and when your youngster is to be picked up and delivered. If he is the first to be picked up and the last to be delivered, you must decide if he's spending the summer on a bus or at a camp.

Check out the waterfront supervision. How many counselors for how many children? Is the instruction given by a qualified person? How many children in a group? Must your child participate in every activity?

Often the wrong choices are made because your youngster's friend is going to a camp. You're investing your child's time and your money. Make a thoughtful selection—don't just go with the flow.

The lace on my sneaker broke. I have visited not one of these facilities. Some are recommendations from mothers who have had children in these programs. Others I read about.

For those of you in search of more bucolic surroundings, here's a random list of day camps that involve a bus ride. *Note:* Prices and dates are subject to change.

Billdave Summer Day Camp, 206 E. 85th St., New York, NY 10028 (tel. 535-7151)
Price: $1,275 for 4 weeks to $2,175 for 8 weeks, including transportation and hot lunch
Ages: 4 to 12

This camp is located in Riverdale, NJ (25 minutes from Manhattan). Their sleep-away camp (for boys) is located in Sebago, Maine ($1,950 for 4 weeks; $2,950 for 8 weeks plus transportation). Both camps are accredited members of the American Camping Assn.

Cavaliers Summer Day Camp, 19 W. 96th St., New York, NY 10025 (tel. 580-1755)
Hours: Monday through Friday from 8am to 4:30pm
Prices: $2,000 for 5 weeks, $2,600 for 8 weeks
Ages: 4 to 12 (coed)

Bring a brown bag. Door-to-door transportation is provided to Old Tappan, New Jersey. Swimming, tennis, baseball, soccer, and basketball

Champions Sports Club (tel. 427-3800), see "Burn-Off" section

Children's Aid Camp at East Harlem Center, 130 E. 101st St., New York, NY 10029 (tel. 348-2343)
Ages: 6 to 12 years

The fees here are on a sliding scale, according to parents' income. Chaperoned sleep-aways for the older children.

🍎 **Hillard Day Camp,** P.O. Box 155, Hartsdale, NY 10530 (tel.
914/949-8857)
Prices: About $2,875 for end of June through end of August,
weekdays
Ages: 3 to 12
   Team sports and games. Swimming, raft races, pony riding,
archery, miniature golf, nature studies, music, drama, and dance.
Hot lunch is served. Menu sent in advance. Door-to-door transportation is provided from Manhattan to Westchester.

🍎 **Mohawk Day Camps,** Old Tarrytown Rd., White Plains, NY
10603 (tel. 914/949-2635)
Hours: Monday through Friday from 9am to 4:15pm, end of June
to end of August
Price: $2,850, plus $210 transportation from Manhattan
Ages: 3 to 12
   Boys and girls are together until they reach the 4½-year level.
Then they're in separate groups. Girls have dance and drama
along with the other activities. These are drawing, model and
hobby shop, nature study, computer programming, swimming,
miniature golf, bowling, field sports, pony rides, and tennis. Lunch
is provided by the camp.

🍎 **Urban Day Camps,** New York City Department of Parks and
Recreation—Manhattan (tel. 408-0204); Bronx (tel. 430-
1824); Brooklyn (tel. 718/965-8939); Queens (tel. 718/520-
5920); Staten Island (tel. 718/720-6864)
Price: $100
Ages: 6 to 14 years
   Citywide recreation programs at more than 40 sites plus field
trips. You must have proof of a medical examination your young-
ster has had within the year.
   Registrants must sign up in person. Registration is from May 1 to
May 16. Call your borough for information.

🍎 **USDAN Center for the Creative and Performing Arts,** 185
Colonial Springs Rd., Wheatley Heights (Long Island), NY
11798 (tel. 772-6060 or 516/643-7900)
Hours: Monday through Friday from 10am to 3:20pm, end of June
through end of August

Price: Theater arts programs are $1,195 and other regular programs are $950; transportation from all boroughs runs about $365 extra; registration, $75

Ages: 8 to 19

Classes in the arts are conducted in a 250-acre woodland setting. There are four student orchestras, four bands, four choruses. All musical instruments for instruction as well as performance. Art, painting, photography, sculpture, ceramics, creative writing, TV and video arts, graphics. Dance is modern, tap, and ballet. Students study a major subject for 2 hours a day and a minor in a "contrasting" field. One hour swim each day in one of three Olympic-size pools. Daily concerts. Bring the brown bag.

SLEEP-AWAY CAMP

This is one listing. It's something special.

Beginnings Professional Entertainment Arts Residency, 16 Second Ave., Pelham, NY 10803 (tel. 914/636-4672)

Price: $695 for 9 days

Ages: 5 to 24

If you feel your child has any interest and/or talent in the performing arts, call director Peter Sklar. Aside from being a delightful, talented man, he has the qualifications: a Masters in Education from Harvard, he has studied at Juilliard and is a professional pianist. More important, he is thirty something, genuinely likes kids, and understands them.

Along with acting, ballet, TV, and stage training, kids enjoy all the other camping activities at a variety of facilities in upstate New York, northeastern Pennsylvania, and northern New Jersey. This is one of a kind—quality all the way.

School Summer Programs

The following is a further sampling of summer programs offered in Manhattan. This is a list of some schools that offer summer programs for fun, education, or both. Learning is fun, remember?

You will see that many of these may accept your youngster by the week, as well as for a month or the season. *Note:* Dates and prices are subject to change

Bank Street School, 610 W. 112th St., between Riverside Drive and Broadway, New York, NY 10025 (tel. 222-6700)
Hours and Price: Mid-June to end of July (2-week minimum), Monday through Friday from 8:30am to 3pm, Wednesdays to 4:30pm; $190 per week, $50 more for 3 to 5:30pm
Ages: 4 to 8
This program includes field trips, swimming at Barnard pool, sports, music, arts and crafts, games, and woodworking. The kids bring their own lunches. Snacks are available. Friday is barbecue day; premises air-conditioned. They also offer a 2-week program for 8- to 10-year-olds that includes trips around the city and a multimedia program for $200.

Brownstone School, 128 W. 80th St., between Columbus and Amsterdam avenues, New York, NY 10024 (tel. 874-1341)
Hours and Price: End of June to the first week of September— Monday through Friday from 9am to 1pm, $110 per week; 9am to 4pm, $146 per week; 8am to 6pm, $177 per week
Ages: 2½ to 8
Field trips around New York and environs (including a weekly trip to Lake Tiorati near Bear Mountain), games, arts and crafts, water sprinkler. Lunch and snacks are part of this program.

Calhoun Summer Days, Calhoun School, 433 West End Ave., at 81st Street, New York, NY 10024 (tel. 877-1700)
Hours and Price: Mid-June to August, Monday through Friday. $125 per week for half-day program for 3- and 4-year-olds; $250 per week for full-day program for older kids (8am to 5:30pm, extended hours available)
Ages: 3 to 12
Swimming, sports, and weekly outings. Kids bring their own lunch. Snacks are available.

Cathedral School of St. John the Divine, A.C.T. Program, 1047 Amsterdam Ave., at 110th Street, New York, NY 10025 (tel. 316-7530)

Hours and Price: Mid-June to August, Monday through Friday from 9:30am to 4pm, $165 per week; extended hours available
Ages: 3½ to 14

A 13-acre oasis where campers garden, play in fields, and eat under the shade of cherry trees. They also have two large indoor gyms for rainy days. There's a 2-week minimum and a nonrefundable deposit per session/per child of $100 which is applied to tuition.

Creative Arts at Convent of the Sacred Heart, 1 E. 91st St., at Fifth Avenue, New York, NY 10128 (tel. 722-4745)
Hours: Mid-June to end of July, Monday through Friday from 9am to 3pm
Price: $1,000 for 6 weeks
Ages: 8 to 15

This is a multi-arts program that includes dance, drama, music film, video, and visual arts. Direction in the theater arts is provided by professionals. There are courses in newspaper, computers, science, and technology. Gymnastics and athletics are offered as well. Brown bags for lunch. The program culminates with an all-day Arts Festival and musical production.

Dalton Early Childhood Program, 62 E. 91st St., between Park and Madison avenues, New York, NY 10128 (tel. 722-5160)
Hours and Price: Beginning of July to mid-August, Monday through Friday from 9am to 4pm, $230 per week (4-week minimum). Add $60 per week for door-to-door transportation
Ages: 4 to 12

Swimming, gym activities, science, sculpture, and outings to the park. They provide lunch with this program. Make reservations in early February with a deposit. This fills quickly! For ball fans (both boys and girls) they also offer a Baseball and Softball Camp: daily games and coaching at Randalls Island from 9am to 12pm for $100 a week. There's also an academic summer school program for high school students.

Fieldston Outdoors, Fieldston Lower School, Fieldston Road and Manhattan College Parkway, Bronx, NY 10471 (tel. 601-0103)

Hours: Monday through Thursday from 8:30am to 3:45pm, on Friday to 2:45pm. Program runs from end of June to beginning of August
Price: $750 for 3 weeks, $1,395 for 6 weeks; transportation extra
Ages: 5 to 11 years

All children are offered swimming, tennis, rafting, hiking, painting, printing, nature studies, music, gardening, caring for farm animals, and trips to historical sites. Brown bags for lunch. For older children whose parents book early (try January) there's a 1-week sleep-away camp in Vermont (additional cost, of course).

Horace Mann Barnard Day Camp, 4440 Tibbett Ave., at 246th Street, Bronx, NY 10471 (tel. 601-3200)
Hours: Beginning of July through mid-August, Monday through Friday from 9am to 4pm
Price: $1,140; transportation to and from Manhattan is additional
Ages: 4 to 12

Swimming, tennis, athletics, crafts, drama, gymnastics, and field trips. They provide lunch. A deposit is required.

Horace Mann Summer School, 231 W. 246th St., Bronx (Riverdale), NY 10471 (tel. 548-4000)
Hours: End of June to beginning of August, Monday through Thursday from 8:45am to 4pm; on Friday to 2pm
Price: About $1,150
Ages: 7th to 12th grades

Classes available in academic subjects and the creative arts. Sports, driver's ed, and typing are also available. The afternoons are for sports and recreation. Lunch may be bought at the school. Additional cost for tennis on 10 to 12 courts is $240 extra (2 to 4pm)

Joy McCormack's All Day Nursery, Battery Park City, 215 South End Ave., New York, NY 10280 (tel. 945-0088)
Hours: Monday through Friday, 8am to 6pm, from beginning of July to end of August
Price: $850 per month for 5 full days, for 18 months and younger; $825 per month for 5 full days, for older kids. For both groups, shorter weeks and/or half-day programs are available for less
Ages: 6 months to 6 years

Here, kids can splash in a wading pool, sandplay in a nearby park, and take rides in a specially built wagon along the Battery Park esplanade. There's storytelling, singing, and barbecues in the backyard of this nursery school which is actually several linked, air-conditioned apartments. Staffers are certified early childhood education teachers.

Trinity Summer School, 139 W. 91st St., between Columbus and Amsterdam avenues, New York, NY 10024 (tel. 873-1650)
Hours: Third week of June to beginning of August, Monday through Friday from 9am to 2pm
Price: $425 to $720
Ages: 12 to 18
Algebra, geometry, precalculus, word processing, driver's ed, biochemistry, physics, you name it.

U.N.I.S. Summer Program, United Nations International School, 24-50 East River Dr., at 25th Street, New York, NY 10010 (tel. 684-7400)
Hours and Price: Mid-June to end of July, Monday through Friday, $110 per week from 9am to noon; $220 per week from 9am to 3:30pm (extended day from 3:30 to 5:30pm $80 extra per week)
Ages: 3½ to 18
Here, children are exposed to a unique international perspective. Program for 3½- to 7-year-olds offers games, swimming, art, drama, cooking, movement, and recreation in a beautiful fully equipped playground. For 8- to 17-year-olds, team sports, karate, rhythmic gymnastics, roller skating, drama, chess, photography, video production, sewing, cooking, and much, much more believe it or not. Academic courses available, too, including math, English, Japanese, French, SAT preparation. Fees for these vary, so call.

Village Community School, 272 W. 10th St., at Greenwich Street, New York, NY 10014 (tel. 691-5146)
Hours and Price: 2½ weeks in June, Monday through Friday from 9am to 3pm for $170 per week; for an extended day (3 to 5:30pm), add $4.50 per extra hour
Ages: 5 to 13
Outings twice a week. Barbecues, baseball, basketball, swim-

ming, volleyball, computers, cooking, drama, mask and mural painting, arts and crafts. Bring the brown bag.

COLLEGES FOR KIDS & PARENTS!

Many colleges and universities have summer and/or school-year programs for kids and/or their parents. Here are examples.

Cornell Adult University, 626 Thurston Ave., Ithaca, NY 14850 (tel. 607/255-6260)
Price: Summer: $635 to $730 for adults, $220 to $330, depending on age of children. This includes housing, meals, and accommodations for 1 week
Ages: 3 to adult
Families can experience campus life together in the summer for week-long stays (yes, in dorms). Little Bears ages 3 to 5 can join the nursery school programs with field trips; children ages 5 to 12 and teenagers can take a host of interesting morning courses and in the afternoon swim, canoe, backpack, all while Mom and Dad take adult courses. This is a unique family experience at a very reasonable cost. Ithaca is beautiful.

Hofstra University, 1000 Fulton Ave., Hempstead, NY 11550 (tel. 516/463-5993)
Price: $100 per course for Saturdays during the school year (fee varies according to subject). Their dynamic summer camp is also available for kids, ages 7 to 15 with the above subjects as well as sports ($550 for 2 weeks)
Ages: 3 to 12
Hofstra offers classes in computer skills, language arts, martial arts, reading, swimming, etc.

Long Island University, C W Post Campus, Northern Blvd., Brookville, NY 11548 (tel. 516/299-2376)
Ages: Grades 2 to 6
Classes for gifted children are held during the school year in advanced reading and study skills (tel. 516/299-2160). Entertainment for children and families is often offered at the Tilles Center (tel. 516/299-2376).

Index

GENERAL INFORMATION

SIGHTS & ATTRACTIONS

EXCURSION AREAS

ACCOMMODATIONS

KEY TO ABBREVIATIONS: *E* = Expensive; *I* = Inexpensive; *M* = Moderate; *VE* = Very Expensive

RESTAURANTS

BY CUISINE

KEY TO ABBREVIATIONS: *B* = Budget; *E* = Expensive; *I* = Inexpensive; *M* = Moderate; *VE* = Very Expensive

BY AREA

SHOPPING

CLOTHING

EVERYTHING ELSE

FROMMER'S CITY GUIDES
(Pocket-size guides to sightseeing and tourist accommodations and facilities in all price ranges)

☐ Amsterdam/Holland $8.95	☐ Minneapolis/St. Paul $8.95
☐ Athens. $8.95	☐ Montréal/Québec City. $8.95
☐ Atlanta $8.95	☐ New Orleans. $8.95
☐ Atlantic City/Cape May $8.95	☐ New York $12.00
☐ Bangkok. $12.00	☐ Orlando $12.00
☐ Barcelona. $12.00	☐ Paris $8.95
☐ Belgium $7.95	☐ Philadelphia $11.00
☐ Berlin. $10.00	☐ Rio $8.95
☐ Boston. $8.95	☐ Rome. $8.95
☐ Cancún/Cozumel/Yucatán $8.95	☐ Salt Lake City $8.95
☐ Chicago $9.95	☐ San Diego. $8.95
☐ Denver/Boulder/Colorado Springs. . . .$8.95	☐ San Francisco $12.00
☐ Dublin/Ireland. $10.00	☐ Santa Fe/Taos/Albuquerque. $10.95
☐ Hawaii $12.00	☐ Seattle/Portland $12.00
☐ Hong Kong. $7.95	☐ St. Louis/Kansas City. $9.95
☐ Las Vegas. $8.95	☐ Sydney. $8.95
☐ Lisbon/Madrid/Costa del Sol $8.95	☐ Tampa/St. Petersburg $8.95
☐ London $12.00	☐ Tokyo. $8.95
☐ Los Angeles $8.95	☐ Toronto $8.95
☐ Mexico City/Acapulco $8.95	☐ Vancouver/Victoria. $7.95
☐ Miami $8.95	☐ Washington, D.C. $12.00

FROMMER'S $-A-DAY® GUIDES
(Guides to low-cost tourist accommodations and facilities)

☐ Australia on $40 a Day $13.95	☐ Israel on $40 a Day. $13.95
☐ Costa Rica, Guatemala & Belize	☐ Mexico on $45 a Day $18.00
on $35 a Day. $15.95	☐ New York on $65 a Day. $15.00
☐ Eastern Europe on $25 a Day $16.95	☐ New Zealand on $45 a Day $16.00
☐ England on $50 a Day. $17.00	☐ Scotland & Wales on $40 a Day $18.00
☐ Europe on $45 a Day $19.00	☐ South America on $40 a Day $15.95
☐ Greece on $35 a Day $14.95	☐ Spain on $50 a Day $15.95
☐ Hawaii on $70 a Day. $18.00	☐ Turkey on $40 a Day. $22.00
☐ India on $40 a Day. $20.00	☐ Washington, D.C., on $45 a Day. $17.00
☐ Ireland on $40 a Day. $17.00	

FROMMER'S CITY $-A-DAY GUIDES

☐ Berlin on $40 a Day $12.00	☐ Madrid on $50 a Day (avail. Jan '92) . . .$13.00
☐ Copenhagen on $50 a Day $12.00	☐ Paris on $45 a Day $12.00
☐ London on $45 a Day $12.00	☐ Stockholm on $50 a Day (avail. Dec. '91)$13.00

FROMMER'S FAMILY GUIDES

☐ California with Kids $16.95	☐ San Francisco with Kids. $17.00
☐ Los Angeles with Kids $17.00	☐ Washington, D.C., with Kids (avail. Jan
☐ New York City with Kids (avail. Jan '92) $18.00	'92). $17.00

SPECIAL EDITIONS

☐ Beat the High Cost of Travel. $6.95	☐ Marilyn Wood's Wonderful Weekends
☐ Bed & Breakfast—N. America $14.95	(CT, DE, MA, NH, NJ, NY, PA, RI, VT) . . .$11.95
☐ Caribbean Hideaways. $16.00	☐ Motorist's Phrase Book (Fr/Ger/Sp) $4.95
☐ Honeymoon Destinations (US, Mex &	☐ The New World of Travel (annual by
Carib). $14.95	Arthur Frommer for savvy travelers) . . .$16.95

(TURN PAGE FOR ADDITONAL BOOKS AND ORDER FORM)

☐ Paris Rendez-Vous $10.95	☐ Travel Diary and Record Book. $5.95
☐ Swap and Go (Home Exchanging). $10.95	☐ Where to Stay USA (from $3 to $30 a
	night). $13.95

FROMMER'S TOURING GUIDES

(Color illustrated guides that include walking tours, cultural and historic sites, and practical information)

☐ Amsterdam. $10.95	☐ New York $10.95
☐ Australia $12.95	☐ Paris $8.95
☐ Brazil $10.95	☐ Rome. $10.95
☐ Egypt. $8.95	☐ Scotland. $9.95
☐ Florence. $8.95	☐ Thailand. $12.95
☐ Hong Kong $10.95	☐ Turkey $10.95
☐ London $12.95	☐ Venice $8.95

GAULT MILLAU

(The only guides that distinguish the truly superlative from the merely overrated)

☐ The Best of Chicago $15.95	☐ The Best of Los Angeles $16.95
☐ The Best of Florida $17.00	☐ The Best of New England $15.95
☐ The Best of France $16.95	☐ The Best of New Orleans. $16.95
☐ The Best of Germany $18.00	☐ The Best of New York $16.95
☐ The Best of Hawaii. $16.95	☐ The Best of Paris $16.95
☐ The Best of Hong Kong $16.95	☐ The Best of San Francisco $16.95
☐ The Best of Italy. $16.95	☐ The Best of Thailand. $17.95
☐ The Best of London $16.95	☐ The Best of Toronto $17.00

☐ The Best of Washington, D.C. $16.95

THE REAL GUIDES

(Opinionated, politically aware guides for youthful budget-minded travelers)

☐ Amsterdam $9.95	☐ Mexico. $11.95
☐ Berlin. $11.95	☐ Morocco $12.95
☐ Brazil $13.95	☐ New York $9.95
☐ California & the West Coast $11.95	☐ Paris $9.95
☐ Czechoslovakia $13.95	☐ Peru. $12.95
☐ France $12.95	☐ Poland $13.95
☐ Germany $13.95	☐ Portugal. $10.95
☐ Greece. $13.95	☐ San Francisco $11.95
☐ Guatemala $13.95	☐ Scandinavia $14.95
☐ Hong Kong $11.95	☐ Spain. $12.95
☐ Hungary. $12.95	☐ Turkey $12.95
☐ Ireland. $12.95	☐ Venice $11.95
☐ Italy. $13.95	☐ Women Travel $12.95
☐ Kenya. $12.95	☐ Yugoslavia $12.95

ORDER NOW!

In U.S. include $2 shipping UPS for 1st book; $1 ea. add'l book. Outside U.S. $3 and $1, respectively.

Allow four to six weeks for delivery in U.S., longer outside U.S. We discourage rush order service, but orders arriving with shipping fees plus a $15 surcharge will be handled as rush orders.

Enclosed is my check or money order for $_____

NAME _____

ADDRESS _____

CITY _____ STATE _____ ZIP _____

0891492